Life-Course Perspectives on Military Service

This edited volume provides a comprehensive and critical review of what we know about military service and the life course, what we do not know, and what we need to do to better understand the role of military service in shaping people's lives. It demonstrates that the military, like colleges and prisons, is a key social institution that engages individuals in early adulthood and shapes processes of cumulative (dis)advantage over the life course. The chapters provide topical syntheszies of the vast but diffuse research literatures on military service and the life course, while the volume as a whole helps to set the agenda for the next generation of data collection and scholarship. Chapter authors pay particular attention to how the military has changed over time; how experiences of military service vary across cohorts and persons with different characteristics; how military service affects the lives of service members' spouses, children, and families; and the linkages between research and policy.

Routledge Advances in Sociology

For a full list of titles in this series, please visit www.routledge.com.

Life-Course Perspectives on Military Service

**Edited by Janet M. Wilmoth
and Andrew S. London**

Routledge
Taylor & Francis Group
NEW YORK   LONDON

First published 2013
by Routledge
711 Third Avenue, New York, NY 10017

Simultaneously published in the UK
by Routledge
2 Park Square, Milton Park, Abingdon, Oxfordshire OX14 4RN

First issued in paperback 2014

*Routledge is an imprint of the Taylor and Francis Group,
an informa business*

Library of Congress Cataloging-in-Publication Data
Life course perspectives on military service / edited by Janet M. Wilmoth
and Andrew S. London.
    p. cm. — (Routledge advances in sociology ; 83)
  Includes bibliographical references and index.
  ISBN 978-0-415-87941-5
 1. Sociology, Military—United States.   2. Veterans—United States—
Social conditions.   3. Life cycle, Human.   4. Life change events.
 I. Wilmoth, Janet M. (Janet May)   II. London, Andrew S.
  U21.5.L525 2013
  306.2'70973—dc23
  2012021173

ISBN 978-0-415-87941-5 (hbk)

ISBN 978-1-138-92085-9 (pbk)

ISBN 978-0-203-07974-4 (ebk)

Typeset in Sabon
by IBT Global.

For all the men and women whose lives have been shaped by military service.

For my father, Carey Walter Wilmoth, Jr., a veteran of the Korean War whose access to the GI Bill and VA home loan program benefited our entire family. Thank you for your sacrifices for, dedication to, and support of your loved ones.

J.M.W.

For my grandfather, Irving Shopnick, a veteran of World War II whom I never knew and whose absence I have always felt, and my spouse, Dr. Alan E. Curle, M.D., a veteran of the All-Volunteer Force whose constant love and support add immeasurably to my life.

A.S.L.

Contents

Figures

Tables

Preface

In 2004, we participated in a conference on "Changing Demographics, Stagnant Social Policies" that was organized by Madonna Harrington Meyer and took place at the Maxwell School of Citizenship and Public Affairs at Syracuse University. Janet presented a paper on demographic trends that will shape future U.S. policy (Wilmoth and Longino 2006) and Andrew presented a paper on race, incarceration, and health across the life course (London and Meyers 2006). During a break in the program, we discussed how the military might be an interesting institutional counterpoint to the penal system, particularly for youth from disadvantaged backgrounds, and how the considerable variation across cohorts in military service experiences might underlie policy-relevant demographic trends. We began to brainstorm about how we could explore these ideas with existing nationally representative datasets. That initial conversation sparked the development of our multifaceted and continually expanding research program that uses a life-course framework to consider the impact of military service on a variety of economic, family, and health outcomes.

As our research program has developed, we have had the privilege of forming collegial relationships with a network of scholars who are interested in understanding military service in lives, many of whom have contributed chapters to this edited volume. Central among those scholars is Glen H. Elder, Jr., whose pioneering work on the life course and World War II veterans has laid a solid theoretical and empirical foundation for this area of scholarship. We are grateful for the expertise, vision, and support that he has generously contributed to our ongoing work. We are also appreciative of the involvement of David Segal and Paul Gade, whose knowledge of military history and institutional operations has been invaluable, and Jay Teachman, whose studies on the influence of military service among more recent cohorts and methodological insights have paved the way for future research. We also would like to acknowledge the efforts made by all of our colleagues who contributed to this edited volume. Each author has enthusiastically engaged with the literature in their substantive areas to provide a comprehensive assessment of the state of knowledge related to military service in lives. They have been open to feedback from the other contributors, responsive to our editorial suggestions, and quick to address our requests. Their patience as we edited the chapters together into a cohesive volume has been much appreciated. It has been a pleasure working with them to produce this volume and we look forward to collaborating with them in the future.

We would also like to recognize the support we have received to advance this area of research. We organized two conferences at Syracuse University, in 2007 and in 2009, which led to the development of this book. Those conferences were supported by the American Sociological Association's Fund for the Advancement of the Discipline and Syracuse University's Department of Sociology, Center for Policy Research, Gerontology Center, and Burton Blatt Institute. In addition, in 2011, the Department of Sociology and the Population Research Center at the University of Maryland-College Park hosted a meeting, with support of the College of Behavioral and Social Sciences Dean's Research Initiative, to initiate conversations about the next generation of longitudinal life-course research and data collection related to military service. Many contributors to this volume were a part of that conversation, as were several others. We hope this volume will provide foundations on which that initiative can build.

We received assistance vetting references, creating the combined reference list, and cross-checking text citations from Kelly Bogart, Martha Bonney, Roseann Presutti, Alison Kirsche, and Janet Coria, all of whom are employed by the Center for Policy Research or the Sociology Department in the Maxwell School of Citizenship and Public Affairs at Syracuse University. Jackie Smith and Yooumi Lee, graduate assistants in the Maxwell School at Syracuse University, provided assistance compiling the index. In addition, Jill McLeigh, who is the Coordinator of the Longitudinal Military Research Program at the University of Maryland, has been crucial in organizing the military study planning group that is trying to move the field forward through new data collection efforts. With this support, we collectively have been able to create a vibrant network of scholars dedicated to using a life-course perspective to understand the influence of military service on lives.

In closing, we wish to acknowledge our spouses—Brian Durkin and Alan Curle—who have patiently endured the personal sacrifices that accompany having their lives linked to scholars who devote enormous amounts of time, attention, and energy to endeavors such as this one. Their willingness to share our interests and support our efforts inspired us to see this book project to completion.

Janet M. Wilmoth and Andrew S. London

Foreword

Glen H. Elder, Jr.

As a young child during World War II, I looked forward to the 4th of July parade, with its dressed-up cars, prancing bands, and colorful floats. Cheerleaders participated, along with a small number of older men, marching slowly in formation. I didn't know who they were or where they came from, but was told that they had served in earlier wars. I wondered about their experiences, their travels to other lands and battlefields. I imagined that some had medals with stories to tell.

Years later, I discovered that we didn't have data at the time to relate military experiences in World War II to post-service lives. Biographical information had not been collected in successive interviews or in retrospective life histories. During the Second World War, the American Soldier project made history by interviewing soldiers overseas, but it contacted them only once and left personal change to the imagination. The investigators could not readily distinguish cause from effect in studies of soldiers' morale or document causal processes over time.

When compared to this state of knowledge, contemporary research on military service in lives represents a highly notable advance, as evidenced by this path-breaking book. There is nothing in the social science literature that approximates its contributions to this field of study with its significance for public policy. At the very center of the advance is the exponential growth of longitudinal samples, a research design that has been suitably described as "the Hubble telescope" of the social sciences, a transformative innovation of the first order in the 20th century. Whether prospective or retrospective, this research design has enabled investigators to trace the effects of military events and experiences across the lives of veterans.

Longitudinal studies of people required a way of thinking about lives through time and space. This need eventually generated a perspective on individual lives and their changing roles and contexts that is now known in the life-course framework as theoretical orientation. People are located in historical time and geographic space; they make decisions and act in ways that shape their lives. They live lives that are intertwined with the changing lives of others, and they experience events and transitions at different times in life. These paradigmatic principles have come to define the life course, with its transitions and trajectories, as a theoretical orientation and flourishing domain of study. The interwoven nature of longitudinal research and life-course models has contributed to the conceptual richness of studies that view military service within the life course. Before addressing this development, some background is in order.

Field surveys were clearly prominent during World War II as the method for obtaining biographical data, but some projects were already in the field collecting longitudinal data. They were motivated by the requirements for studying the development of children, as well as the etiology of health and illness. Psychologists at the Institute of Human Development at Berkeley had launched a set of longitudinal studies of more than 500 children with birthdates in the 1920s. Though initially focused on children, the study members were followed across the Depression and World War II years, and then into later life. Large-scale longitudinal studies came much later. The first major one in the United States, the Framingham Heart Study, was launched with 5,000 adults during 1948 in response to the growing incentive for studies of health and illness.

Neither of these longitudinal projects collected biographical data on military experience, a deficiency that reflected a generalized neglect of the social context of lives during the 20th century. A noteworthy example is the Blau and Duncan (1967) study, the American Occupational Structure, with its focus on the status attainment of successive birth cohorts in the 20th century. This work makes no reference to the influence of military service on the social and geographic mobility of Americans, although 16 million men and women served during World War II and millions more participated in the Korean War of the 1950s. Consistent with this neglect, the study also makes no reference to the social mobility impact of the GI Bill on veterans' lives through access to advanced education and training. Several chapters of this volume tell the story of what we know and do not know about the relation between military service and the social, economic, and geographic mobility of veterans.

Historical focus on the lives of ordinary people did not emerge as a vital field of study until the 1960s. Birth cohorts had just emerged as a strategic concept for studying social change in lives. Norman Ryder (1965) observed that social change influences a birth cohort and the lives of its members according to the life stage they occupy. Children and adolescents were influenced in different ways by their changing world. When coupled with matters of place, birth cohort studies have situated people in particular contexts that have profound implications for their lives, as in eras of economic depression and prosperity, peace and war.

Longitudinal studies during my time at the Berkeley Institute of Human Development in the 1960s paid no attention to these social changes. However, sociological interests prompted my effort to measure these changes and bring them into a study of birth cohorts from the 1920s. All life transitions were defined in relation to chronological age, such as age at entry into active military duty and at exit from the military. Among the college educated, we asked their age at entry and when they completed their education. A sequence of transitions formed a life trajectory, and some transitions became turning points—they changed the direction of lives. World War II was often a turning point for American men who came from disadvantaged backgrounds. It pulled them out of poverty and gave survivors of active duty greater access to life opportunities through higher education. These concepts and others contributed to a rudimentary life-course perspective that drew from many sources. During the 1980s and 1990s, historians began to collaborate with demographers, sociologists, and developmentalists on studies of military experiences in lives.

Conceptual distinctions of the life course provided a way to view military service in terms of a social pathway to young adulthood for young men and women in a particular historical time. There is a usual or typical time for entry into military service, though some young people enter relatively early and others much later. During World War II, young people were subject to military conscription from the age of 18 to the late 30s. By contrast, the Korean War drew most of its recruits from ages 18 to 23, as did the Vietnam War. Overseas duty ranged from "on duty for the duration" in World War II to a period of months in the Korean and Vietnam conflicts. Each of these wars also differed with respect to the public's support at home and the public's reception of returning soldiers. After the Vietnam War had ended, the U.S. military shifted from conscription to an All-Volunteer Force. In these ways and others, historical time has shaped the meanings of military service.

As life-course concepts and theory developed in the 1970s, they tended to influence the design of national surveys and the measurement of concepts through the social scientists who served on advisory panels for major national longitudinal studies (such as the National Longitudinal Surveys). These studies began to include appropriate life-course measurements in their waves of data collection, such as the age grading of life events, although coverage of military service was often limited to only whether the respondent was a military veteran. Looking at these developments from the vantage point of the first decade of the 21st century, sociologist Karl Mayer (2009) has noted the widespread diffusion of a "longitudinal life course perspective" across the social sciences. Longitudinal data collections have increased in exponential fashion and now represent the current gold standard of quantitative social science. Qualitative longitudinal data collections and mixed-method research designs have also become more common in this field.

This book attests to the fruitful marriage between longitudinal research and the life course as a theoretical framework, between concepts and their measurements. It also reveals the continuing neglect of military service in the measurements of prospective longitudinal studies across the last decades of the 20th century. The first major breakthrough in a longitudinal study of American veterans occurred in relation to the men and women who served during and after the Vietnam War era (i.e., from the 1960s on). Retrospective life-history surveys were typically used to obtain information concerning the enduring traumatic impact of service in the Vietnam War, with emphasis on exposure to death, dying, and combat in general. By the 1980s, research had begun to investigate the influence of military service on the timing and order of life events in the transition to adulthood. Studies now extend their reach to aging and health in later life by assessing the long-term effects of military service and combat exposure.

By increasing the potential distance between military service and life outcomes, longitudinal studies have placed greater emphasis on the connecting, explanatory linkages. What are the processes by which exposure to wartime trauma has consequences in later life for chronic disease and mortality? Wartime stresses are known to increase the risk of post-traumatic stress disorder (PTSD), and some studies indicate that PTSD increases the risk of cardiovascular disease and mortality. However, the linking mechanisms are not well documented, owing in large part to inadequate data collection. There is a need for new and better longitudinal data and this book makes a convincing case for a national longitudinal study of veterans within a moving network of linked lives. The study should be designed for research that investigates the causal pathways by which the enduring effects of military service are expressed. A blueprint for such a study is outlined in the concluding chapter of this book.

All lives of military personnel and veterans are linked to other lives, but as Burland and Lundquist's Chapter 8 (in this volume) indicates, this social reality is shown primarily by studies of military families within the relatively short period of the soldiers' military service. The active-duty service member's enlistment, departure for basic training, and deployment overseas, when that occurs, are documented by military records, and perhaps by field surveys. By contrast, longitudinal studies of veterans, frequently over many years, have tended to focus on the individual veteran to the exclusion of significant others, family members, and friends. This limitation may reflect the challenge and cost of collecting data on nuclear family members and friends over time. Whatever the explanation, little is known about veteran families when compared to those of civilians across the life course, or about aging veterans in the changing world of their families. This includes the family impact of veteran disability and caregiving. The enduring ties of veterans to comrades are also generally unknown, along with the meaning of military reunions in their lives.

From one chapter to another in this volume, the life-course perspective identifies highly relevant problem areas for empirical study. Consider Kleykamp's Chapter 7 (in this volume) on labor market outcomes. Few topics have been more frequently investigated than this one, but we quickly learn that research on the labor market outcomes of veterans has tended to ignore employers. How do employers regard honorably discharged young men and their qualifications for employment? How do they regard the employability of combat veterans or the employability of older versus younger veterans, all with a similar level of education? Most men and women serving today have spouses, but studies of their work experiences have not been a priority. Indeed, very little is known about their work experience.

Over the past century, a large percentage of young Americans have served their country by joining the military, typically during their young adult years. This pioneering book tells us what we know about how military experience has influenced their lives, and even more importantly, what we do not know and should know. The reader will encounter more questions than answers, but hopefully these questions will motivate the research agenda of the coming decade and its new research directions.

1 Life-Course Perspectives on Military Service
An Introduction

Janet M. Wilmoth and Andrew S. London

Even before we are born, institutions and social structures begin to shape our lives through their variable effects on our parents and communities. Initially, our families of origin filter the influences of various economic and social forces. As we move through childhood and adolescence, we begin to experience these institutional and structural influences firsthand, through the roles we play as members of our immediate and extended families, as students in educational systems, as worshipers of a given religion, and as patients receiving health care. We arrive on the cusp of adulthood poised to take on new and emergent roles within political institutions, as voting-aged citizens, and within economic institutions, as workers and consumers. As we transition into these and other adult roles, we may experience opportunities related to family connections, higher education, and professional employment, or we may begin to realize the consequences of growing up in disadvantaged circumstances as they play out in constrained educational, employment, and housing opportunities. Some of us will experience spells as inmates in the criminal justice system, while others of us will serve on active duty in the U.S. military.

Life-course scholars have demonstrated that the pathways taken during the demographically dense period of young adulthood (Rindfuss 1991) can leave an indelible mark on the course of human lives. The extant life-course literature demonstrates that these scholars have devoted considerable attention to the influence of family, educational, labor market, and penal institutions on subsequent life-course trajectories and outcomes, including socioeconomic attainment and health. As documented in this volume, a smaller subset of life-course scholars has been concerned with trying to understand the effects of military service on lives.

Glen H. Elder, Jr. is responsible for the most influential early theorizing about the role of military service in the life course (Elder 1986, 1987), and, with a range of colleagues, for empirically demonstrating the importance of military service for life-course studies (Clipp and Elder 1996; Dechter and Elder 2004; Elder and Bailey 1988; Elder and Clipp 1988a,b, 1989; Elder, Gimbel, and Ivie 1991; Elder, Shanahan, and Clipp 1994, 1997; Elder, Wang, Spence, Adkins, and Brown 2010; MacLean and Elder 2007; Pavalko and Elder 1990). As attested by Paul Gade and Brandis Ruise in Chapter 12, as well as in Glen Elders' foreword to this volume and our own comments below, his influence on the field extends beyond his own direct scholarly contributions to his support of many life-course scholars who have taken up questions related to military service. These scholars and other life-course researchers have contributed to this line of research by examining how the effect of military service varies across individual characteristics, service experiences, historical periods, cohort membership, and the timing of military service in the life course (e.g., Angrist 1990; Angrist and Krueger 1994; Gimbel and Booth 1994, 1996; Teachman 2004, 2005; Teachman and Call 1996; Teachman and Tedrow 2004; Wilmoth, London, and Parker 2010). Taken together, this research provides evidence that the U.S. military is a critical social institution that can (re)shape educational, occupational, income, marital/family, health, and other life-course trajectories and outcomes (London and Wilmoth 2006; Mettler 2005; Modell and Haggerty 1991; Sampson and Laub 1996; Settersten 2006). This body of exemplary life-course research aims, in the words of Modell and Haggerty (1991: 205), "to connect the micro- and macro-levels of analysis, thus connecting the soldier's story to that of his *[or her]* changing society."

Despite the existence of this rich body of research, Settersten and Patterson (2006: 5) have argued that "wartime experiences may be important but largely invisible factors underneath contemporary knowledge about aging" (see also Settersten 2006; Spiro, Schnurr, and Aldwin 1997). We contend that the important institutional influence of military service on lives has more generally been underacknowledged among life-course scholars, and more broadly within Sociology and other disciplines that study human lives, including Demography, Economics, Gerontology, and Psychology. This is ironic given that current knowledge about the life course, in particular, and social life, in general, is substantially derived from research based on cohorts that were born during the 20th century, which featured extended periods of peace punctuated by several periods of war and military conflicts. A substantial percentage of men in current old-age cohorts served in the military during World War II, the Korean War, the Cold War, or some combination thereof. Those men, as well as the women and children whose lives are linked to them, were certainly affected by military service and war. Middle-aged adults, who were born during the middle of the 20th century, experienced the transition from the draft era, which included the Vietnam War, to the early years of the All-Volunteer Force period, which were primarily peaceful. After 1990, young adults as well as those at the beginning of middle age, who were therefore at the prime ages for entering military service, were potentially involved in the Gulf War as well as subsequent conflicts, including

Operations Iraqi Freedom, Enduring Freedom, and New Dawn. Importantly, women have increasingly entered the armed forces and directly experienced military service in the most recent decades.

Although rates of participation in the military have declined over the past fifty years as the size of the military has contracted (see Figure 1.1), military service remains a salient pathway to adulthood—particularly for youth from socioeconomically disadvantaged backgrounds (see Bennett and McDonald, Chapter 6 in this volume). The U.S. military remains a primary employer of young and middle-aged adults; in 2010, there were 1,602,000 uniformed military personnel (U.S. Office of Personnel Management 2012). In addition, veterans are a sizeable and policy-relevant demographic group. In 2010, nearly 22 million Americans were veterans, representing approximately 9% of those aged 18 or older (U.S. Census Bureau 2010). The majority (82.5%) of these veterans served during wartime: 9.5% during World War II, 11.8% in the Korean War, 34.9% in the Vietnam War, 15.8% in the Gulf War (8/1990 to 8/2001), and 10.5% in the more recent Gulf War operations (9/2001 or later) (U.S. Census Bureau 2010). Furthermore, as noted above, participation in the military has increased substantially among women; in 2010, nearly 1.6 million American women were veterans (U.S. Census Bureau 2010). However, the extent to which the lives of military personnel and veterans differ from those who have not served in the military has not been systematically documented partly as a result of the dearth of population-level data sources that contain adequate data

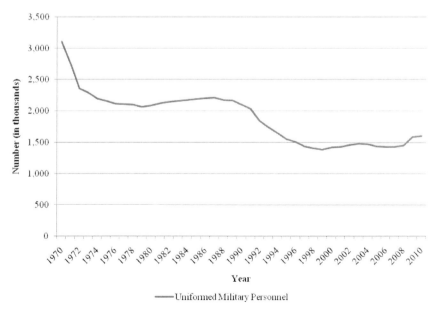

Figure 1.1 Uniformed military personnel, 1970–2010.

on military service experiences and allow for explicit comparisons across these groups. Similarly, we know very little about differences in the lives of nonserving citizens who are linked to active-duty service members and veterans versus those who are not.

THE LIFE-COURSE PERSPECTIVE: RELEVANT PRINCIPLES, CONCEPTS, AND HYPOTHESES

The rich conceptual and theoretical traditions within the life-course perspective provide fertile ground for empirical research (George 2003, forthcoming; Settersten 1999, 2003), including the role of military service in lives. Although there are ongoing debates regarding the scope of life-course scholarship, including how the life-course concept relates to, and differs from, other concepts, such as life span and life cycle (Alwin 2012a,b; O'Rand and Krecker 1990), there is consensus regarding the importance of five major principles that characterize the life-course perspective: *lifelong development, human agency, location in time and place, timing,* and *linked lives* (Elder and Johnson 2002; Elder and Shanahan 2006; Elder et al. 2003). Each of these principles, which are briefly described below, provides a foundation upon which we can begin to understand how military service shapes lives.

First, the principle of *lifelong development* states that human development and aging must be understood as processes that unfold over time. Given that earlier phases of life shape subsequent stages, studies that focus on a given life stage without taking into account the influence of previous periods are limited. For example, when studying health outcomes among veterans and non-veterans, researchers should consider health during childhood and adolescence and its effect on the ability to pass health screening exams required prior to acceptance into the military, as well as veterans' exposure to combat and other risks for service-related injuries. This principle highlights the critical importance of having comprehensive data on military service experiences, as well as longitudinal data that enable researchers to address selection and disentangle aging effects from period and cohort effects.

Second, the principle of *human agency* directs attention to the role that individuals play in their own lives as they actively choose among various opportunities and deal with the constraints that they encounter over the course of their lives. Opportunities and constraints are structured by historical and social circumstances. Consequently, individuals with similar social locations may experience very different opportunities depending on the historical circumstances they face. For example, military personnel who served during World War II and the Korean War and met particular program criteria were eligible for the GI Bill, although access varied by race, regional location, and gender. In contrast, those who served during the post–Korean War period (i.e., the Cold War era) did not have access to the GI Bill until their service was retroactively covered when the GI Bill was reinstated in 1966. Thus, veterans from the Cold War era had fewer opportunities to pursue education upon completion of their military service than prior or most subsequent cohorts.

Third, the principle of *location in time and place* embeds lives in both a historical period and specific geographic (and increasingly online) locations, where various kinds of people are or are not encountered, certain kinds of interactions do or do not occur, and specific values are or are not emphasized. As we age from childhood through adulthood, the influences of historical events are woven into our quotidian lives through social interactions within the families, friendship networks, communities, organizations, and online environments in which we are embedded. Thus, for example, the experience of the Vietnam War depended in part on whether a person was a young adult living on an urban college campus, a mother of a soldier from rural America, a veteran from World War I or II, or a young man serving in the war zone. Similarly, as D'Ann Campbell (in Chapter 3 of this volume) demonstrates, women's experiences in the Civil War and World War II were distinctively shaped by historical time and place. Taking into account this nexus of social, historical, and geographic locations requires methodological approaches that include retrospective life histories and multilevel modeling. Even then, the difficulties involved in measuring and modeling time-varying changes in social structures and individual characteristics remains a daunting challenge for the field.

Fourth, the principle of *timing* focuses on when events and transitions occur in relation to age and other events and transitions. Individuals in different life stages bring various experiences and resources to a given historical event. Consequently, they understand that event and adapt to the new conditions arising from it in different ways. For example, the partner of a commissioned officer who has experienced several tours of duty in Afghanistan is likely to react differently to a deployment than a partner of an enlisted soldier who is being deployed for the first time. This principle also speaks to the importance of when personal life events occur, whether they trigger transitions, and how disruptive they are to ongoing relationships, education, family patterns, and work. Life is characterized by various events that lead to transitions between roles: meeting someone can trigger a transition from being single to partnered; pregnancy can trigger a transition from not being a parent to parenthood; a serious illness can trigger a transition from wellness to a chronic sick role; a war can trigger a transition from civilian status to being a soldier. Sometimes, one event can trigger numerous subsequent, interconnected role transitions that reverberate across the life course; a transition from civilian to soldier during war can lead to a combat role, which can lead to physical or psychological injuries, the emergence of disability, redirection of employment trajectories, the onset of a spousal caregiving role, and marital strain and instability.

The consequences of transitions, including their disruptiveness to already established life-course trajectories, depend in part on whether they are expected or unexpected, as well as if they are considered "on-time" or "off-time." Culturally based, age-graded norms determine whether a transition is deemed to be on-time or off-time. If a transition occurs during the culturally prescribed time frame, then it is considered to be on-time. In contrast, off-time transitions do not coincide with the expected timetable and often are associated with negative consequences. The timing of military service during young adulthood, as well as its timing in relation to the adoption of other salient roles, can have substantial consequences, as will be discussed in more detail below.

Fifth, the principle of *linked lives* focuses attention on the importance of social relationships and the interdependence of lives. As we move through various life stages, the composition of our "social convoy" (Antonucci and Akiyama 1995) shifts as we develop relationships with new members and connections to older members dwindle, evolve, or are severed. Members of our family of origin are often the most enduring members of our social convoy, moving with us through different phases of life. These inter- and intra-generational ties are among the conduits through which events in one person's life impact other people. Additional conduits through which lives are linked include friendships and various types of community relationships (e.g., neighbors, school- or workplace-based peer relationships). For individuals whose lives are linked through various social relationships, events that occur in one person's life can have ripple effects on the entire network. Those effects can be either positive or negative, depending in part on the degree to which members' lives are synchronous or asynchronous. For example, the disruptiveness of deployment for military personnel and their families depends to some degree on life stage; deployments are likely to be less disruptive for a single, childless service member whose parents are healthy than for a partnered service member with young children and/or ailing parents. The armed forces have become increasingly attuned to the importance of families in the lives of military personnel since the shift to the All-Volunteer Force in 1973. Social network members (in particular family members) play a crucial role in recruitment into and retention in the armed forces. As discussed in various chapters in this volume, they are also involved in reintegrating veterans into the larger society and providing care for those with service-related injuries and disability. Although a focus on linked lives offers numerous sociologically rich possibilities to study military service in lives, as we shall see, there has been relatively little empirical life-course research that employs the linked lives principle to explore how the lives of family members, friends, and community members are shaped by the experiences of military personnel and veterans.

Building on these five principles, life-course researchers who study military service in lives have motivated and interrogated two corollary hypotheses that have wide-reaching implications: the *military-as-turning-point* and the *life-course-disruption* hypotheses. Both of these hypotheses emphasize the potential of military service to produce discontinuity in life-course trajectories, for better or worse. They also suggest mechanisms by which participation in the military during young adulthood influences cumulative inequality across the life course.

The *military-as-turning-point hypothesis* states that young age at entry into the military maximizes the chances for redirection of the life course and, assuming no service-connected injury or disability, minimizes disruption to established life-course trajectories. Elder (1986, 1987) argues that early entry into the military is like a social and psychological moratorium, which both delays the transition to adulthood and allows for the maximum utilization of Veterans Administration benefits. More recently, Kelty, Kleykamp, and Segal (2010) have argued that military service during the era of the All-Volunteer Force is one of many pathways to adulthood, rather than a delay or a detour in the process of transitioning to adulthood. Regardless of which theorization is adopted, for youth from socioeconomically disadvantaged backgrounds, military service may be a route out of difficult life circumstances both because the transition to the military "knifes off" certain social ties and patterns of behavior and because it provides a "bridging environment" in which service members can obtain education, training, skills, and resources that put them on different and better life-course trajectories than they otherwise would have followed (Browning, Lopreato, and Poston 1973; Sampson and Laub 1996; see also Bennett and McDonald, Chapter 6 in this volume). While selection into the military on the basis of disadvantaged early-life circumstances would tend to correlate with worse life-course trajectories and outcomes among veterans, it has been theorized that early entrants are precisely the service members who benefit most from the range of service-connected benefits that are available to them and for whom military service is least disruptive. Of course, it is important to bear in mind that service-connected injury and disability can serve as a negative turning point in the life of any man or woman, regardless of age at entry into the armed forces.

The corollary *life-course-disruption hypothesis* suggests that relatively late entry into the military can disrupt established marital, parenting, and occupational trajectories, and that such disruption may have negative consequences for subsequent life-course trajectories and outcomes. Later entrants often come from more advantaged backgrounds, have completed their educations, and are embedded within established families and careers. Because of the timing of military service in their lives, they may have less opportunity to take advantage of GI Bill educational benefits and experience more life-course disruption. Notably among those who serve during war and experience combat, but even among those who are deployed but do not see combat, the physical and psychological effects of military service may intersect with disrupted occupational and family roles in ways that increase strain and the risk of marital disruption. The potentially disruptive consequences of later entry into active-duty service, exacerbated by service-related experiences such as deployment, combat exposure, and service-connected disability, may be particularly significant for men and women activated from the Reserves during times of war, because such occurrences are less expected by them and their family members. This is a particularly salient concern in the context of the contemporary wars in Afghanistan and Iraq.

Implicitly, studies about the influence of military service on lives, in general, and the turning point and disruption hypotheses, in particular, assume a *cumulative exposure model* of the life course, in which adult social conditions mediate the effect of early-life social conditions on adult outcomes (Berkman et al. 2011). In this model, early-life social conditions can directly affect adult outcomes, but often those influences are offset by the circumstances of adulthood, including unique individual experiences, such as the timing of life events and the nature of existing social relationships, as well as macro-level influences, such as participation in social institutions and exposure to formal public policies and informal social norms (Hendricks 2012). Thus, adult social conditions are central to the process of accumulating advantage and disadvantage, in which those with access to resources are able to garner and command additional resources. This differential access to resources accrues and accentuates inequalities across groups over time (Dannefer 1987, 1988; O'Rand 1996, 2002); those who experience advantage are more exposed to opportunity, while those who experience disadvantage are more exposed to risk, which further compounds inequality (Ferraro, Shippee, and Schafer 2009).

The cumulative exposure model focuses on explaining the life course through the analysis of individual-level outcomes. But, as Dannefer and colleagues have pointed out (Dannefer 2012; Dannefer and Kelley-Moore 2009; Dannefer and Uhlenberg 1999), life-course analysis goes beyond the individual level by considering collective and structural/symbolic outcomes. Studies that examine collective outcomes focus on population characteristics, usually through the use of cohorts as the unit of analysis. Such studies consider, for example, intra- and inter-cohort variation in socioeconomic attainment and inequality (Bloome and Western 2011; Crystal and Waehrer 1996) or the timing and sequencing of life events (e.g., Henretta 1992; Hogan 1981; Modell 1989, 1995; Rindfuss et al. 1987). In contrast, studies that consider structural/symbolic outcomes examine the life course as a socially constructed reality that shapes cultural norms and meanings associated with various life events (Kohli 1988). From this perspective, social structure is central to organizing the life course (Cain 1964). In modern welfare states, age-graded policies—such as laws that use age requirements to regulate behavior associated with completion of education, entry into military service, eligibility to vote, and access to public entitlement programs like Social Security—create an institutionalized life course that segments lives into tripartite periods of education, work, and leisure (Kohli 1986, 2007; Meyer 1986; Riley and Riley 1994). This structure shapes the way in which lives unfold and, in turn, gives meaning to those lives. While one can imagine how collective and structural/symbolic approaches could inform the understanding of the interplay between military service and individual lives—a point to which we will return later—the extant literature on military lives rarely incorporates these perspectives.

A CONCEPTUAL MODEL OF MILITARY SERVICE IN LIVES

Building on the life-course perspective and using a cumulative exposure model of the life course, we have organized this volume around the proposition that early-life participation in a particular social institution (i.e., the military) by people with specific characteristics in given historical periods shapes processes of cumulative inequality that lead to later-life disparities in various outcomes (see Figure 1.2). Specifically, we contend that participation in the military can exacerbate, ameliorate, or have no moderating effect on early-life disadvantages. In addition, participation in the military may (re-)shape mid-life educational, occupational, income, marital, and health characteristics that influence later-life trajectories and outcomes. The effects of cumulative inequality are shown in this figure by the solid line running from early-life circumstances to later-life outcomes. This demonstrates how early-life circumstances might continue to have direct effects on later-life outcomes regardless of military service or mid- to late-life characteristics. The discontinuities predicted by the military-as-turning-point and life-course-disruption hypotheses, which have been substantiated in the extant research on the World War II cohort, are indicated by the dashed lines. This represents the notion that the effects of early-life circumstances can be offset by military service, which places

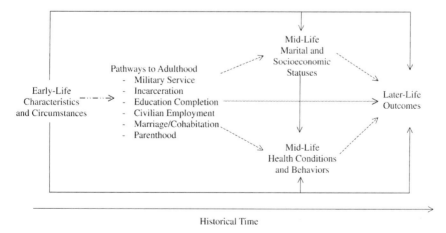

Figure 1.2   Conceptual model of military service in lives.

individuals on a different life-course trajectory that influences subsequent mid-life characteristics, and, ultimately, later-life outcomes. This offsetting effect could be positive or negative, resulting in improvements in or worsening of life circumstances. In the example depicted in Figure 1.2, the effect of early-life circumstances and military service would be either mediated or moderated by mid-life characteristics. The dotted line demonstrates the direct effect military service can have on later-life outcomes, such as effects of experience in a military occupational specialty, combat exposure, or service-related disability, controlling for early-life circumstances and mid-life characteristics. Finally, the line with dashes and two dots is indicative of selection into early-adult trajectories, in general, and military service, in particular. It reminds us of the importance of considering the implications of nonrandom selection into military service (see Wolf, Wing, and Lopoo Chapter 13 of this volume).

Because all of the processes in this model are embedded in historical time, we advocate paying close attention to differences across birth cohorts who experienced military service but lived their lives in different historical periods. It is also important to consider how military service among these cohorts influenced the meaning of various life events, shaped the life course as an institution, and impacted other social trends. Finally, we emphasize the importance of considering the life-course trajectories of those whose lives are linked to service members, including parents, spouses, and children.

A SYSTEMATIC CONSIDERATION OF MILITARY SERVICE IN LIVES: WHAT IS KNOWN AND UNKNOWN?

With this conceptual model in mind, we have developed our own research agenda, funded by the National Institute on Aging and focused on the consequences of military service for men's health trajectories in later life (London and Wilmoth 2006; Wilmoth, London, and Parker 2010). Additionally, in 2006, as we came to appreciate how much was unknown about the life-course consequences of military service, we set out to develop a collaborative working group focused on studying military service and the life course. Initially, we asked life-course researchers who were working with large-scale datasets that included military service measures to think about the ways prior military service might influence what they were studying and to expand their ongoing research to include those variables. Over time, participants who were more explicitly interested in studies that focused on military personnel and veterans joined the group. We organized an initial conference at Syracuse University in 2007, which was partially supported by the American Sociological Association's Fund for the Advancement of the Discipline. At that conference, working group members presented their novel empirical research findings. Glen H. Elder, Jr. provided the keynote address at the conference, and a range of scholars—from graduate students to postdoctoral fellows and assistant professors to senior scholars—also participated. Several papers from that conference were ultimately published in the peer-reviewed literature.

In 2009, we held a second conference at Syracuse University for which participants were asked to prepare a manuscript that reviewed the extant literature on military service in their substantive area, identified gaps in knowledge, and considered avenues for future research. The manuscripts presented at this second conference largely serve as the foundation for this edited volume, although we solicited some additional chapters to address issues that we believed to be critical for a comprehensive assessment of military service in lives. The chapters in this edited volume are designed to raise awareness among researchers, policy makers, and the public about the role of military service in lives. They provide an overview of what is known, and what needs to be known, about the factors that shape selection into and experiences of military service, including gender, race and ethnicity, and sexual orientation, and the influence of military service on various aspects of the life course and aging, including the transition to adulthood, marriage/family formation, socioeconomic attainment, and health outcomes. We asked all of the chapter authors to consider variation across cohorts and demographic change, highlight gaps in the literature, and identify priorities for future data collection. We also encouraged chapter authors to draw upon the major principles of the life course and the model that we outlined above for conceptualizing the role of military service in lives.

While this introductory chapter sets the stage for this edited volume by providing a conceptual framework for thinking about military service in lives, Chapter 2, by Ryan Kelty and David Segal, offers the substantive scaffolding for the remaining chapters. They argue that the role of military service in the life course must be understood in historical perspective, particularly given that the military has changed markedly over time, especially during the last half century. This historical context provides a backdrop against which the military's effects on the transition to adulthood in the late 20th and early 21st centuries can be understood. Kelty and Segal provide a broad review of the literature on who served, how they entered the military, and the impact of service on education, occupational and income attainment, family formation, civic engagement, and health. They also address military-civilian relationships and the changing organization of the American military. The subsequent chapters in the book elaborate upon many of these themes.

Chapters 3 through 5 in this volume consider significant historical changes in the composition of the armed forces with respect to race and ethnicity, gender, and sexual orientation. Each of these chapters examines the contextual and policy changes affecting these specific subpopulations and discusses the ways in which the life-course consequences of military service for these groups may be different from those for White men, who have historically been the most prominent segment of the armed forces.

Chapter 3, by D'Ann Campbell, provides historical evidence about the impact of the American Civil War and World War II on women's lives. By weaving in women's voices from Civil War–era letters and interviews from servicewomen who served during World War II, including WACs (Women's Army Corps), Navy WAVEs (Women Accepted for Voluntary Emergency Service), Coast Guard SPARs (*Semper Paratus*/Always Ready), and Women Marines, along with other historical documents, Campbell demonstrates that women's participation in these wars on the home front and in support of the front lines not only shaped the course of women's lives, but also the course of the wars. She also discusses how women's roles during each war contributed to broader movements for social change that reshaped the context within which generations of women subsequently lived their lives. Chapter 4, by Amy Lutz, provides a detailed historical overview of military service among White ethnics, African Americans, Latinos, Asian Americans, and Native Americans. In addition, she documents how the unique contributions of each group to specific wars facilitated appeals for improved civil rights, which, again, helped to reshape the context for subsequent generations. Chapter 5, by Maria Brown, discusses the historical role lesbian, gay, bisexual, and transgender (LGBT) persons have played in the U.S. military and the changes in the Department of Defense's policies on homosexuals over time. She examines the struggle for the right to serve and issues encountered by LGBT service members and veterans, including the potential life-course effects of being dishonorably discharged because of sexual orientation or gender identity. Brown also considers the role that the massive military mobilizations during the World Wars played in the formation of collective identities and LGBT communities that benefited many who never had direct experience with the military.

The subsequent six chapters in this volume consider the consequences of military service for socioeconomic status attainment, including education, employment, income, and wealth outcomes; marriage and family life; geographic mobility; and health. In each instance, to the extent possible given the extant literature, authors focus on variation by gender, race and ethnicity, and sexual orientation. When appropriate, chapter authors also address questions related to the impact of military service on the lives of those who are linked through marital and family ties to military personnel and veterans. They also review relevant military and government policies that contribute to the distinct characteristics of military and veteran lives.

Chapter 6, by Pamela Bennett and Katrina McDonald, considers how military service shapes adult socioeconomic attainment among disadvantaged youth. They explore the potential pathways through postsecondary education, civilian labor market participation, and military service. Bennett and McDonald conclude that the military is a social institution that can facilitate socioeconomic achievement among adults, but they recognize the risks associated with this pathway into adulthood. They also point out that disadvantaged youth who could benefit the most from serving in the military may be the least likely to enter and stay in the military. In Chapter 7, Meredith Kleykamp summarizes the extant literatures on the labor market consequences of military service for both veterans and their spouses. She notes that the effects of military service on veterans' employment and earnings vary by individual characteristics, the conditions leading to military service, the military experience itself, the societal context of reception, and the policies in place to aid the transition to civilian life. Kleykamp also demonstrates that "trailing spouses" have more consistently negative outcomes than veterans in terms of lower earnings and occupational attainment, along with greater difficulty balancing work and family responsibilities.

Daniel Burland and Jennifer Lundquist pick up on the discussion about the impact of military service on families in Chapter 8 by exploring the "veteran family." They consider variation based on the timing of family formation in relation to military service, the type of military service, and sociodemographic characteristics. Burland and Lundquist effectively use the linked lives perspective to demonstrate that military service has enduring effects on marital stability, children, and spouses, making a strong case that the long-lasting institutional influences of the military extend beyond the military personnel who directly participate in the institution. In the era of the All-Volunteer Force, when many service members make a career in the armed forces, wives, husbands, and children often spend some portion of their lives directly affected by the military. Although some people only experience the military through the memories of a veteran to whom their lives became linked after the service member separated from the armed forces, others directly experience the military as an institutional influence on their own lives, which raises important questions about veteran families, spouses, and children that need to be addressed in life-course research.

The "long arm" of the military in the life course is also evident in Chapter 9, by Amy Bailey, which focuses on issues related to the spatial mobility of active-duty military personnel, veterans, and their family members during the All-Volunteer Force era. She considers how the elevated spatial mobility associated with military service affects individuals, as well as sending and receiving communities, and argues that socioeconomically disadvantaged groups may be disproportionately affected by these spatial mobility dynamics. Similarly, in Chapter 10, Alair MacLean discusses how the military influences health inequalities. She considers positive selection into military service on the basis of health, the risk of physical injury, mental illness, and death among military personnel, as well as the life-course consequences of post-service physical and mental illness, disability, and death among veterans and their family members. MacLean also considers how cohort flow may influence later-life health differences between veterans and non-veterans. Debra Street and Jessica Hoffman expand upon the issue of later-life veteran and non-veteran differences in Chapter 11 by exploring the relationship between civilian entitlement programs and those related to military service. They explain that "dual entitlement" to civilian and military benefits provides an additional safety net that contributes to later-life health and financial security among some veterans. After furnishing details about program policies, Street and Hoffman offer an empirical example to illustrate differences in income, housing wealth, and health insurance between non-veterans, non-career veterans, and career veterans, respectively. They conclude that career veterans, who benefit the most from dual entitlement, are more secure in later life than non-veterans and non-career veterans.

Collectively, the substantive chapters included in this volume synthesize disparate literatures and provide a foundation for considering future needs for data collection and research. The final three chapters broadly consider the state of research on military lives, with an eye toward future challenges for the field and data needs. In Chapter 12, Paul Gade and Brandis Ruise discuss the role of the military services, in particular the U.S. Army Research Institute for the Behavioral and Social Sciences, in sponsoring life-course research on military personnel. They highlight the contributions of several key researchers in this area over the past thirty years, offer additional examples of how the rich conceptual foundations of the life-course perspective can be used to study military lives, and call for more research on the issues addressed in this volume. However, as noted by Doug Wolf, Coady Wing, and Leonard Lopoo in Chapter 13, research on military lives faces serious methodological challenges, particularly related to selection and unobserved heterogeneity. Although these issues are not unique to this area of research, they do make it difficult to determine whether military service, which tends to occur early in the life course, causes variation in subsequent mid- to late-life trajectories and outcomes. Wolf, Wing, and Lopoo discuss approaches to addressing selection and strongly advocate for methodological advances that will be necessary to move the study of military lives forward. As noted by Jay Teachman in the final chapter of this volume, moving the field forward will also require new data collection. He argues that we are beginning to get a handle on how military service shapes some aspects of the life course; however, many important questions remain unanswered. Although some of these questions can be addressed with existing surveys, most do not contain the measures that would be necessary to approach the most pressing substantive and methodological issues in this area of research. Thus, Teachman outlines ten principles that should guide future data collection efforts aimed at supporting research on military service in lives.

AREAS OF FUTURE ENDEAVOR

In closing this introductory chapter, we believe it is essential to challenge scholars to think broadly about how the life course perspective can inform our understanding of the institutional influence of the military on lives. We think it is critically important for the scholarly community to consider the questions we might ask, as well as the necessary data and methods that are needed to thoroughly address those questions. As previously mentioned, much attention has been given to analyzing individual-level outcomes (see for example Camacho and Atwood 2007). Consequently, many of the chapter authors identify additional avenues for research in this vein. We concur that these are important areas for future research endeavors, but we will not reiterate here the many fine points our colleagues have made. Instead, we want to focus on highlighting several areas that are only briefly mentioned, alluded to, or overlooked altogether as potential avenues for future research in the pages that follow. We think that taking up these and similar questions holds great promise for advancing our understanding of military service in lives, while also advancing life-course scholarship more generally.

At the individual level, most research has considered outcomes in a particular domain at a given point in the life course—for example, employment in young adulthood, marriage and divorce during military service, or health status in later life. We need to examine trajectories in each of these domains over a wider span of ages. Additionally, more research is needed on how trajectories in one area are related to those in other areas. For example, do service-connected health changes impact employment trajectories? Is the relationship between health and employment trajectories over time different for veterans and non-veterans? Relatively little is known about the trajectories of homeless veterans and those living in institutions, as they are likely to be missed in traditional household-based surveys. In the chapters that follow, discussion of homelessness and institutionalized populations is notably absent. It is crucial that we consider how to better represent the experiences of these populations in our future studies. The most understudied individual-level area to date concerns the implications of military service for those whose lives are linked to military personnel and veterans. Research on outcomes among spouses and children is becoming more common, but very little is known about how military service affects parents, siblings, and friends. Is the social capital that some military personnel and veterans accrue transmitted intergenerationally? Are attitudes toward military service carried across generations? Does knowing someone who is serving in the military affect support for military operations, social acceptance of veterans, and attitudes towards the generosity of veterans' benefits? Among family members, and possibly veteran peers through clubs and veterans' organizations, many individuals serve as caregivers to and supporters of injured military personnel and disabled veterans. What type of care work do these individuals perform and how does their involvement in caregiving affect their lives? From a developmental perspective, we know little about how military service affects character and moral development. Are those who have served, or who have close ties to service members, more likely to defer to authority, espouse integrity of actions, or engage in civic duties?

At the collective level, it is surprising that we do not know more about the extent to which aggregate changes in the population and other social institutions are due to changing cohort flows in relation to military service. For example, how have changes in military policy affected higher education (Kleykamp 2010) and how much of the improvement in education level among Americans during the 20th century is due to use of the GI Bill? Would the sex differences in overall mortality and certain types of cause-specific mortality (like lung cancer) be as large if the overrepresentation of men with military service in certain cohorts was taken into account? Are patterns of illegal and prescription drug use influenced by the aging of cohorts with particular military service experiences? Examining such questions has become more feasible given recent methodological advances in age-period-cohort analysis that allow for cross-cohort comparisons (Yang and Land 2006; Yang and Lee 2009; Yang et al. 2008); however, data constraints continue to pose obstacles for conducting this research.

We believe one of the most uncharted areas in the life-course scholarship on military service is at the structural/symbolic level. Very few studies have considered how the military shapes the institutionalized life course, as well as the cultural norms and meanings associated with life events and transitions. Social norms regarding the role of military service in the life course have varied across time as the needs for military personnel have waxed and waned along with particular wars and conflicts. Indeed, the debated "deinstitutionalization" of the American life course that occurred during the latter part of the 20th century might in part be due to the shift to the All-Volunteer Force, which made military service a less normative part of the transition to adulthood for young men but an increasingly important part of the transition to adulthood for many women. It remains to be seen whether this deinstitutionalization of the life course has occurred in countries where military service continues to be common, particularly countries like Israel where military service is mandatory and almost every able-bodied youth is required to serve.

Scholars have not given sufficient attention to how the needs of the military establishment can realign gender and race relations, resulting in social change that reshapes the life course. For example, as men were called to battle, women organized the war effort on the home front during the Civil War by running family farms, organizing supplies, and providing care to the sick and injured. During World War II, women were also called upon to work in war-related industries and to play supportive roles within the military. Similarly, racial-ethnic minority group members have played critical roles in all of the nation's wars. These contributions helped to pave the way for the women's and civil rights movements by allowing politically marginalized groups to lay claim to equal rights as citizens who were willing to make sacrifices, fight, and die for their country. Both of these movements profoundly impacted the life chances and choices of women and racial-ethnic minority group members, but the role of military service as a catalyst in these movements is often not acknowledged.

In many ways, the military has been a front-runner in establishing more equitable policies and expanding the role of government in lives. Pensions given to Civil War veterans laid the foundation for the Social Security System, racial integration of the armed forces preceded the end of school segregation, the GI Bill made higher education accessible to the middle, working, and lower classes long before government-subsidized student loans were established, and the recent repeal of "Don't Ask, Don't Tell" may portend further social equality for LGBT persons. Thus, the military is a potential driving force behind social change that affects the course of lives by shaping other institutional structures that people move through as they age. Given this, it is unfortunate that the influence of the military on other institutions is understudied and therefore not well understood.

The military also shapes collective identities and communities in ways that affect the everyday meaning of lives. Migration of rural and urban military recruits to military bases restructures both sending communities—by removing bright, able-bodied youth who might decide to seek opportunities elsewhere instead of returning after military service—and receiving communities, through the geographic concentration of military personnel, their families, and veterans on and around military bases. This geographic concentration allows for the development of military-related subcultures that serve as a source of support for military personnel and their families, while also providing an economic infrastructure that supports the whole community. These subcultures also offer opportunities for groups that might otherwise be marginalized either economically (as is the case for disadvantaged youth) or socially (as is the case for LGBT service members who participated in gay social worlds that began to form on the coasts after the massive mobilizations associated with the World Wars). However, more research is needed to understand the ways in which the military influences communities and the role of military-related subcultures in cultivating collective identities.

As this discussion indicates, there are many potential paths for future research that uses a life-course perspective to study military service at the individual, cohort, and structural/symbolic levels. Pursuing these topics will require the collection of new data at multiple levels. In the fall of 2011, several of the authors who contributed chapters to this volume met at the University of Maryland, along with several other scholars interested in studying military and veteran lives, in order to discuss priorities for future research. We have formed smaller working groups that are charged with exploring the options for additional individual-level data collection related to recruitment into military service, transitions into civilian life, and the long-term consequences of military service across cohorts. Thus, our collective work in moving forward the study of military and veterans' lives continues.

The narrative of an expanding network of scholars that we have traced in this chapter echoes to some extent the narrative provided by Paul Gade and Brandis Ruise with regard to an earlier generation of scholars. Importantly, there is overlap in these groups of scholars. Those who have been at the table over the long term have helped guide us in our work on this volume, as well as more generally, in manifold ways. We hope this volume inspires a new generation of scholars to join the effort to understand the effects of military service from a life-course perspective.

2 The Military as a Transforming Influence

Integration into or Isolation from Normal Adult Roles?

Ryan Kelty and David R. Segal

Military service is an important life-course experience for those who serve. For those who do not, depending on the historical context, lack of military service may also be important. This chapter addresses two fundamental aspects of life-course development with regard to military service.[1] One focus is the consideration of what events or social characteristics of the individual motivate one to pursue a trajectory that includes military service. A second focus centers on how individuals differ in their life-course trajectories during their military service based on different individual social characteristics (e.g., race and ethnicity, gender, social class, and sexual orientation) and the structural characteristics of the military. This application of the life-course perspective includes an examination of how military service acts as a mechanism affecting individuals' life-course trajectories after military service. In other words, this chapter examines who serves, why they serve, and what effect military service has on individuals both while they are in uniform and once they have separated from the military. Our particular focus is on the early-adult life course and the transition to adulthood.

Military service for most is experienced as a transition—a gradual change, generally tied to the acquisition or termination of roles (Settersten 2003). Others may experience important events (e.g., abrupt changes) that influence their life course as part of military service. Examples of events may include experiences of extreme physical trauma or personally witnessing acts of violence to others that causes psychological distress. Of course, the physical and psychological effects from such events occurring during military service can be comorbid. Service-related deaths are events that can have lifelong effects on those linked to the fallen service member.

Scholars who focus on the life-course perspective note that much of the value of this perspective is derived from the understanding that one's life course often combines multiple, interdependent trajectories (Settersten 2003). Thus, this chapter examines not only military service as a work trajectory, but how this trajectory dialectically relates to other simultaneous and successive trajectories—especially during the demographically dense period of young adulthood (Rindfuss 1991) when individuals' family (i.e., marriage and childbearing), educational, and civic engagement trajectories are also experiencing significant development.

The role of the military in shaping the transition to adulthood is best understood in historical perspective, because the composition of those serving and the consequences of service have changed markedly from the 18th to the 21st centuries. These changes have had important effects on youth from different sociodemographic backgrounds. Before the birth of the Republic, military service in the common militia was a rite of passage to adulthood among young men. As the militia waned in the 19th century, military experience became less widespread, setting the stage for dramatic changes in the relationship between America's youth and military service in the 20th and 21st centuries.

Today, a new paradigm for understanding transitions to adulthood among American youth is emerging (Berlin, Furstenberg, and Waters 2010). In the 1950s, it was normative for youth to leave home early because opportunities were plentiful and social expectations supported early transitions to adult roles and independence. Now, it takes much longer for youth to leave home, complete school, enter the workforce, marry, and have children, and the sequencing of these life-course transitions and events is considerably more variable (Settersten and Ray 2010). Yet there are reasons to expect that contemporary transitions to adulthood among those who have served in the military are more stable and orderly than they are for those who have not served, because the All-Volunteer Force is both more career and family oriented than are most civilian forms of employment (Kelty, Kleykamp, and Segal 2010). Thus, in this chapter, we examine military service and transitions to adulthood in relation to both historical and contemporary circumstances.

HISTORICAL CONTEXT FOR CURRENT TRANSITIONS TO ADULTHOOD THROUGH MILITARY SERVICE

During the colonial era, the colonies relied on defense by local militias. According to the Uniform Militia Act of 1792, service in these militias was reserved for free White men, who were usually landowners (Kestnbaum 2000; Mahon 1960). However, during periods of crisis, the privilege of serving in the military was broadened to include those typically excluded from service, and even extended to African Americans at times (Ferling 1981; Kestnbaum 2000; Quarles 1959; Toppin 1975). The part-time nature of this model allowed men to work in their communities unless they were needed for military service, with the added benefit of being cheaper than financing a standing military (Boucher 1973; Coffman 2000). But by 1770, the popular value of obligatory military service was eroding and men began escaping militia duty by paying a fine, which relegated military defense to those who were not of sufficient means to purchase their way out of service (Boucher 1973). Reports of militia ranks being filled by less educated and marginalized lower-class (White) males from early in the nation's history testify to the insidious impact of the system of purchasing waivers for military service (Boucher 1973; Mahon 1983; Segal 1989). Even with its problems, a military model characterized by a small standing Army that was augmented in times of crisis by citizen soldiers recruited through local militia units emerged during the 19th century. In 1871, the National Guard Association was created, replacing most state militias with comparably structured National Guards. These units remained local and under the leadership of their respective state governors, but the new system expressly allowed these units to be federalized as needed (Coffman 2000).

The practice of using Reserve mobilizations and conscription continued through World War I, after which the United States demobilized its large uniformed force and, consistent with the militia model, maintained a very small number of service members in its peacetime military (Segal and Segal 2004). This mobilization model continued to rely on the citizen soldiers of the National Guard as a base from which to build, as necessary, in the case of hostilities. The National Guard was activated during the World War II mobilization, supplemented by a selective national conscription. By the end of World War II, more than 50 million young men had registered for service and 10 million men had been inducted into the military (Segal 1989). World War II saw the first large-scale, systematic inclusion of women in the American military, with more than a quarter of a million women serving in the various female auxiliary military corps (Segal and Segal 2004). Millions of other young men and women worked as civilians in support of military operations. During World War II, the Army remained racially segregated, and the service of African Americans was limited by the number of positions available in all-Black units (see Lutz, Chapter 4 of this volume). Although men (and women) of color could and did serve, they were present in relatively small numbers and typically in less prestigious support roles.

At the end of World War II, the United States maintained, for the first time, a large standing "peacetime" force. Historically, peacetime military participation in the U.S. has represented significantly less than 1% of the population. Although the Cold War military was much larger than any previous peacetime force, it still accounted for less than 2% of the population.

The maintenance of a selective conscription system during World War II and thereafter affected the employment of those who did not serve as well as those who did. Civilian men seeking employment were routinely asked for their registration and classification documents, both to demonstrate that they had complied with the law and were registered for the draft, and to indicate to potential employers the likelihood that they would be drafted. This latter concern had an effect on employers' willingness to invest in recruiting and training workers who then might be called for military service. Veterans were commonly asked for their discharge papers to document that they had met their military obligations and because discharges other than honorable might be indicative of potential problem employees.

The Servicemen's Readjustment Act (the first GI Bill) was established after World War II and provided educational benefits, as well as funds to assist veterans with housing, jobs, and health care. GI Bill benefits were available to all male veterans, but were withheld from women who served until decades after World War II (Segal and Segal 2004). World War II affected the life-course trajectories of a generation of American men (Elder 1986; Mettler 2005; Sampson and Laub 1996). Military service overseas, schooling attained during service, and the benefits of the GI Bill enhanced subsequent educational attainment, occupational status, job stability, and earnings relative to peers who did not serve. This was true for both Black and White men; however, whereas veterans in both groups benefited from service relative to non-veterans, military service did not bridge the racial gap in educational, occupational, or income attainment (Smith, Marsh, and Segal 2011).

During the Korean War, the United States still maintained a male-only draft, but the Army was desegregated and African American participation in the military increased. A majority of some cohorts served, although the numbers were small in comparison to World War II because of the relatively small cohorts born during the Great Depression. For men, the impact of selective service status on civilian employment continued, as did the provision of benefits through the GI Bill.

The male-only draft continued into the Vietnam War. It suffered from flaws in execution, resulting in gross inequities and strong social pressure to reform military personnel staffing policy. A major issue that made implementation of an equitable draft nearly impossible was the disparity between the large baby boom cohorts of men who were of draft-eligible age and the relatively small numbers of men needed for military service. The problem became not whom to select, but how to exclude a large number of young men (Segal 1989). The often socially and politically motivated deferment system was decentralized in the hands of local draft boards for most of the war and produced inequitable results favoring Whites of high social class (Curry 1985). Because of presidential decisions not to mobilize the Reserves, for many young men, enlisting in the military Reserve services became, for the first time in our history, a way to avoid having to go to war. Aside from providing the personnel required through conscription and draft-motivated volunteers, the draft system continued to limit female participation to 1–2% of the force from the end of World War II through the Vietnam War (Segal and Segal 2004).

In 1973, the All-Volunteer Force replaced the draft. Both the militia-based manpower model and the All-Volunteer Force assume an open systems model of the military within American society. The open systems model suggests that those who are drawn into the military provide an essential dialectic link between the military and the host society. This is important in a democracy because it ensures that those expressly trained and equipped for mobilizing significant lethal force have solid links to those whom they are sworn to protect and defend. It also allows for changes in the military to align with changes in the general population. This connective force has been viewed by some as essential for positive civil-military relations in a democracy. Others view the open system as a potential threat to both the military and society. The opposing views are perhaps best summarized by the historical debate between Janowitz (1960) and Huntington (1957).

Janowitz believed that it was critical for the relationship between the military and society to be an open system. For him, an open system legitimates and strengthens the military itself, as well as civilian control over the military—a functional win-win for society. By contrast, Huntington viewed the mission of the military as too important to be distracted or spoiled by civilian interruptions. He called for the military to be separated from society in order that it might be able to focus, train, and implement the mission of military defense. Huntington viewed the separation of military members from society as a functional necessity lest the military be degraded by civilian vices and therefore unable to perform its necessary social functions. Our history indicates societal preferences aligning with Janowitz and other like-minded individuals. The move to the All-Volunteer Force and other subsequent legal and regulatory changes demonstrate even stronger commitments to this preference for a more open system of civil-military relations within the United States.

The initial success of the All-Volunteer Force had much to do with significant increases in the military participation of women and African Americans. For these two groups, expected participation in the volunteer-based military had been grossly underestimated by its architects. Although women had always participated in the military via their connections to men who served and during some periods of war (see Campbell, Chapter 3 of this volume), direct female participation in the military services jumped from less than 2% in 1972 to approximately 5% in 1975, and exceeded 8% by 1980 (Segal and Segal 2004). The admission of women to the national service academies began in 1976. As of 2008, women represented approximately 15% of all military personnel (Manning 2005). African Americans' military participation climbed from 14% in the early 1970s (Kleykamp 2007) to well above 20% by the end of the decade (Eitelberg 1988).

The All-Volunteer Force has motivated more service members to stay for a career, or at least for longer periods of service, than in the draft era. Thus, whereas the conscription era saw the military as a period of transition *from* youth to adulthood, in the volunteer force era, service became a transition *to* adulthood for many who served. Service members who stay longer are more likely to marry and have children than their shorter-serving draft-era predecessors. This has generated issues in negotiating work-family balance, which the military has taken steps to address. It has also meant that more members of veteran families have directly experienced the military as an institution, for better or worse (see Burland and Lundquist, Chapter 8 of this volume). In some instances, among those whose lives are linked to military service personnel, the influences of the military operate early in the life course, over variable but potentially long durations, and during critical periods of child, adolescent, and early-adult development.

Educational benefits continue to be a hallmark of the benefits package for those who have served in the military during the all-volunteer era, although they became contributory programs soon after the end of conscription—a change that lasted until very recently. Although these benefits are available to all service members who are honorably discharged, some service members have opted out. Of those who have contributed to the plan, many have not ended up using the educational benefits they accrued. An updated version of the GI Bill in 2009, the "Post-9/11 GI Bill," provides those who served on or after September 11, 2001, with an enhanced educational benefits package. Service members covered under the new GI Bill receive more money toward tuition and books, a living allowance, and for the first time are allowed to transfer unused educational benefits to their spouses or children (U.S. Department of Veterans Affairs 2010). This has become an incentive to remain in service for people who otherwise might leave to use their educational benefits themselves. Because military service and higher education are typically pursued at similar points in the life course, young veterans may have lower levels of educational attainment than peers who go straight into college. Even so, since its inception in 1944, the educational benefits tied to military service have channeled large numbers of veterans into higher education (see Bennett and McDonald, Chapter 6 of this volume).

The all-volunteer American military of the latter quarter of the 20th and early 21st centuries has had significant effects on service members' transitions to adulthood across a number of domains (Kelty, Kleykamp, and Segal 2010). In the remainder of this chapter, we examine these influences, beginning with a general discussion of military service and its alternatives. We then examine five broad areas through which the military impacts the transition to adulthood for those who serve, which provides a basis for the additional discussion of these topics in subsequent chapters.

First, we note that several sociodemographic groups, defined on the basis of gender, race and ethnicity, social class, and sexual orientation, continue to have differential access to the organization and its benefits. Unlike the militia model, in which most people in a fairly homogeneous demographic category served, in the volunteer force era, a far smaller proportion of a far more diverse population serve. In addition, we note the specific factors affecting the lives of members of the Guard and Reserve services. The current protracted wars on two fronts have stretched our forces, in particular Guard and Reserve service members, who have been returned to their pre–Vietnam War role as an operationally essential military reserve. The total force (active duty, Guard, and Reserve) is still being adjusted in an attempt to meet the needs of the nation, as well as the needs of our service members and their families.

Second, we explore how military service affects family formation, including the timing of marriage and parenthood, family structure, and the influence of military culture on families. Third, we view the numerous ways military service continues to be connected to education. This aspect of military service links with issues of race and ethnicity, class, and gender, as well as recruitment and retention of personnel. Fourth, the connection between civilian labor force participation and military service will be addressed (see also Kleykamp, Chapter 7 of this volume). This is in part a reflection of returns to education that might have been gained through military educational benefits. It is also a reflection, in part, of the national redistribution of the labor force attributable to geographic mobility either during or after service (see Bailey, Chapter 9 of this volume). Finally, because the nature of military service during times of war is inherently dangerous, this chapter examines the impact of physical and mental health issues on service members' transitions to adulthood (see MacLean, Chapter 10 of this volume). In each section, we contrast the roles and early life-course trajectories of those who have and have not served in the military.

MILITARY SERVICE AND ITS ALTERNATIVES

Most people who join the military do so as young adults. For teens coming out of high school, the primary life decision is whether to enter the workforce directly or to delay workforce entry by continuing one's education. In both cases, a military trajectory is possible. For those choosing to go directly to work, joining the military as an enlisted service member is an option. For those who wish to attend school, there are several avenues for using higher education as a springboard into service as a military officer, including ROTC programs at civilian colleges and universities, the federal service academies, or totally civilian education followed by a commission through one of the officer candidate schools. Given the nature of the current military as all volunteer, the individual is free to weigh the merits of each potential trajectory in deciding which to pursue, although clearly some have more viable options than others. The following sections address the two competing alternatives to military service in early adulthood— education and civilian employment. Further, each section discusses how military service influences individual trajectories in education and civilian employment for those who do volunteer for military service.

Education and the Military

Most people who join the military do not make it a career. In recent generations, the educational incentives tied to the GI Bill have been a strong motivation for military service. However, because military service and higher education are typically pursued at similar points in the life course, young military veterans may have lower levels of educational attainment than peers who go straight into college.

Research on the educational attainment of veterans in the mid-20th century suggests that men who had served in World War II and the Korean War achieved higher levels of education than their non-veteran peers. By contrast, military service during the Cold War effectively disrupted education, with non-veteran educational attainment increasing relative to veterans across the 1950s and 1960s (McLean 2005). Following this pattern, male veterans of the Vietnam era achieved lower levels of education than their peers who did not serve (Cohen, Segal, and Temme 1986; Cohen and Temme 1986). This reversal may be due in part to the advent of programs for federal aid to higher education not tied to military service that increased markedly in the 1960s (McLean 2005; Segal 1989) and in part to changes in the nature of GI Bill educational benefits. Due to the scale of the wars pre-Vietnam and the relative support they received from the American public, a substantial number of men served who were well positioned to attend college and well received on college campuses following their service. At the peak of World War II GI Bill use, benefits were equivalent to 53.9% of monthly wages in manufacturing. By contrast, in 1975, Vietnam-era GI Bill enrollees received only 34.3% of average monthly manufacturing wages, raising the opportunity costs for GI Bill use (Mattila 1978).

Data from the National Longitudinal Survey indicate that at least through the first decade of the All-Volunteer Force, the Cold War pattern of educational attainment persisted. Veterans of the volunteer force lagged educationally behind their peers who did not serve, and the longer they served, the more they fell behind (Cohen and Temme 1986; Cohen, Warner, and Segal 1995). This was true for Black and White veterans, and for male and female veterans (Cohen, Segal, and Temme 1986). Black veterans did show a positive educational trajectory across the life course, although one not sufficiently strong to overcome the negative effects of military service (Cohen et al. 1995). At the intersection of race and gender, African American women veterans do not differ significantly from White women veterans in terms of years of education or percent earning a college degree, although among non-veterans, White women are more likely to earn college degrees than Black women (Cooney, Segal, Segal, and Falk 2003). Taken together, educational benefits accrued by service members during or after their service demonstrate inconsistent effects on veterans' life-course outcomes depending on era, race, and gender.

The Civilian Labor Force and Military Service

The military offers its most junior enlisted personnel higher pay and better benefits than are available to nonserving age-matched peers. Their relatively young age and relatively low educational attainment makes competing in the civilian labor market more challenging for this group. However, these relative benefits decrease over time, and White veterans earn less in their subsequent civilian lives compared to their counterparts who did not serve (Angrist 1998). Veterans who served as officers tend to fare better, earning, on average, a 10% wage premium over their non-veteran peers (Hirsch and Mehay 2003). Black veterans have tended to achieve more in terms of their educational attainment, income, and occupational status than their peers who did not serve, and in some instances have caught up with White non-veterans by the later years of their working lives (Smith, Marsh, and Segal 2011).

The military's pay and benefits structure is based on rank and years in service, and as such it is a much fairer employment environment than the civilian labor market in terms of monetary and nonmonetary compensation. The pay gap between White and African American service members is significantly smaller than in the civilian labor market (Booth and Segal 2005). This factor is a leading cause for the significant overrepresentation of African American women in the armed services. Not only does the military treat racial minorities more fairly than the civilian sector in terms of promotion and compensation, it also compensates women much more evenly with men. Differences in pay by race and gender do exist, but the gap is considerably narrower within the military than in the civilian labor market.

As we mentioned above, a very small percentage of age-eligible youth tend to serve in the military, and most who serve do so for a limited amount of time and do not make a career out of military service. For them, military service may indeed be a transition between school and the civilian workforce. Even for those who serve for a career, the restrictions on upper age limits due to the premium placed on relative youth in the military means that virtually all military personnel will leave the service at an age too early, and a pension too small, to fully retire. They are likely to have to transition to civilian work roles.

Vietnam-era veterans have more negative earnings outcomes compared to military veterans of the Korean War and World War II eras. For example, most World War II veterans experienced a positive progression in their careers after separation from service, whereas Vietnam veterans showed several negative effects due to military service. Vietnam veterans have been observed to earn less than their civilian contemporaries (Angrist 1990). They are also more likely to have changed careers and are significantly less satisfied with their careers and finances than their civilian counterparts (Bookwala, Frieze, and Grote 1994). This cohort effect likely reflects the adjustment difficulties experienced by a largely conscripted military force serving in an unpopular war during a time of tremendous social change in our society. The lack of clear support and respect afforded many Vietnam veterans, in conjunction with physical and psychological wounds, appears to have had systematic impacts on their transitions to education and work following their service.

More contemporary studies on veterans' civilian workforce attainment in the All-Volunteer Force era examine differences by race and gender. The proportion of women veterans who had obtained a Bachelor's degree in 1990 (14%) was approximately one-third that of women who have never served in uniform (Cooney et al. 2003). Women veterans in 1990 also had higher rates of unemployment than nonserving women and this difference was consistent among White and African American women (Cooney et al. 2003). In 1990, women veterans were estimated to have a 12.5% "tax" on their earnings and an 11.7% disadvantage in their family income compared to women with no military service, and these effects were net of education and race. Fifteen years later, however, in 2005, analyses of veteran status on earnings by gender estimated that women who serve earned approximately $7,000 more each year than female non-veterans (Holder 2007).

In 2005, male veterans also outperformed their civilian counterparts with respect to earnings, but with a much more modest boost ($3,000 per year) above non-veterans (Holder 2007). However, White veterans' earnings lagged behind nonserving peers for the first few years after separation from service (Phillips et al. 1992). A consistent pattern in the relationship between veteran status and earnings indicates African American and Hispanic veterans fare better than White veterans relative to each group's nonserving counterparts (Cooney et al. 2003; Holder 2007; Phillips et al. 1992). Thus, although there does seem to be a later-life income benefit to military service, the relative benefit is greatest for racial and ethnic minorities.

One difference between the current wars in Iraq and Afghanistan and other post–Korean War conflicts has been a dependence on Reserve forces that has not been seen since World War II. In mid-2008, 40–50% of American military personnel serving in combat theaters were drawn from the Reserve components (i.e., the National Guard and federal Reserve forces) (DeAngelis and Segal 2009). These weekend warriors, many of whom joined the Reserves on the assumption that they would train for one weekend a month and two weeks during the summer unless needed for missions, such as natural disasters, found that they had to transition from their primary civilian roles—occupational and familial among them—to military roles involving long and frequent combat deployments. Such life-course disruption associated with transitions to military roles after other roles have been established has been shown to have long-term negative consequences in earlier cohorts (Elder 1987; Elder and Clipp 1988a,b; Elder, Shanahan, and Clipp 1994). With the increased rate of mobilization of Reserve component personnel for the wars in Iraq and Afghanistan, the impact of such deployments on the financial well-being of these personnel has become an issue, and it will be decades before we know the full impact it has had on their later-life health and financial security (see Street and Hoffman, Chapter 11 of this volume). Because some reservists are unemployed, underemployed, or in school prior to mobilization, on average, the earnings of reservists increase when they are activated. Moreover, their earnings increase with length of active-duty service. However, some reservists experience earnings loss with activation, and, on average, earnings decline when the reservists are demobilized (Government Accountability Office 2009; Loughran, Klerman, and Martin 2006). Equally important, reservists may return from combat zones with physical or psychological wounds. They may also find that they lack the support systems that facilitate the transition back into civilian roles that are available to regular military personnel.

An increasing option for post-service civilian employment is that of civilian contract work. This growing industry is divided in a few different ways. First, there is a division between private security firms—those that use guns to secure people or physical assets—and those that contract their labor without the use of lethal weapons. Second, there is a distinction between those who are in skilled trades (e.g., electronics, intelligence, mechanical) and those who work in unskilled service-oriented jobs (e.g., cooking, cleaning, maintaining physical grounds). Many who serve in the unskilled jobs on bases outside of the United States are third-country nationals—citizens of neither the United States nor the country in which they are working as a contractor.

There are several major differences between serving in the military and working as a contractor. For one, the pay differential between the two groups can be quite large and favors the skilled, but not the unskilled, contractors. The benefits packages are also different, but many feel that the military personnel make out better on this dimension. Contractors are also perceived to be exposed to less risk, have more autonomy and flexibility in their work, maintain more control over their work contracts, and experience less work-family conflict with regard to number of household moves required (if any), time away from family, and vacation time (Kelty and Schnack 2012). Several recent studies indicate that the integration of civilian contractors with military units has a negative impact on retention attitudes—potentially affecting service members' work trajectories (Kelty 2008, 2009; Kelty and Segal 2007). The increase in pay and reenlistment bonuses for military personnel with skills that are highly valued in the growing civilian contractor market is evidence that the military, as an institution vying for the best talent in an open system of employment, is having to restructure in order to deal with the emerging threat of personnel leaving the military to pursue contractor employment. One particularly interesting example of this phenomenon was the spike in Special Forces personnel with more than ten years of service electing to leave for jobs with contracting agencies (Burgess 2008). Whereas these individuals have historically tended to remain in service until reaching their twenty-year mark, at which point their all-or-nothing retirement benefits would activate, now they are increasingly being offered compensation packages that motivate termination of service. Aside from the loss of personnel generally, we do not yet know whether these losses are equal across subgroups defined by race, ethnicity, class, gender, and sexuality, or whether the pull is felt more strongly by some groups than others. Regardless, for some, the option to parlay one's experience in the military into direct application with a civilian contracting organization creates relatively easy transitions from military to civilian work within one's employment trajectory.

SOCIAL CHARACTERISTICS: WHO SERVES?

In this section, we turn our attention to issues of the selection of military service by individuals with different social/structural characteristics, such as gender, race, ethnicity, social class, and sexual orientation. We provide only an overview of each here to emphasize that the experience of military service in one's life-course trajectory varies by these important characteristics. Fuller discussions of these issues are found in other chapters within this volume.

Gender

Military service has historically been a masculine role. Legal reforms in 1967, in conjunction with more recent reforms associated with the initiation of the All-Volunteer Force, lifted official ceilings on women's participation, although many restrictions remained in place that helped keep female participation lower than it might otherwise have been. Public acceptance of women serving in the armed forces has increased dramatically since the advent of the All-Volunteer Force in the early 1970s. In part, this is because the military is embedded within its host society and reflects the more progressive attitudes toward women in the workforce that we find in the general population. Another factor is the personnel needs of the military in the all-volunteer context (Segal and Segal 2004; Titunik 2000). As a consequence of the shift to an all-volunteer model based on market dynamics rather than the draft system, it has been in the military's interest to normalize and support increased female participation in the military.

The Marine Corps employs the fewest women of all service branches (6%), followed by the Army and the Navy at approximately 15% each. By far, the Air Force has the largest number of women, approximately 20%. However, in raw numbers, the Air Force and Army each employ a substantial number of women, approximately 60,000 combined (Manning 2005).

The differential treatment of women at the institutional and interactional levels has several important effects on transitions to adulthood and the pursuit of careers. First, the current ground combat exclusion that prohibits women serving in small ground units (e.g., Army branches of infantry, armor, and artillery below the battalion level) limits the number of women who can serve, and structurally constrains female officers and enlisted personnel from the most prestigious units and jobs in the military. This affects service entry and both the rate and height of their ascent in the organization should they choose to remain for a career (Stewart and Firestone 2001). Second, the hypermasculine culture of the military devalues feminine qualities and characteristics (Miller 1997; Snyder 2003). This devaluation leads to both physical and symbolic violence against women, which is a significant source of motivation for leaving military service among many female service members (Miller 1997). Third, mentorship is important in fostering maturation of young professionals. The significant increase in more senior women in both the officer corps and enlisted ranks provides many more role models and mentors who share important social and cultural experiences.

The above-mentioned challenges that military women face make them more likely than men to leave the armed forces after a short period of service. For these women, military service leads to a transition to other adult occupational, familial, and educational roles rather than a transition to a military career. However, as we shall see below, these choices vary by race and ethnicity, as well as by gender. Although the military appears to be leading the way in providing gender-equitable employment opportunities relative to the civilian labor market, even at the highest levels of the employment ladder, there remains room for improvement—especially in reducing work-family role conflict among female service members.

Race and Ethnicity

During the early debates on the end of conscription, critics of the volunteer force concept argued that recruitment on the basis of labor market dynamics would place the burden of military service disproportionately on the shoulders of economically disadvantaged groups: the poor and racial-ethnic minorities (Janowitz and Moskos 1974; Marmion 1971).

The architects of the volunteer force had expected that the end of conscription would not affect the racial composition of the force. However, in marked contrast to both the militia era and the pre–Korean War conscription era, African American participation in the military increased dramatically in the 1970s and remained around 22% from 1980 through 2001. Since the war in Afghanistan began, African American participation has declined, dipping below 20% in 2006 for the first time in over a quarter of a century. By contrast, African American participation in the civilian labor force since the late 1970s has remained constant between 11 and 13% (Segal, Thanner, and Segal 2007). Some hypothesize that Black youth may prefer the immediate benefits of the military, including its more rigorous meritocratic structure, relative to increased educational acquisition or civilian labor force participation (Teachman, Call, and Segal 1993a). For many young African Americans, joining the military remains a transition to an adult military role, rather than a step taken prior to assuming alternative adult roles in the civilian labor market.

Hispanic participation in the military has risen sharply since the early 1990s. From the inception of the All-Volunteer Force until 1994, Hispanics represented less than 6% of military personnel. An upward trajectory began in the late 1980s and has continued to the present, with the population identifying as Hispanic more than doubling to nearly 13% in 2006 (Segal, Thanner, and Segal 2007). In contrast to African American trends, levels of Hispanic military service mirror their increasing participation in the civilian labor force during this time period, only falling behind in recent years. When adjusted for those qualifying for military service on the basis of education, Hispanics are actually slightly overrepresented in the military compared to the civilian labor force (Segal et al. 2007). Differential racial-ethnic participation in various branches of the military is consequential for whether military service represents a transition to a military career or a step toward alternative careers. The Marine Corps has the smallest career force of the branches; the Air Force has the largest. Thus, the concentration of Hispanics in the former suggests that service is likely to represent a transition to alternate nonmilitary adult roles for young Hispanic men and women.

Social Class

Analysis of those serving in the All-Volunteer Force reveals a pattern of over-representation from somewhat lower socioeconomic backgrounds. Members of the armed services also exhibited moderately lower levels of academic performance than those who qualified but did not serve. Not surprisingly, those who served as officers had higher levels of high school performance and came from higher socioeconomic status backgrounds than enlisted personnel. The overrepresentation of African Americans in the All-Volunteer Force noted earlier is primarily a reflection of their disproportionate representation in the less affluent strata of society (Segal, Burns, Falk, Silver, and Sharda 1998). However, those from the bottom quartile of the socioeconomic distribution are underrepresented in the military, largely because of the educational, physical, mental, and moral requirements[2] for service. The top quartile is also underrepresented primarily because of self-selection. As a consequence, the volunteer force is composed of personnel drawn from the broad middle range of the socioeconomic distribution, with a mean socioeconomic status somewhat below that of the broader society. These patterns have been consistently noted since the earliest decades of the volunteer force (Bachman et al. 2000). Thus, while military service might be playing a larger role in the transition to adulthood for women and for racial and ethnic minorities than it did in the past, and might do so in the future for sexual minorities, it is now less inclusive across the socioeconomic spectrum than in the militia era or at the time of World War II and Korean War conscription.

Sexual Orientation

Homosexuals have served in the U.S. military since the Revolutionary War, although they have faced severe discrimination for much of our history (see Brown, Chapter 5 of this volume). Homosexuals were officially prohibited from military service beginning in 1950, and this prohibition lasted until January of 1993 when President Clinton signed the "Don't Ask, Don't Tell, Don't Pursue" policy on sexual orientation in the military. Don't Ask, Don't Tell, as it was popularly known, allowed homosexuals to serve provided that they did not engage in homosexual acts or disclose their sexual identity (Bowling, Firestone, and Harris 2005; Segal and Bourg 2002). Initially, the prohibition against homosexuality in the military was based on moral grounds, but in more recent decades it was recast as a national security issue related to unit cohesion and morale. Thus, until its recent repeal in September of 2011, members of the lesbian, gay, and bisexual community did not have the same access to military service either for an adult role or for a transition to other adult roles as did the exclusively heterosexually behaving community.

Prior to its repeal, many questioned the equity of the "Don't Ask, Don't Tell, Don't Pursue" policy's enforcement, arguing that in times of crisis, such as our current engagements in Iraq and Afghanistan, the military is much less likely to discharge for homosexuality due to personnel needs. Even so, there has been a fair amount of public debate over the dismissal of homosexual service members, especially Arabic linguists, in recent years. Those who opposed the policy argued that it violated human rights and the U.S. Constitution, while also placing homosexuals in the position of second-class citizens—similar to claims made by African Americans in the past and women currently.

Don't Ask, Don't Tell allowed closeted homosexuals to serve in the military, but effectively suppressed, at least publicly, adult roles tied to committed relationships among same-sex partners. Given the frequent relocations, housing restrictions, and physical and psychological risks (addressed below) that are associated with military service, the inability of same-sex partners to fully engage their roles as significant others presents numerous challenges for these service members. Some of these challenges are not present for their civilian counterparts, or if they are, they can be addressed differently in civilian life than in the less tolerant military institution. With the recent lifting of the ban on homosexuals serving openly in the military, the conflict between work and family trajectories for the minority of service members who are homosexuals has been reduced.

FAMILY TRAJECTORIES

Prior to the current era of the All-Volunteer Force, the military was composed primarily of young, single men. During the conscription era, men tended to either postpone marriage and fatherhood until after their military service or, at times, get married to avoid conscription. In either case, military service was largely decoupled from family roles. The volunteer force is older and more career oriented than the prior conscription-era force. Policy makers have recognized that the modern military still recruits individuals, but it retains—or fails to retain—families. Military and familial trajectories are now more closely linked, which increasingly leads to work-family role conflict among military members. Such conflicts, and other intersections of military service and family life, vary by gender, age, sexual orientation, route to active-duty service (e.g., activation from the Reserves versus voluntary transition after high school), and duration in the military, as well as other social characteristics.

Marriage

The number of service members who are married, as well as the number of dual-service couples (i.e., with both partners serving in uniform), increased after the advent of the All-Volunteer Force. However, the growth in marriage has not been linear. The percentage of married enlisted soldiers climbed from 40% in 1973 to a peak at 57% in 1994. After declining and then rising again over the next ten years, the percentage in 2005 was 52% (Department of Defense 2005). In 2002, nearly 12% of marriages among service members involved dual-service unions. At that time, only 7% of male service members were married to women who also served, whereas 49% of female service members were married to men in uniform (Segal and Segal 2004). The significant difference in dual-service marriage rates by sex is due in part to the underrepresentation of women in the military.

Military personnel are slightly more likely than their civilian peers to be married; however, they are less likely than their age peers to be married when they enter the military (Segal and Segal 2004). They enter single, but marry young. Military service is more compatible with the husband and father roles than the wife and mother roles. Female officers and enlisted service members are less likely to be married than their male counterparts (Department of Defense 2005). In 2002, men in the junior enlisted ranks were nearly twice as likely to be married as civilians aged 18 to 24 (Adler-Baeder, Pittman, and Taylor 2005; Segal and Segal 2004). Interestingly, the racial differences in family formation that appear in the civilian population are absent in the military (Lundquist 2004).

Divorce rates differ dramatically by gender, race, and rank among military personnel. In 2005, the marital dissolution rate (per 100, per annum) among male service members was nearly twice as high among enlisted personnel (2.8) than among officers (1.5). Among women, the difference exceeded a two-to-one ratio between enlisted personnel (7.3) and officers (3.6). In both cases, divorce rates among military women are significantly higher than among military men, but they are especially high for enlisted personnel (Karney and Crown 2007).

During the early years of the volunteer force, divorce was higher among military personnel than their civilian counterparts, but this was in part a consequence of earlier age at marriage of the military personnel (Lundquist

2007). There was also a pattern of relationships between race and divorce in these rates that ran counter to civilian trends. Although African Americans have higher civilian rates of marital dissolution than White civilians, the pattern was reversed in the military. Compared to White civilians, White enlistees were 50% more likely to divorce, whereas African American enlistees were more than 10% less likely to divorce compared to African American civilians. Lundquist (2006) attributes the closing of the racial gap in marital dissolution within the military to an equalizing of the constraints faced by the families involved. Military men are less likely to be divorced than their age-matched civilian counterparts, whereas women in uniform are significantly more likely to be divorced than their civilian counterparts (Karney and Crown 2007; Pollard, Karney, and Loughran 2008). Among service members over age 25, there are large gender differences in the percentage of first marriages, which is consistently lower for military women in their first marriage than for civilian age-matched peers—the reverse pattern of that found among military and civilian men. In particular, in one study, older service women (ages 40–49) were approximately half as likely to be in their first marriage (27.2%) as civilian women in the same age group (49.2%) (Adler-Baeder, Pittman, and Taylor 2005). The apparent gender differences in divorce rates are one reflection of the differential effects of role conflict experienced by male and female service personnel compared to civilian peers.

Despite the stressors associated with deployments, there is no strong evidence prior to the current wars that they increased divorce among male service members, although female members have had higher divorce rates than their civilian peers (Pollard et al. 2008). Indeed, there is some evidence that deployments may strengthen military marriages (Karney and Crown 2007). However, data collected since the beginning of the wars in Afghanistan and Iraq show that the divorce rate among service members, as a group, has climbed from 2.6% in 2001 to 3.6% in 2009 and 2010 (Bushatz 2010). Additionally, recent findings show that once service members leave the military, they experience higher rates of marital dissolution than their civilian peers. This suggests that the military is able to buffer against the stressors on marriages while individuals remain in service, but once the structures and support of the military are no longer present veterans' marriages are negatively impacted (Pollard et al. 2008).

There are a number of stressors experienced by military families that may contribute to the observed marital patterns: financial stress, spouse employment, housing/neighborhood quality (off-post), access to services, separation from family and friends (i.e., social support networks), frequent relocations, and risk of death/injury (Cooney 2003; Karney and Crown 2007; Segal 1986). There are also potential benefits of military service for marriage. Supportive family policies in supportive communities, with professional development opportunities to improve human capital through training, education, and leadership, can increase financial prospects through military promotions and post-service work, while also contributing to personal development and growth. Each of these outcomes may improve the resilience of marriages and family solidarity more generally (Karney and Crown 2007). There is also evidence to suggest that the suite of benefits available to military personnel and their families buffers against some of the stressors known to increase marital dissolution in the civilian population (Watanab, Jensen, Rosen, Newby, Richters, and Cortês 1995).

Childbearing

Nearly three-quarters of married military personnel have dependent children (Segal and Segal 2004). However, in part due to conflicting role demands, military women are less likely than military men to have children (Segal and Segal 2004). The Department of Health and Human Services compared civilian and military men and women on age at first birth. They found that active-duty military and civilian men had nearly identical mean ages at the birth of their first child (25.0 and 25.1 years, respectively). However, among women, mean age at first birth was 1.5 years younger for those in the military than for civilian women (23.6 and 25.1 years, respectively) (Department of Health and Human Services 2007). This is in part a reflection of earlier age at first marriage among military women, perhaps because of the volunteer force's increasingly family-friendly policies (Lundquist and Smith 2005). Couples in dual-service marriages are less likely than single-service couples to have children (Segal and Segal 2004). Among all active-duty personnel, regardless of marital status, 44% of service men and women had dependent children in 2002. Comparable proportions of Black men (53%) and women (52%) in uniform had children. White service men (44%) were more likely to have children than White service women (33%); similar parenthood rates were observed among Hispanic service men (42%) and service women (34%) (Department of Health and Human Services 2007).

The Influence of Military Culture on Families

Military culture pressures family members to conform to normative service standards in order to positively reflect upon the family's service member, and by extension their unit and commanders. This pressure is felt by spouses and children, but especially by female spouses of officers, who regularly engage in a variety of volunteer activities to support the community and their husbands' units, such as family readiness groups, youth activities, and unit social events (Harrell 2001). Despite a long history of hypermasculine traditions that manifest themselves in overt and subtle ways, the military's adoption of family-friendly policies seems to have encouraged and supported family formation and growth. Ironically, progress made by the military toward gender equality in some senses has outpaced gender equality in families. The fact that the military allows women to do most of the things that men do, while society (and the military) still expect women to play the major role in childrearing, makes it difficult for women on active military duty to meet the demands at the intersection of those roles. Thus, military women are more likely to divorce or to leave active duty. This contributes to the perpetuation of the hypermasculine image of military culture, as well as the relatively small number of dual-career military couples.

CIVIC ENGAGEMENT AND THE MILITARY

Military service may instill, enhance, or transform civic attitudes and engagement. Military service is itself a service to the nation and a form of civic engagement, a motivation for many who voluntarily choose to join the military (National Research Council 2003). Military service and training may influence civic attitudes and behaviors by inculcating the values of duty and selfless service, encouraging the development of organizational and leadership skills, and connecting individuals to social networks through fraternal and veterans' organizations (Nesbit and Reingold 2008). Veterans have been shown to have higher levels of political and civic participation. Although there is variation by race, ethnicity, gender, and other social characteristics, veterans are more likely than their civilian peers to vote, work on political campaigns, donate, sign petitions, and volunteer (Ellison 1992; Leal 1999; Nesbit and Reingold 2008; Teigen 2006).

Several studies indicate that many of the forms of civic engagement observed in the World War II generation may not extend to more recent cohorts of veterans (Krebs 2004; Mettler 2002; Putnam 2000). Early work on Vietnam-era veterans' civic engagement found that although veterans were more alienated than civilian peers, veterans as a group demonstrated higher levels of political activism and civic participation than did their non-veteran peers. In addition, contrary to the generally observed decline in political activism with age, it is the older Vietnam-era veterans who are more active than younger veterans of this period. Additionally, college graduates of the Vietnam era differ in their political activity as a function of veteran status; college graduates who served in the military are more likely to engage in political activity than graduates who did not serve (Louis Harris and Associates 1980). Thus, even though alienation was elevated among Vietnam-era veterans, it did not translate into withdrawal from civic engagement.

A more recent study of the connection between military service and civic engagement focused on young men graduating from high school between 1976 and 1995 (Segal et al. 2001). High school graduates from the years 1976 to 1985 who joined the armed forces demonstrated a significant increase in trust in government from their senior year to two years post-graduation. Neither their college- nor non-college-bound nonserving peers showed an increase in trust in government over this same two-year period, suggesting a positive effect of military service on trust in government. Men graduating high school between 1986 and 1995 with a high propensity to serve in the military had significantly higher levels of trust in government than those not interested in military service. In addition to starting with higher levels of civic interest than their peers who were not inclined to serve in the military, across the twenty-year period examined (1976–1995), men who served increased their level of interest in government during the first couple of years after high school. Veterans' increased level of interest in government following high school was higher than that of their civilian peers who attended college (Segal et al. 2001).

The modern military professional was socialized to forego pursuit of personal political agendas for the greater good of the military mission (Hunter et al. 2004; Ulrich 2002). This may be best exemplified by General George C. Marshall, who refused to vote because he considered voting as a military officer a conflict of interest. He has been singled out as a paragon of the idea of separating military and politics for the sake of military effectiveness and civil-military relations more generally. In some cases, as in Vietnam, this model of unquestioning loyalty to civilian authority proved tragic. In more recent military engagements, both active and retired[3] military leaders have been much more outspoken and critical of national policy on military matters.

In the early 1990s, General Colin Powell openly challenged presidential policy on America's involvement in the Balkans in an Op-Ed article in the *New York Times*, and also publicly disagreed with the administration on the issue of gays in the military (Roman and Tarr 2001). In the current engagements in Iraq and Afghanistan, Lt. Col. Paul Yingling wrote an article in the *Armed Forces Journal* entitled "A Failure in Generalship," in which he offered numerous criticisms of American generals who had "miscalculated both the means and ways necessary to succeed in Iraq" (Yingling 2007). He extended his criticisms to Congress, arguing that it has failed to create a supportive and effective environment for military success in its current conflicts. In 2007, seven Army noncommissioned officers jointly published an Op-Ed essay in the *New York Times* recounting their assessment of the war from a hands-on perspective, concluding with clear criticisms of America's use of military power in Iraq, including a call to withdraw American forces. Their support of a troop withdrawal in Iraq was contextualized by the closing statement: "This suggestion is not meant to be defeatist, but rather to highlight our pursuit of incompatible policies to absurd ends without recognizing the incongruities" (Jayamaha et al. 2007). Although challenges from service members to civilian authority and policy positions are not novel, they do appear to be growing in frequency and to be more public in nature (Jayamaha et al. 2007).

Building Citizens of Character

Military training and education are designed to do more than build technical competence in one's career field. Training, education, and service in general are also critically focused on building character. It is not enough to merely act; one must choose to do the right things for the right reasons. Emphasis is placed on moral-ethical development across the spectrum of professional military education (i.e., formal schooling and training). This function of military service can be observed in many ways. For example, each of the federal military academies states as part of its mission the development of moral-ethical leaders for service in our nation's military and beyond. Each academy has specific programs in moral-ethical character development in addition to infusing character building into many of their military and academic experiences (e.g., West Point's weekly seminars on Professional Military Ethic Education). The following quote, taken from the U.S. Air Force Academy's vision statement, is an example of this fundamental emphasis on character in military education and training:

> Since the nature of the military profession requires officers to have high ethical and moral standards, cadets are challenged to reflect upon their beliefs and values from the moment they arrive (U.S. Air Force Academy 2010).

The military's emphasis on moral-ethical development is not limited to officers. In addition to all training and education programs for enlisted personnel incorporating character building as an integrated component, the different services also have officially espoused values that emphasize moral-ethical development. An example is the set of seven Army values: loyalty, duty, respect, selfless service, honor, integrity, and personal courage. This philosophy is summarized in its definition of "integrity": "Do what is right, legally and morally. Integrity is a quality you develop by adhering to moral principles. It requires that you do and say nothing that deceives others" (U.S. Army Medical Services 2010). By making moral-ethical character development an explicit goal of service, the military influences the development of its members in ways that are strikingly different from most civilian employers. The hope is that this development intersects with other trajectories, both co-occurring and subsequent, to make these men and women better parents, significant others, citizens, and workers.

PHYSICAL, COGNITIVE, AND PSYCHOLOGICAL HEALTH OUTCOMES

The nature of military service, especially in times of war, exposes those who serve to potential physical and mental harm (see MacLean, Chapter 10 of this volume). Through January 3, 2012, the Department of Defense reports 31,921 service members wounded in Iraq during Operation Iraqi Freedom, and another 15,157 wounded in Afghanistan and surrounding locations during Operation Enduring Freedom (Department of Defense 2012). The most likely cause of physical injury (death and nonlethal wounds) in both Iraq and Afghanistan are improvised explosive devices (65% in Iraq, 60% in Afghanistan) followed by artillery/gunshot (9% in Iraq, 16% in Afghanistan) (Department of Defense 2011e). Two of the major physically debilitating injuries suffered by military personnel in the current engagements are traumatic amputations and burns. As of September 2010, the Congressional Research Service reports that across all four branches of service 1,621 service members have suffered amputations—1,033 of which are classified as major limb amputations (Fischer 2010). Several hundred more service members have suffered serious burn wounds in Operation Iraqi Freedom and Operation Enduring Freedom (Atiyeh, Gunn, and Hayek 2007).

In both Iraq and Afghanistan men have been significantly more likely than women to be killed or injured in action (Department of Defense 2011e). Whites are killed and wounded in greater numbers than their proportional representation across all services. Hispanics are wounded less, but suffer fatalities more, than their proportional representation, and African Americans are underrepresented in both casualty statistics relative to their proportion of the force. The underrepresentation of African Americans is attributed to greater participation in the noncombat arms specialties. The disproportionate casualty statistics across races/ethnicities clearly create disparate impacts for members of different groups in their abilities to benefit from military service either on career paths or through transitioning into civilian employment and other adult roles. Such differences in fatality and casualty rates also have implications for the lives of those who are linked to service members, such as parents, spouses, and children.

The "invisible wounds" of cognitive and psychological trauma among service members are also major health outcome concerns that can influence the transition to adulthood. The incidence rate of traumatic brain injury has been officially calculated at 178,876 diagnoses between 2000 and 2010, with 20% classified as moderate, severe, or penetrating (Fischer 2010). Women, Hispanics, enlisted personnel, and those *not* in the active federal forces (i.e., Guard, Reserve, retired) are more likely than their counterparts to report post-traumatic stress disorder (PTSD) and depression (Tanielian and Jaycox 2008). A recent RAND report estimates 300,000 service members who were deployed in Iraq and Afghanistan suffering from PTSD or major depression, along with 320,000 affected by probable traumatic brain injury (Tanielian and Jaycox 2008).

Suicide rates among military personnel have typically been lower than civilian rates. Recent Department of Defense figures indicate that 2008 marks the first time since Vietnam that the rate of suicides in the Army (128 deaths, or about twenty per 100,000 soldiers) has been higher than in the civilian population (Ritchey 2009). In addition to suicides among active military personnel, male veterans are twice as likely as their non-veteran peers to die by suicide. White veterans are more likely to die by suicide than are Black veterans (Kaplan et al. 2007). Suicide among service members and veterans is strongly related to the presence of PTSD, major depression, traumatic brain injury, and limitations in activities of daily living (Kaplan et al. 2007; Tanielian and Jaycox 2008). Such challenges are likely to affect service members' transitions to civilian life and their broader life-course trajectories, as well as the life chances and choices of those with whom their lives are linked.

Service members report alarming failures to acquire available treatment for their cognitive and psychological disorders. Nearly half of those surveyed reported seeking psychological or counseling help for PTSD or major depression. Of those suspecting they had a traumatic brain injury, 43% were never seen by medical professionals for this condition (Kaplan et al. 2007; Tanielian and Jaycox 2008). Many suspect that the culture of the military, like the civilian culture in America, motivates people to avoid seeking help from medical professionals for cognitive and psychological disorders. Fear of negative impacts on career, personal stigmatization, and peers' loss of confidence are cited as major motivations in the decision not to seek professional help (Ritchey 2009; Tanielian and Jaycox 2008). The negative implications associated with these high rates of nontreatment for cognitive and psychological trauma on work outcomes, future health, including higher rates of substance abuse and suicide, and relationship success (especially related to families) cannot be overstated (Tanielian and Jaycox 2008).

Sexual Harassment and Sexual Assault

Sexual harassment and sexual assault affect a significant number of men and women in the United States, both within the military and in the civilian population. These serious issues have been given much more attention in the military over recent decades. Comparisons across the civilian and military populations are quite challenging, due to reporting differences between the two populations for sexual harassment and assault. Comparisons over time within the military are also difficult because the military has changed its reporting format several times in recent years. Even with these challenges, we are able to obtain a fairly clear understanding of the breadth and impact of these events on current military personnel and veterans.

Both men and women experience sexual harassment and sexual assault (referred to jointly as "military sexual trauma") while they are serving in the military; however, rates are much higher among women. In a 2006 study conducted by the Defense Department, 33% of women in uniform related experiences of sexual harassment versus only 6% of male service members. Incidents of sexual assault were reported by 6.8% of military women versus 1.8% of men. Junior enlisted personnel, compared to all other ranks, were most likely to acknowledge military sexual trauma. Across all four branches of the military, service members in the Army were most likely, and those in the Air Force least likely, to report experiences of sexual harassment and assault (Lipari et al. 2008). The rate of military sexual trauma among female veterans is estimated to be 20 to 30%[4] versus estimates between 2 to 4% among male veterans (Polusny and Murdoch 2005; Zeiss 2009).

Racial differences in exposure and type of military sexual trauma have been identified. Whereas White female service members report more incidences of "softer" military sexual trauma, such as crude behavior and sexual and gender harassment, their Black peers are more likely to report experiences of more aggressive behaviors, such as unwanted sexual attention and sexual coercion. White female service members reported having less psychological distress compared to Black female personnel following experiences of military sexual trauma (Buchanan et al. 2008).

Experiences of sexual harassment have led to increased turnover among female service members, even when job satisfaction, organizational commitment, and marital status have been taken into account (Sims, Drasgow, and Fitzgerald 2005). Even within the officer corps, sexual harassment has been identified as a significant motivation for women to separate from service (Sims et al. 2005).

Health outcomes associated with exposure to military sexual trauma include negative effects on both physical and mental health. A recent study using 2003 Veterans Health Administration data found that women veterans who reported experiencing military sexual trauma also presented with diagnoses of PTSD, as well as dissociative, eating, and personality disorders. Male veterans who reported experiences of military sexual trauma were found to have higher levels of dissociative and personality disorders. Male veterans who suffered military sexual trauma had a significantly higher likelihood of being diagnosed with adjustment disorders than women veterans who experienced military sexual trauma. Men and women veterans who experienced military sexual trauma were more likely to be diagnosed with alcohol and anxiety disorders than their same-sex veteran peers who did not experience military sexual trauma, and for both disorders the association was stronger among women (Kimerling et al. 2007).

The risk of developing PTSD from military sexual trauma is at least as high, if not higher, than the risk of developing it from exposure to combat (Himmelfarb, Yeager, and Mintz 2006; Kang et al. 2005; Wolfe et al. 1998). Among veterans who have experienced military sexual trauma, women are nearly three times more likely than men to be diagnosed with PTSD. Women veterans who experience military sexual trauma are also up to five times more likely to develop PTSD than women who experience civilian sexual trauma (Himmelfarb, Yeager, and Mintz 2006; Suris et al. 2004).

In addition to negative impacts on mental health, military sexual trauma has been shown to reduce physical health. Behaviors associated with experiences of military sexual trauma (e.g., substance abuse and risky behavior) expose these veterans to increased physical health risks, such as liver disease, chronic lung disease, weight-related disorders, and HIV/AIDS. In addition, male and female veterans who experienced sexual harassment or assault while in uniform have attempted suicide or intentionally harmed themselves at more than two times the rate of veterans who have not experienced military sexual trauma (Kimerling et al. 2007).

Taken together, the risks of physical and psychological trauma associated with military service place active-duty service members and veterans at higher risk for role disruption or challenging transitions to adulthood. These traumas affect transitions to a number of adult roles, but perhaps most importantly, they can interrupt normative transitions and relationships related to employment and family. Such service-related health problems might influence employment in a particular field or affect whether the veteran can work at all, as well as impacting processes of marriage and family formation and maintenance.

CONCLUSION

Over recent history the American military has become a smaller, more professionally oriented force than it had been previously. The policy of relying on volunteers to fulfill the personnel requirements of the military has thus far been successful in meeting the operational needs of the nation's defense. Much of the success of our military is due to larger numbers of racial-ethnic minorities and women serving than were expected. The increased benefits and pay associated with the all-volunteer model have been successful in retaining a large number of service members on career paths. Since the early 1970s, the military has become increasingly an adult role of choice rather than merely a means of transitioning to other adult roles in civilian society.

The title of this chapter asks whether military service facilitates integration into or isolation from normal adult roles. We think the answer to this question is contingent. On the one hand, enhancing human and social capital through service is a key aspect contributing to the success of the military in developing service members in their work roles while they are in uniform, as well as preparing them for their transition to civilian roles post-service. The educational benefits of the GI Bill, combined with training and leadership experience, as well as the social networks built during one's service, provide a strong complement of knowledge, skills, and abilities that veterans can leverage in the civilian world. Preferential hiring of veterans by government agencies and other employers is another benefit of service that helps to integrate veterans into normal adult work roles. The revolution in family-friendly policies within the military in recent decades supports transitions to normative family roles (i.e., spouse and parent) among those who serve, and among their civilian spouses as well. The development of moral-ethical principles, the increase in civic-mindedness, and the strengthening of related civically conscious behavior through military service also support those in the military and veterans in additional adult roles during their unfolding life course.

On the other hand, military service has the potential to disrupt current and future adult roles. There is evidence that military service causes some to forego additional formal education. Military service also presents risks to physical and mental health, both of which can cause significant disruption in acquiring or maintaining other adult roles across the life course. The most extreme example of this disruption would be loss of one's life in service to the country. In this case, role loss extends to the service member's entire family. Additionally, the potential effects of military service on one's life course, positive and negative, are significantly tied to key social characteristics, such as gender, race, ethnicity, social class, and sexual orientation, and these effects have varied considerably across time. As a result, the potential benefits, as well as the potential harms, associated with military service are not equally available to all members of society, or even all who serve.

Many of the points discussed in this chapter indicate that the military is oriented toward a more inclusive, better integrated model of civil-military relations. The military has made several organizational changes in recent decades to mirror (or compete with) civilian society. Pay and benefits have increased, and now include more opportunities to secure education while in service. The positive effects of military service on civic engagement make veterans an important bridge between the military and civilian spheres; their efforts to support, critique, and educate others on military-related issues are potentially important in ways that have not yet been fully appreciated.

The U.S. military has taken steps to maintain, or even exceed, the standards of equality based on race, ethnicity, social class, and gender that are found in civilian society. Although significant changes in expanding opportunities for service to racial-ethnic minorities and women have occurred in recent decades, some discrimination remains due to what have been argued to be operational necessities. Most notably, systematic discrimination continues via ground combat-related restrictions for women, whereas discrimination against homosexuals was only recently addressed, and much remains to be seen about how the repeal of Don't Ask, Don't Tell plays out in the lives of service members. It is true that women and homosexuals are moving toward more full access to the benefits of military service (e.g., new military specialties, more powerful social networks, promotional and other career opportunities, and formal recognition of same-sex relationship roles), but these increased opportunities come with the physical, psychological, and cognitive risks of military service.

What would it mean to allow women into all military specialties, eliminating the ground combat exclusion? As a practical matter, we are witnessing this in our current operations in Afghanistan and Iraq. Women are excluded from units intended to engage in ground combat (i.e., infantry, armor, artillery), yet, as military police, they accompany infantry units on searches of houses and their occupants in order to honor the Muslim prohibition on men touching unrelated women. It is noteworthy that the risk of injury, death, or capture—key concerns motivating female exclusion from the battlefield—are now highest among those in the transportation corps, from which women are not restricted and where they currently perform jobs with high levels of skill and professional competence.

What are the implications of the repeal of the Don't Ask, Don't Tell policy? It is doubtful that enlistment will dramatically increase among homosexuals, but it is an important step in affirming equal employment conditions for the men and women who volunteer for selfless service in our military. Additionally, it provides lesbian, gay, and bisexual service members, and potentially their family members, access to resources and benefits from which they might otherwise be excluded. The military has long recognized the importance of cohesion for unit morale and effectiveness. Trust is an important factor in developing cohesion among service personnel. The end of the institutionally sanctioned discrimination against homosexual personnel is important, for as Kier argues, "any form of discrimination toward organizational members is pernicious in an organization that performs group tasks and depends on the integration of all individuals and units" (Kier 1999: 46–47). Service members seem to understand this—as there are many reports of homosexual service members coming out to friends and soldiers in their units without creating chaos in the ranks. Although there will undoubtedly be incidents of gay-bashing—the military still experiences hundreds of racial incidents per year, more than a half century after racial integration—the repeal of Don't Ask, Don't Tell is likely to have positive effects in retaining quality lesbian, gay, and bisexual soldiers who might otherwise separate from service, as well as improving their morale and performance.

To the extent that both women and homosexuals are more fully included and provided equal opportunities for leadership and promotional opportunities, and have access to all military specialties, one would expect that individuals in these groups would be more inclined to join, and, once in service, more likely to serve for a career. Given that military retirement benefits begin at twenty years of service, electing for career service places individuals on a trajectory for possible retirement with full benefits in the early forties, with experience, training, education, and social networks that will ease the transition to the world of civilian work. Conversely, to the extent that any given subpopulation is disproportionately either pushed or pulled out of service prematurely, they forfeit opportunities to benefit from the rather generous benefits and retirement packages offered to military personnel. This is potentially important over the long term because career veterans appear to experience better later-life health and financial security than their non-veteran and non-career veteran counterparts (see Street and Hoffman, Chapter 11 of this volume).

In regard to social class, the distribution of those in uniform is being truncated at both ends of the scale, drawing disproportionately from the middle quartiles in society. Although remaining open to people of all classes, the military still rejects those who fail to qualify on educational standards, and relatively few in the upper social class self-select into military service. Though the military does act as a transforming social agent, many are either precluded from or self-select out of the experience of military service.

For those who experience physical or psychological trauma during their military service, there is a high probability of serious disruption to or strain in their transitions to adult roles. In addition to the primary stress of trauma experienced during service, these experiences often lead to stress proliferation and the emergence of secondary stressors later in life (Pearlin et al. 1981). It is not simply that one, for example, loses a leg, but that this loss also affects self-concept, stresses personal relationships, and may impact the types of civilian jobs one can perform. Traumas affecting cognition, which are common in those injured by improvised explosive devices, may affect educational attainment, as well as the ability to perform some important skills needed for employment. Physical independence may also be affected as a direct result of military service, impacting numerous roles in the lives involved, as well as the lives of others.

An interesting case to consider is the role of our National Guard and Reserve men and women. These service members straddle the fence between military and civilian work roles. In this capacity, they deal with "interruptions" to their civilian work and family roles when called on for training and deployments. At the same time, the role as service member enjoys high levels of prestige in society, which provides all the benefits discussed above that are associated with the GI Bill and veterans' status for employment preference. Moreover, their positions with current employers are legally safeguarded during their absence for military service. Guard and Reserve service is "part-time" in the sense that these men and women work regular civilian jobs and serve in a limited capacity when not mobilized for deployment. As such, they are able to serve later into the life course before reaching mandatory retirement based on years served. In these ways, the experiences of our Guard and Reserve service members interact in unique ways with the contingencies of life-course effects examined in this chapter.

Finally, examination of the military service at the macro level through the open system model helps us understand how military service facilitates or constrains integration into other adult roles among those who serve. There have been significant improvements in inclusiveness across a number of important social characteristics. These improvements have at times set the standard for civilian society (e.g., racial integration in the military preceding racial integration in the U.S. generally), and at other times, the military follows the lead of civilian society (e.g., improved equality for women and homosexuals). As such, the United States has aligned itself with a model of civil-military relations that seeks to integrate the military (and those who serve) with society rather than create a more strictly enforced segregation between those who serve and the rest of society.

Questions arose in the mid to late 1990s about a culture gap between military and civilian society (Ricks 1997), but a major interdisciplinary research effort showed primarily the kinds of schisms that are likely to appear between any profession and its clientele, rather than the "chasm" that former Secretary of Defense William Cohen feared (Feaver and Kohn 2001). The publication of the major report of this effort in the wake of the events of September 11, 2001, virtually guaranteed that little attention would be paid to it. The issue reemerged in late 2011, as the war in Iraq was winding down. But again, although both military personnel and civilians agreed that civilians do not understand what military personnel go through, and military veterans have experienced problems reintegrating into civilian society, the military continues to be seen as a trusted and valued institution. Almost half of non-veterans surveyed said they would advise a young person to join the military (Pew Research Center 2011). It is difficult to imagine any other occupation that would garner that level of support.

Military service can provide numerous benefits to individuals across multiple social roles and periods of the adult life course. It also poses significant risks for those who serve in terms of the disruption or termination of roles and the threat of injury and death. At present, the U.S. military appears committed to supporting service members during their time in uniform and in preparing them for successful transitions to civilian life post-service. Those who serve self-select for military duty, which impacts the diversity of the military across all categories. For those who do elect to serve, the military provides the potential for positive life-course trajectories to those who can successfully negotiate the risks.

NOTES

1. This research was supported in part by the U.S. Army Research Institute for the Behavioral and Social Sciences under Contract W91WAW09C0077. The views presented in this chapter are those of the authors and not of the Army Research Institute, the Department of the Army, or the Department of Defense. We also acknowledge support from the Eunice Kennedy Shriver National Center for Child Health and Human Development, grant R24-HD041041, to the Maryland Population Research Center.
2. The moral requirement for military service is generally oriented toward lawfulness—i.e., does one have a criminal record?
3. Here, retired is meant to include all those who have separated from the military, without regard to qualification for retirement benefits.
4. Estimates for male and female veterans' rates of military sexual assault are obtained from studies of veterans applying for benefits through Veterans Affairs hospitals. These estimates should be viewed cautiously because they are not necessarily reflective of all veterans' experiences. For a summary of military sexual trauma rates among veterans, see Himmelfarb, Yaeger, and Mintz (2006).

3 Women's Lives in Wartime

The American Civil War and World War II

D'Ann Campbell

The course of each man and woman's life is shaped at the nexus of historical events and personal biography. Arguably, of all the historical events that influence individual lives, wars have the greatest impact—especially for those who participate in or are otherwise subject to military battles. Contemporary Americans tend to think of wars as happening in esoteric, far-away, foreign places, like Korea, Afghanistan, Vietnam, Iwo Jima, Guadalcanal, and Normandy. Consequently, the impact of wars on individuals often seems removed from the everyday lives of Americans whose only contact with them is through letters from the battlefield, the memories of surviving veterans, and the mass media. What happens to American lives when the invaded and devastated land is right here in Virginia and Tennessee, when the casualty rate is ten times higher than is typically the case in contemporary wars, and when there are American lives at stake on both sides? To answer such questions, we must look at the American Civil War. Alternatively, what happens to American lives when there is a massive, protracted war mobilization, when civilians are required to make daily sacrifices due to rationing, when individuals who do not typically directly participate in war efforts are needed to enlist in the military and work in war-related industries? In this case, we must look to World War II. In both of these wars, the historian's perspective allows for a broader definition of the impact of wartime that takes the experiences of women into account.

Historical research is usually conducted in a specific geographic area such that the historian can link together multiple records that are only available locally; the bias is toward long-term residents. Most of the documentation available deals with men, especially those with greater wealth, who were involved in more official financial, legal, and political affairs. It also biases the literate. This adds a class bias, but historians and archivists in recent decades have made special efforts to study poor people and, when possible, draw on oral history to overcome this bias. Historians have only recently turned away from battlefield action to study the home fronts in more depth, so the literature remains uneven. For example, there is very little scholarship on the impact of World War I on women. Consequently, that war will not be discussed in this chapter. There is more evidence about how the Civil War and World War II had dramatic impacts on the lives of some exposed women, and subtle effects on the great majority. However, the historian's knowledge of the impact of war on American lives is far thinner with respect to World War II than it is for the Civil War—we have statistical surveys and oral histories for World War II, but we lack the depth of the Civil War sources and the thousands of scholars who have pored through the documents and letters of the 1860s. Following the usual practice in social history, this chapter will rely on narrative, using multiple, scattered reports by historians, rather than attempt a standard review of the literature (Abbott 2005; Gabaccia 2010).

This chapter will focus on the impact of two different wars on women's lives, situating women's experiences within the broader historical events influencing their families and communities. In much of America during the 19th century, especially in the rural South, the life course of women was deeply embedded in traditional family life. This was so even during wartime, although women were often called upon to take on new roles and perform nontraditional tasks to support themselves and their families. Thus, when considering women in wartime, historians often take what might be considered a "linked lives" approach and focus on women's roles in their families and how their lives changed as a consequence of the wartime absences of the men to whom their lives were linked. The women themselves were not in combat, but military service was less of an individual affair than a community effort. Therefore, the close link between the soldiers and the home front during the Civil War meant that men's wartime service had a greater impact on women during the Civil War than during 20th-century wars. Nevertheless, wars have always affected women's lives. During World War II, the increased participation of women in formal military roles and war-related industries changed the nature of war's impact on women's lives.

THE CIVIL WAR

Better social organization in the North facilitated much more complex activities by women—as typified by national organizations such as the Sanitary Commission and the United States Christian Commission. In these organizations, women played major roles and learned organizational skills that were applied after the war to charitable endeavors, as well as the prohibition and woman suffrage movements. The war did not significantly alter the life course trajectories of most women in the North, where life continued more or less as normal. The impact of absent men on families was temporary, with scarcely a ripple in terms of the pool of eligible spouses, for example (Mitchell 1995). The large volume of volunteer work undertaken by Northern women seems not to have had permanent effects beyond a few leaders (Attie 1998). The disruption caused by death and severe war wounds was profound for the women affected, but did not alter the system of widowhood, except that the widows received government pensions.

The systematic efforts of communities and governments to provide aid to soldiers' families and pensions for the wounded and widows provided a new level of financial security for the survivors, setting the stage for the later development of the welfare state (Skocpol 1992). However, the administration of these benefits was racially biased despite the fact that the statutes establishing pensions for Union Army veterans were color-blind (Logue and Blanck 2008). Historians have not noted any shift in family or life-course patterns in response to the availability of pensions. To encourage enlistment in 1862, the Lincoln administration broadened the number of family members eligible for assistance and increased the amount of compensation for widows and orphans, which opened the way for a permanent, if limited, welfare state (McClintock 1996).

The impact of the Civil War on women in the South, both Black and White, was far more dramatic than in the North. In the South, it was a total war in the sense that virtually every sector of society and economy became involved. To call women "civilians" is technically correct, but substantively inaccurate; in total war, everyone is engaged in and contributes to the war effort. As Robert E. Lee explained a month before Appomattox: "Everything in my opinion has depended and still depends upon the disposition and feelings of the people . . . the difficulties and sufferings of their condition" (Lee and Dowdey 1961: 913).

The geography of devastation was highly uneven. Most areas saw no fighting at all. In a given state, the invading armies operated along lines of transportation, with towns and cities that were crossroads becoming targets. Half of the cities of the Confederacy saw military action and a dozen suffered major destruction. The rural areas rarely endured major damage, save in the famous efforts by Sherman to ruin portions of Georgia (about 20% of the state) and by Sheridan in devastating the Shenandoah Valley of Virginia. However, the loss of farm infrastructure was about the same whether or not enemy armies came near—that is, across the South, farms, buildings, and implements fell into disrepair and, by war's end, most livestock was gone. The loss of infrastructure and productive capacity meant that rural women throughout the region faced not only the absence of able-bodied men, but a depleted stock of material resources that they could manage and operate themselves. During four years of warfare, disruption, and blockades, the South used up about half its capital stock. The North, by contrast, absorbed its material losses so effortlessly that it appeared richer at the end of the war than at the beginning (Paskoff 2008).

An insight into the linked lives aspect of men's wartime service and the impact of war on women comes from looking at an important ingredient in the letters from Confederate soldiers: food. Southern soldiers accustomed to high-calorie peacetime diets were sometimes more afraid of starvation than of Yankees. Inadequate nutrition helped bring on depression, lethargy, and night blindness, and made the soldiers more susceptible to infectious disease. The situation steadily worsened in the Confederate Army, but even more threatening to morale were the letters from home, which reported that the food situation was even worse there, with actual starvation a real threat (Frank 2008). As a young Confederate woman told her man in 1863:

> Two more months of danger, difficulties, perplexities, and starvation will lay [Mother] in her grave. . . . Lilly has been obliged to put her children to bed to make them forget they were supperless, and when she followed their example, could not sleep herself, for very hunger (Dawson 1960: 343).

Temporary food deprivation probably does not leave permanent damage, but the memory of the experience does have a lasting effect in making people far more cautious. Such an enduring result is often pointed out with regard to survivors of the Great Depression (Lumey and Vanpoppel 1994).

Women's Roles during the War

Women in both the North and the South were involved in providing supplies for soldiers. In the North, perhaps 20,000 women's societies were established. The more modern Yankees put a higher priority on organizational skills and had more latitude to use them, regardless of resources and urbanization. In contrast, middle- and upper-class Southern women had more resources before the war, but used them less effectively during the war (Brown 2000). The Confederate supply system was poorly organized and resourced; soldiers often relied on homemade supplies of clothing and bandages. It was also generally confined to small cities, and, importantly, failed to meet the escalating needs of soldiers and civilians (Whites 1995).

Half the women in the North lived on farms, as did a large majority in the South. The role of women in the adjustment of the rural economy was probably more important than any other economic contribution. Some women replaced soldiers by taking on farm jobs not customarily done by women (Anderson 2007). How many and in what roles—these are the sorts of questions that letters can answer, as women asked questions and soldier spouses sent back detailed instructions on farm management (Bahde 2009). Women were aided by teenagers and older men; when available, hired labor became more important. Some farm work was reduced in scope or postponed, like maintenance and expansion; in the North, new machinery, like reapers, replaced some soldiers. A common solution was to reduce the scope of operations or shift the mix of crops and animals, which in the South only compounded shortages. The new roles for women were difficult and unwelcome. Confederate military wages were too low and erratic to count for much. Farm women did not revel in their newfound autonomy; rather, many found their new responsibilities overwhelming. Numerous women and their children were forced to rely on kin and relief institutions in order to survive. The life stage of widowhood and receiving assistance in old age was normative; in the prime of life, these were severe shocks. Women without kin or community to rely on suffered even greater hardships while their husbands were away.

Although little is known about how altered gender roles among this group of women were handled immediately after the war, women generally accepted the changes as necessary during wartime (Giesberg 2005). In many cases (especially in the South), women abandoned the farms and merged into the households of relatives, or even became refugees. We lack even rudimentary quantitative estimates of exactly what mix of strategies farm families used (Frank 2008). The adoption of new work roles for farming in the North was temporary; there was no visible long-term impact. The effect in the South was greater, given that 250,000 men never came home. That number represented 30% of all Southern White men aged 18 to 40. In the aftermath of the War, prosperity and normality never returned for many farm women in the South.

Brown (2000) shows a significant impact of the Civil War on upper- and middle-class Southern belles. The war let many break free from the restrictive roles defined for them by men in the Antebellum period; many sustained their newfound freedom by means of greater self-reliance in the Reconstruction era. Compelled by the strictures of society to be feminine, uneducated, and unskilled, Southern White women met the challenges brought about by the war by redefining who they were and what they could do. As their men marched off, women kept financial accounts, oversaw farm and plantation work, and tried to make ends meet. After the war, amid poverty and loss of property, women pursued new occupations, entering the workplace as teachers, seamstresses, and factory workers. Before the war, being an "old maid" was a grave threat to the normal life course. In the aftermath of the war, it became almost a norm (Faust 1996: 139–152). Many welcomed the "blessed singleness" of not having to marry (Jabour 2007: 273–280). For those who did marry, divorce rates rose, suggesting a greater willingness to break social customs. Partly as a consequence of the Civil War, the concept of the "New Woman" emerged. Self-sufficient and independent, the New Woman stood in sharp contrast to the image society had defined forty years earlier.

The most dramatic contradiction between patriotic and private lives came with marriage. America's family orientation was reflected in the conscription laws. The Yankees' substitute system allowed families to choose which member went to war and which stayed home. The Confederacy was less flexible, leading to a heavy flow of appeals from women that a particular draftee be spared to them (Rable 1989). The patriarchal family system was the norm in the South, and very prevalent in the North as well. Such appeals publicly put patriotism in tension with family well-being and the private needs of the family.

How did patriarchal families cope with the absence of the patriarch; was there a long-term impact on gender relations? Some historians have suggested that the severe strains resulting from the war-related absence of men could only partially be overcome by letters and furloughs. The inability of traditional patriarchs to protect and provide for the minimal needs of their women and children was pronounced in the South, but also was a factor in the North. Nevertheless, female roles and norms remained largely unchanged in the White South because they were embedded in the basic continuity of a class, race, and gender hierarchy (Rable 1989). The verdict is less clear regarding Northern women. There is some evidence that they became more assertive in issues such as childbearing. For example, a two-child norm was reached surprisingly early among White native-born couples in Northern towns following the Civil War (David and Sanderson 1987).

Sacrifice was central to the roles of women at war and became a permanent badge of prestige that protected the status of women who lost most of their financial support. In both the North and the South, the first duty of patriotic women was to send their men off to war, as explained by a Boston newspaper in May 1861:

> The affluent send their sons and the fondest mothers shed tears of joy as boys leave for the field. Wives smother their emotions of tenderness and gird on the sword of their husbands for the fight, while the maiden who was but the gay butterfly of society takes the needle and ends in equipping troops for the contest (*Boston Evening Gazette* 1861, cited in Perkins 1942: 1073).

However, when the Confederate cause appeared problematic in Kentucky in 1862, invading Confederate armies failed to enlist the number of volunteers they sought. "Enthusiasm is unbounded," Confederates discovered, "but recruiting at a discount; even the women are giving reasons why individuals cannot go" (U.S. War Department 1880: 895). Willingness to have men go off to war did not just involve the original departure. Even more important was the continuous flow of support from the women toward their soldiers, which helped maintain morale and minimize desertions. When Vermont private Wilbur Fisk went absent without leave from his hospital bed to spend more time at home, his bride insisted he return. Additionally important was the question of reenlistment. Soldiers who felt they had performed their patriotic duty wanted to come home. Would the women approve or would they send them back to war? How many women echoed the Massachusetts mother who instructed her sons in February 1864: "Dear boys don't be discouraged. Yours is a holy cause, a just cause, and may the God of battles watch over and protect you is my constant prayer" (Culpepper 1991: 30–31).

There was a long-term benefit to encouraging husbands and sons to fight in the war. Sending a son or husband off to war entitled Northern women to a prestigious social status that had financial benefits in terms of wartime aid and postwar pensions, whereas Southern women gained social and political visibility and protection. Victorious invaders, who had already defeated the Confederate men and who now occupied the same public spaces as Southern women, often noted that the women were more fervent rebels. Nannie Haskins said in Clarksville, Tennessee, in 1863: "I never see [a Yankee] but what I roll my eyes, grit my teeth, and almost shake my teeth at him, and then bite my lip and turn away in disgust" (Wiley 1975: 152). The problem for Confederate patriots was that the Union Army took control of larger and larger areas; the women left behind could not be openly patriotic, so they reacted by being more covert—some became spies and smugglers. They formed an effective female mutual support network that continued to function after the war (Brock 1991).

The great majority of Southern White women were loyal to the Confederacy. However, when the Confederacy seized control of Unionist areas, especially in Appalachia, the women there helped the resistance. Unionist women in rural East Tennessee petitioned political leaders, spied on the Confederates, and secretly nursed and aided Union soldiers. They ran an underground railroad of Unionists and prison escapees, visited prisons and hospitals with food and other supplies, and moved their families to safer locations as necessary. These new roles did not survive the war, but they additionally reveal a willingness among women to move well beyond conventional gender norms in the name of patriotism (Strasser 1999).

During the Civil War, it was simply assumed by everyone that warfare was synonymous with manhood and that women could never be soldiers. Women who located themselves near military encampments—including nurses—risked being considered disgraced as sexually immoral. A Philadelphian wrote home in 1862: "There is a spirit of criticism & I might say sort of slur thrown out to those young ladys which attend the Hospitals" (Gallman 1990: 71). In the South, upper-class belles were eager to become nurses, but were turned away. That was a role traditionally assigned to slaves and it was inconceivable to the patriarchy that well-bred ladies should become involved (Jabour 2007).

Death as a Part of the Life Course

War and death seem inextricably linked. Historians warn that assuming there was always such a linkage may well be an artifact of how we think about warfare today. The question is how people at the time thought of death, and how they linked the question of death to war, in general, and their own life course in particular. During the mid-19th century, people were familiar with death firsthand. Infant mortality was high, and there were far more fatal diseases that struck during childhood and middle age, with death normally occurred at home, rather than in antiseptic hospitals or speeding ambulances. Death was omnipresent, and the rituals surrounding death were central to the notion of family and community. The challenge was to be prepared for death, to die in a suitable way, and to be buried by the community. The anonymous pauper's burial was almost the cruelest fate; even worse was the fate of the unknown soldier. When the sad news arrived from Spotsylvania, Margaret Scott wrote her sister:

> He was shot in the head and died instantly, oh how like a knell it rings in my ears. . . . He lays in a battle field far away without one moment's warning and could not send no message to the wife he loved so well (Coffin 1993: 261).

Sudden, unexpected death was a horrible thing to contemplate—a person would not have time to prepare his soul. Yet sudden death from bullet or shell became the common way young men died in 1862. The challenge for the soldiers—and for their communities—was how to redefine the proper death so that the casualties of war could be fitted into their rituals. The Northern solution was to expand the religious rhetoric to frame the death of a soldier as a heroic community sacrifice for a higher cause. Abraham Lincoln used the occasion of the dedication of the first national cemetery at Gettysburg to rededicate the nation to a new birth of freedom—it was the dead who had given their lives so that the nation might live. It was the duty of the living to finish the work for which they had given the last full measure of devotion. Theologically, Yankee soldiers were mostly postmillennialists, which meant that they understood the need to purify the nation before Christ's Second Coming. Fighting—dying—helped hasten the day. Julia Ward Howe's "Battle Hymn of the Republic" underscored the religious message: "Mine eyes have seen the glory of the coming of the Lord. . . . As He died to make men holy, let us die to make men free" (Faust 2008: 165).

Religious Americans saw death not as the end of life, but as an integral part of the life course, especially for those who had recently experienced the Second Great Awakening and believed they were going to see their loved ones again in heaven. Letters and diaries reveal that families coped with death by drawing on a religious worldview rooted in a firm conviction that they would be reunited with loved ones in heaven. Stressing that the time and manner of death was determined not by fate, but by a personal God, loved ones helped soldiers to be prepared for death at any moment. When the dreaded letter arrived, they sought evidence that the deceased had left a testimony of dying in Christ. Comforted by their certainty of everlasting bliss, letters described heaven in detail. Some letters depicted heaven as a place where the saved gathered around the throne to worship God, and others focused on reunion with families in a life stage that resembled the Victorian home. Far from representing the beginning of a secular approach to death and dying, the Civil War marked the continuation of a religious understanding of death (Faust 2008; Miller, Stout, and Wilson 1998; Scott 2008).

Wartime deaths were substantial on both sides of the conflict; about one-tenth of Yankee soldiers and one-fourth of Confederate troops died in uniform. However, in sharp contrast to the images conjured up, only 22%

of the deaths came on the battlefield; 66% were due to disease and accident and 12% to complications from wounds. Thus, most deaths took place in hospitals—and were more likely witnessed by female nurses than by male comrades. Some historians have suggested the high Southern casualty rates helped create religious revivals—religion as an escape mechanism. Whether Civil War soldiers were in fact as fatalistic about death as their spouses is unclear, but it has been suggested that a surge of female piety may have produced the revivals. Perhaps most of the concern with death came from civilians. Soldiers rarely thought about death—they were much more worried about getting wounded. Death might be in Fate's domain, but nonfatal wounds were not. By 1862, death for the soldier had been incorporated into community and religious ritual, whereas nonfatal wounds were never part of it. Some Republican politicians were known for years to "wave the bloody shirt," but they were talking about battle deaths, not injuries or war-related harm to civilian women, elders, and children. Civilians living in the Confederate states faced the alarming risk of death through murder, pillage, or starvation. There was no glory in that; it was not sanctified by the community. Civilians became increasingly terrified that such dishonorable death might indeed be their fate if their men did not rush home to take care of them. As one wife wrote in desperation:

> Last night I was aroused by little Eddie's crying . . . and he said 'Oh Mamma! I am so hungry.' And Lucy, Edward, your darling Lucy; she never complains, but she is growing thinner and thinner every day. And before God, Edward, unless you come home we must die (Wiley 1943: 214).

Consumption and Survival

Reduced consumption was forced by a fall in purchasing power. Both Washington and Richmond printed paper money, with the resulting inflation hurting consumers. In the Confederacy, the collapse of the transportation and marketing systems caused reductions in household consumption, with no compensating benefit to the war effort. One result was bread riots that broke out across the South, including in Richmond. The situation in Georgia was representative. Food supplies grew critically short because of the failure of the river and rail systems, the absence of men who would normally be growing crops, and the miscalculation of planters who continued to grow cotton instead of food. Hoarding was common, as flour sold for exorbitant prices. Those who suffered most were middle- and lower-class women and children, many of whom were eventually near starvation from the lack of basic necessities. Unable to get help from their impoverished neighbors, and frustrated by government inaction, some took matters into their own hands. Beginning in 1863, in at least twenty-three incidents across Georgia that are known to historians, they raided stores and captured supply wagons to seize necessities, such as bacon, corn, flour, and cotton yarn. The severe deprivations and the failure of the ruling class to do anything about them proved the helplessness of the Confederate nation. Thus, women commonly determined that the survival of their families was much more important than the continuation of the Confederacy. In various ways, women challenged Confederate authority and undermined the war effort (William and Williams 2002).

After the summer of 1863, the Confederate armies began to evaporate away slowly. Desertions and absences without leave claimed up to half the nominal soldiers, and new enlistments had been reduced to a trickle. When home front morale broke, Confederate soldiers felt compelled to desert. If soldiers represented their communities—not just the Confederate nation itself—then the needs of their home communities came first. Indeed, demands from women that husbands return immediately to protect them from starvation or slave insurrection had become a factor by mid-1863, and grew more insistent month by month. Confederate recruiters reported as early as 1863 about deteriorating conditions in backcountry parts of South Carolina:

> The tone of the people is lost; it is no longer a reproach to be known as a deserter; all are ready to encourage and aid the efforts of those who are avoiding duty, and to refuse information to and thwart and even resist those who seek to make arrests (U.S. War Department 1888: 769–770).

Slavery and Freedom

No change in American history was more dramatic than the emancipation of 4 million slaves during the Civil War, which particularly influenced the daily lives and life-course trajectories of African Americans living in the South. Most important was freedom itself—the freedom to make their own decisions about their own lives and the freedom from compulsion and control by White masters. No more were they subjected to the hated gang labor system or the threat of sale. There was the freedom to move about, to relocate, and to vote and engage in politics, although it took more than a century for many of those freedoms to be fully realized. Most Blacks had previously lived on plantations with twenty or more slaves in group housing, doing gang labor under the direction of a Black driver, a White overseer, and a White owner. Now, they refused to work in gangs. Most became sharecroppers on former plantations or wage-earning farm laborers. Freedwomen were determined to reunite their families and control their own labor. Often kept on separate plantations prior to the war, husbands and wives reunited. In the aftermath of the war, they formed a family system strikingly similar to that of poor Whites, choosing their own surnames (Frankel 1999; Gutman 1976; Schwalm, 1997).

The transition from slavery to freedom was a complex process. Many slaves handled it on their own when Union armies approached, usually by departing the plantation to a nearby town or refugee camp to validate their new freedom of movement. Often, the transition was supervised by a federal agency, the Freedmen's Bureau, which had a clear-cut agenda of moving refugees off welfare and out of the camps to paid labor on former plantations. The Bureau's employment and relocation efforts also involved the apprenticeship of young children based on traditional White age and gender roles (Farmer-Kaiser, 2007). Booker T. Washington, who was 9 years old at the time, later recalled Emancipation as a communal event:

> As the great day drew nearer, there was more singing in the slave quarters than usual. It was bolder, had more ring, and lasted later into the night. Most of the verses of the plantation songs had some reference to freedom. . . . Some man who seemed to be a stranger (a United States officer, I presume) made a little speech and then read a rather long paper—the Emancipation Proclamation, I think. After the reading, we were told that we were all free, and could go when and where we pleased. My mother, who was standing by my side, leaned over and kissed her children, while tears of joy ran down her cheeks. She explained to us what it all meant, that this was the day for which she had been so long praying, but fearing that she would never live to see (Washington 1901: 19–21).

Freedmen's Bureau agents complained that freedwomen were not working as they should according to prevailing views of Black women among White men. Because they were refusing to contract their labor, free Black women violated the free labor principles of White men. The Bureau thought that free labor was the alternative to slavery and that meant Black women had to sign work contracts. Officials demanded that husbands sign contracts obligating the whole family to work; unemployed freedwomen were considered "vagrants" and were ineligible for relief. The beliefs of the men who ran the Bureau were to a degree softened by the feminine sensibilities of the many women abolitionists who became involved, so the Bureau made some exceptions (Faulkner 2004). These included certain married women with employed husbands, and some "worthy" women, widowed or abandoned, who had large families of small children and thus could not work. "Unworthy" women, meaning the unruly and, especially, prostitutes, were usually subjected to punishment for vagrancy (Farmer-Kaiser 2004).

Without the whip, the hours worked per year by Blacks fell 28%: men worked 16% fewer hours; women and children worked 40% fewer (Ransom and Sutch 2001). The South as a whole had been impoverished by the war, but in terms of consumption, Blacks saw about a 30% increase in their standard of living in the transition from slavery to freedom and now had the opportunity to make their own choices about what to buy (Ransom and

Sutch 2001). Thus, compared to Whites living in the North as well as in the South, the Civil War had more profound, long-lasting, and positive impacts on the life chances and choices of African American men and women.

WORLD WAR II

World War II involved a multitude of new experiences that shaped life-course trajectories and outcomes for 16 million men in uniform. Sampson and Laub (1996) found evidence that wartime service was a turning point in the transition to young adulthood for men. They report that overseas duty, in-service schooling, and GI Bill training between the ages of 17 and 25 raised postwar occupational status, increased job stability, and improved economic well-being independent of childhood differences and socioeconomic background. Indeed, young men from disadvantaged families benefited most from their years in uniform (Sampson and Laub 1996). Like women in general, gay men and lesbians experienced new, emergent opportunities as a consequence of the war mobilization (see Brown, Chapter 5 of this volume). However, many soldiers experienced negative consequences. Pavalko and Elder (1990) found higher rates of divorce among veterans than non-veterans, although World War II did not produce a change in long-term trends for divorce rates. Due to disruption in established life-course trajectories, men and women who joined in their 30s had the hardest time readjusting (Campbell 1984, 1990; Elder and Clipp 1988a,b).

Although the chapters in this volume document many life-course consequences of military service in different historical periods, relatively little life-course research is available on male veterans of World War II and even less can be found on women veterans (but see LaRossa 2011; Mettler 2005). Was this service a critical event in the lives of servicewomen (Elder 1985; Hareven 1978; Rossi 1985)? Chafe (1972), in the early days of the feminist revolution, argued that the wartime experience of paid employment enabled the emergence of feminism decades later. However, critics thoroughly refuted his claims, which Chafe himself eventually withdrew. Housewives who took war-related jobs were adding to their workload, and, on the whole, welcomed the chance to return to the status of housewife after the war. This was especially apparent among those with an enlarged pool of savings and employed husbands, which enabled much better living conditions. Given that, for some women in this cohort, the baby boom was seen as their reward, not their punishment. Looked at another way, the war enabled millions to achieve a new lifestyle, based on the companionate family with numerous children, some degree of affluence and mobility, and much better housing in family-oriented suburbs rather than apartments designed to allow the husband to walk to work (Campbell 1984).

The changes in higher education brought about by the GI Bill have been widely celebrated, but some points related to the impact of the GI Bill on women's lives need highlighting (Altschuler and Blumin 2009). The nation's campuses became heavily male as veterans flooded onto them, sharply reducing the opportunities women had for leadership positions and restricting career chances for single women. The famous 1946 film *It's a Wonderful Life* is a dystopia, showing the horrors of an alternative society, and the worst horror is that the heroine would have become a shriveled up, frightened spinster librarian. In contrast to Chafe's debunked claim, it can in fact be argued that the war and immediate postwar experience had the effect of postponing the emergence of the feminist movement (Rupp and Taylor 1987).

Military service was not entirely new for American women—the Army had employed nurses in uniform since 1901. During World War I, nursing expanded and there were 11,500 additional short-lived billets in the Navy only lasting for the duration of the war (Godson 2001). Nevertheless, the World War II expansion of numbers and roles was dramatic. Some 350,000 women served in uniform, including 140,000 WACs (Women's Army Corps), 100,000 Navy WAVES (Women Accepted for Voluntary Emergency Service), 23,000 Marines, 13,000 Coast Guard SPARs (based on the Coast Guard motto *Semper Paratus* combined with its English translation "Always Ready"), 60,000 Army nurses, and 14,000 Navy nurses (Campbell 1984). Below, I describe these servicewomen in terms of personal background, work life, war service, and postwar experience. This discussion is based on various historical sources, including surveys taken at the time on women serving in the Army (Stouffer et al. 1945) as well as a questionnaire covering 150 topics that was filled out by women veterans who were selected in a snowball sample from volunteers at reunions and their wartime friends who did not attend the reunions during the 1984–1986 period (Campbell 1990; Ivie 1992). The questions in the latter study replicated those included in a 1985 survey of male veterans from the Oakland/Berkeley area (Elder 1987; Elder and Clipp 1988a,b).

Personal Background and Work Experience

The military wanted its men young and inexperienced; men could volunteer for the Marines at 17 years old or be drafted at 18 years old for the Army. In contrast, women recruits were selected on the basis of maturity, not youthful zeal (Campbell 1984). Women had to be at least 20 years old to volunteer for the military, and the average age at entry was nearly 24 years overall, and almost 25 years for nurses. A 1985 survey of women veterans reported a mean age of entry of 23 years (Louis Harris and Associates 1985). The women in my study (Campbell 1990) reported their family background as "average," but were an upscale group; one-third had fathers who were managers or professionals and only one in six felt her family had been worse off than the average family during the depression. One-fifth of the women came from broken families, which is about the same proportion as all women of similar age in 1943. Women just turning 20 years old when joining were more likely than older women to come from blue-collar backgrounds. Less than 10% were from farming families; two-fifths grew up in small towns. Almost three-fourths had mothers working as homemakers. Three in ten reported that their fathers had served in the military; three in five had siblings presently serving.

The South was seriously underrepresented (with only 14%) because it had fewer hospitals and high schools. Perhaps more important was the military mystique: in the South, military service connoted bayonet charges, not typing pools. Being a military wife was a high-prestige role for a Southern woman, but donning a uniform was not. As the director of the Marine Corps Women's Reserve discovered, "service in women's military organizations is a newer idea in the deep South than in other parts of the country and more at variance with their customs and traditions" (Meid 1964: 60). The servicewomen were much better educated than their civilian sisters; over half had educational experiences beyond high school. Schooling, of course, did not necessarily guarantee self-assurance: "I was very young and dumb and frightened when I went in," confessed a WAVE who joined at age 20. At the time of volunteering, fewer than 10% of the women were married. Lack of a job was not a factor. The women joined at the height of the wartime job boom; seven in eight had been working full-time, whereas 9% were at home and 3% were full-time students (Campbell 1990: 254).

Recalling their motivations four decades later, 84% of the WACs, WAVES, SPARs, and Women Marines highlighted their patriotic motivations; 40% also expressed the wish "to try something different," and 25% mentioned the desire for adventure and travel; 31% noted that they had a relative in the service. Escape was a motivation for 12%; fewer than 10% recalled utilitarian career goals. The nurses had additional reasons for joining. On the one hand, they knew how vital their skills were during war (Sarnecky 1999). Although nearly all recalled patriotic reasons, over half also reported wanting "to use their skill." One nurse spoke of her uncle who had died in World War I due to a lack of nursing care. On the other hand, one-third came for "adventure" or because their "friends had joined" (Campbell 1990: 255). Surveys of veterans show that 40% of the women had to overcome the opposition of close relatives; only half said their closest male friends were supportive, whereas over three-fourths of their closest female friends had supported their decision (Treadwell 1954). "My own family didn't like the idea of my dressing like a man and joining the Army, but now they are proud of me," said a 30-year-old married WAC in 1943 (Campbell 1990: 254). A wartime study of Marine women reported that 29% served for reasons of patriotism, 26% out of a desire for change, 14% from an interest in training, and 3 to 7% for other reasons—having relatives in service, a desire for discipline, the need to replace a brother, searching for a spouse, or the need for group life (Meid 1964).

Before service, over half of the nurses were working in civilian hospitals, two in ten were private-duty nurses, and less than one in ten had just finished their training. Nurses were needed in the war effort; nearly half of the eligible civilian nurses in the country joined the Army or Navy Nurse Corps, which was the highest service rate of any occupational group, male or female, by far. Often, a civilian hospital decided to form a unit and recruited its best people (Kalisch and Kalisch 1978). At least some nurses enrolled in the Red Cross Reserve without realizing that made them liable to call-up for active duty. One subject reported that she was "stunned" at being called up and sent to the jungles of New Guinea. She never fully adjusted: "I hated Army life—its protocol, its insensitivity to . . . quality care and the control over my total life" (Campbell 1990: 256). However, on the whole, the nurses knew what they were doing and they were eager to join. Often, when a major hospital decided to set up an entire general hospital of doctors and nurses, it mobilized as a team. The entire group was then sent to the European theater, to the South Pacific, or to the China/Burma/India theater. As one woman noted, "We were really like a 100-girl family in the 40th General Hospital" (McMinn and Levin 1963: 146).

War Service: A Critical Life Episode

Elder (1987) explains that joining the military, especially during wartime, is an acceptable break from occupational, educational, and familial obligations. As the following quotes from Campbell (1990: 256) demonstrate, for the youngest women, the war came at a critical juncture in their lives. One woman noted: "I was fresh out of nursing school ready to take on the world." A nurse explained: "I was old enough to take life in stride and young enough to survive it." A third reflected: "I put off finishing college until after the war—became involved in what was involving the whole world—got an on-site practical education and met people." One nurse summed up what many were thinking: "I knew that I should volunteer for this unique opportunity regardless of what it would be like."

Despite the publicity photos of WACs in overalls servicing airplane engines, the vast majority worked at clerical or technical jobs scarcely different from those held by civilian women. Indeed, the jobs for WACs were somewhat more sex-stereotyped than those the women had before entering the service. Separated from civilian men and women, and largely segregated at very large bases in remote areas, the women developed their own esprit. They created a "family life atmosphere" in their units and discovered that "new friends remained friends forever" (Campbell 1990: 257; see also Campbell 1984; Craighill 1966; Treadwell 1954).

Postwar Experiences

The usual life-course sequence for women in the middle of the 20th century was school-work-marriage-family building. Those who had completed college before volunteering to serve in the military seldom sought schooling after the war ended—most graduate and professional programs accepted few women. However, about one-third of the nurses and half of the others took advantage of the GI Bill to obtain their undergraduate degrees; the other nurses generally felt they had completed their highest level or that being in their late 20s or early 30s made them too old to return to school. Almost all of these veterans obtained jobs after the war, seven in ten married, and three-fifths had children. By the time they were ready to return to school, their GI Bill benefits had expired.

The handful of women who entered the military already married had the most difficulty readjusting to civilian life and were the most likely to report health issues related to military service (Ivie 1992). Although some women veterans suffered psychological challenges, as did many of the men, the health issues reported by women were physical. Women who entered the military in their 30s were often given the most opportunities to lead, to learn new skills, and to be sent overseas, even in combat support areas. For whatever reason, these women were least likely to return to the workforce after the war and were also the most likely to report medical problems that were related to their military service (Campbell 1984). This may have been due to the added stress of these assignments. Men in the same age range also often had the most difficulty reintegrating (Elder 1987).

Three out of eight non-nurses said that wartime service had given them useful job skills, especially in administration. One woman reported: "The grades attained [in the WAC] groomed me for a supervisory position when I returned to my old job" (Campbell 1990: 257). Even more valuable was the self-understanding, discipline, and confidence the women gained. "Before World War II, I was a conservative New England school teacher," reported a WAC lieutenant who joined at age 30. "During service people gave me opportunities to use my talents: my self-esteem rose. I came out of the service a confident person not afraid to tackle anything" (Campbell 1990: 257).

Although some women veterans found jobs, rejoined the military, or raised families, others floundered for a while as they tried to make the transition back to civilian life. Army psychiatrists were especially worried that women veterans would require longer readjustment than men:

> Even more than men, these women have become unsuited to their former civilian environment because the change in their pattern of life was more radical. . . . Most of them have matured; have broader interests and a new and finer sense of values (Craighill 1966: 226–230).

Some employers seemed reluctant to hire women veterans and were not sure that women were entitled to the same benefits as men. Likewise, after Korea and Vietnam, servicewomen seem to have gained little or no boost to their civilian careers (Warner 1985).

Nurses had the hardest time adjusting to postwar civilian life. Nurses gained maturity and new skills from their wartime service. They often performed tasks that no civilian nurse would be deemed capable of doing. We "came out of the war with far more experience than our civilian counterparts. We had been at the forefront of medicine with the new drugs [and] daring surgical techniques." Most had been given "more responsibilities at a younger age in the military" than they would have in civilian life. Therefore, they were shocked upon returning to civilian life to discover that they were offered only poorly paid, low-status positions involving menial work of the sort corpsmen had done. Indeed, autocratic civilian hospital administrators gave nurses less authority, offered fewer channels for promotion or advancement, and refused to provide Social Security or retirement benefits. One nurse, who found civilian nursing "restrictive and boring," had five jobs in four years. She reported: "Civilian nursing to me was too restrictive, routine, and not progressive." Another decided: "I knew I couldn't work in a civilian hospital after returning from the Army Nurse Corps." When they were not treated as they had become accustomed to as military officers, marriage, and escape, was a quick solution. By early 1947, 22% of all nurse veterans had married, and a total of 38% had left the profession (Campbell 1990: 259; McGuire and Conrad 1946: 45, 305–306; Randolph 1946: 95–97; Sharritt 1946: 849–851; U.S. Department of Labor 1948: 9).

There is mixed evidence regarding the broader social integration of servicewomen separating from military service. Women were excluded from some veterans' groups, such as the Veterans of Foreign Wars (Campbell 1984). However, two-thirds of the servicewomen reported that they had attended at least one reunion, and evidence suggests that doing so had positive effects on their long-term health (Ivie 1992). Male veterans with emotional problems at the time of discharge were more likely to attend reunions than veterans without emotional problems (Elder and Clipp 1988a,b). For women, there are no links between military experiences or exit problems and attending reunions (Ivie 1992).

Was the war a more important influence on their future lives than the Great Depression? For the majority of civilians, the Great Depression was more decisive. For these female veterans, when asked where they would place their World War II military service as an influence when considering the most important events in their lives on a scale of 1 (worst) to 10 (best), the average ranking was 8.7 for nurses and 8.1 for the other female veterans. Two-thirds of the nurses and one-half of the non-nurses ranked World War II as a 9 or 10. Clearly, their military experiences made an impression, and for some, they were transformative. The long Depression years, when they grew up, were hardly forgotten; 31% said the war had "more to do with the kind of person" they are now, 13% said the Depression, and an unexpectedly high 56% said "both." One Wave looked at the positive contributions of both: "The Depression made me appreciate the value of a job and money and saving. World War II made me appreciate the value of all persons and all ways of life." A Marine was more sober: "The Depression was a traumatic experience for me. I was a frightened person. The years in the Marines built up my self-confidence and security." Balancing out the two eras, a WAVE saw the war as "another 'suffering' episode," but this time, "it was I who benefited through deprivations. More fight than fright. I was to rear five children, divorce after twenty years, remarry, and [end up] a widow. To take life and better it, not give up as I felt in the Depression" (Campbell 1990: 262).

FURTHER RESEARCH

The battles and the generals have all been covered at length in historical scholarship. In recent decades, the "new military history" has demonstrated the richness of the intersection of social history and the military experience. Although this chapter has shown some of the work that has been done, perhaps it will be useful to look at what has not been done. For the Civil War era, we know more about the deaths than the lives of the veterans, and far too little about the lives of their wives and widows. Historians have begun to use the very rich trove of pension records for Northern veterans and widows, which are filled with personal testimony, to analyze the war's impact on marriage (McClintock 1996, 2002). They have only just begun to mine the very rich lode of pension records to study the impact of the amputations and debilitating sicknesses on the life course of veterans (Logue and Blanck 2008). We have only one study of the psychiatric impact of the Civil War, based on the records of Northern mental hospitals (Dean 1997). Other states have good records and we can expect many more studies. Prisoners of war have been studied in relatively great depth for the Civil War (Chesson 1996) and for Korea and Vietnam (Dean 1997), but astonishingly, we still lack studies on the experiences of male prisoners of war in the World Wars. There were few women prisoners of war in World War II, but there are several studies (Norman 1999), whereas for men, we know much more about the German prisoners of war in the United States than the 93,000 Americans held by the Germans (Hasselbring 1991; Kochavi 2005).

Confederate veterans and their widows seldom received pensions, and thus did not generate the paper trail that historians need; it is much harder to study the impact of the war on their social and psychological conditions. The "Lost Cause" myth helped to reintegrate Confederate veterans to an honored role in Southern society, with amputated limbs considered a badge of honor. However, we do not know how the psychiatric symptoms experienced by Confederate soldiers were handled. The "Lost Cause" vision of heroic failure may also have served as a collective "screen memory" overlaying less acceptable recollections that required tremendous energy to "forget" (Mitchell 1988).

Historians have begun to explore the impact of women's roles in the Civil War on postwar activism, especially the transition from abolitionism to the temperance movement. A representative leader was Annie Turner

Wittenmyer (1827–1900), sanitary agent for the Iowa State Sanitary Commission, who became the first president of the Woman's Christian Temperance Union in 1874 (Ginzberg 1990). We have numerous examples of Civil War organizers becoming postwar activists, but in the case of World War II, there was exceedingly little carryover from wartime organization to postwar activism. The only compelling evidence comes from nurses, who broke away from control by the American Red Cross to form their own professional organizations. The women of the WACs, WAVES, SPARS, and Marines seem to have been disillusioned by their negative public image during the war and did not transition into significant organizational activity (Campbell 1984). Housewives and volunteer workers during the war, who were tightly controlled by national organizations like the USO and the Red Cross, did not develop independent organizational skills (Knapp 2000). For that matter, male veterans were not well organized either. They certainly were not nearly as well organized as the veterans' movements that emerged after the Civil War and World War I (Pencak 2009).

The most astonishing lacuna involves historical studies of the impact of the World Wars on male veterans (but see LaRossa 2011; Mettler 2005). We have full-scale studies using oral history and interviews of women veterans, but the coverage of men from a social science perspective is haphazard. The best we have are longitudinal projects that began in the 1930s and carried through the 1940s and beyond. There are numerous oral history projects underway—just in the nick of time—but they lack the systematic analytic framework that has been applied to the servicewomen of World War II (Campbell 1990; Ivie 1992; Ryan 2008). The interviews conducted with World War I veterans (and held at the Army War College) are too haphazard to be useful. There is still time for systematic interview work with Korean War veterans, but no major projects are underway. Thus, historical research has begun to provide a more detailed picture of the impact of war on men's and women's lives, but much remains to be studied. In particular, there is much to be learned about how recent historical changes in women's roles within the military have affected women's, men's, and children's lives.

As this chapter demonstrates, women's participation in the Civil War was linked to the military enlistment of male kin, including husbands, fathers, brothers, and uncles. As such, they were limited to managing the home front and tending to sick and injured soldiers. Through the middle of the 20th century, women's lives continued to be influenced by war through participation in these traditional roles, although they increasingly experienced the direct effects of service in the limited roles that were available to them during World War II, the Korean War, and the Vietnam War. With the advent of the All-Volunteer Force in 1974, women have been granted access to a wider range of training opportunities and roles within the military. The service academies have been opened to women, and women's rate of participation in the military has been increasing, particularly among women of color (see Kelty and Segal, Chapter 2 of this volume; Wilmoth and London 2011). As of 2005, 7% of veterans were women (U.S. Census Bureau 2007); in 2010, nearly 1.6 million American women were veterans (U.S. Census Bureau 2010). Although women continue to be barred from direct combat positions, the changing nature of enemy engagement in Iraq and Afghanistan is blurring the lines between combat and support positions. Consequently, women are increasingly experiencing and being harmed by enemy engagements, and there is ongoing debate about whether to eliminate the restriction on women serving in direct combat roles. The implications of these changing military roles for women and their families are unclear. The shifting nature of women's military roles highlights the necessity for long-term life-course research on the impact of military service on not only the men and women who have served, but also those whose lives are linked to them through marriage, family, and community.

4 Race-Ethnicity and Immigration Status in the U.S. Military[1]

Amy C. Lutz

The racial-ethnic composition of the United States military has changed over time as demand for personnel has waxed and waned during periods of war and peace, recruitment and enlistment policies have changed, and the demographic characteristics of the U.S. population have shifted. This chapter provides a historical overview of military service among White ethnics, African Americans, Latinos, Asian Americans, and Native Americans. I pay particular attention to how the roles members of each group have been allowed to play have changed over time, the unique contributions of each group to specific wars, and the relationship between military service and calls for improved civil rights. This is followed by a description of the relative rates of military service across various racial-ethnic groups, as well as consideration of issues related to race, ethnicity, and immigrant status in the contemporary military. This chapter sets the stage for considering how race, ethnicity, and immigrant status might intersect with military service within particular birth cohorts to shape the various life-course outcomes considered in subsequent chapters.

A BRIEF RACIAL-ETHNIC HISTORY OF MILITARY SERVICE

White Ethnics in the Military

Immigrants and the adult children of immigrants have a long history of participation in the U.S. military. From the Revolutionary War to World War II, a large percentage of the immigrants and their American-born adult children (referred to hereafter as the second generation) who served in the military were White ethnics. In the Revolutionary War, many Irish and German first- and second-generation immigrants fought alongside the colonists, although some campaigned on the side of the British. Particularly in the Mid-Atlantic states, Irish and German ethnics comprised a large percentage of recruits to the American forces and, in some cases, participated in all-Irish and all-German battalions. Neimeyer (1996: 37) estimates that "roughly one out of every four continental soldiers was of

Irish descent," noting that the colonists drew parallels between Irish and American revolutionary ideals to recruit the Irish to their cause. Germans, who settled in large numbers in the state of Pennsylvania, comprised, on average, 13% of Pennsylvania's regiments (Neimeyer 1996). Many of the well-known military leaders who fought in the Revolutionary War were born in Europe, including Kościuszko (Polish/Lithuanian), Pulaski (Polish), Lafayette (French), and von Steuben (Prussian) (Holm 1996). During the Mexican American War, a battalion of Irish soldiers known as the St. Patrick Battalion/San Patricios famously changed sides to fight with the Catholic Mexican forces. Irish and German ethnics also fought in the Civil War. Both the North and the South recruited immigrants to serve in the military; however, Irish and German immigrants tended to fight on the Union side due to their settlement patterns (Neimeyer 1996). Although most fought in regular military units, there were predominantly Irish or German regiments also (Burton 1988).

By the turn of the 20th century, immigration trends had shifted and new immigrants to the United States tended to come from Southern and Eastern Europe. Many of these newcomers fought in World War I. Although only those immigrants who had applied for citizenship were eligible for the draft at that time, the majority of immigrants who had not applied for citizenship registered and served (Sterba 2003). Such noncitizen combatants were able to acquire citizenship while they were in the service (Mangione and Morreale 1992). Given that the United States fought on the same side as Italy, Italians made up a large number of the recruits, in total comprising nearly 12% of the Army (Mangione and Morreale 1992). Eastern European Jews were another important group of immigrants who fought in World War I. About 200,000 Jews served, and the vast majority of them were of Eastern European origin (Sterba 2003). Indeed, at the end of World War I, a survey by the American Jewish Committee found that 97% of the Jewish soldiers who served in the war were immigrants or children of immigrants, and three-quarters had originated from the Russian Pale (Sterba 2003). Despite such high levels of immigrant participation in World War I, anti-immigrant sentiment was growing in the United States and, shortly after the war, the quotas created by the National Origins Act of 1924 severely curtailed migration from Southern and Eastern Europe (Portes and Rumbaut 2006).

First- and second-generation immigrants also served in World War II. Among them were Italians, who were the largest group of new immigrants at the time, "numbering perhaps six million residents in 1940" (Pozetta 1995: 64). Despite the fact that they were fighting on the side opposed to their home country, more than 500,000 Italians served on behalf of the U.S. during World War II (Mangione and Morreale 1992). After World War II, migration from Eastern and Southern Europe did not resume in large numbers. Although the Hart-Cellar Act did away with the National Origins Quotas in 1965, European migration has never reached the levels recorded during the early part of the 20th century. Instead, the Act paved the way for immigration to the United States from new source countries, particularly Asia and Latin America.

For those White ethnics who served during World War II, veteran status provided many benefits that helped to launch them into the American middle class (Mettler 2005). The end of World War II marked a period of increased home ownership and suburbanization into segregated White residential enclaves, particularly among families of veterans who received Veterans Administration loans for housing. The combination of the GI Bill, federal housing policies, and banking practices created greater opportunities for social mobility among White veterans than Black veterans, who were excluded from housing in the newly created White suburbs. Jewish veterans also faced discrimination as a result of the Home Owners Loan Corporation's color-coded housing practices. Although the home ownership rate increased for both Blacks and Whites between 1940 and 1950, it increased more for Whites (Bennett 1996). Bennett (1996: 298) notes that "[w]ithout a doubt, the GI Bill . . . accelerat[ed] 'white flight'" as White veterans took their housing benefits to the suburbs and Black veterans bought the homes in the cities that Whites had left behind.

During the Vietnam era, through college and other types of deferments, Whites were more successful in avoiding wartime service than other racial-ethnic groups, such as African Americans and Latinos (Armor 1996; Mariscal 1999). The subsequent transition to the All-Volunteer Force in 1974 was associated with increasing rates of military service by racial-ethnic minorities (Levy 1998). Yet how the experience of military service has differed across race and immigrant generation has not been fully explored in the literature. Considering the different social, economic, and political circumstances of Whites and racial-ethnic minorities in America underscores the importance of understanding how experiences of military service, and the effects of military service on lives, have varied for service members from different racial-ethnic and immigrant groups who served in different historical time periods.

African Americans in the Military

In the early years of the United States, guidelines generally stated that participation in the military was for Whites only; however, in practice, Blacks were allowed to join whenever the military needed manpower. As such, African Americans have fought in every American war. In the Revolutionary War, George Washington initially banned Black participation, but when the British offered to free slaves who fought on their side, Washington changed his mind and allowed free Blacks to fight with the colonists (Moskos and Butler 1996). In 1792, Blacks were prohibited from joining militias (Young 1982), and during the War of 1812, they were officially excluded from participation. However, the need for additional troops meant that over 3,000

Blacks eventually fought in that war (Moskos and Butler 1996). During the Civil War, African Americans were initially prohibited from joining the Union Army, but the need for additional troops led Union forces to change this policy and admit Blacks into the military (Young 1982). As a result, about 180,000 African Americans fought in the Union Army during the Civil War and another 29,000 served in the Union Navy (Dorn 1989). After the Civil War, the Army created four all-Black units (Mershon and Schlossman 1998), and the 1862 Militia Act allowed African Americans to serve in state militias (Young 1982). In 1863, the Conscription Act, which initiated the draft, included African Americans (Young 1982).

However, by World War I, segregation had become rampant in American institutions, including some that were previously integrated, such as the Navy, which, during the 1890s, began to segregate by occupation. Blacks were informally and quietly assigned to positions of menial labor, which would keep them segregated from other sailors (Mershon and Schlossman 1998). The Army had traditionally maintained four Black regiments since the days of Reconstruction. These units had fought in the Spanish American War, as well as in battles against Native Americans. However, the four traditional all-Black units were not sent to Europe during World War I (Mershon and Schlossman 1998). Among Black Army draftees in World War I, most were excluded from combat duty and held positions in which they performed menial labor. Few African Americans advanced to become officers. Discrimination and lack of training meant that there were few Black officers to lead Black soldiers; as a result, Black soldiers were almost always led by White officers, including many who discriminated against their own men (Mershon and Schlossman 1998).

World War II marked another turning point for Black participation in the military, both because large numbers of African Americans served during that war and because the war itself became a catalyst for a social movement that would demand equal rights for Black soldiers. Participation by Blacks varied across the different branches of military service. Most African Americans served in the Army, as they still do today. At that time, over 900,000 African Americans served; at the height of Black participation during World War II, nearly 9% of the Army was Black (Dansby and Landis 2001), which was approximately equivalent to their representation in the male population of the United States at the time (9.5%) (U.S. Census Bureau 1940). Fewer, but not insubstantial, numbers of African Americans served in the Navy and Marines. Approximately 167,000 Blacks served in the Navy during the war, making up roughly 4% of that service (Dansby and Landis 2001), whereas approximately 17,000 served in the Marine Corps, comprising about 2% of that service (Dansby and Landis 2001). Across all branches, African Americans generally continued to serve in segregated units during this period.

During and after World War II, the National Association for the Advancement of Colored People (NAACP) and other organizations concentrated their efforts on the desegregation of the military. The "Double V" campaign, which sought victory over enemies abroad and Jim Crow policies within the United States, was started by an editorial in the *Pittsburgh Courier*, an African American newspaper (MacGregor 1981). By the end of the war, the military began experimenting with racial integration. As a result of the positive outcomes of such integrationist experiments, the Navy chose to end segregation of African Americans in its general service, including the desegregation of sleeping quarters and mess halls (Mershon and Schlossman 1998). However, in practice, the Stewards' branch, which comprised the manual labor positions to which African Americans were confined during the war, remained segregated (Mershon and Schlossman 1998). Although the Army also experimented with racial integration on a small scale and desegregated its recreational facilities, by the end of the war, it had reaffirmed its policy of maintaining segregated units (Mershon and Schlossman 1998).

The proportion of African Americans in the military grew during and after World War II. Despite segregation and widespread discrimination, a survey of soldiers reported that African Americans found life in the military to be more satisfying than did Whites (Mershon and Schlossman 1998). Additionally, although the Navy lost a large proportion of African Americans after the war (Mershon and Schlossman 1998), fewer Blacks than Whites were discharged from the Army at that time (Dansby, Stewart, and Webb 2001). Voluntary enlistment of African Americans into the armed services, particularly the Army, continued, even after the war's end. Six months after the end of World War II, 17% of new enlistees were African American, although only about 11% of the 18- to 37-year-old male population in the U.S. was Black (Young 1982). As a result of such trends, the proportion of Black soldiers in the military grew.

In 1948, President Harry S. Truman issued Executive Order 9981, which created a policy of racial equality in the military. The order stated:

> It is hereby declared to be the policy of the President that there shall be equality of treatment and opportunity for all persons in the Armed Forces without regard to race, color, religion, or national origin. This policy shall be put into effect as rapidly as possible, having due regard to the time required to effectuate any necessary changes without impairing efficiency or morale (Truman 1948).

Executive Order 9981 also established a presidentially appointed committee to examine racial inequality in the military, as well as to create and alter military policies related to civil rights. Whereas previous policies had sought to put an end to racial discrimination in the military, they did not define segregation as a form of discrimination. Truman and the President's Committee on Equality of Treatment and Opportunity were clear in specifically defining segregation as a form of racial discrimination. Truman "saw black civil rights as a matter of national security" (Skrentny 2002: 16), and, because racial policies in the military were not statutory laws, he could pursue desegregation of the military without congressional legislation (Mershon and Schlossman 1998). Desegregation in the Navy and the Air Force began to take hold as these branches worked with the President's Committee to desegregate their units. However, the Army and the Marines resisted desegregation efforts.

Whereas the GI Bill may have contributed to increased residential segregation, Bennett argues (1996) that it played a key role in the integration of institutions of higher education. In addition to attending Black institutions, where enrollment vastly increased, many Black veterans attended Northern and Western institutions where governmental vouchers provided financial incentives for their admission. The sheer numbers of Black veterans applying for college after World War II was more than the institutional capacity of Northern and Black colleges, which created pressure for desegregation of Southern colleges (Bennett 1996). Further, the experience of fighting for equality in Europe in the war and receipt of the same federal educational benefits for service initiated a powerful call for change in educational institutions by Black veterans (Bennett 1996). Integration of Ole Miss began with an Air Force veteran, James Meredith, under the strategic leadership of Medgar Evers, who was also a veteran. Many of those involved in the legal teams working for educational desegregation—leading up to, including, and following the Brown case—were veterans (Bennett 1996).

The Korean War was the first war fought under a policy of troop integration. In practice, many units remained segregated during the war, but, by the end of the war, integration was nearly complete. In fact, the Korean War led the Army to begin to see desegregation as a solution to problems of manpower and inefficiency. Similarly, the Marine Corps moved toward integration as a way to ease personnel shortages during the war. By the beginning of 1954, only 10,000 out of 250,000 African Americans in the military continued to serve in segregated units (Young 1982).

Despite formal integration, the Vietnam War was marked by racial strife. One prominent issue was racial inequality in the draft. The military allowed college students to defer service; such deferments largely allowed the White middle class to avoid the draft. Given that lower-class men and Blacks made up a large portion of the troops who served during the Vietnam War, allegations were made that "blacks and the poor were serving as cannon fodder" (Armor 1996: 9). Some civil rights activists became strong opponents of the war, in part because the inequalities in the draft meant that large numbers of African Americans were fighting and disproportionately bearing the risks and injuries associated with combat exposure. Throughout the Vietnam War, military installations—both in the United States and abroad—became sites of race riots (Mershon and Schlossman 1998). Some of this strife arose because there was rampant discrimination against Black soldiers. For example, after the assassination of Martin

Luther King, Jr. some White soldiers burned crosses and flew Confederate flags on bases in Vietnam (Terry 1971). Despite continued discrimination in the military, Blacks tended to reenlist at a greater rate than Whites (Stern 1971), which further contributed to growth in the population of African Americans in the armed forces.

In 1971, the Pentagon created the Defense Race Relations Institute (DRRI), which subsequently was renamed the Defense Equal Opportunity Management Institute (DEOMI). This Institute was originally created to "cope with the racial turbulence then afflicting the military" (Moskos and Butler 1996: 56). That mission evolved, such that DEOMI increasingly became involved with equal opportunity training, which is mandatory for all military personnel. The program has been labeled "the single most ambitious training program . . . ever implemented in the United States" (Dansby, Stewart, and Webb 2001: xxiii). Today, equal opportunity training emphasizes an "overarching American identity," rather than multiculturalism, as the aim is to create an underlying unity among soldiers (Moskos and Butler 1996: 58). The armed services take this training seriously and view racial harmony as an important step toward the broader goal of cohesive units and combat readiness. As Moskos and Butler (1996: 53) note, "The Army treats good race relations as a means to readiness and combat effectiveness—not as an end in itself." For example, hate speech tends to be punished only when it causes problems within the ranks, rather than at every utterance.

In 1973, as the Vietnam War came to an end, the military did away with conscription, marking the beginning of the era of the All-Volunteer Force. Concerns were raised that, in the context of a volunteer force, the overrepresentation of Blacks and low-income individuals would become even greater, as middle-class Whites would have little motivation to join the military (Armor 1996). Indeed, with the advent of the All-Volunteer Force, the proportion of Blacks in the military did grow substantially (Levy 1998). Participation by African Americans in the 1991 Persian Gulf War, fought exclusively with volunteers, was high (Buckley 2001). Throughout the All-Volunteer Force era, levels of participation by Blacks have remained high; however, the roles occupied by African Americans have changed. For example, Black service members in the All-Volunteer Force have been "more concentrated in non-combat support units" and some have suggested that African Americans now "rea[p] the benefits of military service without unduly bearing its ultimate burdens" (Gifford 2005a: 206, 201). African Americans made up about a third of noncommissioned officers in the 1991 Persian Gulf War (Buckley 2001) and were also overrepresented as noncommissioned officers in Operation Iraqi Freedom in 2003–2004 (Gifford 2005a). In both Operation Iraqi Freedom and Operation Enduring Freedom in Afghanistan, African Americans have been underrepresented in casualties (Gifford 2005a, Zweig et al. 2011). Today, use of GI Bill educational benefits by African American veterans is high and seems to particularly facilitate graduate education. African American veterans make up

20% of military graduate students, but only 11% of nonmilitary graduate students, and they are the only racial-ethnic group for whom the difference is statistically significant; differences among undergraduates are within 3% for all racial-ethnic groups (Radford and Weko 2011). Since 2006, the number of African Americans in the armed forces has declined (Department of Defense 2010c). Currently, 6.3 and 0.3% of veterans aged 65 and older are Black men and women, respectively, but those percentages are expected to increase to 11.7 and 2.0% by 2030 (Wilmoth and London 2011).

Latinos in the Military

Latinos also have a long history of service in the military, although their service has historically not been well documented. Dansby, Stewart, and Webb (2001: xix) note that "Hispanic soldiers participated in major battles from the War of 1812 to the present," but that "the number of Hispanic Americans serving in the military before the Vietnam War can only be estimated" as the military did not keep records on Hispanic or Latino ancestry prior to that time. The Department of Defense (1989) estimates that 9,000 Mexican Americans, serving in both the Confederate and Union armies, fought in the Civil War, with the Union Army creating exclusively Mexican American cavalry units in both California and Texas.

Latinos also fought in both World Wars. Rochin and Fernandez (2002: 9) estimate that "[m]ore than 4,000 Hispanics were trained for military service" in World War I, but many were given menial tasks during the war. Although many Latinos served in integrated units, Puerto Ricans tended to serve in six segregated units on the island and in the Panama Canal Zone, including a Black Puerto Rican unit, the 365th (Villahermosa 2002).

One estimate based on surnames indicates that approximately half a million Latinos fought in World War II (Allsup 1982). Mexican Americans, in particular, served in disproportionate numbers relative to other ethnic groups, in part because a large proportion of the population was of draft age and they were unlikely to occupy the jobs for which deferments were granted (Steele 2008). Not only did Mexican Americans serve during World War II, but about 15,000 Mexican citizens also served (Zamora 2005). These included some citizens from Northern Mexican border states who specifically crossed into the United States in order to join the military (Griswold del Castillo 2008); by 1943, Mexico and the United States also had a military agreement that required military service of nationals within the other country's borders (Schwab 2002). Mexico was an Ally during World War II, declaring war on the Axis powers after Germany sank two Mexican tankers in 1942 (Schwab 2002), yet there were relatively few opportunities for Mexican nationals to fight for their country overseas. The one exception was for Mexicans to serve as pilots in the 300-member Squadron 201 of the Mexican Expeditionary Air Force, which trained in the U.S. and fought in the Pacific against the Japanese (Schwab 2002).

Latinos mostly served in integrated units with Whites (Department of Defense 1989) or in all-Black units, depending on their skin tone (Dansby, Stewart, and Webb 2001). However, Puerto Ricans still tended to serve in segregated units, such as the 65th Infantry Unit (Villahermosa 2002), as they had during World War I. Although mostly serving in integrated units with Whites during World War II, many Mexicans, who made up the largest numbers of Latino recruits, experienced a sense of "double consciousness," which Griswold del Castillo (2008: 57) refers to as a sense of "considering [one]self a patriotic American" while also experiencing discrimination and "second-class citizenship" in the United States. Griswold del Castillo (2008) notes that the war became a watershed moment in relation to Mexican American civil rights. Mexican Americans built on the activism that had taken place during the 1930s while drawing on the moral imperative to end intolerance in Europe that was created by World War II and arguing for the end of discrimination against them in the U.S. In addition, for the first time, during this period, Mexican Americans experienced greater equality with Whites in both military service and factory work in the defense industry at home.

Mexican Americans long felt their citizenship status was questioned by Anglo Americans. Participation in World War II was a platform on which some organizations made claims regarding the "authenticity" of the citizenship of Mexican Americans (Griswold del Castillo 2008). For example, the Congreso del Pueblo de Habla Espanola promoted service in the military among Mexican Americans, saying "We are also children of the United States. We will defend her" (Griswold del Castillo 2008: 50). Upon returning home from World War II, Mexican American veterans played key roles in both new and existing civic and civil rights organizations, such as the League of United Latin American Citizens (LULAC), the American GI Forum, the Mexican American Political Association (MAPA), and the Community Service Organization (CSO) (Griswold del Castillo 2008). After the war, Navy veteran Cesar Chavez joined the CSO and eventually took a leadership position in that group. He also brought other Mexican Americans into the organization. His experience in leadership within that organization helped him to build the farmworkers' association and become a key figure in fighting for Mexican American civil rights (Griswold del Castillo 2008). Veteran status (after World War II and the Korean War) played an important role in building up the social standing of Mexican Americans because it provided them access to the educational benefits of the GI Bill and priority in credit and loans for housing (Morin [1963] 2008). Mexican Americans had greater opportunities than African Americans for integrated housing with non-Hispanic Whites because Mexican Americans were often considered White and therefore less subject to color-coded housing policies (Steele and Griswold del Castillo 2008).

During the Korean War, the all–Puerto Rican 65th Infantry Regiment served again. However, as was the case during World War II, most Latinos served in integrated units (Department of Defense 1989). By the time of the Vietnam War, the 65th Infantry Regiment had become integrated (Villahermosa 2002). During the 1960s, Latino military service was shaped by President Johnson's War on Poverty, which promoted military service as a type of career socialization and opportunity for low-income individuals, while also meeting the growing need for soldiers to fight in the Vietnam War (Mariscal 1999). One such program was Project 100,000, a Defense Department program that lowered the educational criteria for military service to allow those who were originally not deemed fit for service to be retested or accepted under lower standards. Consistent with War on Poverty rhetoric, this policy was implemented for the purpose of "upgrad[ing] the educational and skill level of disadvantaged youth and assist[ing] them in finding jobs and a future in our society" (Greenberg 1969: 1). Those scoring low on the Armed Forces Qualification Test (AFQT), however, were often placed in infantry units. Large numbers of those who were originally deemed mentally unfit for service on the basis of the AFQT were Spanish speakers (Mariscal 1999). Many Puerto Ricans and Latinos from South Texas were among those who received low scores on the AFQT exam at first, but were later deemed fit to serve under different standards (Mariscal 1999). Previously (since the 1950s), the Army had a program in Puerto Rico whereby recruits would be trained in English before undergoing basic training on the mainland; however, that program was abandoned with the creation of Project 100,000 (Mariscal 1999).

There is evidence that Latinos were overrepresented both among those who served during the Vietnam War and among the causalities of that war. The importance of Latino service in Vietnam is underscored by the fact that Rodriguez (along with Johnson) is one of the two most common surnames on the Vietnam War Memorial (Mariscal 1999). Mariscal (1999) reports that Puerto Rico ranked fourteenth in the highest number of casualties and fourth in the number of combat deaths, but twenty-sixth in terms of overall population size, and also quotes a George McGovern speech noting that 15% of casualties from California and 10% from the Southwest were people of Mexican descent.

Like African Americans, few Latinos were able to get draft deferments (Mariscal 1999); however, among Latinos, there was less antidraft activism than among African Americans and Whites. Ybarra (2004: 210) notes that some Latinos felt that their "American-ness" was questioned by Anglo Americans despite their patriotism and that they had to prove their loyalty to the United States by "earning their citizenship" through military service. Ybarra (2004) interviewed Mexican American veterans of the Vietnam War. Although that war was marked by racial strife in the ranks, Ybarra's interviews suggest that Mexican Americans had a very different experience of the war in that respect than African Americans. His interviewees, despite acknowledging discrimination and disillusionment about race and class in the U.S., indicated that the greatest hostility was between Blacks and Whites. Given that the war coincided with the Chicano civil rights movement, he reports that veterans recalled an increasing awareness and pride in Chicano identities and culture, as well as strong ties among Chicanos in service, while also creating opportunities for them to build bonds with Black, White, and other Latino servicemen. He also noted how the Spanish language supported the combat effort when Mexican American radiomen in Vietnam used Mexican slang in communicating with each other to prevent enemies from understanding their messages. Likewise, he found that soldiers expressed a sense of growing political awareness over the course of the war, not only about issues within the U.S., such as civil rights, but also concerning U.S. policies toward Latin America.

In recent years, Latinos have tended to be underrepresented in the military (Armor 1996). Research by the Pew Hispanic Center indicates that Latinos tend to be overrepresented among personnel who "most directly handle weapons," whereas they tend to be underrepresented in "technical occupations such as electronics and communications" (2003: 5). Gifford (2005a: 220) found that Latinos' propensity to volunteer for combat-oriented positions, such as in the Marine Corps, is associated with the rate at which they incur casualties. During the 2003–2004 Iraq Conflict, under "high intensity conditions," such as the invasion, they incurred a disproportionate share of casualties, although their share of casualties was proportional to their service rates during other conditions, such as the occupation stage. In recent years, the military has been actively recruiting Latinos and working with Latino organizations and media outlets in their efforts (Miles 2004). Zweig et al. (2011) found that Latinos are underrepresented in casualties incurred during Operation Enduring Freedom in Afghanistan relative to their numbers in the U.S. population. However, future research should investigate whether this is due to their underrepresentation in the military, generally, or some other factor, such as their roles in the conflict.

Latinos are a growing portion of the veteran population. In 2010, approximately 5.3 and 0.6% of veterans 45 to 64 years old were Latino men and women, respectively, but by 2030, those percentages are expected to increase to 8.2 and 1.7% (Wilmoth and London 2011). Given the dearth of research on Latinos in the military in different historical time periods, it is difficult to say the extent to which the meaning and life-course consequences of military service has differed for Latino members of the armed services and their wider communities across time. Determining the life-course consequences of such service among Latinos is another area ripe for further research.

Asian Americans in the Military

Although Asian American participation in the U.S. military has not been well documented, it is known that Filipinos have been joining the armed services since shortly after the turn of the 20th century. The Philippines became an American colony after the Spanish American War, in which the United States intervened in both Cuban and Filipino movements for independence from Spain, defeating the Spanish militarily. In the Treaty of Paris of 1889, the United States and Spain negotiated the agreement to transfer the Philippines to the U.S. without the consent of the Filipino forces or people. Thus, the Philippines continued to be at war, although with the United States rather than with Spain. Coverage of massive Filipino civilian casualties and details of extreme violence in the American press resulted in criticism of the U.S. role in fighting the Filipino anticolonial forces by much of the American public. Even before the end of the Philippine-American War, Filipinos began serving in the U.S. military, first as Philippine Scouts in the Army, and shortly thereafter, in 1904, in the Navy (Posadas 1999). The numbers of Filipinos in the Navy grew over time, eventually comprising 5.7% of enlisted personnel in 1922 (Posadas 1999). From the end of World War I until 1932, Segal (1989) indicates that the Navy began replacing African Americans with Filipinos in steward and messmen positions. Posadas (1999) suggests that there was greater job security for Filipinos in the military than in other types of jobs in the U.S., despite the lack of opportunities for advancement for most Filipinos in the Navy.

In 1934, the Tydings McDuffie Act made the Philippines a commonwealth, in large part as an exclusionary effort to decrease migration from the Philippines to the United States (Lee and Yung 2010). Previously Filipinos could migrate as U.S. nationals; however, during this period, they were subject to the national origins quotas and given an allotment of only fifty people per year. The Philippines had "the lowest quota the United States assigned to any country in the world," with the exception of those countries, such as China, which were entirely excluded (Lee and Yung 2010: 281–282). Filipinos on the islands thus maintained an ambiguous status as U.S. nationals who were neither U.S. citizens nor fully independent citizens of the Philippines; moreover, foreign-born Filipinos in the United States became ineligible for naturalization.

Between 200,000 and 300,000 Filipinos fought with the United States during World War II (Nakano 2006). In 1941, Franklin D. Roosevelt brought the Philippine Commonwealth forces under the auspices of the U.S. military. In 1942, Congress allowed for the naturalization of foreigners serving for the United States during the war; until 1946, this included overseas naturalizations (Nakano 2006). The policy was somewhat amended with respect to Filipinos due to fears of mass immigration; it was applied only to those serving as Philippine Scouts, rather than to all veterans who served in the Commonwealth (Nakano 2006). Filipinos who were living in the U.S. served in the segregated 1st and 2nd Filipino Infantry Regiments in the Pacific, and in integrated units in Europe (Posadas 1999; Takaki 2000). Lee and Yung (2010: 296) note that "[i]n California, 16,000 or 40 percent of the state's entire Filipino population registered for the first draft, and 7,000 . . . served," with service members gaining citizenship through "mass naturalization ceremony[ies] for soldiers," and that changes in the law allowed wartime industries to become open to Filipinos in the United States. Filipino bravery became well known in the U.S. after the fall of Bataan (in the Philippines), when the Japanese forced about 75,000 Filipino and American soldiers to march about seventy miles to concentration camps under inhumane and torturous conditions, with thousands dying during what is often called the Bataan Death March (Takaki 2000). However, Takaki (2000) notes that Filipino soldiers faced discrimination in the United States. In Maryville, California, for example, residents refused Filipino soldiers and their wives accommodations in hotels, theaters, and restaurants, or required them to be segregated. This persisted until Colonel Robert H. Offley told the local Chamber of Commerce that there would be repercussions for noncooperation with the military and continued discrimination against Filipino service members and their families (Takaki 2000).

In 1945, the Bureau of Veterans Affairs indicated that veterans who had fought in the Commonwealth qualified for benefits; however, a few months later, in the 1946 Rescission Act, Congress withdrew access to those benefits, saying that the services provided by those veterans "were not to be considered as active military service for the purposes of veterans benefits" (Nakano 2006: 137). In 1946, after a delay due to World War II, the Philippines gained independence from the United States, and in that same year, the Luce-Celler Act granted Filipinos who had migrated to the U.S. the right to American citizenship (Lee and Yung 2010). In 1947, the Philippine Military Bases Agreement allowed the United States to keep its military bases in the Philippines and recruit up to 1,000 Filipino nationals per year for service in the U.S. armed forces; this quota was increased to 2,000 Filipino nationals during the Vietnam War (Burdeos 2008; Posadas 1999). After President Truman signed Executive Order 9981, which created a policy of racial equality in the military, African Americans began to have greater opportunities within the military and left the low-status work as stewards in the Navy and Coast Guard to which they had previously been disproportionately assigned. In 1953, the Navy and Coast Guard began recruiting stewards from the Philippines (Burdeos 2008). Among Filipinos, even those with high skills, there was a massive response to this selective recruitment, and many joined the Navy in response to this perceived opportunity (Burdeos 2008).

The struggle over veterans' benefits continues today for Filipinos who served in the Philippines during World War II. It has been ongoing since 1946, when the United States decided that veterans' benefits for them should be discounted to about half what American veterans received (Nakano 2006). Additionally, they were tied to an inaccurate valuation of the peso; however, the formula for this benefit calculation was changed in 1966 in an effort to gain support for the Vietnam War (Nakano 2006). In 1990, to make amends for injustices in naturalization policies toward Filipino veterans of the U.S. military in the Philippines, Congress extended the right to naturalize to Filipino veterans of World War II even if they lived outside the U.S. (Aoki and Takeda 2009; Nakano 2006). By 1998, 28,000 elderly Filipino veterans had migrated to the U.S. (Nakano 2006). Ineligible for Veterans Administration benefits and pensions, many were living in poverty. To try to improve their circumstances and achieve justice, they initiated a social movement to secure their benefits. Thus far, they have been successful in gaining access to war-related compensation, SSI benefits (if living in the U.S.), and the right to care at Veterans Administration hospitals and nursing homes, but not to non-service-related disability or pension benefits (Aoki and Takeda 2009).

Other Asian Americans also served in the U.S. military during World War II. For Chinese Americans, World War II marked a change in status. During World War II, 13,499 Chinese Americans served in the military, which represented 22% of all adult males of Chinese descent in America (Takaki 2000). Similar to the experiences of Mexican Americans, many Chinese Americans had their first experiences of social integration through their military service and participation in related wartime industries. Because China was an ally of the United States against Japan, people of Chinese descent slowly began to be seen as "Americans" and were afforded new opportunities that extended beyond the boundaries of America's Chinatowns (Takaki 2000). Restricted from migration by the Chinese Exclusion Act, barred from naturalized citizenship and land ownership (among the foreign-born) in some places, and subjected to violence and ghettoization in American cities, people of Chinese ancestry were now recast as "friends" (Takaki 2000). *Time* magazine ran an article at the time to inform Americans how to see the difference between Chinese "friends" and Japanese enemies based on physical characteristics, and stores in Chinatown posted signs that read, "This is a Chinese shop" (Takaki 2000: 111, 113).

As with much of the propaganda issued by the Axis powers during World War II that focused on the treatment of minority groups in the United States (Skrentny 2002), Japan emphasized the hostile treatment of Chinese Americans in attempting to persuade China to fight against the U.S. (Takaki 2000). In the face of such propaganda, and with evidence of large-scale participation of Chinese Americans in the military and in other wartime efforts, along with an intense lobbying effort and a visit by Madame Chiang Kai-shek, the United States repealed the Chinese Exclusion Act in 1943 and gave China a small annual quota of 105 immigrants (Takaki 2000).

Over 30,000 Japanese Americans, mostly children of immigrants, served in the U.S. military during World War II (Inada and California Historical Society 2000). Some were volunteers or had been serving in the military prior to the war, whereas others were drafted from internment camps (Muller 2001). At the time of the bombing of Pearl Harbor, about 158,000 Japanese Americans lived in Hawaii, where they made up about a third of the population (Takaki 2000), and another 126,000 lived on the mainland, mostly on the West Coast (Nakasone 1999). Conscription was already taking place before the bombing and 1,400 Japanese American children of immigrants in Hawaii had been drafted and were serving as part of the 298th and 299th Infantry Regiments of the Hawaiian National Guard, which had already been federalized by the time of the Pearl Harbor bombing (Nakasone 1999). Due to the federalization of the Hawaiian National Guard units, the state created a new Territorial Guard in which 300 Japanese American children of immigrants served, mostly from the University of Hawaii ROTC (Nakasone 1999). Following the bombing of Pearl Harbor, Japanese Americans in the Territorial Guard were discharged, although other Asian Americans in the unit remained. Despite being discharged, the Japanese Americans who had served in the Territorial Guard continued to serve as the "Varsity Victory Volunteers" (Nakasone 1999). The drafting of Japanese Americans into the U.S. military was halted immediately after Pearl Harbor and, for some time, those eligible for the draft were classified as 4C (enemy aliens). However, later, the conscription of Japanese Americans was resumed (Nakasone 1999; Rosen 1997), and by 1944, Japanese Americans were being drafted directly from the internment camps (Muller 2001).

After the attack on Pearl Harbor, 120,000 people of Japanese ancestry, including some American citizens, were placed in internment camps. This defied intelligence reports at the time, which suggested that people of Japanese ancestry in the U.S. posed no risk (Takaki 2000). Over 2,000 Latin Americans of Japanese descent were also brought to the U.S. by South American allied countries, mostly from Peru, to be interned along with Japanese Americans (Nakasone 1999). Although Japanese Americans living on the mainland were interned, those living in Hawaii were not, in part because of practical considerations related to the large size of the Japanese population in Hawaii, and in part due to the need for their skills and labor to rebuild Pearl Harbor (Takaki 2000). A segregated combat unit, the 100th Infantry Combat Battalion, was formed from the soldiers who were part of the federalized Hawaiian National Guard units (298th and 299th) and draftees (Inouye 2000; Nakasone 1999). More than 90% of the soldiers in the 100th were children of immigrants (Inada and California Historical Society 2000). In 1942, 1,432 Japanese Hawaiian soldiers were sent to Fort Shelby, Mississippi, and Camp McCoy, Wisconsin, for training as part of the segregated 100th Infantry Battalion, before being sent for a short time to North Africa and later to fight in Italy (Nakasone 1999; Rosen 1997). Although most of the officers in the 100th were White, one of their leaders was Lieutenant Kim, a Korean American. The 100th fought in Monte Cassino and Anzio Beach in Italy, with substantial casualties (Rosen 1997).

In early 1943, President Roosevelt approved the creation of a fully segregated Japanese American combat unit. Over 11,000 Japanese Americans in Hawaii volunteered for what was originally a call for 2,500 volunteers. Ultimately, the 442nd Infantry Regiment of about 4,000 soldiers was created. This Regiment included the 522nd Field Artillery Battalion and the 232nd Combat Engineer Company (Inada and California Historical Society 2000; Inouye 2000), as well as an antitank company, a cannon company, a service company, a medical detachment, and the regimental band (Nakasone 1999). Senator Daniel Inouye (2000), who served in the 442nd and was among the first to enlist, reported that 1,000 Japanese Americans volunteered on the first day.

The decision to segregate Japanese Americans in the military, rather than integrate them with White troops, took into account the potential reactions of both White and Black enlisted soldiers. Although framed as an opportunity to show Japanese Americans' loyalty, Muller (2001: 49) notes that the military decided to segregate the unit because of concerns about the "psychological effect" of integration on White soldiers and because the integration of Japanese American soldiers would "emphasize" the segregation of Black soldiers, who were viewed by top officials as "increasingly bitter" about their segregation in the war.

As the 100th fought, the 442nd, comprising both Japanese Hawaiians and Japanese Americans from the mainland, who had enlisted from the internment camps, began training at Fort Shelby, Mississippi, and later joined the 100th in Benevento, Italy (Inada and California Historical Society 2000; Izumigawa 2000; Rosen 1997). Within the 442nd, there was originally some friction between the two groups of Japanese Americans, but after the Japanese Hawaiians visited one of the internment camps and realized the conditions under which their mainland counterparts had volunteered, tensions dissipated (Rosen 1997). The 100th and 442nd combined into the 442nd Regiment, but the 100th still kept their name because they had distinguished themselves so much in battle.

In 1944, after fighting in Italy, the 100th/442nd served in France in the Vosges Mountains. There, after an eight-day battle during which they captured the towns of Bruyeres and Biffontaine, without receiving recognition by the military, they were sent to rescue a unit of about 275 men from Texas, the 1st Battalion of the 141st Regiment, which is now often called the "Lost Battalion" (Crost 1994; Nakasone 1999; Rosen 1997; Sterner 2008). Although two other battalions from the same regiment were previously unable to do so, the 442nd was ordered by General Dahlquist to fight in extremely dangerous forested conditions (Crost 1994), which made many feel that the general viewed them as expendable (Sterner 2008). In successfully rescuing the group after five days, the 442nd suffered massive casualties, with 161 killed, 43 missing, and 2,000 wounded (over 40% with serious wounds) (Inada and California Historical Society 2000; Nakasone 1999; Rosen 1997). When only 500 of about 4,500 men of the 442nd presented themselves to General Dahlquist upon his request, he asked, "Where are the rest of the men?" Colonel Virgil S. Miller cried as he replied, "Sir, this is all that's left" (Rosen 1997). Questions still remain about whether the decision to send the 442nd to the rescue of the "Lost Battalion" was

racism or a case of sending the best men (Rosen 1997). The regiment ultimately lost more of its own members than it saved in the rescue (Nakasone
1999). During the war, the 442nd had a 315% turnover rate because of
losses, with 9,486 casualties during seven campaigns (Inada and California
Historical Society 2000; Rosen 1997).

The 100th/442nd was ultimately the most highly decorated unit of
World War II, with 18,000 individual medals and 9,486 Purple Hearts
(Rosen 1997). However, during the war, only one Medal of Honor was
granted to a member of the 100th/442nd despite numerous recommendations (Crost 1994). In 2000, nineteen members of the 100th/442nd were
given the Congressional Medal of Honor. A street in Bruyeres is also named
after the regiment and monuments in Biffontaine and Monte Cassino honor
the 100th (Crost 1994).

In addition to those who served in Europe, Japanese Americans—both
Nisei, American-born children of immigrants, and *Kibei*, American-born
children educated in Japan—served in the Military Intelligence Service in
the Pacific, as linguists and interrogators (Crost 1994). The U.S. government began recruiting Japanese Americans for this work in 1941, before
the bombing of Pearl Harbor, and initially trained sixty men at a language
school in the Presidio in San Francisco. The facility was moved to Minnesota after Executive Order 9066 required the internment of the Japanese
on the West Coast. By the end of the war, about 6,000 persons had been
trained (Crost 1994; Inada and California Historical Society 2000; Nakasone 1999). Military Intelligence Service Staff Sergeant Min Hara (2000)
describes how he and seven others volunteered for the position from an
internment camp in Arizona and underwent a twenty-six-week-long training program in the Japanese language. Japanese American Military Intelligence Service agents translated documents, battle plans, and maps, and
also interrogated prisoners in the Pacific. Their contributions should not be
underestimated, as the Japanese military used Japanese rather than codes
in their communications under the mistaken assumption that the United
States did not have the capacity to translate them (Crost 1994; Rosen
1997). Among those serving as linguists in the Military Intelligence Service
were "four officers and 194 enlisted men" of the 100th/442nd, who volunteered to serve in the Pacific after fighting ended in Europe (Crost 1994:
271). At least two Japanese American Military Intelligence Service agents
were involved in translating Japanese documents on bombs for the Manhattan Project (without knowing the reason at the time) which helped the
U.S. military determine whether Japan had made progress on the creation
of an atomic bomb (Crost 1994). The Japanese American Military Intelligence Service agents also played a large role after the war with respect to
interrogating prisoners, searching for prisoners of war in Japan, checking
the language in Japanese war documents, helping to draft the new constitution. assisting with the Japanese surrender and occupation, and providing
translation in war crimes trials (Crost 1994).

In 1944, when the United States military began drafting young men from the internment camps, more than 300 resisted, which resulted in federal charges of draft evasion against them (Muller 2001). Most of these cases resulted in convictions; of the twenty-three whose charges were dismissed, all were returned to the internment camps following the verdict (Muller 2001).

After the war, children of Japanese immigrants became more engaged in Hawaiian politics. Nakasone (1999) has argued that Japanese Americans' strong record of military service played a role in the postwar success of Japanese Americans from Hawaii in state and national political races, as well as in the acceptance of Hawaii as a state. Members of the 100th/442nd maintained contact with one another by organizing several veterans' clubs in Hawaii (Nakasone 1999). The connections between military service, community organizing, and political careers, which are exemplified among Japanese Americans in Hawaii during this period, is an understudied aspect of life-course scholarship.

Korean immigrants were in a unique position during World War II. Because their homeland had been occupied by Japan since 1910, they were highly supportive of the United States in the war. Nevertheless, like Japanese immigrants and their children, they were often treated by the U.S. government as "enemy aliens" (Takaki 2000). Korean participation in the war took several forms, from purchasing large numbers of war bonds to translating documents from Japanese, which they had learned in school in Korea during the occupation, into English; many also served in the Korean "Tiger Brigade" unit of the California National Guard (Takaki 2000). Those who were working in the defense industry in Hawaii were forced to wear badges indicating their Japanese classification; however, ultimately, they were allowed to include a printed notation on their badges: "I am Korean" (Takaki 2000: 127).

Since World War II, Asian Americans have continued to serve in the U.S. military. Many Japanese Americans who had been part of the Military Intelligence Service also served during the Korean War (Crost 1994). The Department of Defense has estimated that 35,000 Asian Americans/Pacific Islanders served during the Vietnam War (Mariscal 1999). Fighting in Asia not only engendered conflicted feelings among some Asian American soldiers, but also made them targets of racism for some other American soldiers (Mariscal 1999). Between 1953 and 1992, the Navy and Coast Guard recruited about 45,000 Filipino nationals directly from the Philippines (Burdeos 2008). In 1973, after a Senate investigation of civil rights issues in the Navy, the Navy changed its policy and allowed Filipinos to enter all occupations rather than recruiting Filipinos only as stewards. In 1992, the United States and Philippines terminated the Military Bases Agreement and the U.S. stopped recruiting Filipino nationals into the American military (Espiritu 2003). The large-scale participation of Filipinos in the Navy has contributed to a thriving Filipino American community in San Diego, where Filipinos have typically done their Navy training. Additionally, Filipinos with ties to the Navy continue to make up a large component of Filipino communities in the U.S. (Espiritu 2003).

Native Americans in the Military

Prior to the arrival of Europeans in North America, Native American warfare was different from that of Europeans, both in terms of motives and tactics (Holm 1996). With the arrival of Europeans in North America, colonial military forces began to evolve and become "syncretized" with tribal traditions and "tribal warriorhood began to mesh with the newer tradition of service in White men's armies" (Holm 1996: 64). Fighting in North America also created changes in the military strategies of Europeans. For example, American frontier militias (the name "militia" itself comes from a Native American term) shifted from the rigid block formations of European-style warfare to guerilla-like techniques with less infantry that resembled Native American fighting in the Indian Wars (Holm 1996).

At the beginning of the Revolutionary War, Native Americans tended to fight on the British side. After three years of fighting, Congress made a treaty with the Delawares, initially bringing about 400 Native Americans to the American side, with additional tribes joining later (Holm 1996). After the war, the desire for American expansion met the reality that existing military power was not strong enough to overpower all of the Native American tribes living on the frontier. Thus, Secretary of War, Henry Knox, created a system whereby only the federal government could enter into a treaty to obtain Indian land, and the military would act to prevent and punish violence between Whites and Native Americans; however, in actuality, the violence over land between Whites and Native Americans continued (Holm 1996). From the late 1700s to the mid-1800s, the American military adopted a strategy of dividing Native Americans by pitting traditional adversaries against one another. The military also built strategic alliances with specific tribes, such as the Cherokees, Choctaws, Chippewas, Osages, and Pueblos (Holm 1996).

About 20,000 Native Americans fought on both sides of the Civil War (Holm 1996). For those living in Indian Territory, including the Cherokees, Creeks, Chickasaws, Choctaws, and Seminoles, divisions created by their displacement through the Indian Removal Act of 1830, as well as religious differences and conflicts over slaveholding, continued into the Civil War. These divisions led to members of the same nation fighting on opposite sides of the war, mostly as allies of the Northern and Southern armies, rather than as a part of them (Confer 2007; Holm 1996). The Confederacy, offering the Five Nations in Indian Territory opportunities that they could never get from the U.S. government, made intensive recruiting efforts, whereas the U.S. government engaged in actions that might be seen as pushing them away, such as ending federal annuities, removing troops from federal posts in the West, and only belatedly and haphazardly allowing Native Americans to join the Army (Confer 2007). Some Native American leaders made treaties with the Confederacy, whereas many within the tribes chose to fight with the North or defect from the Confederate units to join the Northern Army (Holm 1996). In 1862, the Union created three Indian Home Guards, which mostly fought in Indian Territory (Holm 1996). In addition, some Osages and many Eastern Cherokees fought with the South; other Native Americans fought on the Northern side, including the Iroquois in the 132nd New York State Volunteer Infantry and the Chippewa in Company K of the Michigan Sharp Shooters (Holm 1996). While fighting with either the North or the South, Native Americans often served without adequate pay, food, or weapons (Confer 2007). In the West, the Civil War marked a time of great violence and chaos in the Indian Territories as the federal troops who were assigned to uphold treaties regarding Native American lands left to fight in the war (Confer 2007; Holm 1996). Ultimately, the U.S. government required greater reparations from Native Americans at the end of the war than from the Confederacy, despite the fact that many Native Americans had fought on the Northern side.

In 1866, Congress passed legislation creating the Indian Scouting Service, and until 1943, allowed Native Americans to enroll in this newly created branch of the U.S. military (Holm 1996, 2006). A year before the Indian Scouting Service ended, the Army Special Forces adopted the use of its insignia as its own (Holm 1996). One remnant of the Indian Scouting Service that has remained a part of the military, even during contemporary wars, is the notion that Native Americans are naturally good scouts because of a perceived closeness to the land. This stereotype continues to influence the assignment of Native Americans to highly dangerous scouting and search missions during wartime (Holm 2006).

During the reservation period of the late 19th and early 20th centuries Native American cultural practices were being repressed by both the American government and Christian missionaries (Meadows 1999). Part of this repression involved efforts to abolish Native American songs and dances. Some Native American tribes, such as the Southern Plains Indians—Kiowa, Apache, and Comanche—had strong pre-reservation traditions of military or men's societies, which honored veteran warriors through song and dance ceremonies (Meadows 1999). However, circumstances of reservation life, including cultural repression and the absence of warfare, and, therefore, a lack of veteran status, led to the decline of such military societies.

Nearly 17,000 Native Americans participated in World War I (Holm 1996). Federal and church authorities were unable to suppress the traditional song and dance send-off and return celebrations, which drew on pre-reservation cultural practices and honored the warriors (Meadows 1999). Of the Native Americans who served, from 75 to 85% volunteered; relatively few were drafted (Meadows 1999). Overall, Native Americans served at twice the rate of the general population (Holm 1996). The Indian Office called for Native Americans to be in integrated units with Whites, although some Native American tribal leaders wanted separate units (Holm 1996). In practice, some served in all or mostly Native American units once they arrived in Europe, mostly in France. These units included Apache scouting units; Company E of the 142nd Infantry; the 158th Infantry, which drew a large number of Native Americans from the Arizona National Guard; and the 358th Infantry in the 90th Division (Holm 1996; Meadows 2002). Choctaws (mostly in the 142nd in France) served as code talkers, who used coded forms of their native language to send telephone messages that Germans would not be able to decode (Holm 1996; Meadows 2002). Members of other tribes, including the Comanche, Sioux, Osage, Cheyenne, and Cherokee, also conveyed messages in their native languages, although it is not known whether they used codes or simply spoke in their native languages (Meadows 2002).

A very large number of Native Americans, about 25,000, participated in the military during World War II, and many more, about 50,000, went to work in defense- and other war-related jobs off of the reservations (Holm 1996; Meadows 1999). Compared to other ethnic groups, Native Americans' rate of participation in World War II was high (Meadows 1999). Of Native Americans who served, 90% were in the Army (Meadows 1999). As in World War I, sixteen or more tribes furnished code talkers during the war (Meadows 2002). The largest group was the Navajo, of whom approximately 400 participated in Marine divisions in the Pacific, although relatively small numbers also served in the Army and Navy (Meadows 2002: 241; Naval History and Heritage Command 2010). Seventeen Comanche were selected to participate in the 4th Signal Company, 4th Signal Division to use codes in the Comanche language in Europe during the war (Meadows 1999) and eleven Hopi used codes in the 223rd Battalion of the Army in the Pacific (Meadows 2002). In addition, seventeen Chippewa/Oneida and nineteen Sac and Fox were recruited to be involved in military communications, but it is not known whether they developed a code based on their languages (Meadows 2002). Members of other tribes also participated in military communications in their languages without developing a specific code (Meadows 2002). Native American reservations also served as sites for military training, and one reservation was used for the internment of Japanese Americans during the war (Meadows 1999).

Outgoing and returning soldiers received ceremonies and homecoming celebrations, including song and dance, to honor their warrior status. Holm (1996: 4) notes that a "war-related ceremony shares the returning warriors' guilt and battle-induced stress with the community and reaffirms individual and community identity." World War II had a much larger impact than World War I on the revival of military societies within Southern Plains Indian communities because of the large number of men involved. In addition, 29,700 Native Americans served in the Korean War (Meadows 1999). The substantial number of veterans returning from World War II and the

Korean War led to the revival of traditional song- and dance-based ceremonies. Some old military societies, such as the Blacklegs Society and the Little Ponies, and dances, such as the Gourd Dance, were revived, and new societies were created, with an associated resurgence of Native American identity based on traditional cultural practices related to honoring warrior status (Meadows 1999). The American Indian Veterans Association (AIVA) was also created after World War II for all American Indian veterans; however, that organization eventually split into more tribally based groups (Meadows 1999). Although Native Americans also joined other veterans' organizations, such as the Veterans of Foreign Wars (VFW), some Native Americans felt that those organizations did not provide a supportive social environment for them and that there was too great a focus on drinking alcohol (Meadows 1999).

Meadows (1999) notes that the postwar revival of military societies and other warrior cultural elements coincided with the Relocation and Termination Acts, which threatened to terminate the relationships between tribes and the federal government. This created another impetus for ethnic resurgence and revival of specific tribal cultural practices. Many of the songs and dances that evolved in this period included both traditional elements and features that emphasized veteran status within the U.S. military, such as military uniforms, insignia, captured flags, and other war trophies (Meadows 1999).

The Kiowa, in particular, saw a resurgence of traditional military societies and a reemergence of war dancing at powwows in the form of the Gourd Dance, which is associated with veteran status, accompanied by Kiowa songs (Meadows 1999). The cultural revival of Kiowa forms of the Gourd Dance and songs to honor veterans also extended to other tribes in a pantribal context, even though other tribes also historically had their own unique forms of the Gourd Dance (Meadows 1999). Given the revival and subsequent spread of the Kiowa Gourd Dance to other tribes, Powers (1980: 217) has suggested that the reemergence of the Gourd Dance since the 1950s has come "to symbolize what it means to be Indian rather than what it meant to the Kiowa." In addition to the military societies, women's auxiliary societies were also created and revived to support the activities of the military societies (Meadows 1999). Although the threat of treaty termination and the revival of military ceremonies related to participation in war strengthened some cultural practices and collective identity, amalgamation and urbanization threatened tribal cultural practices for many and led to increased numbers of Native Americans living off of the reservations (Holm 1996).

About 42,000 Native Americans served in the Vietnam War (Holm 1996). There is evidence that this service may have had long-term consequences for many of these Native Americans. For example, Native American and Native Hawaiian veterans were more likely than White or Japanese American veterans to suffer from post-traumatic stress disorder (PTSD), possibly because many were involved in combat as a consequence of their service in the Marines (Friedman 1998). However, Native American soldiers returning from Vietnam experienced a very different homecoming than did soldiers from other ethnic groups; in Native American societies, every soldier is honored both upon leaving and returning and continually throughout his or her lifetime through powwows, song and dance, and military societies (Meadows 1999). That said, the rotation system of twelve months and twenty days used in the Vietnam War, unlike World War II, meant that soldiers did not enter and return as cohesive units. Thus, during the Vietnam War, soldiers often returned home alone. This contributed to a situation in which larger numbers of Native American and other veterans had weaker ties with the others in their unit, communicated with them less often after the war, and dealt with their war experiences in isolation after their return (Holm 1996). Other contextual and political factors also influenced the experiences of Native American veterans. For example, urbanization of Native Americans after World War II meant that many veterans were more isolated than in prior postwar eras, and the military took longer to recognize the concerns of Native American veterans than it took to acknowledge the concerns of other racial and ethnic groups (Holm 1996).

Delay in official response to the concerns of Native American veterans motivated tribes to take action to respond to emergent needs. In 1981, the Vietnam Veterans' Intertribal Association (VEVITA) was created. This organization created a Gourd Dance society and sponsored the first National Vietnam Veterans Powwow (Holm 1996). The work of these organizations has continued; during Operation Desert Storm, military societies continued to honor the Southern Plains Indian soldiers who were leaving or returning with powwows, songs, and dances and tribes without military societies have also engaged in ceremonies to honor or heal (Meadows 1999). Thus, one of the unanticipated consequences of Native American participation in the U.S. military is its contribution to the ongoing preservation of traditional Native American culture as well as voluntary initiatives to respond to the needs of community members.

RACIAL-ETHNIC AND IMMIGRANT PARTICIPATION IN THE CONTEMPORARY MILITARY

The historical profiles of racial and ethnic participation in the military provided above suggest how social and institutional changes affect the life chances and life choices of differently situated social groups and individuals, as well as the ways that the military, as an institution, and war, as a societal event, have contributed to historical change. They also provide the background for a discussion of the representation of racial and ethnic minority groups, as well as immigrants, in the contemporary All-Volunteer Force.

One way to examine the representation of different racial-ethnic groups is to compare the percentage of different groups in the military with their percentage in the military-aged (17–35 years) general population. If the percentage of a given group in the military is markedly greater than that of the general population, we can say that it is overrepresented in the military; if its percentage in the military is markedly lower, we can say that it is underrepresented. For example, historically, from 1940 to 1973, Blacks were less likely to join the military than Whites (Fligstein 1980). In 1970, the percentage of Blacks in the military was 9.8%, whereas the percentage of Blacks in the military-age general population was 11%—making Blacks slightly underrepresented in the military (Ruggles et al. 2008; U.S. Census Bureau 2008). However, later research has concluded that during the All-Volunteer Force era Blacks have been overrepresented in the military (Kane 2006).

Table 4.1 shows the percentage of different racial-ethnic groups in the military and the general population for the years 1980/1981, 1990, and 2000.[2] In 1981, Blacks were somewhat overrepresented in the military, whereas Whites and Hispanics were somewhat underrepresented. By 1990, Whites were overrepresented in the military, whereas Blacks, Hispanics, and Asian Americans were underrepresented. In 2000, Hispanics remained underrepresented, and Blacks had become overrepresented.

My own research (Lutz 2008) using the 1988 National Educational Longitudinal Study (NELS) investigates military service by the year 2000

Table 4.1   Racial-Ethnic Composition of United States Military and Military-Aged General Population

	1981 Military	1980 General Population	1990 Military	1990 General Population	2000 Military	2000 General Population
White	72.4%	78.3%	85.1%	72.7%	65.9%	63.1%
Black	19.8%	12.0%	7.7%	12.7%	19.8%	13.0%
Hispanic	3.7%	7.1%	4.4%	10.5%	7.9%	16.5%
Asian American	2.0%	1.8%	1.6%	3.2%	3.6%	4.6%
Native American	0.7%	0.7%	1.2%	0.8%	1.0%	0.8%
Other	1.4%	0.1%	0.0%	0.1%	1.9%	0.2%
Two or more Races	n/a	n/a	n/a	n/a	n/a	1.9%

Sources: Binkin et al. (1982); Ruggles et al. (2008); DEOMI (1990, 2000).

among a cohort of eighth graders in 1988 who became eligible for military service in the mid-1990s. I found that there were social class differences, but no significant racial-ethnic distinctions in terms of ever having served in the military. In addition, children of immigrants, whether born in the U.S. or abroad, did not significantly differ in their likelihood of having served in the military compared to the native-born with two U.S.-born parents. However, I did find some differences in service by ethnic origin among Latinos. Puerto Ricans and Mexican Americans, whose rates of military service did not substantially differ, were significantly less likely than Latinos of other national origins to have served. Overall, my research suggests that, in 2000, the likelihood of service in the military among people in their mid-20s did not vary substantially by race and immigrant generation, particularly once other factors were taken into account. My findings are somewhat similar to those of Elder et al. (2010) based on the ADD Health data, although they found that African American males were more likely than White males to join the military instead of entering the labor force.

In 2010, active-duty forces in all services, including the Army, Navy, Air Force, Marine Corps, and Coast Guard, comprised the following ethnicities: 70% White, 17% Black, 1.7% American Indian or Alaska Native, 3.7% Asian American, 0.6% Pacific Islander, 2.1% multiracial, and 4.9% who were of an unknown race (Department of Defense 2010c). Like the U.S. Census Bureau, the military asks whether personnel are of a "Hispanic ethnicity," in addition to asking about race. Among active-duty service members, 10.8% identified as Hispanic. There is variation in the racial-ethnic composition across armed services. Overall, the Navy has a greater proportion of racial-ethnic minority service members (37.9%) than any other branch (Department of Defense 2010c). However, there are more Blacks in the Army than in any of the other armed services—Blacks comprised 21.5% of active-duty Army enlisted members and 13.7% of Army officers in 2010. The greatest overall number and proportion of Asians are in the Navy, where they make up 5.8% of enlisted personnel and 4.1% of officers. Among American Indians and Alaska Natives, the greatest number and proportion are in the Navy, where they comprise 5.3% of active-duty enlisted personnel and 0.7% of officers (Department of Defense 2010c). The Defense Department's 2010 report does not list proportions of White or Hispanic members by service branch, but in 2006, the largest number of individuals who identified as Hispanic were in the Army, whereas the highest percentage of Hispanics was in the Marine Corps, where they made up 13.1% of all active-duty personnel (DEOMI Research Division 2006). Among Whites, the greatest number were in the Army, but the greatest proportion was in the Coast Guard, where Whites made up 79% of active-duty personnel (DEOMI Research Division 2006). Overall, the proportion of active-duty minority members in the military has decreased since 2006 (Department of Defense 2010a).

By 2009, nearly 8% of the active-duty members of the armed forces were immigrants, among whom almost 81% were naturalized citizens (Stock 2009: 3). Like native-born Americans, immigrants living in the U.S., including undocumented immigrants, are required to register with the Selective Service (Stock 2006). For those with permanent residency, military service is a way to expedite citizenship. Substantial legal changes have been made since September 11, 2001, to bring more immigrants into the American military (Hattiangadi et al. 2005; Stock 2009). Stock (2009: 3) has suggested, "Without the contributions of immigrants, the military could not meet its recruiting goals and could not fill its need for foreign-language translators, interpreters, and cultural experts." Hattiangadi and colleagues (2005) have also found that noncitizens have lower rates of attrition from the military than citizens, which may be an indication of the relatively equitable reward structures and the ability to maintain legal status within the military as opposed to outside of it. In July 2002, President Bush used his authority under the Immigration and Nationality Act to expedite the citizenship of noncitizens who had been serving honorably in the military since September 11, 2001, "regardless of their length of residency or immigration status" (Stock 2009: 5). Between 2001 and 2010, more than 65,000 immigrants serving in the military have become U.S. citizens (U.S. Citizenship and Immigration Services 2010), and many have been given posthumous citizenship, including some undocumented immigrants "who ended up in the military by accident or through the use of false documentation" (Stock 2009: 5). Such access to citizenship has direct implications for surviving veterans, but also for the family members of surviving and, potentially, deceased service members. The National Defense Authorization Act, passed in November of 2003, also allows naturalization proceedings to take place outside of the United States, thereby permitting military personnel serving in places like Iraq and Afghanistan to become U.S. citizens while serving abroad (Batalova 2008; Stock 2006). The Act also extends naturalization benefits to the "Selected Reserve" and "Ready Reserve," and provides other benefits to immigrants who serve (Stock 2009). U.S. Citizenship and Immigration Services (2010) announced in FY 2010 that 11,146 service members were naturalized, which is the largest number in any year since 1955.

Hattiangadi and colleagues (2005: 5) have argued that because "much of the growth in the recruitment-eligible population will come from immigration," immigrants and their families are "one overlooked source of military manpower." However, this may be changing. In 2006, military enlistment statutes were revised by Congress to make it easier to recruit immigrants into the military when it serves national interests. This allowed for the creation of the Military Accessions Vital to the National Interest (MANVI) program (Stock 2009). In 2009, the military specifically recruited refugees and other documented immigrants with Eastern European, African, Arabic, and other Asian language skills, as well as other specialized skills, through this program. Expedited naturalization was offered as an incentive for joining. By the end of the decade, Congress had authorized special immigrant visas for Iraqi and Afghan translators, contractors, and other employees of the U.S. government and their families (Stock 2009). Additionally, in his 2011 memorandum outlining the use of prosecutorial discretion in immigration cases, the Director of U.S. Immigration and Customs Enforcement explicitly focused on service members and their families, noting that a factor to consider in the use of such discretion is "whether the person, or person's immediate relative, has served in the U.S. military, reserves, or National Guard, with particular consideration given to those who have served in combat," further noting that status as "veterans and members of the U.S. armed forces" are among the "positive factors that should prompt particular care and consideration" (Morton 2011: 4–5).

The Department of Homeland Security indicates that thousands of military spouses are unauthorized. This is related to the 1996 changes in immigration law that made it difficult for immigrants to legalize their status and imposed bars on reentry to the U.S. for those with past immigration violations (Preston 2010). It remains to be seen whether and how policy makers will address this specific intersection of immigration policy and military service. Should the DREAM Act, which would allow for the naturalization of undocumented immigrants who came to the U.S. as children, pass eventually, it would likely have a considerable impact on military recruiting. Under the as of yet unpassed Dream Act, a precondition for becoming a Legal Permanent Resident is two years of service in the military or at least two years of higher education, depending on the degree program (Batalova and Fix 2006; Stock 2009). Thus, it is likely the future research on military service and the life course will need to consider immigrants and their families to a greater extent than past research has done.

DISCUSSION AND CONCLUSION

As this review has shown, historically, the U.S. military has served as an institution of both racial-ethnic exclusion and inclusion. The relationship between military service and various civil rights movements is complex and greater scholarly attention should be devoted to understanding how racial-ethnic and immigrant participation in the military services has contributed to social change in the United States. Experiences in military service and related wartime industries has served as a catalyst to campaigns for civil rights, and veterans have played important leadership roles in organizations that have worked toward greater racial justice and equality. The institutional role of the military itself, though, is far from straightforward; for some groups and individuals, the impetus toward civil rights is related to experiences of unequal, unjust treatment and segregation, whereas for others it arose from gaining greater access to new roles that had previously been unavailable or to the double consciousness of experiencing both simultaneously. Ways of thinking about access to privilege through military service by different racial-ethnic groups have also shifted over time as the privilege of serving became replaced by the privilege of avoiding military service.

As an organization, the contemporary military strives for racial unity within its ranks. However, little is known about how diversity and racial integration shape racial relations within the military or how they affect wider communities or the lives of community members. There is a dearth of research on how the racial and ethnic composition of the military impacts the communities that send recruits, as well as those that receive military personnel and veterans. Bailey (Chapter 9 of this volume) notes that military bases and their surrounding neighborhoods tend to be "among the most residentially integrated communities in the country," which may shape other aspects of race relations among military personnel and their families (see also DeFina and Hannon 2009; Farley and Frey 1994). Lundquist's (2008) work indicates that African Americans, in particular, find military housing to be a satisfying aspect of military life, and that Blacks and Latinos in the military report high levels of satisfaction relative to Whites. Yet, simultaneously, the military remains stratified by race and class; those from the most disadvantaged backgrounds are likely to face greater risks. Within the context of a rank-based system of authority, many members, particularly in the lower ranks and combat units, may pay an extraordinarily high price for their service. How different groups of service members make sense of the complexity of racial equality and race relations within the institution of the military is an important area for future research.

Further research needs to be done on how race, ethnicity, and immigration status impact the likelihood of military service, the lives of service men and women as well as those linked to persons who serve, and the communities from which military service members leave and veterans return. New data and perspectives will be helpful in this regard. Further efforts might investigate how race, ethnicity, and immigration status are related to roles within the military, the paths by which individuals make their way into those roles, and the consequences of military service. Other studies might look more closely at differences in participation, roles, and consequences across race-ethnicity and immigrant generation. Given the dearth of research, particularly on Asian and Latin Americans in the military, a great deal of detailed investigation across a range of domains is needed to understand their experiences. Finally, much research on the military has focused on active-duty service members, and even more particularly on those whose active duty occurs during wartime, but 40% of troops are Reserves and racial-ethnic minorities may be overrepresented among them (Segal and Segal 2005). This is not necessarily a new phenomenon, given the previously mentioned federalization of National Guard troops in the past, but it continues to be an underexplored topic of research.

NOTES

1. Some material included in this chapter was previously published in Lutz (2008).
2. I compare IPUMS (Integrated Public Use Microdata Series) data for 1980, 1990, and 2000 (Ruggles et al. 2008) with military data for 1981, 1990, and 2000. The 1981 military data are taken from the work of Martin Binkin and colleagues (Binkin et al. 1982), whereas the military data from 1990 and 2000 are from the Defense Equal Opportunity Management Institute (DEOMI 1990, 2000).

5 Military Service and Lesbian, Gay, Bisexual, and Transgender Lives

Maria T. Brown

The relationship between the U.S. military and the lesbian, gay, bisexual, and transgender (LGBT) community is more complex than it first appears. Historically, the American military has both denied the existence of homosexual[1] service members and had a hand in shaping what some have termed an "official gay identity" (Lehring 2003) and the coming out process (Bérubé 1990). Department of Defense policies and practices have evolved over time. In different periods, military policies and practices have focused to differing degrees on excluding and discharging homosexuals on the basis of past or current same-sex sexual acts, as well as targeting same-sex attraction, self-identification, gender difference, or some combination of desire, behavior, and identity (Bérubé 1990; Burrelli and Feder 2009; Shilts 1993). Volunteers and draftees were not intentionally excluded from military service based on homosexual *identity* until World War II, although they were tried sometimes for homosexual acts before that time (Chauncey 1989). Discharges based on homosexuality were not considered dishonorable until after World War II (Mettler 2005). Importantly, during times of war, enforcement of policies to exclude homosexuals from the military was often relaxed.

There is evidence that in some historical periods, widespread homosexual behavior among men in some branches of the military was well known to both service members and military leaders. As Chauncey (1989: 294) has shown through the use of transcripts from a Navy investigation of homosexuality at the Newport Naval Training Station in 1919–1920, "large numbers of sailors were able to have sex with men identified as 'queers' without affecting their image of themselves as 'normal' men." In fact, the sexual culture that prevailed at the time allowed naval investigators, like other "straight" men, to engage in gender-appropriate homosexual behavior with "queer" men (i.e., they played the male role in the encounter) as part of their investigations and give testimony to that effect in court without apparent concern about impugning their own masculinity or raising questions about their own sexual identity. The existence of these enclaves and subcultures of homosociality and homosexuality in the military were known to civilians, and having access to them away from the scrutiny of family, friends, and hometown community members was often a motivation for some men and women to join the service.

The evidence is clear that homosexuals have played a role in shaping the American military from the Revolutionary War to the present (Shilts 1993). There are a variety of excellent publications on the history of gays and lesbians in the military. Some of these texts limit themselves to a discussion of the history of gay men or lesbians during World War II, as this was the largest military deployment in American history and it played a large role in shaping gay and lesbian communities in coastal cities (Bérubé 1990; Hampf 2004). As John D'Emilio (1989: 458) has written, "World War II was something of a nationwide coming-out experience. It properly marks the beginning of the nation's, and San Francisco's, modern gay history." Other texts provide a longer-range overview of this history, encompassing multiple peacetime and wartime developments, or focusing on difference branches of service (Herek 1993; Jones and Koshes 1995; Shilts 1993; Zeeland 1993, 1996, 1999). Because many early gay rights activists were also active in the Vietnam-era antiwar movement, they were more interested in getting gays and lesbians out of the military than in reforming military policy to allow homosexuals to serve openly (Shilts 1993). As a result, although the texts summarized in this chapter make frequent reference to the modern gay rights movement (Belkin and Bateman 2003; Lehring 2003; Rimmerman 1996; Shilts 1993), the struggle to obtain the right to serve openly in the American military has not received substantial attention (Katz 1976; Marcus 2002; White 2009).

As other chapters in the volume document, considerable research has investigated the consequences of military service, its effects on educational and occupational attainment, as well as other life-course outcomes, and the potential of military service to function as a positive or negative turning point in the life course. The influence of military service on heterosexual marriage and family, and the lives of those linked to veterans through marital and family ties, has also been examined in the extant research to some extent (see Burland and Lundquist, Chapter 8 of this volume). However, to date, the specific ways that homosexual desire, behavior, and identity (Laumann, Gagnon, Michael, and Michaels 1994) intersect with military service to shape lifelong development and various life-course trajectories and outcomes has not been systematically investigated. Similarly, the ways that the lives of the men, women, and children linked to gay and lesbian active-duty personnel and veterans in different historical periods have been affected by those connections have not been explored.

This chapter begins to address some of these gaps in the literature by exploring the linked histories of the gay community and the American military, the history of U.S. Department of Defense's policy on homosexuals and military service, why people with same-sex attractions would join an institution that was not welcoming to them, and the role that the military has played in the formation of collective lesbian and gay identities and community. This chapter also describes some of the different issues faced by LGBT service members and veterans, such as the struggle for the right to serve and the potential life-course effects of being dishonorably discharged because of sexual orientation or gender identity. The chapter concludes with a brief discussion of directions for future life-course research that includes the experiences of LGBT service members and veterans.

LINKED HISTORIES OF HOMOSEXUALITY
AND THE U.S. MILITARY

The influence of homosexuals on the United States military dates back to the days of the Revolutionary War (Shilts 1993). For example, Baron Frederich Wilhelm Ludolf Gerhard Augustin von Steuben was a Prussian engaged by Benjamin Franklin to review George Washington's troops and provide guidance on how the Army could be improved. Steuben accepted the invitation even though he was not guaranteed a salary and had to pay for his own transportation from Europe to the American colonies. Steuben most likely accepted the offer because of looming charges in Europe that he had "taken familiarities with young boys" (Shilts 1993: 8). He arrived in America with a young male companion, purportedly his secretary and interpreter. However, because this young man proved inadequate, Steuben was assigned two young colonels from Washington's Army to serve as his interpreters. Based on historical readings of their personal correspondence, these two men appear to have been lovers and may have been assigned to Steuben out of recognition of their similar orientations (Shilts 1993). Steuben went on to become famous for introducing discipline to the American Revolutionary Army (Shilts 1993). At the same time Steuben was training the Army in drilling techniques, on March 11, 1778, the Army dismissed Lieutenant Gotthold Frederick Enslin for homosexual behavior (Shilts 1993). This juxtaposition reveals the paradoxical history of homosexuals in the American military; as pivotal as their participation has been during any number of wars and missions, homosexuals have almost always been rejected by the military establishment. The military benefits from them even as it denies them a primary acknowledgement of citizenship— the opportunity to openly enlist in the armed forces and serve the nation (Lehring 2003).

Homosexual service members have continued to play important roles throughout U.S. military history. Shilts (1993) provides a variety of examples, including that of Stephen Decatur and Richard Somers, lovers who fought the Barbary pirates aboard the USS *United States* in 1798, and Major General Patrick Ronayne Cleburne of the Confederate Army during the Civil War. Somewhat paradoxically, psychiatrist Harry Stack Sullivan, who was homosexual, became involved in shaping and implementing the military's screening policies and practices in the early 1940s, which were ultimately used to exclude homosexuals from service (Bérubé 1990; Wake 2007). Although Sullivan did not originally include homosexuality in the screening guidelines he helped to develop, by mid-1941, Washington bureaucrats had modified the original screening plans to include "homosexual proclivities" as a disqualifying deviation, and draft boards were directed to refer suspected homosexuals for closer examination by Regional Medical Advisory Board psychiatrists. This influence of psychiatry reflected the ascendance of the medical model of homosexuality during the middle of the 20th century and the view that homosexuality was a mental disorder. Ultimately, Sullivan was involved in the dissemination of these guidelines for screening draftees (Bérubé 1990).

Another pivotal figure in American military history was Lieutenant Tom Dooley, medical officer on the *Montague* in August of 1954. At that time, the *Montague* was charged with transporting refugees from North Vietnam to South Vietnam in Operation Passage to Freedom before the beginning of American involvement in the Vietnam War (Shilts 1993). Recognizing that refugees were carrying a variety of microbes that could expose American soldiers in the refugee camps to a host of infectious diseases for which they had no immunity, Dooley established a network of health care clinics in South Vietnam, improving the general health of the refugee population and revitalizing America's international image (Shilts 1993). He was the youngest Navy doctor in history to receive the Legion of Merit award and was awarded the "Officier de l'Ordre National de Vietnam" by the President of South Vietnam (Shilts 1993). Dooley (1956) wrote a best-selling book, *Deliver Us from Evil: The Story of Viet Nam's Flight to Freedom*, based on the diaries he kept during Operation Passage to Freedom, and he was named one of Gallup's most admired men in the United States in 1959 (Shilts 1993). Ironically, Lieutenant Dooley's transfer to the *Montague* was his commanding officer's attempt to move suspected homosexuals out of his command and avoid a homosexual purge of the Navy's medical staff (Shilts 1993). Ultimately, the rumors of Dooley's homosexuality resurfaced and he was forced to resign his commission with the Navy (Shilts 1993). He continued working to improve the health of people in Southeast Asia until his death from cancer in 1961.

U.S. DEPARTMENT OF DEFENSE POLICY ON HOMOSEXUALITY

At the same time efforts were undertaken to investigate and remove homosexuals from the military during various historical periods (Chauncey 1989), policies on who qualified as a "true" or "latent" homosexual, who deserved to be discharged, and who should be treated and retained in the armed forces have evolved over time (Bérubé 1990). Before World War I, certain types of homosexual behavior were considered criminal and service members, particularly men and women whose appearance or mannerisms

were deemed inappropriate for their gender, were imprisoned for homosexual behavior. As a result, although military policy officially targeted
homosexual acts, in effect it was also targeting individuals who appeared to
"be" homosexuals, or who embodied homosexual identity. Military policy
continued to explicitly target homosexual behavior rather than homosexual identity through World War I, even though psychiatrists such as Albert
Abrams advanced the idea of excluding people from military service based
on homosexual orientation or identity as early as 1918:

> [When] recruiting the elements which make up our invincible Army, we
> cannot ignore what is obvious and which will militate against the com-
> bative prowess of our forces in this war . . . the homosexualist is not only
> dangerous, but an ineffective fighter. . . . It is imperative that homosexu-
> alists be recognized by military authorities (Shilts 1993: 15).

It was not until World War II that the military acted to prevent people with
"homosexual tendencies" from entering the military (Shilts 1993). The World
War II mobilization was the largest in American history. Such large numbers of men registered for the draft in the fall of 1940 that the armed forces
could afford to exclude groups that they felt would undermine discipline and
morale (Bérubé 1990). At that time, the Department of Defense believed that
they needed better screening techniques for identifying and excluding homosexuals from military services than had been used previously.

As suggested in the biographical sketch of Harry Stack Sullivan provided
above, the relatively young discipline of psychiatry played a central role in
formulating regulations to identify and prevent the enlistment of homosexual men in the armed forces (see Bérubé 1990 for a detailed history of
the role of psychiatry in structuring the identification and management of
homosexuals during World War II). In an effort to legitimize the discipline,
psychiatrists lobbied heavily during World War II to redefine homosexual
behavior as a manifestation of mental illness rather than or in addition to
a criminal activity (i.e., sodomy). Consequently, Department of Defense
policies for dealing with homosexuals evolved from courts-martial and
imprisonment in World War I to dishonorable discharges during World
War II (Belkin and Bateman 2003; Bérubé 1990; Shilts 1993). In addition, the screening procedures that were put in place in the middle of the
20th century represented the beginning of efforts to exclude and discharge
homosexuals on the basis of feelings or identity rather than acts (Bérubé
1990; Shilts 1993).

As concern about homosexuality grew, so did concern about "reverse
malingerers"—homosexuals who so desired to serve their country that they
would lie about their true "tendencies" (Bérubé 1990; Shilts 1993)—and
malingerers—"normal" draftees who would feign homosexuality to avoid
being drafted (Bérubé 1990). However, draft records were not confidential,
and with the stigma that would come with a psychiatric diagnosis of "sexual

psychopath," draftees would have to be very desperate to avoid enlistment before they would falsely claim homosexuality (Bérubé 1990). The price of falsely declaring oneself a homosexual was high, and the stigma and social implications of being seen as a homosexual could ruin a person's life. "Blue" discharges, which were issued to those deemed unfit for service for a variety of reasons, including homosexuality, chronic alcoholism, criminal behavior, drug addiction, and undesirable traits or habits (Mettler 2005), were similar to dishonorable discharges and felony convictions in their impact on the lives of individuals who received them. Such discharges could haunt the subsequent life course, and could have long-term negative repercussions for recipients and their families in terms of employment, income, housing, and access to adequate health care (Beauchamp, Skinner, and Wiggins 2003). Such discharges likely created barriers to service-connected benefits, which, in tandem with the other negative consequences they entailed, may have contributed to later-life financial and health insecurity for some LGBT veterans (see Street and Hoffman, Chapter 11 of this volume).

Anti-LGBT regulations have always been adaptable to the prevailing historical circumstances, regardless of whether they were based on conceptualizations of homosexuality as criminal behavior or mental illness. During wartime, homosexual discharges from the armed forces decreased through lack of enforcement of existing policies or because those policies were formally suspended. Enforcement depended to some extent on the number of service members needed during a particular conflict. During peacetime, discharges of homosexuals have tended to increase (Bérubé 1990; Gershick 2005; Lehring 2003; Shilts 1993). Even this general trend is manifested inconsistently, as we have seen during recent conflicts in Iraq and Afghanistan, during which the number of discharges may have decreased because of wartime conditions; nevertheless, the people still being removed were often highly trained, highly skilled individuals like Lieutenant Dan Choi or Chief Petty Officer Stephen Benjamin—both skilled linguists discharged during a time when the military desperately needed linguists to translate insurgent intelligence (Benjamin 2007). Lehring (2003: 4) argues that this inconsistency in military discharge policies undermines the government's claim that allowing homosexuals to serve threatens "morale, good order, and discipline." Gershick notes:

> They consider us less than human because of our sexual preference. But when manpower is low or we're needed because there's a crisis going on, then it's okay if you're a homosexual. Then you'll be considered a soldier (2005: 85).

Policies that aim to keep homosexuals out of the military reflect and reinforce the homophobic attitudes and prejudices that many service members internalize and believe as a result of their socialization in a society in which heteronormativity is hegemonic. Such policies help to create a context that puts LGBT service members at risk and makes them more vulnerable to violence that targets real or perceived "otherness." This vulnerability is manifested in "queer bashing" or anti-gay violence at the hands of service members (Bérubé 1990; Herek 1993; Johnson and Buhrke 2006), as well as the harassment and sexual assault of women who are perceived to be lesbian and are pressured or forced to have sex with male peers to prove they are not. Examples of these types of incidents include the 1992 murder of gay sailor Allen Schindler aboard the USS *Belleau Wood* at the hands of two shipmates who had learned he was gay (Shilts 1993); the harassment and 1999 murder at Fort Campbell of Army Private First Class Barry Winchell, who was murdered in his sleep for dating a transsexual woman (Rowe 2009); and the 2009 murder of Navy Seaman August Provost, who had recently been accused of being homosexual (AVER 2009).

These incidences of anti-gay violence are extreme examples of the negative impact that discrimination in the military can have on LGBT service members. Such discrimination can also have adverse consequences on the lives of LGBT veterans. The effects of military bans on homosexuality and gender variance differ based on historical context and biographical specificities, as well as the particular service experiences and the types of discharges received. Same-sex desire, behavior, and identity may have emerged before, during, or after service, with different life-course consequences. At the nexus of homosexuality and military service, there is likely to be substantial heterogeneity in experiences. These different types of military service experiences among LGBT service members and veterans likely vary by cohort and policy regime, although there are probably similarities in strategies for managing same-sex desire, behavior, and identity or gender difference that are present to some degree across cohorts.

WHY ENLIST IN THE MILITARY?

Why would someone want to serve in an institution that does not seem to want them? This is a simple question with a complicated answer. Military service has not always been voluntary, but people have always volunteered to enter the military. Prior to the All-Volunteer Force era, people voluntarily joined the military for a variety of reasons, including patriotism, family tradition, a sense of duty, access to educational and other benefits of the GI Bill when they were available, escape from structural racism, and the pursuit of options not available in rural communities or depressed local economies. Other young men hoped that the military would "make a man out of them" (Bérubé 1990) or "prove they are men" (Shilts 1993: 32)—in other words, they hoped that the discipline of military service would enable them to ignore and overcome their attraction to people of the same gender or to transcend the feelings of discordance between their gender identities and their bodily sexual characteristics. When they could, women entered the military in pursuit of alternative lifestyles, enhanced opportunities, and adventures. As noted by D'Ann Campbell (Chapter 3 of this volume), some women joined during World War II to escape, although what they were escaping remains unnamed. Like men, women who desired women sometimes entered the military in search of other women who were like them.

In the U.S., as in many nations, military service is seen as an indication of patriotism and, for some, an affirmative duty of citizenship (Lehring 2003; Mettler 2005). Many draftees and volunteers have historically come from cultural and familial backgrounds in which military service is a tradition. During World War II, some gay draftees and lesbians volunteering for military service were in a "double bind"—they wanted to serve their country, but knew that the military found them undesirable and unfit for service. They knew that they could be discharged if their homosexuality was discovered, as these quotes from Bérubé (1990: 4, 23) indicate:

> Everyone in my age group went into the service that year—and you would have been ashamed if you didn't go in [Billy DeVean].

> We were not about to be deprived the privilege of serving our country in a time of great national emergency by virtue of some stupid regulation about being gay [Charles Rowland].

Like these men, many other young homosexual men and women felt a patriotic duty to serve their country. If they did know they were homosexual and that the military had policies to exclude them, they may have lied about their homosexuality during their draft or enlistment interviews to avoid being stigmatized at home, because their admissions were not confidential, or they may have felt it was their right and a duty to serve their country (Bérubé 1990). Some may have felt motivated or compelled by family tradition to serve, even if they did not want to join and were not compelled by the draft to do so. Regardless of their acknowledged sexual or gender orientations at the time they made the decision to join the military, many young people, like Army Captain Anthony Woods, a decorated gay veteran of Operation Iraqi Freedom, chose to follow in the footsteps of their immediate and extended families (Bedwell 2009). This identification with military service as an obligation, an honor, or a family tradition may be stronger, or may be part of their conscious identity earlier in life, than their recognition of sexual or gender identity.

Sinclair (2009) argues that LGBT persons pursue careers in the military to prove that they are worthy of the right to serve and to justify their existence. Using U. S. Census data, Gates (2004) estimates that in 2000, 2.5%, or approximately 36,000 active-duty personnel, and 3.8% of veterans (1 million) were gay men or lesbians; however, the Census only counts adults who are living with their same-sex partners, so these estimates are certainly low because they exclude single lesbians and gay men.

Data from the 1990 Census indicate that lesbians (6.6%) are more likely to serve in the military than are heterosexual women (1.4%), whereas gay men (16.9%) are half as likely to serve as heterosexual men (32.3%) (Cahill, South, and Spade 2000). In the 2000 Census, lesbians comprised 9.3% of female active-duty personnel, compared to about 3% of the adult female population (Gates 2004). Lesbians are more likely to serve either because military service gives them employment opportunities that they might otherwise have trouble accessing in the civilian workforce (Shilts 1993) or because they have trouble fitting traditional female roles in civilian society. For example, in a last-ditch effort to find a legitimate social role for her "masculinity," Renee joined the military. Encountering a fairly open network of lesbians, she came to accept herself as a lesbian during the course of her military service and stated her belief that people look at her and see a lesbian (Seidman 2002: 52).

MILITARY SERVICE AND THE FORMATION OF GAY IDENTITY AND COMMUNITY

The State and institutions of the State, such as the military, define who is a citizen by deploying discourses of science, medicine, tradition, or religion (Lehring 2003). The labeling as deviant and exclusion of homosexuals by the military and other institutions of the State is rooted in religious and moral judgments about same-sex sexual behavior and serves to deny gays and lesbians access to a key marker of American citizenship. As Steven Seidman (2002: 181) has written, "For a fully abled adult to be excluded from military service because of his or her race, national origin, or sexual identity publicly marks the individual as an outsider."

The public denial of citizenship by the State and the procedures the military and other institutions put in place to screen for the presence of homosexuality were critical in shaping an "official gay identity" in modern American culture:

> The process of creating an *official* gay identity, as we have seen, has two parts: (1) the creation of the homosexual subject [by the State] who comes to understand that it is he or she who is being categorized as "homosexual" and (2) the identification of individuals by the authorities and the requirement that these individuals account for and justify their conduct and demeanor, now construed as misdeeds. It is in the course of accounting for oneself publicly that the process of producing an *official* lesbian or gay identity is completed (Lehring 2003: 72).

The emergence of an "official gay identity" was born in part from the State's intensified interest in and desire to exert social control over human sexuality—via medical/scientific discourses, the military and, during the

McCarthy era, the State Department—and to criminalize deviance in the ranks of the citizenry (Lehring 2003).

Lehring (2003: 15) defines identification as the "process by which a person comes to realize what groups are significant for him [or her], what attitudes concerning them he [she] should form, and what kind of behavior is appropriate." The process of identity itself is "located *in the core of the individual* and yet also *in the core of his communal culture,* a process which establishes, in fact, the identity of these two identities" (Erikson 1968: 22). Although some men and women enlisted in the military in order to access homosexual communities and subcultures that were known to them, many male draftees or female volunteers during World War II had no name for their sexual feelings toward members of their own sex; many had never heard of the term "homosexual" before their draft/enlistment interviews and had not met other men or women who acknowledged same-sex attraction (Bérubé 1990; Shilts 1993). Thus, before encountering the label "homosexual" as a possible way to name their feelings, before being made to hide their feelings in order to enlist, and before finding others who were also hiding similar feelings, most young World War II soldiers had no homosexual, gay, or lesbian identity:

> I didn't recognize lesbians at that time. I didn't even recognize myself by that name. There were some women who were more masculine, who had shorter hair, carried themselves differently. At that time, my head said tomboy. I'd never met anyone who said they were a "lesbian" (Gershick 2005: 3).

> I was asked the big question 'Are you a homosexual?' And I certainly said no and I didn't believe I was (Bérubé 1990: 23).

> And like everyone else, of course, I said no. Because I truly did not know what 'homosexual' meant. We called it more or less being 'queer' or 'fruit' (Bérubé 1990: 24).

The massive draft and military deployment during World War II had a significant effect on men and women with same-sex sexual desires as individuals, as well as on the formation of homosexual, gay, and lesbian collective identities and community. Participating in military service during World War II raised awareness about the existence of other gay men and lesbians, and provided an environment—military bases and ships—to begin building community. Rather than following the recommendations of the classification system, classification officers frequently made job assignments based on the perception that a service member was homosexual (i.e., if the recruit's skills, interests, or mannerisms reflected gay stereotypes) and conventions about the kind of work that homosexuals preferred or at which they excelled (Bérubé 1990). Gay and lesbian recruits could also exercise a certain degree of agency in pursuing these assignments in the hopes of finding sympathetic, rather than hostile, co-workers. For example, members of the Women's Army Corps (WACs) and Women Marines who were perceived as butch or homosexual might be assigned to the motor pool, which was also one of the few nontraditional assignments available to Black women (Bérubé 1990). Enlisted men perceived as effeminate or homosexual might be assigned clerical positions (Bérubé 1990). Black service members were generally assigned to noncombat work and, if perceived as effeminate or gay, were typically assigned to service positions, like cooks, mess attendants, or supply clerks (Bérubé 1990). These stereotyped assignments contributed to the formation of community among homosexual service members. Importantly, this community was based on a collective sexual identity that had not previously existed for many of these young Americans:

> In the 1930s "to come out" or "to be brought out" had meant to have one's first homosexual experience with another person. But, by 1941, gay men and women were using "coming out" to mean that they had found gay friends and the gay life, and were saying that circumstances in their lives, not just their first sexual partner, had brought them out. . . . The massive mobilization for World War II relaxed the social constraints of peacetime that had kept gay men and women unaware of themselves and each other, "bringing out" many in the process. Gathered in military camps, they often came to terms with their sexual desires, fell in love, made friends with other gay people, and began to name and talk about who they were (Bérubé 1990: 5–6).

The different branches of the armed forces provided entertainment to their troops through all-soldier variety shows, which included female impersonation routines (Bérubé 1990). These female impersonator roles often attracted gay soldiers or led to insinuations that the soldiers willing to perform in drag were gay. Ultimately, they contributed to the building of gay community in all of the branches and to the development of drag as a cultural art form in the larger gay community during and after the war (Bérubé 1990; Chauncey 1994; Shilts 1993).

In addition to the community they created together on military bases and ships, homosexual service members built social networks and published underground newsletters, communicating with one another about places where they might congregate safely off-base or in war boom cities while they were on leave (Bérubé 1990; Shilts 1993):

> There was a hysteria that ran underground from the Pentagon to the Statler, Mayflower, and Willard hotels. . . . Everybody beamed at everyone else, particularly on Pennsylvania Avenue after dark. . . . They all thought of themselves as part of an adventure, so for the first time in a decade they were united, proud, and rather gay (Bérubé 1990: 98).

In some cities, like New York and Seattle, visible gay communities and subcultural institutions had existed for decades, and complex, visible, and knowable forms of social organization and interaction had been developed (Chauncey 1994; Paulson and Simpson 1996). Service members who passed through these cities during military mobilizations often participated in the gay urban worlds that they encountered or sought out.

Military service often results in geographical separation between service members and their families of origin or spouses (see Bailey, Chapter 9 of this volume). For some, particularly those with same-sex sexual desires or feelings of difference, this separation may be part of the appeal of joining the military; serving provides a socially legitimated reason to leave home at a relatively young age. Many service members return to their communities of origin and families once they complete their service, but some do not. The choice to stay away after completing service commitments may be easier for some soldiers than for others, and likely depends on many factors, such as personal history, the stage of the life course during which they entered and left military service, and the time period in which they served. It is well documented that many World War II veterans returned home to their pre-service relationships and marriages after their tours of duty. However, it is also well documented that some who had participated in same-sex sexual behavior during the war stayed in coastal cities in order to continue to do so. In cities like New York, Washington, Seattle, and San Francisco, they found thriving subcultures, and helped to establish or expand gay neighborhoods where they could maintain the sense of community that they had become accustomed to in the military. As one veteran put it:

> I can't change, have no desire to do so, because it took me a long, long time to figure out how to enjoy life. . . . I'm not going back to what I left (Bérubé 1990: 244).

Choosing to stay in a place where the possibility of being LGBT seemed feasible undoubtedly had profound consequences on the life-course trajectories of these LGBT individuals, just as the decision to go back home likely had profound consequences for others. The efforts of those who stayed and helped build gay and lesbian communities and institutions reverberate across the generations; LGBT youth from later generations have gravitated to those places in search of "family," safety, connection, and inclusion. The lives of these LGBT youth are linked, historically and distally, to the men and women who came before them. The social and political organizing that has emerged from those communities has had a profound effect on social change and has helped create opportunities for LGBT persons in America.

LIFE-COURSE EFFECTS OF BEING DISCHARGED FOR HOMOSEXUALITY

Service members accused of homosexuality during World War I and in the 1920s and 1930s were likely to be court-martialed for sodomy; if found guilty, they might be imprisoned or receive a less-than-honorable discharge (Belkin and Bateman 2003; Shilts 1993). During World War II, members of the armed forces were much more likely to receive "blue" discharges for homosexuality than they were to be court-martialed; however, they may also have been returned to service depending on the branch in which they served and the policies in place at the time, as policies shifted rapidly during the war (Belkin and Bateman 2003).

At the end of World War II, the Federal government was having trouble maintaining the existing Veterans Administration model. The Veterans Administration was a centralized, hierarchical, independent agency in which the Veterans Bureau, the Bureau of Pensions, and the National Home for Disabled Volunteer Soldiers had been combined in 1930. Fifteen years later, unable to meet the demand for GI Bill benefits as veterans began coming home from World War II, the Veterans Administration modified its structure (Bérubé 1990; Mettler 2005). By April of 1945, the Veterans Administration had modified its policies regarding "blue" or undesirable discharges, which had historically not been considered either dishonorable or honorable (Mettler 2005). The GI Bill originally extended eligibility to all veterans with any type of discharge status that was not dishonorable. However, the 1945 changes included instructions that "blue" discharges for homosexual "acts or tendencies" should be considered dishonorable (Bérubé 1990). Veterans with "blue" discharges were subsequently denied GI Bill benefits (Mettler 2005). These instructions were reissued by the Veterans Administration in 1949, even though, in 1946, the House Committee on Military Affairs in the House of Representatives criticized this policy as inappropriate and determined that the Veterans Administration had no right to reinterpret these discharges or pass moral verdicts about any soldier's history (Bérubé 1990; Mettler 2005).

These less-than-honorable discharges deprived veterans and their families of all services provided by the Department of Veterans Affairs and any pension income for which they might otherwise have been eligible (Cahill, South, and Spade 2000; Grant 2010). The loss of access to such benefits and income obviously disadvantaged gay men and lesbians who were discharged for homosexuality. The penalties for such discharge are hard to quantify, as are the life-course consequences of the stigma from a less-than-honorable discharge for homosexuality and the loss of resources that it entailed. Moreover, the forfeiture of GI Bill benefits may have been more significant for some veterans than for others, depending on the benefits available to their cohort (see Bennett and McDonald, Chapter 6 of this volume). To the extent that access to such benefits would have contributed to a positive turning point in the lives of some gay men and lesbians from disadvantaged backgrounds, or better outcomes overall, the loss of opportunity was substantial. For some veterans, the lack of access to educational benefits, housing subsidies, and health care may have been less substantial, but such losses may have been compounded by the stigma and social disadvantage that such a discharge would carry in the civilian world.

Importantly, Williams and Weinberg (1971) found that receiving a less-than-honorable discharge for homosexuality and being labeled as a deviant did not always have a negative impact on the life course. This would particularly be the case if such a discharge helped propel an individual into an existing or emergent gay subculture in which they were ultimately able to thrive. The Williams and Weinberg sample may have contained people who served during World War II, the Korean War, and the Vietnam War, but their sample is unlikely to have been representative of the gay men and lesbians who served during those periods. It was drawn from the membership of "homophile groups" or homosexual advocacy groups (Belkin and Bateman 2003), and may therefore have disproportionately represented those who took a path from dishonorable discharge to a gay community and to activism on behalf of others in that community. Thus, it may not be reflective of all veterans who received dishonorable discharges for homosexuality during those periods. In some cases, then, being dishonorably discharged for homosexuality could be seen as a *positive* turning point in the life course if it propelled an individual into a supportive "queer subculture" of same-sex relationships and an LGBT community that they may not otherwise have sought out. For some, a shift out of a normative context into a supportive subculture, however that occurs, can be a positive turning point. Some social gerontologists may argue that from the life-course perspective, these nonnormative pathways though life should not be considered positive. Such an argument highlights a flaw in the life-course paradigm in that the institutionalized life course is rooted in heteronormative assumptions about what comprises a "valid" life course, and subsequently silences the experiences of sexual minorities (Brown 2009).

After World War II, policies continued to evolve in each of the armed forces. In general, discharges based on homosexuality increased and were predominantly dishonorable (Belkin and Bateman 2003; Gershick 2005; Shilts 1993). Discharge rates varied over time and with respect to whether the U.S. was engaged in military conflict. In total, the U.S. armed forces discharged over 100,000 men and women for homosexuality between 1941 and the late 1980s, which is between 1,500 and 2,000 men and women per year, on average (Bérubé 1990).

From 1993 through 2011, the Department of Defense policy regarding homosexuality was known as "Don't Ask, Don't Tell" (DADT). This policy was considered a compromise between President Clinton's desire to eliminate the military's ban on gays in the military and the Department of Defense's efforts to ensure the maintenance of order, discipline, unit cohesion, and morale, which they believed would be undermined by allowing gays and lesbians to serve openly (Belkin and Bateman 2003). DADT stated that military service was not a constitutional right, that success in combat required "military units that are characterized by high morale, good order and discipline, and unit cohesion," and that homosexual tendencies or the intent to commit homosexual acts are threats to these characteristics (Belkin and Bateman 2003: 177). Under DADT, service members could be separated from the military for engaging in, soliciting others to engage in, or attempting to engage in homosexual behavior; stating they were homosexual or bisexual; or marrying or attempting to marry someone of the same biological sex. Having been found to engage in any of these behaviors, a person could only prevent separation by proving that the conduct was a departure from normal behavior; that the behavior was forced or coerced; that retention would be consistent with the unit's interests in terms of good order, proper discipline, and morale; or that there was no intent to engage in homosexual behavior in the future nor did the person appear to have a tendency to be a homosexual (Belkin and Bateman 2003). DADT also suspended the traditional practice of questioning recruits about homosexuality, but reserved the right to reinstate questioning about homosexuality in the future if the Secretary of Defense found it necessary to enforce the rest of the policy.

It is estimated that more than 14,300 service members were fired under DADT between 1993 and the repeal of the policy in 2011 (Servicemembers Legal Defense Network 2009a; Servicemembers United 2011). The nature of these discharges for homosexuality was determined by the circumstances surrounding each individual case, although many fell into the category of other-than-honorable (OTH). Thus, the effect of the discharge on the life course would vary by type of discharge, as well as with the evolution of the benefits available to veterans, active-duty and Reserve service members, and their families:

> Service members with OTH discharges risk losing most, if not all, veterans' benefits; the Veterans Administration (VA) is supposed to make a case-by-case decision when a veteran with an OTH discharge requests assistance. Veterans with OTH discharges also face substantial prejudice in civilian employment and, in many states, an OTH discharge bars collection of unemployment compensation when they are discharged from the military (Servicemembers Legal Defense Network 2007).

Unfortunately, we do not know much about the positive or negative effects of dishonorable discharges among many gay and lesbian service members, although we do know that some service members' lives are cut short when they commit suicide in response to military investigations into their sexual orientation (Shilts 1993). We also do not know enough about the effects of military service on the lives of those LGBT persons who complete their service under the conditions that prevailed at the time. There is a critical need for life-course studies that address the consequences of military service for LGBT persons who served in different historical periods. Such studies must develop conceptual models that allow for the possibility that non-(hetero)normative trajectories and outcomes might be beneficial for

LGBT individuals and should consider comparing LGBT persons with military service histories to LGBT persons without them.

THE STRUGGLE FOR THE RIGHT TO SERVE

As social attitudes and laws regarding homosexuality have changed, and LGBT persons have become more effective at organizing and advocating for themselves, gay and lesbian service members have become less willing to remain hidden among the ranks or to accept blue discharges (Holobaugh and Hale 1993; Seidman 2002). There is an extensive history of veterans' efforts to fight blue or dishonorable discharges (Lehring 2003; Rimmerman 1996; Shilts 1993). Some service members defend themselves by denying the accusation of homosexuality, whereas others respond by challenging the military's policies of exclusion based on homosexuality (Lehring 2003; Rimmerman 1996; Shilts 1993). A recent and well-known example of a service member who challenged the military's exclusionary policies is Lieutenant Dan Choi, who came out publicly as a gay man in 2009 to challenge Don't Ask, Don't Tell, and was honorably discharged in July 2010 (Conant 2010). Fluent in Arabic, Lieutenant Choi was a graduate of West Point and a founding member of Knights Out (Meyer 2010). Knights Out is an organization of West Point alumni, faculty, and staff who advocate for the right of LGBT soldiers to serve openly (Knights Out 2010).

The assumption that homosexuals are not fit to serve in the military, that their presence in the ranks would undermine morale, and that they would compromise the safety of their fellow soldiers has been extensively debated and disproven (Belkin and Bateman 2003; Jones and Koshes 1995; Rimmerman 1996; Shawver 1995). For the past two decades, there has been a considerable amount of debate about the validity of the most recent version of the military's ban on gays and lesbians in the military (Belkin 2008; Belkin and Bateman 2003; Belkin and Embser-Herbert 2002). Congress voted in 2010 to repeal DADT, but they did not require the military to allow open service by gay, lesbian, and bisexual service members. Instead, they laid out a process by which a ban on open service would be lifted. In doing so, Congress required certification by the Joint Chiefs of Staff that a repeal of the ban would not undermine traditionally accepted indicators of military readiness (i.e., recruitment, retention, morale, and order). These new regulations were slated to be issued on September 20, 2011, lifting the ban on open service. However, the absence of an express congressional order to allow open service leaves an opening for future presidents to call for new regulations that could involve reinstating DADT or a similar ban (Dao 2011).

Contrary to the Department of Defense's assertion that the presence of known homosexuals would threaten discipline, morale, or order, the Palm Center has conducted multiple studies of the effect of lifting bans on homosexuality in the military in other countries. Among those countries that allow gays and lesbians to serve openly are allies, like Great Britain and Canada, whose troops have fought alongside American troops in Afghanistan and Iraq. A recent study of the twenty-five nations that currently allow gays and lesbians to serve in the military reached the following conclusion:

> Research has uniformly shown that transitions to policies of equal treatment without regard to sexual orientation have been highly successful and have had no negative impact on morale, recruitment, retention, readiness, or overall combat effectiveness. No consulted expert anywhere in the world concluded that lifting the ban on openly gay service caused an overall decline in the military (Frank et al. 2010: 2).

Gay and lesbian service members and veterans have created support networks for coping with the stress of being closeted in and after service, as well as the legal issues surrounding, and the consequences resulting from, discharge from service. Organizations providing advocacy and support to LGBT service members and veterans include the Gay, Lesbian, and Bisexual Veterans Association (GLBVA); the Servicemembers Legal Defense Network (SLDN); and the Transgender American Veterans Association (TAVA).

DIFFERENT ISSUES FOR LESBIANS, BISEXUALS, AND TRANSGENDER SOLDIERS AND VETERANS

Gay men, lesbians, bisexuals, and transgender individuals experience different issues during military service and different effects on the life course as the result of anti-gay military policies, even if they are not dishonorably discharged. Because Don't Ask, Don't Tell specifically targeted homosexual and bisexual behavior and identity, retirees from active-duty or Reserve service who identified as homosexual or bisexual, or who engaged in same-sex relationships, were theoretically at risk of losing their Veterans Administration benefits if their relationships were discovered by the military or the Department of Veterans Affairs (Cahill, South, and Spade 2000; Servicemembers Legal Defense Network 2007). However, there are no known cases of veterans being recalled to active duty for prosecution under Don't Ask, Don't Tell, and the policy was not enacted to target veterans (Servicemembers Legal Defense Network 2007).

While Don't Ask, Don't Tell was in effect, some gay, lesbian, bisexual, or transgender veterans may have feared negative repercussions if their sexual orientations or gender identities had been exposed, even if Don't Ask, Don't Tell did not legally apply to them (Grant 2010; Servicemembers Legal Defense Network 2007). As a result, they may not have sought medical care when they needed it, or they may have sought some health care services outside of the Veterans Administration system. Additionally, their same-sex partners could not qualify for any services within the Veterans Administration even if those services would have been available to opposite-sex spouses of veterans. Now that Don't Ask, Don't Tell has been repealed, it is still doubtful that same-sex partners or spouses will qualify for the Veterans Administration services available to opposite-sex spouses, as the Federal government does not recognize same-sex marriage, even if that marriage is performed in a state that does legally allow it. Health care costs for these veterans, then, can still be higher than for heterosexual veterans, and their partners can still lose access to pension and survivors' income (Cahill, South, and Spade 2000; Grant 2010). These outcomes would be particularly devastating for veterans wounded as a result of service, as well as their families.

Retired service members and veterans seeking psychological services may have also feared the loss of Veterans Administration benefits if they disclosed their sexual or gender identities. Veterans suffering from post-traumatic stress disorder (PTSD) or other effects of combat or service-related trauma may have had difficulty in treatment because of their reluctance to be completely honest with their mental health providers; they may also have certain risk factors, like low self-esteem, which make them less resilient in dealing with the effects of trauma (Davison et al. 2006). However, because most studies of veterans do not include data on sexual orientation or gender identity, we do not know the impact of these factors on resilience or mental health among veterans.

Lesbian and heterosexual women veterans are more likely to be dealing with long-term emotional and psychological effects of sexual trauma or sexual harassment experienced during service than are men (D'Amico and Weinstein 1999). Women, if they were not willing to "prove" their heterosexuality by engaging in sex on demand with service men, were suspected of or investigated for lesbianism, or were at risk of being caught up in anti-gay purges, such as those that occurred during World War II. Some have suggested that women in the military are treated as either dykes or whores (Gershick 2005, Hampf 2004; Herbert 2000; Shilts 1993). As one woman service member explained:

> [O]n several occasions I was approached, before I was married. "Everyone says you're a lesbian. You gotta sleep with me, or you gotta sleep with someone on the team" (Gerschick 2005: 207).

Lesbians are more likely to serve in the military than straight women, and have also been more likely to be caught up in anti-gay purges than gay men, particularly during periods when the status of women in the military was most contested (Bérubé 1990; Shilts 1993). Anti-gay persecution of women is complicated by sex-based discrimination within the military, resistance among the ranks and leadership to gendered integration, and the assumption that women who wish to serve are lesbians (Rimmerman 1996):

> Somebody had ignited a magnesium flare—the signal normally used to issue a distress call—in a rear passageway outside the back door of the female berthing area . . . it was clear that the fire had not been an accident and that whoever had set it knew what he was doing. The women suspected it was an attempt to intimidate the new crew members. The episode reminded Carole that during their orientation a captain had noted that there would be men on board the ship who would not welcome them (Shilts 1993: 322).

Bisexuality is basically invisible in the literature, although Bérubé (1990) does discuss transient same-sex relations that occurred during boot camp and military deployment in World War II. The invisibility of bisexuality in the literature makes it difficult to distinguish between bisexuality as a chosen identity and the same-sex sexual activities of heterosexual men looking for sexual release or heterosexual women looking for affection, sexual release, or protection (Bérubé 1990). Bisexuality is generally not distinguished from homosexuality in military policies. Bisexuals risk detection and discharge, and the loss of benefits, when they engage in same-sex relationships, but are otherwise invisible to the military community.

The issues faced by transgender veterans are very different from those faced by gay, lesbian, or bisexual veterans. Witten (2005) examines the lived experiences of gender-variant individuals in the military, the variety of gender identities that individuals claim, and the ways that the military reacts to individuals who identify outside of the male-female gender dichotomy. Witten reports:

> On an institutional level, this study finds that the U.S. military has taken the stand that non-traditional gender identities fall under the aegis of disease, in particular psychopathology and that individuals claiming such identities are therefore to be removed from service or to be prevented from entering the service wherever and whenever possible (2005: 9).

Witten (2005) supports this claim with documentation from the Army Medical Services Standards of Medical Fitness, which lists "transexualism, exhibitionism, transvestitism, voyeurism, and other paraphilias" as reasons to reject individuals for "appointment, enlistment, and induction" (2004: 13, Section 2–30). This medical construction of transexualism as evidence of being unfit to serve is related to the medical model of homosexuality, which was adopted by the military during the 1940s. According to the Servicemembers Legal Defense Network, military regulations effectively prohibit service by transgender persons. . . . The military medical system does not recognize the World Professional Association for Transgender Health's Standards of Care for Gender Identity Disorders and will not provide the medical support necessary for transitioning service members (2009b).

Individuals who identify as transgender, but have not transitioned surgically are considered unfit to serve on the basis of mental illness, and those who have already undergone genital surgery may be denied the right to serve (Servicemembers Legal Defense Network 2009b). Transgender individuals were also at risk of being investigated under the Don't Ask, Don't Tell policy, simply because gender nonconformity is often conflated with sexual orientation (Servicemembers Legal Defense Network 2009b). The majority of transsexual veterans surveyed by the Palm Center report that they were not able to transition until they left the military, and 70% were not using the Veterans Administration hospital system (Bryant and Schilt 2008). The majority of requests made to Veterans Administration hospitals for medical gender transition treatments were denied (Bryant and Schilt 2008). Effectively, then, transgender and transsexual veterans, whatever the nature of their termination from the military, have historically been unable to take full advantage of the GI Bill health benefits that they earned during active-duty or Reserve service:

> I was told by a religious clerk that I should just go away because I was an insult to the brave real men who were there for treatment (Bryant and Schilt 2008: 9).

Policies related to medical services for transgender and transsexual veterans may be changing. Recently, the Department of Veterans Affairs released a new directive regarding the respectful delivery of health care to transgender and intersex veterans enrolled in or eligible for care in the Veterans Administration health care system (U. S. Department of Veterans Affairs 2011a). The Veterans Health Administration (VHA) Directive 2011–024 states that

> VA provides health care for transgender patients, including those who present at various points of their transition from one gender to the next . . . including: those who have had sex reassignment surgery outside of VHA, those who might be considering surgical intervention, and those who do not wish to undergo sex reassignment surgery, but self-identify as transgender (U.S. Department of Veterans Affairs 2011a: 1).

Sex reassignment surgery and plastic or reconstructive surgery that is considered "strictly cosmetic" is still not provided by the Veterans Health Administration (U.S. Department of Veterans Affairs 2011a); however, this new directive does categorize the following as "medically necessary care" for enrolled or eligible intersex or transgender veterans: "hormonal therapy, mental health care, preoperative evaluation, and medically necessary post-operative and long-term care following sex reassignment surgery" (U.S. Department of Veterans Affairs 2011a: 2). The directive includes language that respects a veteran's self-identified gender and also establishes certain sex-specific health care screenings and treatments as recommended care for transgendered or intersex veterans, such as breast cancer and prostate cancer screening in male-to-female transsexual patients aged 50 or older (U.S. Department of Veterans Affairs 2011a). Unless it is renewed, this directive expires in November of 2012.

CONCLUSION

Ultimately, because American military institutions have traditionally ignored, excluded, rejected, or punished sexual minorities, we know very little about how the military experience affects the life-course trajectories and outcomes of LGBT veterans who have served in different historical and policy contexts. We also know very little about the life-course trajectories and outcomes of those whose lives are linked to LGBT veterans. As is the case with heterosexually identified persons, it is likely that military service affects multiple domains of, and has the potential to function as a positive or negative turning point in, the lives of LGBT persons. Thus, there is a substantial need for life-course studies that focus on these issues among LGBT veterans and their families.

The majority of the information available about the effects of Don't Ask, Don't Tell is focused on the impact on active service members' right to privacy, rather than on the life-course effects of discharge resulting from the policy (Belkin and Bateman 2003; Rimmerman 1996; Servicemembers Legal Defense Network 2007). More research needs to be conducted on the effects that anti-gay military policies have had on the life-course trajectories and outcomes of LGBT service members and veterans later in life, and the different ways and degrees to which different groups within this population have experienced these effects.

With the repeal of DADT (Herszenhorn and Hulse 2010), we can look forward to the day when lesbian, gay, and bisexual members of the active-duty and Reserve services in the U.S. can serve without fear of dishonorable discharge or loss of GI Bill benefits because of sexual orientation. However, this policy change will not protect transgender service members and veterans from facing discrimination when serving or attempting to serve. Additionally, the lifting of DADT does not guarantee that anti-gay violence between service members will stop.

We need to conduct research following the repeal of DADT to determine if repeal will simply change the visible composition of the armed forces in the U.S. or if it will truly eliminate homophobia within the ranks and leadership of the military. As a comparison, we could examine whether legislating gender or racial integration of the American military has successfully resulted in true integration within the ranks and leadership of the different branches and eliminated sexism and racism in the institution as a whole. However, although some would argue that the exclusion of homosexuals from the military is similar to the exclusion of Blacks or women, Butler (1993) would caution against making these comparisons, as the social and cultural histories and current realities of these groups are very different.

What we do know is that societal attitudes toward homosexuality have changed, and continue to change, and there is evidence that younger service members have attitudes more favorable toward serving alongside gays and lesbians than may be held by older generations (Belkin 2003; Johnston 2007). This shift in attitudes may have influenced military leaders in eventually supporting the repeal of DADT. Finally, we should explore the potential effects that lifting this policy will have, or arguably should have, in terms of the benefits and services available to LGBT service members and veterans, their same-sex partners, and their families.

NOTES

1. Use of the term "homosexual" may be considered problematic in light of current understandings of human sexuality and gender. However, Department of Defense policy has historically dealt primarily with the question of "homosexuality," rather than distinguishing between gay men and lesbians or dealing with the complexities of desire, behavior, sexual identity, bisexuality, gender variance, and transgender identity. Despite this lack of attention to the nuances of gender and sexuality in military policies, it is noteworthy that the perception of individual service members as being homosexual was often based on gender deviance (Bérubé 1990; Chauncey 1989).

6 Military Service as a Pathway to Early Socioeconomic Achievement for Disadvantaged Groups

Pamela R. Bennett and Katrina Bell McDonald

It is generally believed that disadvantaged youth—defined here as those from low socioeconomic backgrounds, those with low levels of education, and those from racial and ethnic minority groups—often find themselves trapped on trajectories characterized by "cumulative disadvantage," whereby disadvantages in childhood contribute to disadvantages later in the life course and, perhaps, even grow more acute over time. Such disadvantages include poor educational training in low-quality schools, residence in poor and segregated neighborhoods, and restricted access to health care and useful social networks, to name a few. By the time youth in such circumstances complete high school, if in fact they do, they have effectively been excluded from the kinds of social resources that are necessary for them to close the gap between themselves and those from more privileged backgrounds. The reality of that gap comes into full focus for these youth when, after leaving high school, they must choose a trajectory to economic independence (a major transition into adulthood) and find that some pathways are closed to them.

Since the mid-20th century, a mechanism by which disadvantaged groups often overcame their disadvantage has severely eroded. Relatively rare are the blue-collar, semiskilled jobs that provide a middle-class standard of living to those without a college education. Today, movement up from low socioeconomic status generally is best achieved through postsecondary education. However, unfortunately, much research has documented substantial academic, financial, and informational obstacles to college entry and graduation among youth from disadvantaged backgrounds (Bennett and Xie 2003; Kahlenberg 1996; Manski and Wise 1983). Thus, although a college education is a mechanism for upward mobility, it is one that is relatively off-limits to those most in need of its benefits.

Entering into military service is another path to economic independence and socioeconomic attainment available to the disadvantaged. African Americans and those from socioeconomically disadvantaged backgrounds are overrepresented at some points during the contemporary All-Volunteer Force era, although they were substantially underrepresented in other historical periods when they were only allowed to serve in segregated units (see Lutz, Chapter 4 of this volume). These groups are significantly more

likely than similar Whites and economically advantaged persons to opt
for military service (Elder et al. 2010; Kleykamp 2006). However, those
patterns may be changing, as evidenced by the fluctuating proportion of
military personnel who are African American (Kelty, Kleykamp, and Segal
2010; Kleykamp 2006; see also Lutz, Chapter 4 of this volume). The trend
for Hispanics has gone in the opposite direction; they have shifted from
being underrepresented in the military to being somewhat overrepresented,
depending on whether the population is restricted to high school graduates (Kelty, Kleykamp, and Segal 2010). Yet Hispanics are more likely than
similar non-Hispanic Whites to enter the labor market rather than enlist in
the military (Kleykamp 2006), and Hispanic participation in the military
likely varies by ethnicity and generation, as discussed by Lutz (Chapter 4
of this volume).

Similar to the ways in which postsecondary education can have a
transformative effect on those who experience it, military service can
substantially alter the lives of those from disadvantaged backgrounds,
because it can disrupt processes of cumulative disadvantage. Elder (1986:
234) describes military service as a "turning point" in the lives of disadvantaged men who served in World War II; their experience in the war
served to "redirect" their life trajectories from ones in which childhood
disadvantage begat disadvantage in adulthood. Sampson and Laub (1996)
describe military service as separating disadvantaged service members
from their pasts, while providing an alternative environment in which
to develop new ways of thinking and being. Moreover, by accumulating human capital through military training, service members are able
to transform themselves from low-skilled to skilled workers in the labor
market and command higher earnings (see Kleykamp, Chapter 7 of this
volume). Through the educational benefits provided via the various GI
bills that have been in effect since the middle of the 20th century, individuals can transition from high school to military life and then into
the ranks of the college-educated. Through either path, the military can
facilitate the social mobility of disadvantaged persons and arrest the process of cumulative disadvantage in their lives. Military service may also
disrupt the intergenerational transmission of disadvantage. By providing
a means for service members to raise their own socioeconomic status,
military service helps to make possible that which their children require
for a more advantaged life.

Below, we evaluate the alternative pathways along which disadvantaged
youth can pursue financial independence in adulthood. They involve three
institutions—the labor market, the military, and postsecondary education. Use of one or more of these institutions yields five routes to early
socioeconomic achievement. Military service is involved in three of the
five, as depicted in Figure 6.1. The importance of sequencing and ordering
is evident in this discussion, as it is in other examinations of life-course

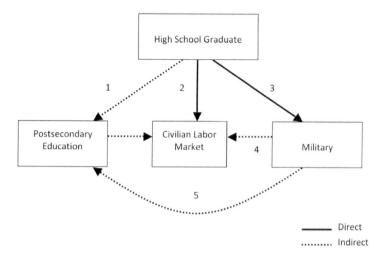

Figure 6.1 Pathways to early socioeconomic attainment.

trajectories and outcomes. Youth may take the pathway that has become most idealized in the United States; that is, they can go directly to college after high school and then take their college credentials to the civilian labor market. This is the pathway least available to the population of young people of interest here. For those unable or unwilling to attend college immediately after high school, the remaining four pathways represent reasonable alternatives. Thus, the second option is that youth may enter the labor market directly from high school and secure employment and wages based upon their relatively low levels of education and skill. Third, youth can pursue a military career by entering and remaining in the military. Fourth, youth can enter the military directly after high school and then take their upgraded skills to the civilian labor market. Finally, youth can enter the military and then use the educational benefits it provides to obtain college education that they then put to use in the labor market. Throughout this chapter, we describe the employment opportunities and challenges that await high school graduates in the civilian labor market and contrast them with the benefits and costs of military service to understand what role it might play in the socioeconomic attainment of disadvantaged youth.

PATH 1: IMMEDIATE PURSUIT OF POSTSECONDARY EDUCATION

In his address to the Hispanic Chamber of Commerce in March of 2009, President Barack Obama commented on the growing need for bachelor's degrees for entry into the fastest-growing occupations. He noted that in fewer than ten years, "four out of every ten new jobs will require at least some advanced education or training" (Obama 2009). This portends the continuation, and possible worsening, of the bifurcation of the American labor market into relatively high-paying jobs that require some postsecondary education and low-wage jobs that do not. Moreover, while the president and others are focused on increasing the number of people who hold college degrees, Rosenbaum (2001) warns us against "college-for-all" thinking. Such thinking leads us to overlook those who have only high school credentials—a population he refers to as the "forgotten half," a term borrowed from Howe (1988). Given historical and contemporary problems with access to college among racial minorities and economically disadvantaged persons, and the possible role that military service has and can play in redirecting the life-course trajectories of disadvantaged youth, we devote the majority of this chapter to the other pathways for socioeconomic achievement that are more accessible to disadvantaged groups.

PATH 2: IMMEDIATE ENTRY
INTO THE CIVILIAN LABOR MARKET

Prior to the economic restructuring of the U.S. labor market, high school graduates had a reasonable chance of securing employment at living wages (Harrison and Bluestone 1988). Blue-collar jobs did not require college education, provided on-the-job training, and paid salaries and wages with which men, primarily, could purchase homes and provide for their families. The shift from blue-collar to service-sector jobs that began in the late 1960s eroded a valuable segment of the occupational base for those without the ability or desire to attend college. During the 1970s and 1980s, blue-collar jobs were replaced with low-skilled jobs in the service sector that offered lower wages, lower rates of unionization, fewer if any benefits, and less stability (Nelson and Lorence 1988; Sassen 1990; Wilson 1987). At the same time, low-skilled jobs relocated from cities to suburbs. This shift placed employment opportunities at greater distances from low-skilled workers, who often lacked access to private vehicles or adequate public transportation, and thereby depressed their employment and wages (Kain 1968; Lyson and Tolbert 1996).

Industrial restructuring has had negative labor market consequences for socioeconomically disadvantaged persons, generally. However, some research suggests that the growing spatial mismatch between low-skilled jobs and less educated job seekers has been particularly harmful to the

employment prospects of African Americans and Latinos, who are disproportionately located in America's cities (Holzer and Danziger 2001; Stoll
1998). Because Blacks, and Hispanics to a lesser extent, have been and
continue to be constrained by residential segregation, they are less able
than Whites to leave areas of job decline for areas of job growth. In a
study of unemployment in Detroit in 1980 and 1990, Mouw (2000: 747)
found that the suburbanization of employment had no effect on employment among Whites, but increased unemployment among Blacks by 3.3
percentage points, which, he notes, "is comparable to the national impact
of a recession." Mouw's study is consistent with Wilson's (1996) observations of the mismatch between jobs and residential locations of Blacks
in Chicago, where 60% of job growth occurred in counties where Blacks
comprised only a small fraction of the population. More recent national
data indicate that the spatial mismatch between jobs, on the one hand, and
Blacks and Latinos, on the other, has declined, but only by modest amounts
(Raphael and Stoll 2006).

Beyond industrial restructuring and spatial mismatch, African Americans become aware of the difficulties of securing employment well before
they graduate from high school. As a result, African Americans are more
likely than Whites to be confronted with the decision to enter the military versus the civilian labor market. In a study of Baltimore youth,
Entwisle, Alexander, and Olson (2000) found that White adolescents had

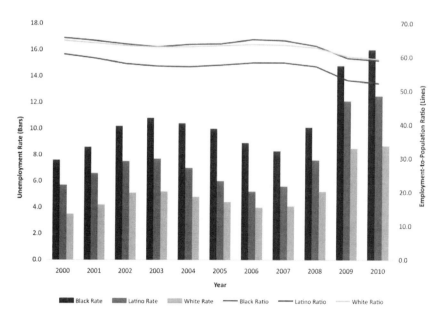

Figure 6.2 Unemployment rates and employment-to-population ratios for Whites,
Blacks, and Latinos—2000–2010.

substantially higher employment rates than Blacks, despite the fact that Black youth evidenced greater effort at finding jobs. This race gap in youth employment could not be explained by either Black-White differences in family socioeconomic background or school performance. Consequently, Entwisle, Alexander, and Olson (2000: 284, 291) concluded that "[r]ace was the most consistent predictor of job-holding between ages 13 and 17" and worried that "a lack of work for inner-city or minority adolescents could create labor market disabilities for them" as adults. No doubt, their concern extends to Latinos, who had unemployment rates between those of Whites and Blacks in 2006 (Catanzarite and Trimble 2008). Those same patterns of racial and ethnic inequality in unemployment will confront youth as they graduate from high school and enter the labor market as adults. Figure 6.2 displays employment and unemployment data by race over time for persons 16 years old and older. Compared to Whites, Blacks and Latinos have consistently higher rates of unemployment, although only Blacks have lower employment-to-population ratios relative to Whites.

Added to the complications created by the decline and geographic movement of entry-level jobs are problems associated with the expansion of the American criminal justice system. Pattillo, Weiman, and Western (2004: 1) open their book, *Imprisoning America: The Social Effects of Mass Incarceration,* with this startling account:

> The growth of the U.S. penal system over the past twenty-five years has significantly altered the role of government in poor and minority communities. Between 1920 and 1975, the state and federal prison population totaled around .10 of 1 percent of the population. After half a century of stability in imprisonment, the incarceration rate increased in every single year from 1975 to 2001. At the beginning of the new millennium, the proportion of the U.S. population in prison had increased four-fold over twenty-five years. If jail inmates are also counted, the U.S. penal system incarcerated a total of .69 of 1 percent of the population in 2001.

Figure 6.3 depicts the dramatic rise in incarceration in the United States beginning in the 1980s. Although the risk of incarceration has risen for Blacks, Latinos, and Whites since the mid-1970s, the increases have not been equal. Between 1974 and 2001, the percentage of Whites expected to go to prison increased from 1.2 to 3.4%. Among Latinos, it rose from 2.2 to 10%, and among Blacks it increased to a staggering 18.6% from 7.0% (Bonczar 2003). As increasing numbers of people were imprisoned, racial disparities in incarceration grew, such that by 2008, Blacks and Latinos were substantially more likely to be arrested and jailed than Whites (see Figure 6.3).

At the start of the opening decade of the 21st century, the lifetime chances of going to state or federal prison for White males was 5.9%,

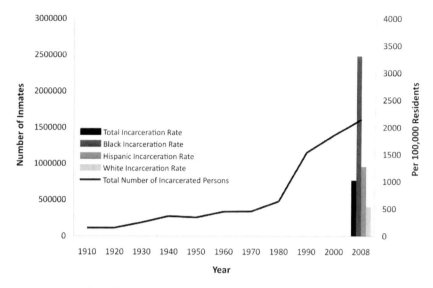

Figure 6.3   Number of inmates and incarceration rates in the United States, 1910–2008. *Source*: Justice Policy Institute (2000) and Sobol et al. (2010).

whereas the chances for Latino and Black men were substantially higher, at 17.2 and 32.2%, respectively; the chances of incarceration for women are much lower for all race and ethnic groups (Bonczar 2003). Even though the risk of incarceration is greatest among those with the lowest levels of education, almost a fifth of African American high school graduates born between 1965 and 1969 are expected to have gone to prison by the time they reached their early 30s, compared to 3.6% of White graduates (Pettit and Western 2004). Indeed, in 1999, Black men without a college education were more likely to go to prison during their lifetimes than serve in the military, whereas the reverse was true for their White counterparts (Pettit and Western 2004). Toward the close of the first decade of the 21st century, 537 of every 100,000 Whites were incarcerated, whereas 1,275 Hispanics and 3,310 Blacks per 100,000 were imprisoned (Sabol, West, and Cooper 2009). As Pager (2007: 3) notes, "[p]rison is no longer a rare or extreme event among our nation's most marginalized groups. Rather it has now become a normal and anticipated marker in the transition to adulthood."

Clearly, the expansion of the criminal justice system has resulted in substantial numbers of (overwhelmingly male) persons from disadvantaged backgrounds with criminal records. For some of those who are imprisoned, it is not hard to imagine how processes of cumulative disadvantage might be set in motion early in the life course. Of the various consequences associated with having such a negative credential, the most persistent are tied to employment in the civilian labor market. The pervasiveness of incarceration, combined with employers' aversion to hiring people with criminal backgrounds, depresses employment rates among all groups. Yet even the effect of a criminal record varies by race. White job applicants *with* criminal records are just as likely as Black applicants *without* convictions to have received responses from potential employers to their job inquiries; moreover, employers try to determine whether an applicant had a criminal background more often when the applicant is Black than White (Pager 2007). Thus, the combination of rising incarceration rates and the increasing use of criminal background checks even for entry-level jobs combine to depress the employment rates of disadvantaged groups, especially African American men.

Yet it is unclear whether minorities with clean records will fare significantly better than those with prior convictions, even if recent efforts to limit employers' inquiries into the criminal backgrounds of applicants are successful. For example, employers who do not run criminal background checks are *less* likely to hire young Black men than those who do (Holzer, Raphael, and Stoll 2006). This suggests that employers simply assume that young Black men have been involved with the criminal justice system and exclude them from consideration when there is a lack of information about the presence or absence of a criminal record. It seems, then, that Black men must navigate a labor market in which those with a history of incarceration will find it difficult to secure employment, whereas even those without criminal records will be assumed to have prior convictions. Under either scenario, Black men are disadvantaged in the competition for jobs. Although we have little evidence on how well Latinos with criminal records fare in the labor market, there appears to be little reason to suspect that they are unaffected by the possession of such discrediting credentials.

Additionally, racial and ethnic discrimination continues to shape the competition for entry-level jobs (Holzer 1999). Numerous studies document the myriad ways in which employers place African Americans, especially those from urban areas, at or near the bottom of their hiring queues while also using recruitment methods that draw few Black applicants (Kirschenman and Neckerman 1991: 231; Neckerman and Kirschenman 1991). In contrast to employee referrals, interviews and the use of skill tests appear to improve the chances that Black applicants are hired. Presumably, interviews provide Black applicants an opportunity to engage in impression management (Goffman 1959) to combat the negative assessments that employers hold of low-income Black workers generally. Regarding experiences in Chicago, Kirschenman and Neckerman (1991: 231) write:

> Black job applicants, unlike their White counterparts, must indicate to employers that the stereotypes do not apply to them. Inner-city and lower-class workers were seen as undesirable, and Black applicants had to try to signal to employers that they did not fall into those categories, either by demonstrating their skills or by adopting a middle-class style of dress, manner, and speech.

Interestingly, Pager (2007) observed a similar effect in her study of the labor market consequences of a criminal record. Given an opportunity to interact with employers in person, testers who acknowledged criminal records were able to overcome the associated stigma as evidenced by more callbacks than when the same testers applied without in-person contact. In effect, the interview is the space in which African Americans and ex-offenders may transform themselves from discredited to employed (Goffman 1959, 1963).

Racial and ethnic discrimination in the labor market is not limited to African Americans, of course (see Pager, Western, and Bonikowski 2009). Precisely because Latinos share with Blacks a number of axes of disadvantage—low levels of education, non-White racial origins, and residential location—immigration scholars worry that they may experience downward intergenerational socioeconomic mobility in contrast to the upward mobility historically experienced by European immigrants (Portes and Zhou 1993). Indeed, in an audit study of employer behavior with respect to entry-level positions in Chicago and San Diego, Kenney and Wissoker (1994) found that Hispanic job-seekers were substantially less likely to be interviewed and offered jobs than non-Hispanic Whites who were matched with them on education, work experience, presentation, and other characteristics.

Unlike the vast majority of Blacks, Latinos must also confront issues surrounding legal status and citizenship given that approximately 40% of Hispanics are foreign-born (Ramirez 2004). To the extent that legal status issues complicate the ability of Latinos to secure employment at decent wages, increased political pressure on employers to verify the eligibility of prospective employees to work in the U.S. have surely made it more difficult. In 1997, the federal government launched the voluntary Basic Pilot/Employment Eligibility Verification Program, which provided employers a fast and free means of checking the legal status of potential hires. That program has evolved into the current E-Verify Program. Although participation remains voluntary for the vast majority of employers (U.S. Citizenship and Immigration Services 2011a: 4), the number of employers who use it reached 387,000 in mid-2011 (U.S. Citizenship and Immigration Services 2011b). No doubt, part of the increase in employer participation was spurred by efforts of elected officials in jurisdictions like Frederick County, Maryland, where the county government approved by unanimous vote a requirement that contractors who do business with the county must affirm that neither they nor any of their subcontractors employ workers who are not authorized to work in the United States. The county plans to pursue regulations that *require* contractors to use the E-Verify system, thus transforming a voluntary program into a requirement in order to conduct business with the county government (Tully 2009). Although undocumented workers are the targets of work eligibility verification efforts, suspicion about the status of Hispanics generally may impact the labor market experiences of U.S.-born Latinos and those with legal status. Therefore, the potential benefits that flow from military service may be a compelling alternative to the civilian labor market for Hispanic citizens and permanent residents.

In sum, the labor market prospects of persons with only a high school diploma are more limited today than they were in the past. The industrial base of the U.S. economy has weakened, and a substantial proportion of labor-intensive jobs, both skilled and unskilled, have either been replaced by technology or have been moved to other countries where labor costs are lower. With that said, one should avoid painting an overly pessimistic portrait for *all* high school graduates from disadvantaged backgrounds. Surely, some graduates succeed in securing employment in jobs that pay livable wages and that may even have internal job ladders to higher-paying positions. However, such experiences appear to be the exception rather than what can be expected by today's typical high school graduate. Long-term social problems, such as racial and ethnic discrimination, along with relatively more recent challenges like spatial mismatch, rising rates of incarceration, and increased pressures on immigrant workers make achieving financial independence by a quick and relatively early life-course transition from high school to the labor market even more difficult.

PATH 3: A MILITARY CAREER

An alternative pathway from high school to early socioeconomic achievement is through military service. Currently, the military asserts that its "[e]ntry-level pay and benefits are hands down superior to entry-level jobs in the civilian sector," and invites anyone to "try to find an entry-level job [in the civilian sector] that starts at $1300/mo, pays for food, housing, medical, education, [provides] thirty days paid vacation, and many more benefits" (O'Brien 2008). This compensation package is noteworthy, particularly when juxtaposed with entry-level positions in the service sector of the civilian labor market. However, increases in the financial rewards to military service have come with greater expectations for those who seek to serve. Unlike earlier eras, the military is not a destination of last resort for those whose education and work ethic are too poor to succeed in the civilian labor market. Today, one must *qualify* for military service. To serve in the U.S. armed forces, and thus to pursue a military career, one must meet a number of enlistment standards set by the Department of Justice.[1] Of particular concern to us are the ways in which the educational, aptitude, citizenship, and morality restrictions may create barriers to entry for men and women from disadvantaged groups (see Kelty and Segal, Chapter 2 of this volume).

Rising rates of incarceration are as problematic for military service as for securing employment in the civilian labor market. Multiple minor criminal offenses or a single felony conviction can jeopardize a career in the military. Zero-tolerance policies and the use of school resource officers in public schools have had the effect of translating what was once considered poor student conduct into criminal offenses. Schools that serve primarily poor and minority students appear to utilize such policies and law enforcement personnel more often than predominantly White and middle-class schools (Theriot 2009), which works only to disproportionately usher poor and minority students through the "school-to-prison pipeline" (Wald and Losen 2003: 11). Such an early life-course trajectory may lock them out of military careers.

Citizenship and legal status comprise another important enlistment requirement that may have a disproportionate effect on access to the military among racial minorities, especially Latinos. Based on 2000 census data, about 15.9% of all noncitizens are of military recruitable age (18–24 years old). This works out to be about 2.9 million persons, half of whom are from Mexico (Hattiangadi, Quester, Lee, Lien, MacLeod, Reese, and Shuford 2005). Of all noncitizens in this age group, approximately half are without legal status (see Figure 3 in Hattiangadi et al. 2005); thus, they are, for the most part, not eligible to join the military (see Lutz, Chapter 4 of this volume). The remainder may do so and seek naturalization. Indeed, legal residents from Mexico contribute the largest number of noncitizen military service members. Moreover, from 1995 to 2003, Latin American countries accounted for ten of the top twenty countries from which legal resident enlistees came (see Table 12 in Hattiangadi et al. 2005). In 2002, Latinos accounted for only 10% of citizens in the armed forces but comprised 37% of noncitizen enlisted persons (see Figure 14 in Hattiangadi et al. 2005).

For Latino citizens, the pool of benefits offered by the military are the same as those available to other groups. However, for noncitizens, the military offers additional and important benefits. As has been true throughout the history of the U.S. military, noncitizens who are legal permanent residents are permitted to serve, and have done so since the Revolutionary War. Currently, approximately 47,000 noncitizens serve in the military, National Guard, and Reserves, with about 8,000 enlisting each year (Hattiangadi et al. 2005). The military provides them a path to citizenship in exchange for their service. In this way, military service can be a truly transformative experience for legal residents who become American citizens, as it allows them to come into possession of most of the same political rights enjoyed by all citizens, along with the ability to sponsor other members of their families for citizenship.

In addition to moral, citizenship, and legal status standards, enlistees must meet educational requirements to join the military. Although a high school diploma is not required for service, the military enlists few people who do not possess this credential, either in the form of a traditional diploma, GED, or certificate. Moreover, potential enlistees must demonstrate a level of math and verbal proficiency by achieving a minimum score on the Armed Forces Qualification Test (AFQT). Myriad military occupations are available to enlisted persons, with access determined by level of education and AFQT score.

In 2010, estimated annual base earnings for enlisted persons ranged from $16,794 to $18,824 in the first year. With full medical and dental benefits, the total annual compensation package was $21,550 to $23,736 ($30,586 to $48,743 with dependents). In year four, total compensation increases to between $39,208 and $52,000 ($41,092 to $57,064 with dependents). Enlistees who remain in the military for a full twenty years can earn between $103,475 and $130,777 ($105,923 to $135,733 with dependents), which includes a substantial housing allowance (Department of Defense 2010a). These figures make clear that the military not only offers base earnings that are comparable to those high school graduates obtain in the civilian labor market ($16,296 in 2008), the standard of living offered by the military through its insurance, housing, and dependent benefits is substantially higher (U.S. Census Bureau 2009).

A career in the military is not a given, even for those who meet enlistment standards. Although the barriers to entry are relatively low, remaining in the military until retirement—after a minimum of twenty years of service—requires continuous upgrading of knowledge and skill. Failure to do so, as evidenced by the inability to achieve particular milestones (e.g., completion of courses, passage of tests, promotion) can lead to separation from the military. In other words, military personnel who do not demonstrate continuous progress are denied the opportunity to reenlist. Thus, unlike the civilian labor market, the military offers a comfortable standard of living via competitive and stable earnings, substantial benefits, and job training; however, all such benefits are contingent on continuous qualification for military service. Not only must a prospective enlistee qualify to enter the military, he or she must qualify to remain there. If accomplished, a career in the military can drive lifelong development that often transforms the life-course trajectories of service members from disadvantaged backgrounds, as well as those to whom service members are linked.

PATH 4: MILITARY TO CIVILIAN LABOR FORCE

Those enlistees unable or unwilling to devote twenty or more years of their lives to military careers can take the skills they acquire in the military into the civilian labor market. Unfortunately, we know relatively little about how disadvantaged veterans fare in the labor market. Most research on the socioeconomic outcomes of veterans makes comparisons at the broadest level (e.g., veteran versus non-veteran) without giving detailed attention to differences among veterans with respect to race, ethnicity, and socioeconomic background. The research that does exist strongly suggests that the effects of military service vary across socioeconomic groups, as well as the historical contexts in which service occurs.[2]

In the early 1970s, the prevailing expectation was that persons without military experience would obtain higher levels of education and command higher wages than those who served in the military. It was also expected that this pattern characterized the socioeconomic outcomes of veterans from disadvantaged backgrounds. Yet Browning, Lopreato, and Poston (1973) hypothesized the opposite—that among disadvantaged groups, veterans would command higher incomes than non-veterans. These researchers conceptualized the military as a "bridging environment" in which disadvantaged groups acquire training, skills, and socialization to military ways of being that would pay dividends in the civilian labor market.

Although the question is not settled, research suggests that disadvantaged veterans enjoy an economic premium relative to similarly situated non-veterans, and may even benefit from military service more so than members of advantaged groups in terms of the magnitude of earnings differences between themselves and civilians. For example, Little and Fredland (1979) and Xie (1992) found that Black and Latino World War II veterans enjoyed a larger premium in earnings than that observed for White veterans, as did veterans with low levels of education relative to better-educated veterans. Research by Teachman and Tedrow (2004) showed that the long-term economic benefit of World War II service was larger for non-White veterans than White veterans. More recently, in a study of veterans in New York City, Kleykamp (2009a: 281) found that "Black veterans with administrative experience were treated more favorably than their civilian peers" in the job market. Based on analyses of the outcomes for Vietnam veterans, Hirsch and Mehay (2003) report that White veterans saw a modest wage penalty, whereas Blacks realized gains. Additionally, the effect of military service may vary *among* racial-ethnic minorities, as suggested by Browning, Lopreato, and Poston's (1973: 80) finding that "the income gains accruing to Mexican American veterans [were] substantially greater than those to Black veterans." Consistent with the idea that military service can separate service members from troublesome pasts are Sampson and Laub's (1996) findings that even veterans with episodes of delinquency in their youth have benefited socioeconomically from military service.

Not all research supports a positive relationship between military service and the labor market outcomes of minorities. Some studies show either neutral or negative effects. White (2008), whose interest is in military personnel who transition to police occupations, found that military service had no bearing on performance on standardized police exams among Black veterans. Phillips et al. (1992: 356) cautioned that the positive effects of military experience on earnings that they observed for Blacks and Hispanics were not a "significant value-added effect," and "to the extent that there was a positive earnings differential for Blacks, it diminished over time."

The experience of veterans in the All-Volunteer Force (AFV) that began in 1973 may tell us the most about what recent high school graduates may be able to expect in the labor market relative to civilians. Angrist (1998) examined earnings and employment among veterans during the 1980s. Although he found that service members commanded higher earnings than civilians, and veterans earned higher wages than non-veterans, the effect of military service varied by race. White veterans experienced an earnings shortcoming relative to non-veterans in the years immediately after their service, but a much lesser deficit several years later. In contrast, non-White veterans experienced "modest" positive effects on earnings and employment throughout the entire observation period of eight years. We await additional studies of the labor market effects of military service in the AVF era that can speak to the experiences of veterans in the 1990s and 2000s. It will be important for such studies to take the range of military service experiences into account, as well as the diverse racial, ethnic, nativity, and socioeconomic backgrounds that characterize the population of service members.

In sum, disadvantaged young adults who decide to separate from the military and join the civilian labor force can expect to have acquired additional human capital and, potentially, socialization to military ways of being that may help them achieve and sustain financial independence. Whether due to the use of military experience as a screening tool by employers (de Tray 1982; Xie 1992) or because veterans possess better hard and soft skills than non-veterans, disadvantaged persons appear to have a better chance of attaining financial security for themselves and their families via military service than with a strictly civilian career. To the extent that the premiums disadvantaged veterans enjoy are due to the ability of military service to "knife off" problematic personal histories (Sampson and Laub 1996) or turn around the lives of disadvantaged persons, it becomes a mechanism for weakening the process of cumulative disadvantage across the life course (Elder 1986).

PATH 5: FROM THE MILITARY TO COLLEGE AND THEN TO THE CIVILIAN LABOR FORCE

One of the major benefits of military service is its provisions for acquiring postsecondary education, a benefit that dates back to Title II of the Servicemen's Readjustment Act of 1944. Among other things, the Act that became known as the "GI Bill of Rights" permitted World War II veterans to obtain additional education upon their return. The educational provisions were rather generous. With respect to postsecondary education in particular, veterans were entitled to four years of what amounted to full tuition and fees, which were paid directly to the college or university of their choice (Radford 2009), thereby sparing veterans the complications of seeking reimbursement for educational expenses.[3] The lack of a cap on tuition placed even the most expensive colleges and universities within the reach of veterans, so long as they academically qualified for admission. Additional support came in the form of a stipend to offset any personal expenses that veterans incurred during their studies. Stipends covered "about half of the opportunity costs of not working for a single veteran and about 70% of the opportunity cost for a married veteran" (Bound and Turner 2002: 790). In evaluating the effect of the GI Bill thirty years after its creation, the then-administrator of Veterans Affairs noted that "no veteran benefit in history . . . has contributed more to the life-long welfare of America's veterans, their families, and [the] country than veterans' education and training programs" (Veterans Administration 1977: 7). Indeed, almost 8 million individuals increased their human capital through the original GI Bill, which facilitated their reentry into the civilian labor market (Veterans Administration 1977).

The generosity of the GI Bill has varied with each major military conflict (see Table 6.1). Starting with the post–Korean Conflict GI Bill, this pathway to college was available to those who served in the military during times of peace as well as in times of war (Altschuler and Blumin 2009). Comparisons of educational benefits over time indicate that no GI Bill between the first and the most recent one has been as generous as the original (Altschuler and Blumin 2009; Radford 2009). Nevertheless, substantial numbers of veterans have made their way from the military to postsecondary educational institutions with GI Bill support.

Currently, two GI bills provide benefits to veterans—the Montgomery GI Bill (created in 1984) and the Post-9/11 GI Bill (created in 2008). The Montgomery GI Bill is the controlling benefits package for veterans who completed their service prior to September 11, 2001. Unlike the World War II GI Bill, the Montgomery GI Bill provides a fixed amount of money for educational expenses, which is intended to cover tuition, fees, books, supplies, and living expenses. Evaluations of the Montgomery GI Bill, relative to the original, show declines in the value of its educational benefits given increases in the cost of postsecondary education over time (Bowman, Volkert, and Hahn 1973). Whereas the original bill fully covered the cost of tuition and fees at public and private colleges, the Montgomery GI Bill covers, on average, 100% of tuition at public colleges, but only 47% of tuition at private colleges, based on college costs reported by the College Board. As of the 2009–2010 academic year, in-state tuition and fees at public four-year colleges averaged $7,020 compared to an average of $26,273 for private (not-for-profit) colleges and universities (Baum and Ma 2009).[4] In 2009, the Montgomery GI Bill paid a total of $12,312, disbursed in monthly installments, to veterans who qualified to receive the full educational benefit. Importantly, participation in the Montgomery GI Bill requires a contribution of $1,200 by the service member in the first year of service, which may be a barrier to uptake for some veterans.

The Post-9/11 GI Bill is available to those who served after September 11, 2001, including those who began service prior to, but remained in the military after, that date. Revelations of the declining value of GI Bill educational benefits over time have spurred reforms that make postsecondary

Table 6.1 Postsecondary Educational Provisions across GI Bills, 1944–2009

	Original	Korean	Post-Korean	MGIB-Active Duty	MGIB-Selected Reserve	Post-9/11
Effective Date	6/22/1944	8/20/1952	6/1/1966			8/1/2009
Service Period	9/16/1940 to 7/25/1947	6/27/1950 to 1/31/1955	2/1/1955 to 5/7/1975	Variable, but with earliest service date on 1/1/1977	First service period starting 6/30/85 and later	Active duty on or after 9/11/2001 for at least 90 aggregate days
Eligibility	90 days	90 days	181 days	Variable across four categories of eligibility; requires contribution of $1,200 in first year	Six-year obligation to Selected Reserve made after 6/30/85; officers required to serve another 6 years	Variable, but with full benefits after 36 months or 30 days with service-related disability; graduated scale from 90 days to 35 months
Period of Eligibility	9 years	8 years	8 years	10 years	14 years	15 years
Entitlement	1 year of training plus 1 month for each month on active duty to maximum of 48 months.	1.5 times the amount of time served on active duty to a maximum of 36 months	1.5 times the amount of time served on active duty to a maximum of 36 months; additional time allowed for completion of pre-college coursework.	Maximum of 36 months	Maximum of 36 months	Maximum of 36 months

Tuition, fees, books	Cost of tuition up to $500	$110/month	$100 (in 1966) to $220 (in 1972)	$1,368/month for those with 3+ years of service; $1,111/month for others	$333/month	Tuition and fees up to the highest in-state tuition for public education institution, plus up to $1,000 for books and supplies
Stipend	$50–75/month	Included in above	Included in above	Included in above	Included in above	Equivalent to the "basic allowance for housing" for an E-5 with dependents
Job training	$50–65/month plus maximum of $100 for tools	$70/month with no additional benefit for tools	$80–168 with no additional benefit for tools; $50/month for tutoring to a maximum of $450	Yes	Yes	No
Housing	No additional benefit	No additional benefit	No additional benefit	No additional benefit	No additional benefit	Yes, except for those on active duty
Disbursement of benefits	Tuition and fees paid directly to educational institution	Benefit paid in monthly installments to service member	Benefit paid in monthly installments to service member	Benefit paid in monthly installments to service member	Benefit paid in monthly installments to service member	Tuition paid directly to educational institution; other benefits paid to service member
Transferability	None	None	None	Yes, during active commitment	None	Yes, during active commitment

Sources: Bowman, Volkert, and Hahn (1973); U.S. Department of Veterans Affairs (2010).

Note: "Post-Korean" is applied to veterans who served during the post-Korean and Vietnam eras. Veterans who served during the post-Korean War period between 1955 and 1965, also sometimes referred to as the "Cold War Era," did not have access to the GI Bill. When the program was reinstated in 1966, veterans who had served during this period were retroactively covered.

education substantially more affordable for veterans and service members. The Post-9/11 bill demands no "buy in," so service members are not required to make contributions to receive benefits, and the period during which they may use their benefits is longer compared to that of the Montgomery GI Bill (Radford 2009). Although there remains a limit on what the military will pay for tuition and fees, that amount is now flexible (i.e., place-specific) rather than fixed. In other words, the benefit will pay up to the amount of tuition charged by the most expensive public college or university in the veteran or service member's state of residence, though it may be used at either a public or private institution (Radford 2009). Additionally, the Veterans Administration has returned to the practice of paying benefits directly to educational institutions rather than reimbursing beneficiaries. In another move back to its historical roots, the military once again provides additional funds to service members enrolled in college, this time in the form of the "basic allowance for housing," which currently amounts to $1,950 per month for an individual with dependents (Department of Defense 2010b).

Just as the composition and total value of benefits in GI bills have changed over time, so have their effects on the educational attainment of veterans. There appears to be consensus that the GI Bill increased the educational attainment of veterans of World War II, the Korean War, and the Vietnam War (see Angrist 1993; Bound and Turner 2002; Stanley 2003). However, there is evidence that the use of the GI Bill was not uniform across the population of veterans; those who enlisted at younger ages from middle- to upper-class families were more likely to use the World War II and Korean War GI Bill educational provisions than those who were older at enlistment and from working-class families (Stanley 2003). Those findings are underscored by the experiences of "Cold War"–era veterans, who served after the end of the Korean War between 1955 to 1965. During these years, no GI Bill was in effect, although when the program was reinstated in 1966 these veterans were retroactively covered. As a result, Cold War veterans evidenced lower levels of education than civilians, net of background characteristics, even among those who had planned to attend college (MacLean 2005). Their levels of education were also lower than other Cold War veterans who had access to the GI Bill's educational benefits because their enlistment date was prior to February 1, 1955, which was used as the cut-off date for eligibility for the Korean War GI Bill (Stanley 2003).

There is less agreement about whether the positive effects of the GI Bill extend to veterans of the All-Volunteer Force era (see Angrist 1993 for positive effects and Teachman 2007a for negative effects). Moreover, not all sociodemographic groups benefited educationally from the provisions in GI bills. Research shows that substantial benefits flowed to those from higher socioeconomic backgrounds (Stanley 2003), those who used their benefits in colleges versus vocational-technical schools (Angrist 1993), Whites nationally (Bound and Turner 2002), and both Whites and Blacks outside the Southern region (Onkst 1998; Turner and Bound 2003).[5]

Socioeconomically disadvantaged persons and racial minorities confronted many of the same obstacles that they faced in other contexts in relation to utilizing their educational benefits for postsecondary education. Poor-quality elementary and secondary education provided to African Americans, Latinos, and low-income Whites surely made it difficult for them to meet the academic requirements for admission to most colleges and universities. Moreover, even though the stipends provided to veterans covered a substantial portion of the earnings that GIs deferred by going to college, veterans from low-income families likely found it too difficult to make up the portion of deferred wages that was not covered by the GI Bill. Ultimately, Stanley (2003: 704) concludes that "GI bills may have made college more accessible for the children of the middle and upper middle class, but apparently they had little effect among those of the working class."

African Americans and Latinos faced an additional roadblock to using their benefits for college education—racial and ethnic discrimination. The combination of *de facto* segregation in the North, *de jure* segregation in the South, and a tradition of discrimination against Mexican Americans in the Southwest meant that many Black and Latino veterans were actively denied the opportunity to use the educational provisions they had earned. For this and other reasons, most Black veterans who sought a college education turned to Historically Black Colleges and Universities (HBCUs) (Turner and Bound 2003). However, due to insufficient financial support, HBCUs could neither physically nor academically meet the full demand for college education among these veterans. Consequently, approximately 20,000 Black veterans were denied admission to HBCUs in addition to countless others who were excluded from White institutions (Olson 1974).

Less is known about the means by which Mexican American and other Hispanic veterans overcame the roadblocks they faced, but it is clear that they confronted many. In *The American GI Forum*, a book named after a veterans' organization founded by veteran Hector P. Garcia to fight for the rights of Mexican American and other veterans, Ramos describes the circumstances that awaited Hispanic veterans when they returned from World War II (see also Lutz, Chapter 4 of this volume):

> [T]hese servicemen returned to a society that had historically denied Mexican Americans and others the full benefits of citizenship to which they were rightfully entitled, and they quickly found that the war had done little to change this. . . . Aside from informal manifestations of prejudice and discrimination . . . returning Mexican-American servicemen came to experience more directly than ever before the discriminatory injustice and neglect of American institutions. Supposedly equal beneficiaries of the entitlements attendant to the GI Bill, these returning servicemen frequently found themselves denied the generally prompt and adequate receipt of the bill's financial, educational, and health benefits afforded to their Anglo counterparts (1998: 2).

Such denials of the rights of Black and Hispanic veterans were facilitated by the Veterans Administration's use of local administrators to approve and disburse benefits (Altschuler and Blumin 2009; Ramos 1998). Reliance upon local administrators, many of whom engaged in discriminatory behavior, meant that qualified Black and Latino veterans had access to benefits that many could not readily use, at least not for a college education (Altschuler and Blumin 2009; Herbold 1994; Humes 2006). The GI Bill, with its race-neutral provisions but discriminatory implementation in various historical periods and contexts, was the embodiment of the duality of America's relationship to its non-White citizens. Martin Luther King, Jr. would symbolize this duality nearly twenty years after the establishment of the original GI Bill, using the metaphor of a promissory note, stating

> When the architects of our republic wrote the magnificent words of the Constitution and the Declaration of Independence, they were signing a promissory note to which every American was to fall heir. This note was a promise that all men, yes, black men as well as white men, would be guaranteed the unalienable rights of 'Life, Liberty and the pursuit of Happiness.' It is obvious today that America has defaulted on this promissory note insofar as her citizens of color are concerned. Instead of honoring this sacred obligation, America has given the Negro people a bad check, a check which has come back marked 'insufficient funds' (1988 [1963]: 224).

The history of the GI Bill in relation to Black and Hispanic soldiers makes it clear that America failed to honor the obligation it had to those it sent to war; it created a means for upward social mobility rarely accessible to African Americans and Latinos on their own, but then placed those means in the hands of people who insisted upon keeping these veterans "in their place." Although the Veterans Administration's check was good, too few colleges and universities were willing to accept it. Consequently, Onkst (1998: 532) concludes that the original GI Bill "did little to assist Southern Black veterans in their attempt to improve their lives during the postwar period." Less is known about the effects of the GI Bill on the educational attainment of Mexican American and other Latino veterans, but given the obstacles to its use, we can safely assume the effect was far less than it could have been.

To be sure, formal barriers to institutions of higher education no longer exist. African Americans (and Latinos) have access to the full range of four-year colleges, as evidenced by the proportion of Blacks who attend HBCUs relative to other colleges. Estimates from nationally representative data show that approximately 30% of 1990 Black high school graduates who enrolled in college attended non-HBCU four-year colleges and another 5.8% enrolled in four-year selective colleges compared to 22.2% who elected to attend HBCUs (Bennett and Lutz 2009). Moreover, African Americans were more likely to enroll in non-HBCU unselective and selective colleges than Whites from similar backgrounds (Bennett and Xie 2003). Despite formal access, obstacles to postsecondary education continue to confront the socioeconomically disadvantaged among all racial and ethnic groups (Carnevale and Rose 2004; Heller 2002; St. John 2003). However, to the extent that their low rates of college attendance are rooted in lack of financial (Orfield 1992) and social capital (Jordan and Plank 2000; Plank and Jordan 2001; Stanton-Salazar 1997), the educational provisions obtained through military service can help overcome those challenges. For racial minorities and those from low-income families, the Montgomery and Post-9/11 GI Bills make the pathway from the military to college to the labor market a realistic mobility strategy among contemporary veterans.

DISCUSSION AND CONCLUSION

In this chapter, we have been concerned with the options available to disadvantaged high school graduates for early socioeconomic achievement, and in particular, their prospects for becoming financially independent given its importance in the transition to adulthood. One recognized pathway to this objective is through postsecondary education. Unlike many other places in the world, there is almost a universal aspiration (if not expectation, unfounded as it may be) among U.S. high school graduates for a college education. That President Obama recently lamented that "[i]n a single generation, America has fallen from 2nd place to 11th place in the proportion of students completing college" speaks to the difficulty of achieving that goal, particularly among certain segments of the population (Obama 2009). As the president works to help the United States "take the lead once more" in the percentage of students who complete college, we must also keep in mind those graduates who either cannot or do not wish to attend college, at least not immediately after high school.

Although it is certainly true that any *individual* high school graduate may find employment at a job that pays good wages, offers benefits, and provides opportunities for advancement, this is not the experience most high school graduates can expect. As Rosenbaum (2001: 1) notes, "[a] crisis [has emerged] in the American labor market. . . . [High school graduates] either experience enormous difficulty getting jobs or take dead–end jobs that offer low status, little training, and pay too low to support a family. . . . Even at age thirty, a large portion of high school graduates continue to hold low–paying, high–turnover jobs." Based on this and other assessments, including our own, there appears to be little in the civilian labor market to interrupt the process of cumulative disadvantage, whereby childhood challenges place youth on trajectories that lead to potentially greater disadvantage in adulthood.

There are institutional elements in the military that can facilitate early socioeconomic achievement among disadvantaged groups. Military service is inseparable from employment and training. Not only does the military offer wages that are, at the current moment, competitive with or superior to those found in the civilian labor market, it also guarantees (in fact, *requires*) improvements in human capital via skills training, especially if a service member seeks a career in the military. There is also a built-in pathway to a college education via GI bills, should a service member desire to seek a college degree. It is here that the military stands apart from the labor market, but alongside colleges and universities with respect to disadvantaged persons—it makes possible a number of options that are either not found in the labor market or are not readily accessible there. These options are to (1) pursue a twenty-year or longer military career, which fosters lifelong development, (2) serve for a period of time and then enter the labor market with skills acquired in the military, or (3) attend college after military service. Pursuing one of these options creates the context in which disadvantaged persons can exercise greater control over their lives than appears possible via low-wage jobs in the civilian sector. Similar to the way a college degree opens doors to opportunities that are otherwise unavailable without it, military service paves roads to various opportunities for socioeconomic achievement unlikely to be otherwise accessible to disadvantaged persons, including one that leads to college campuses. Not only can these opportunities, if taken, arrest the process of cumulative disadvantage for an individual service member, it can also interrupt the intergenerational transmission of disadvantage by raising the starting position of his or her children.

Lest we paint an incomplete portrait, an assessment of the opportunities available through military service should not stand unconfronted by an assessment of its potential costs. Acknowledgment of the risks that accompany military service is especially required at the present moment, when the dynamics of the geopolitical landscape can have severe repercussions for men and women who serve. Involvement in prolonged military conflicts like the wars in Iraq and Afghanistan can weaken the appeal of military service or, at least, alter the calculus an individual makes when considering whether to serve. In some circumstances, military service can lead to injury and disability that can compound early-life disadvantage rather than mitigate it. Evidence that households that include a disabled veteran experience higher levels of poverty and material hardship than households that include a nondisabled veteran underscores this reality (Heflin, Wilmoth, and London 2012; London, Heflin, and Wilmoth 2011).

Unlike the present moment, the early years of the All-Volunteer Force comprised a period in which military service carried relatively little risk. Although several major military conflicts occurred during this time, all were characterized by their short duration and low numbers of casualties (see Figure 6.4).[6] For example, the involvement of combat forces in the invasions of Granada (1983) and Panama (1989), the Persian Gulf War (1990–1991), Somalia via the Battle of Mogadishu (1993), Bosnia–Herzegovina

(1995–2004), and Kosovo (1999) each lasted less than a year, although forces were sometimes deployed somewhat longer for humanitarian and/ or peacekeeping missions. The initiation of military conflicts in Afghanistan and Iraq created a more hazardous climate in which entrance into the armed services carried with it a greater risk of harm, disability, and death than it had since Vietnam. Moreover, a given cohort of men and women in the military may be placed in harm's way more frequently than has been true in the past should military action become the modal response to perceived threats and actual acts of terrorism.

We also emphasize once more that military service is not a path to socioeconomic achievement merely to be chosen. Although military service offers valuable opportunities to those from disadvantaged backgrounds, one must qualify for military service and repeatedly demonstrate sufficient merit to remain there. Given the mental, physical, intellectual, familial, and moral barriers to entry, it is clear that military service is not a path that all disadvantaged persons can travel. Moreover, a military career is possible only for those capable and willing to continuously upgrade their skills—a

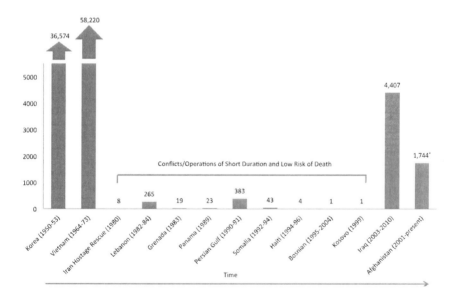

Notes:
Number of deaths in the Korean War including non-theather deaths is equal to 54,246.
Data for Korea through Haiti come from Leland and Oboroceanu (2010).
Data for Bosnia and Kosovo come from Diehl (2009).
Data for Afghanistan and Iraq come from the Department of Defense (2011a, b).
*As of December 31, 2011.

Figure 6.4 Number of military deaths in a selection of American wars, conflicts, and operations.

requirement that persons from disadvantaged backgrounds are unlikely to confront in the labor market. Those who are most in need of the very benefits and possibilities that military service offers may be among those least likely to meet requirements to enter and stay in the military. Thus, as they transition to adulthood, some youth continue to face limited pathways to financial security, which will contribute to ongoing cumulative disadvantage across their life courses and may increase financial and health insecurity in later life (see Street and Hoffman, Chapter 11 of this volume), as well as possibly disadvantaging the lives of those who depend upon them.

There is a substantial need for additional research that draws on the pathways framework we have articulated in this chapter to investigate the role of military service in the lives of men and women from disadvantaged backgrounds. Different pathways into service are likely to be associated with different experiences of active-duty service, as well as different short- and long-term consequences of military service (see Wilmoth and London, Chapter 1 of this volume). There are likely to be substantial consequences of military service for labor force, family, and health trajectories, all of which will shape later-life outcomes among disadvantaged youth. These consequences are likely to affect the racial and ethnic communities with which disadvantaged youth identify, as well as the geographic areas they come from prior to, and return to after, military service. The next chapters in this volume consider these life-course domains in more detail, offer a number of suggestions for future research, and provide a discussion of the kinds of longitudinal data that will increasingly be needed to allow for the investigation of the mechanisms by which military service shapes the life-course trajectories and outcomes of disadvantaged youth, as well as those from more advantaged backgrounds.

NOTES

1. Individual branches of the military may institute standards that exceed those of the Justice Department. See Asch, Buck, Klerman, Kleykamp, and Loughran (2009) for a detailed discussion of enlistment standards.
2. See MacLean and Elder (2007) for a recent review of studies on variation in the effects of military service across military eras.
3. Veterans could also use the GI Bill to complete high school, pay for job training, or attend vocational schools. Most veterans who used their educational provisions did so for these purposes.
4. The percentage of tuition and fees covered by educational provisions are the authors' calculations based on a Montgomery GI Bill monthly payment of $1,368 for nine months and the average cost of public and private colleges (U.S. Department of Veterans Affairs 2010). Members of the Selected Reserve receive a substantially smaller monthly payment from the Montgomery GI Bill, which means that it covers a much smaller percentage of college costs.
5. See Altschuler and Blumin (2009: Chapter 5) for a treatment of the GI Bill in relation to women's opportunities.

6. For a comparison of risk associated with military service, death rates are preferable to number of deaths. For example, there were 9.5 deaths (theater and nontheater) for every 1,000 service members during the Korean War. The death rate for the Vietnam War was slightly higher, at 10.3 persons per 1,000 service members, but it was only 0.9 for the Persian Gulf War. Additionally, Figure 6.4 does not represent the full extent of the risk associated with military service. It does not, for example, reflect the number of military persons who were wounded in combat or missing in action, nor does it reflect noncombat harms, such as increased risk of military sexual trauma, disability, suicide, unemployment, and criminal involvement (MacLean 2010; see also MacLean, Chapter 10 of this volume).

7 Labor Market Outcomes among Veterans and Military Spouses

Meredith Kleykamp

Veterans typically serve in the military during young adulthood when civilian peers are gaining education and work experience. This often puts veterans "behind" their peers who follow more normative age-patterned transitions from school to nonmilitary work, although it may have specific benefits for individuals from disadvantaged backgrounds (see Kelty and Segal, Chapter 2 of this volume, and Bennett and McDonald, Chapter 6 of this volume). To gain a fuller portrait of how veterans fare in the labor market after service, it is important to examine key turning points and outcomes at a single point in time, such as enlistment or separation from service, as well as trajectories over time in their experiences while serving in the military, post-service earnings, and occupational attainment. Nearly three decades of scholarship concerning the effects of military service on veterans' employment and earnings has produced inconsistent findings, partly because of methodological challenges (e.g., selection bias, data constraints, and others) (see Wolf, Wing, and Lopoo, Chapter 13 of this volume). This body of research suggests that veterans sometimes outperform their non-veteran peers, but more typically, they come from behind and face bumpy paths back toward parity with civilians. These trajectories vary in terms of personal biography, specific military experience, and historical context.

By definition, spouses' lives are intimately linked with each other. The fateful decisions of the service member and of the military constrain the personal developmental trajectories of military spouses. Military service has both short- and long-term consequences for veterans' and spouses' employment and earnings over a lifetime. These consequences are historically conditioned and likely vary based on the timing of marriage, military service, and other family roles. Yet we know very little about how the work-life trajectories of military spouses evolve over the long term. However, in light of the high percentage of All-Volunteer Force–era active-duty service members who are married, life-course scholars are increasingly asking how military service constrains the labor market outcomes of military spouses, who are mostly wives, given the skewed gender distribution of the armed forces. These studies paint a consistent picture of limited career mobility, lower wages, dampened aspirations, and difficulty balancing work and family as a "trailing spouse."

As these two bodies of research continue to tackle basic questions about the labor market consequences of military service for veterans and their spouses, they must also move forward to better understand *why* such outcomes take place. A renewed focus on mechanisms might lead researchers to attend to the influences of employers, public attitudes toward veterans, contextual effects of labor market conditions on veterans' readjustment, veterans' job search strategies, post-service education, and the physical and mental transformation veterans experience during service. Such a focus might also identify the set of mechanisms that operate to undermine the labor market success of military spouses. New questions can only be adequately answered with new forms of, and approaches to, data collection, possibly including the use of experimental research designs, new surveys of subpopulations, and better inclusion of the military population in national surveys in both number and in the information collected. Although the lack of large-scale, nationally representative, longitudinal data is a very real challenge (see Teachman, Chapter 14 of this volume), scholars must identify alternative approaches to researching these questions until such new data become available.

This chapter draws on insights from the life-course perspective (see Wilmoth and London, Chapter 1 of this volume) to better understand why and how military service influences veterans' and spouses' employment; the importance of the age-patterning of events and experiences, the role of historical change, and the concept of linked lives provide a framework for studying veterans' and spouses' employment outcomes. In the literature on the life course, work is often the central activity organizing the early and mid-life adult life course. Military service in the contemporary All-Volunteer Force constitutes a form of work for those who make it a career and a prelude to civilian work for those who spend only a few years in service. Military service influences the life course in varied ways. Thus, this chapter emphasizes how veterans' post-military labor market trajectories and outcomes are contingent on individual characteristics, including race, gender, and educational attainment; the conditions leading to military service, particularly conscription or voluntary enlistment; the military experience itself, such as whether it occurred during peacetime or wartime and the particular occupational specialty held; the societal context of reception and whether veterans were returning from popular or unpopular conflicts; and the policies in place to aid the transition to civilian life. This chapter also provides an overview of what we know about the employment trajectories and outcomes of military spouses.

The rest of this chapter summarizes prior research on the post-service labor market outcomes of veterans and the labor market consequences of being married to someone who serves in the military. Following a review of these two literatures, I offer a number of suggestions for future research on these issues, identify several mechanisms that are high priorities for further research, and briefly discuss the kinds of data needed to inform this new research agenda.

RESEARCH ON VETERANS' LABOR MARKET OUTCOMES

Decades of research on the labor market outcomes of veterans reveal several key insights about who benefits from military service and suggests reasons why. Veterans and non-veterans appear to have different labor market outcomes, including labor force participation rates, employment rates, and earnings. However, the "effect" of military service on these outcomes is conditioned by personal biography, the nature of military service itself (e.g., length, occupational specialty, service branch, officer/enlisted status), and historical context. Addressing substantive questions regarding the effects of military service on labor market outcomes is complicated by the need to untangle the transformative effects of military service from selection effects in producing observed veteran/non-veteran differences in employment and earnings. Methodological constraints remain a primary challenge in this area of research (see Wolf, Wing, and Lopoo, Chapter 13 of this volume).

Historical Context

The social context of military service has changed dramatically over the past several decades. The consequences of serving during the large-scale World War II mobilization of nearly 16 million young men differ substantially from the consequences of serving in the much smaller, conscripted forces of the Korean and Vietnam wars (U.S. Census Bureau 2003). Fewer still served in the All-Volunteer Force during the 1980s and during the hot peace of the 1990s or the wars in Iraq and Afghanistan, which have been fought with an active-duty force of about 1.4 million people (Department of Defense 2011c). Historical context sets the conditions under which individuals enter the service, including whether service is compulsory or voluntary, what the opportunity costs of serving are, and who else is likely to be serving in the military. Historical context also influences the nature of the military experience and training. Is the training purely of a military nature, or is there occupation-specific training that may transfer into later civilian work? Is the in-service experience during peacetime or war, and are those who serve at great risk of facing combat? History also provides a context of reception for new veterans coming back into civilian life. Are veterans welcomed back or met by a skeptical and suspicious public? Are jobs readily available or do veterans experience limited opportunities for work or further training and education? In each era, there exists a constellation of benefits provided by the state to current and former military members to ease the transition from soldier to civilian, and these policies change in response to the public's perception of veterans' needs and merit. Each of these macro-level factors influences the ways in which military service shapes post-military labor market experiences. All of these considerations make it challenging to generalize from research on one generation of veterans to another, or to specify "the" effect of military service.

Studies of World War II veterans generally find an earnings advantage among those who served compared to those who did not (de Tray 1982; Fredland and Little 1985; Goldberg and Warner 1987; Little and Fredland 1979; Martindale and Poston 1979; Sampson and Laub 1996; Villemez and Kasarda 1976). These outcomes are for a generation who served in a popular war in which most men eligible to serve did so (Angrist and Krueger 1994). Because of the massive manpower mobilization of World War II, men who did not serve often had disqualifying conditions, leading to negative selection in this population. In this light, it is easy to see how additional studies that use more stringent methods of accounting for this selectivity find little to no positive effect of military service on later earnings among World War II veterans (Angrist and Krueger 1994). Given the popularity and pervasiveness of the war experience, policies—most notably the GI Bill—facilitated the transition to the civilian economy for large numbers of returning veterans (Angrist and Krueger 1994; Bound and Turner 2002; Dechter and Elder 2004; Mettler 2005; Stanley 2003; Teachman and Tedrow 2004; Turner and Bound 2003; Wilson 1995; see also Bennett and McDonald, Chapter 6 of this volume).

Contrast the experience of the "Greatest Generation" with that of Vietnam veterans, who served in an unpopular war, staffed in large part by draft-induced volunteers or conscripts selected through an unfair process that allowed the well-off and college-enrolled populations to avoid service. The combination of a process that negatively selected young men *into* service and the experience of serving in a confusing and publicly unpopular war influenced their outcomes relative to non-veterans. Nearly all analyses of the "returns to service" among Vietnam veterans find a substantial earnings penalty (Angrist 1990; Berger and Hirsch 1983; Bryant, Samaranayake, and Wilhite 1993; Hirsch and Mehay 2003; Martindale and Poston 1979; Savoca and Rosenheck 2000; Teachman 2004, 2005). Being drafted exacerbated the negative impact of military service in Vietnam (Card 1983; Hirsch and Mehay 2003; Teachman 2004). Furthermore, returning home with a stigma of drug addiction, combat stress, and negative sentiment generally had dramatic negative consequences for the employment experiences of Vietnam veterans compared with their non-veteran peers, many of whom increased their human capital through college deferments (Bordieri and Drehmer 1984; D'Anton 1983; Starr et al. 1974).

The shift to an All-Volunteer Force had implications for the post-service outcomes of veterans. Just as the World War II and Vietnam-era drafts produced positively and negatively selected forces, respectively, the contemporary All-Volunteer Force likely generates a highly selective force—but it is less clear how the selectivity of these men and women relates to their civilian labor market chances. The dual selection process, whereby individuals self-select into enlistment and the military selects those deemed qualified for service from this pool, combined with the selectivity for those who choose to remain or depart military life, complicates research on the consequences of military service. Among the current generation of military personnel and veterans, outcomes likely differ both on the basis of personal biography and its influence on the decision to enlist and on the specific occupational experiences that service members have within the military.

Personal Biography

Personal characteristics are among the most stable mediators of the influence of military service on later-life outcomes across historical context. Both the "returns to service" literature and the life-course paradigm identify a normative age-patterning and sequencing of military service and other major events, such as college enrollment, marriage, and labor force attachment, with differing consequences depending on the age-patterning of these life events. Various elements of personal biography influence who chooses to join the military, when, and in lieu of what other activities. Personal biography also references how the unfolding of other life events interacts with and shapes longer-term occupational and earnings trajectories after military service. Below, I briefly summarize the individual-level characteristics that have been found to have the most influence on how military service affects civilian labor market outcomes: race, education, and gender (see Lutz, Chapter 4 of this volume, and Bennett and McDonald, Chapter 6 of this volume).

Diversity of the Effects of Military Service

Race and Ethnicity

One of the more consistent findings across generations of veterans is the fact that the effect of military service appears to be more positive—or at least less negative—among racial and ethnic minorities (Browning, Lopreato, and Poston 1973; Lopreato and Poston 1977). World War II veterans who came from more disadvantaged backgrounds, including those with low levels of education and racial-ethnic minorities, showed higher post-service earnings and employment than their more advantaged peers (Fredland and Little 1985; Little and Fredland 1979; Moskos and Butler 1996; Teachman and Tedrow 2004). Even among the Vietnam-era generation, there appears to be a positive effect of military service on the earnings of Blacks and among the less educated, whereas Whites and more highly educated veterans suffered an earnings penalty (Berger and Hirsch 1983; Martindale and Poston 1979; Rosen and Taubman 1982; Teachman 2004). Among veterans of the All-Volunteer Force era, these results appear to hold; overall, there seems to be a negative impact of military service on labor market outcomes, but this disadvantage is smaller among Black men and men with less than high school education (Angrist 1998; Hirsch and Mehay 2003; Phillips et al. 1992; Teachman and Tedrow 2004, 2007).

Education

One of the major reasons that military service is purported to provide advantages is the provision of extensive educational benefits to those who serve (see Bennett and McDonald, Chapter 6 of this volume). Most well-known is the Montgomery GI Bill. However, other educational benefits that accrue during and after the completion of service have allowed thousands of military personnel to increase their human capital attainment, which has sometimes improved their opportunities for post-military employment. Military service sometimes enables, but sometimes constrains, educational attainment, and this is one of several key mechanisms linking military service to post-military labor market outcomes.

Prior to the Vietnam War, World War II and Korean War veterans gained more education than their peers. Vietnam veterans fell behind the educational attainment of their peers, at least at the time of discharge; however, Vietnam veterans closed some of the attainment gap over time (Bound and Turner 2002; Card 1983; Cohen, Segal, and Temme 1986; Little and Fredland 1979; Teachman and Call 1996). In the All-Volunteer Force era, Teachman (2007a) found a diversity of ways by which military service actually hindered educational attainment. As access to higher education expanded among civilians, military service became an alternative to, rather than a step toward, college. Veterans had lower levels of education than peers at discharge, and unlike Vietnam-era veterans, All-Volunteer Force veterans fell farther behind the educational attainment of peers over time. Only officers, African Americans, and those who had higher Armed Forces Qualification Test (AFQT) scores or were older at entrance into the military have been able to reduce this educational deficit (Teachman 2007a). To the extent that these educational differences influence civilian employment and earnings, it appears that military service may be hindering socioeconomic advances among today's veterans by limiting educational attainment.

Gender

Research specifically investigating the consequences of military service among women is sparse, and only a few studies have addressed questions related to the post-service economic outcomes of female veterans. Unlike racial and ethnic minorities, female veterans appear to face an earnings penalty. Prokos and Padavic (2000) found that female veterans earned less than their non-veteran peers after controlling for demographic and human capital differences. However, they also found that older, pre–All-Volunteer Force women veterans earned a premium, which suggests that military service among "trailblazing" women was relatively advantageous at a time when fewer female non-veterans were working, particularly in male-dominated occupations. Cooney et al. (2003) found no advantage to military service among Black women and a veteran disadvantage among White women. They conceive of these effects not as a reflection of the effect of military service, but as indications of the different relative opportunity structures for nonserving Black and White women. If the civilian opportunities for Black women are more limited than those for White women, then Black veterans may appear more advantaged relative to Black non-veterans than do White veterans relative to White non-veterans. Mehay and Hirsch (1996), using data well suited to control for the selectivity of female veterans, found a 9% wage penalty among all female veterans, with a 12% penalty among Whites and a 2% penalty among Blacks relative to their respective same-race non-veteran peers.

Research on women veterans does affirm the racial aspect of the bridging or positive turning point hypothesis, which predicts that those from disadvantaged backgrounds will benefit more from military service. Available evidence does suggest that women of color are less disadvantaged by their service. However, the available studies do not investigate employment specifically, nor are they able to tease out the mechanisms generating low earnings among veteran women. This is unfortunate, because the "greedy" nature of military service, family roles, and civilian work likely intersect in complex ways to influence female veterans' labor force participation, employment conditions, and, by extension, their wages. Research on the consequences of military service among women is much needed, but has been hampered by the relatively low numbers of female veterans in available datasets.

Military Experience

Historical context partly shapes the nature of the military experience. However, in order to understand variations in the post-military experiences of veterans, it is important to distinguish between the context facing all those who served and the particular experiences that vary across individuals within a given cohort. It is especially important to consider occupational experiences. Some military specialty occupations will have more direct transferability to the civilian labor market, and this will alter the expected post-service labor market experiences of veterans. Occupational differences also condition the likelihood of experiencing combat and the risk of mental or physical injury. Exposure to combat has emerged as a key turning point in the lives of those who serve and appears to have long-term consequences for health and labor market outcomes (Ikin et al. 2009; Settersten 2006).

Military Occupations

All military members are assigned to some kind of occupational specialty. These range from purely military roles, such as infantryman, submariner, tank operator, and artillerist, to ancillary roles, such as cook, musician, photographer, clerk, nurse, and phlebotomist. The range of military occupational specialties includes jobs with virtually no equivalent in civilian society, as well as those that are highly transferable (so much so that they are increasingly "privatized" and delegated to civilians to perform) (Mangum and Ball 1987, 1989). Thus, some service members gain extremely valuable skills and training, which they can parlay into civilian employment. For others, military experience is less directly exchangeable in the civilian labor market. As a consequence, service may represent lost time for some service members during which their non-veteran peers accumulate valuable experience in the labor market (Hisrch and Mehay 2003; Teachman and Tedrow 2007).

Assignment into a military occupation is a complex process that incorporates enlistee preferences with military needs, and the relative weight of these two factors varies by historical context and national security needs. Military occupation is not randomly assigned, nor is it determined purely at the discretion of the military. Some occupational specialties require minimum scores on qualification tests, usually demanding higher levels of aptitude for noncombat arms specialties that have some of the highest degrees of transferability. Additionally, volunteers typically request particular occupational specialties and have some degree of input into what kind of occupational path they will pursue in the military. Although assignment to particular occupations may be largely determined by military needs under systems of conscription or during times of war (Gimbel and Booth 1996), in a volunteer force, recruit choice also plays a role. Unpacking how military occupational experience influences post-military labor market experiences is challenging because of the complexity in the process of matching military recruits to military jobs and variation in the transferability of military occupational experiences.

Relatively few studies address these issues. Magnum and Ball (1987, 1989) examined the transferability of military occupational experiences and found that roughly 50% of veterans were able to transfer their military training into civilian work. However, they also concluded that there is a need to better understand how military occupational experience conditions post-service employment and earnings. Bryant and Wilhite (1990) showed the importance of distinguishing the effects of military training from simple tenure in the military. They also found significant differences in the returns to military experience by service branch; Air Force veterans had the highest returns, whereas Army and Marine training did not offset the loss of experience relative to civilian peers. Past generations of veterans with experience in the combat arms may not have had many civilian alternatives upon

discharge, except perhaps law enforcement. In more recent years, the proliferation of private military contractors (such as Blackwater USA, now Xe,
Halliburton/KBR, L-3 MPRI, DynCorp, Titan Corp., and others) is likely
facilitating the transition out of the military for many veterans, and the
growth of this industry is aided by highly trained soldiers who bring their
skills to the market place (see Kelty and Segal, Chapter 2 of this volume).

Wartime and Combat Exposure

Not all who serve in the military do so during a time of war, and not all
wartime veterans experience combat. Historical context certainly shapes the
risks involved in military service; those who volunteer or are called to fight
wars face dramatically different risks to life and limb from those who serve
during peacetime (although the risks of military training are nontrivial). Even
during wartime, there have always been both frontline and support roles,
each with different levels of risk. Soldiers in the wars in Iraq and Afghanistan
are facing a blurring of the line between frontline and support roles.

As Gimbel and Booth (1996) demonstrated among Vietnam veterans,
not all who serve do so in a combat arms specialty, not all in combat specialties are assigned to combat zones, and not all assigned to combat zones
experience combat at the same levels. Exposure to combat is a multistage
process, with personal attributes influencing the risk of exposure at each
stage. Their findings suggest that those with lower measured aptitude for
complex noncombat positions were at greater risk of being assigned to combat arms jobs. Those exhibiting more aggressive behavior and good stress
management skills also had greater combat exposure. Thus, combat veterans were a heterogeneous group. Some had characteristics that both led
them into combat jobs and put them at risk of poor outcomes after military
service. Others, who had a more assertive temperament that was suited to
combat, may have had personal traits that allowed them to better navigate
and manage combat exposure and post-combat life.

Combat exposure appears to have long-lasting negative effects on health
and well-being, and possibly through them, on labor market outcomes
(MacLean and Elder 2007; see also MacLean, Chapter 10 of this volume).
However, some research has found positive consequences of combat. In particular, those veterans who found something positive in their combat experience, such as camaraderie or resiliency, had fewer post-traumatic stress
disorder (PTSD) symptoms and likely had an easier long-term adjustment to
civilian life (Elder and Clipp 1988a, 1989; MacLean and Elder 2007).

WHY DOES MILITARY SERVICE INFLUENCE LATER
WORK OUTCOMES? SOME PROPOSED MECHANISMS

The robust body of research examining the economic returns to military
service suggests several mechanisms that may generate differences in veteran

and non-veteran employment outcomes. These include selectivity, loss or gain in human capital, bridging, and signaling. These explanations mostly map onto the influences of history, biography, and military experience, but articulating the connections between empirical findings and proposed theoretical explanations highlights fruitful areas for further research. However, these perspectives engender indeterminate predictions; each can lead to an expectation of military service as an enhancement or hindrance to labor market success. Moreover, the ways that these mechanisms operate varies by length of service as well as race, and possibly by other factors also.

Military Service as Enhancement

The selectivity hypothesis posits that veterans appear advantaged in the civilian labor market because military enlistment standards result in a positive selection of military service members on characteristics that are valued by civilian employers. Personal biography and historical context help shape selection. Veterans may also gain an employment advantage from the specialized on-the-job training they receive, especially for highly technical specialties in electronics and communications (Angrist 1993; Mangum and Ball 1987, 1989). Veterans may gain other skills and experiences valued by civilian employers, including opportunities to engage in leadership and supervisory roles. These latter two mechanisms suggest the ways that military service may increase human capital among veterans.

Military service may actually alter individual ideology, work habits, and other attitudes and behaviors to make veterans more attractive to employers (Browning, Lopreato, and Poston 1973; Lopreato and Poston 1977; Xie 1992). This idea has been termed the "bridging hypothesis" because it suggests military service acts as a bridge between a disadvantaged background and a more advantaged social position. Consistent with the bridging hypothesis, military service may alter life-course trajectories by cutting individuals off from negative influences and exposing them to new, positive environments and social networks (Elder 1986; Laub and Sampson 1993; Sampson and Laub 1996). Since the 1990s, little research has investigated the role of military service in altering personal and social networks, although it is a potentially large and important mechanism linking military service and labor market success.

Military service exposes individuals to new sources of job networks through various personal ties and friendships, which can serve as the weak ties to information about employment opportunities that prior research indicates are critically important resources for job-seekers (Granovetter 1973). Furthermore, military personnel, civilian government employees, and civilian contractors are fully integrated and interact on a daily basis in the military. These interactions expose military persons to the kinds of civilian jobs that would utilize their expertise. The military also offers extensive career counseling as individuals leave the service. Many companies advertise for employment through these transition offices, which gives separating personnel privileged access to employment opportunities. Finally, military service typically involves moving away from home to different locales. For some, this geographic mobility may offer exposure to new sources of employment opportunities. For example, those enlisting from rural areas may gain exposure to the wide variety of work available in urban areas, and military service-related mobility may facilitate relocations to areas with more economic opportunities (see Bailey, Chapter 9 of this volume).

Prior military experience may serve as a signal to employers regarding the employability of an individual, offering a credential akin to a diploma (the "sheepskin effect") (de Tray 1982; Xie 1992). Evidence of an honorable discharge might signal to an employer something about an applicant's qualifications for employment that is not available for non-veteran applicants. If veterans are thought to be positively selected from the population, particularly the population segments comprising typical applicants for a given job, veterans may gain a hiring benefit from this credentialing. An honorable discharge provides information about what minimum standards an individual met during service in order to join the military and the minimum performance standards met to be honorably discharged. Such information is typically not available for non-veteran applicants, because most civilian firms do not have the military's formal and all-encompassing criteria for hiring. Some information about a non-veteran's performance might be signaled via letters of recommendation from prior employers; a favorable letter is, perhaps, akin to an honorable discharge. With some notable exceptions (Berger and Hirsch 1985; de Tray 1982; Savoca and Rosenheck 2000), most empirical studies have not explicitly evaluated the signaling perspective. However, this frame of reference highlights how veteran outcomes depend on societal and other institutional influences as much as on individual characteristics, because social actors receive and interpret the meaning of signaled information.

Military Service as Hindrance

Much research finds military service has a positive effect on later work life, but some studies find little or no evidence of a veteran premium in employment and/or earnings. This research suggests that military experiences may not translate well into civilian job experiences. Veterans may suffer in the civilian job market when their experiences do not have civilian equivalents, or if civilian employers do not understand how to evaluate prior military experience. Veterans may face disadvantages in hiring from the loss of human capital in the form of years of civilian work experience (Angrist 1998; Angrist and Krueger 1994; Bryant, Samaranayake, and Wilhite 1993; Bryant and Wilhite 1990). Veterans' training and skills in the military may have little corollary in the civilian world and their experience may not be relevant to civilian employers (Barley 1998). However, explanations for the veteran "penalty" that center on the transferability of military experience in the civilian labor market have not provided a clear test of how the nature of military work experience conditions the returns to military service in hiring or income. Analyzing a cohort of military veterans who left service in 1971, Goldberg and Warner (1987) showed that military experience equaled civilian experience only in selected occupational areas, such as medical fields and in electrical/mechanical repair. However, these results may be outdated given the restructuring of the economy and the military in the past thirty years.

Selectivity plays a major role in studies finding a labor market penalty for military service. If veterans (or some subpopulation of veterans) are actually *negatively* selected from the population, then they may in fact face disadvantages relative to their peers in searching for civilian employment (Angrist 1990; Berger and Hirsch 1983, 1985). Similarly, although signaling may partly explain a veteran premium, the same rationale can be used to explain a penalty for military service. Although some positive information may be conveyed to employers through the signal of veteran status, negative information may also be conveyed. In either case, employers use information on prior military service to evaluate applicants, but we know very little about the meaning they take from that information or how they use it to make hiring and pay decisions.

One specific piece of information about prior military service comes from the nature of the military discharge. Veterans with other-than-honorable discharges likely face challenges in finding civilian work. Any veteran with such a discharge would probably face a substantial penalty in seeking employment and would have to explain the circumstances leading to the discharge. In particular, this issue negatively impacts lesbian, gay, bisexual, and transgender veterans discharged under the Don't Ask, Don't Tell policy, as well as veterans discharged for homosexuality in other historical periods (see Brown, Chapter 5 of this volume). Furthermore, such other-than-honorable discharges limit access to some veterans' benefit programs, such as the GI Bill and retirement benefits (see Bennett and McDonald, Chapter 6 of this volume, and Street and Hoffman, Chapter 11 of this volume).

Studies that include substantial controls for selectivity, through the use of matching methods, instrumental variables, or fixed effects using sibling pairs often find that veterans earn less than their civilian peers for several years after service, but they eventually catch up. In the long run, they show no differences in relation to non-veterans. Thus, some of the concern about negative returns to service may be the result of focusing on a short follow-up period and not observing the employment and earnings trajectories of individuals over a long enough period of time (Teachman 2004).

Length of Military Service

Life-course trajectories differ based partly on whether interaction with institutions and social relations are stable (or transitory) and predictable (or unpredictable) (Dannefer and Kelley-Moore 2009). Those who spend a career in the military establish a stable, predictable work trajectory, which also provides a number of structural benefits. For career service members, the military is their labor market, and within this labor market, career trajectories are highly predictable and stable because the rules for pay and promotion do not change often. The majority of research on labor market outcomes among veterans emphasizes the experiences of the non-career veteran, who spends some period of time, typically four to eight years, in the military and then moves into civilian work. Few studies examine the labor market outcomes of military retirees, who are often too young to completely retire from work life, but whose twenty-plus years of military experience may limit civilian earnings because of the low degree of transferability of a military career (Danzon 1980; Goldberg and Warner 1987). Earlier research has found that military retirees entered the civilian market with lower earnings than their peers, but their earnings eventually caught up five to ten years after retirement from the military (Borjas and Welch 1986). More recently, Loughran (2002: 5) found that more recent military retirees have lower relative earnings than those from earlier cohorts, which indicates a "low level of relative wage growth for retirees over the course of their civilian careers." Wage growth among military retirees relative to civilians was estimated to be 2 to 5%, which is a much lower figure than previous research suggested. The generous military pension was designed to counteract any negative consequences related to spending a career in military service, and it does serve as a financial buffer that allows some retirees to pursue second careers of interest at lower pay. It also allows retirees to work less than their peers, which may account for much of the earnings differential between military retirees and civilians (Cooper 1981). Furthermore, there are numerous nonfinancial benefits available to those who retire after twenty or more years of service, including generous health care benefits (see Street and Hoffman, Chapter 11 of this volume).

Variation by Race and Ethnicity

The value of prior military service in the civilian labor market may also differ by race and ethnicity. Racial-ethnic minorities serve in the military at higher rates than Whites (see Lutz, Chapter 4 of this volume), which suggests that military service offers an alternate source of stable employment to those who are often disadvantaged in the civilian labor market (Department of Defense 2006; Moskos and Butler 1996). Some research has found that racial-ethnic minority veterans, on average, have higher rates of employment and earnings compared with their non-veteran peers (Angrist 1998; Bryant, Samaranayake, and Wilhite 1993; Phillips et al. 1992; Seeborg 1994; Teachman and Call 1996). These same results have not been found for White military veterans, who have been shown to face disadvantages relative to their civilian peers in earnings. Blacks may show positive returns to military service because the military positively selects Blacks on characteristics that would make them more employable as civilians (Mare and

Winship 1984). A similar selectivity explanation suggests that employers may understand that racial-ethnic minority veterans may be more selective than their non-veteran peers and treat them differently than non-veterans in hiring and wage-setting. Racial-ethnic minority veterans may also be preferred by employers who feel that military service actually alters the attitudes, skills, and behaviors of those who serve. If such personal changes are perceived to be more advantageous for racial-ethnic minorities, then employers may also exhibit preferential treatment for veterans. Little to no research to date has focused attention on the perceptions and behaviors of employers that influence observed patterns of veteran employment.

RESEARCH ON MILITARY SPOUSE
LABOR MARKET OUTCOMES

The evolution of the contemporary All-Volunteer Force has led to an increase in the number of service members who are married (Segal and Segal 2004). At the same time, women's participation in the paid labor force has been growing. The combination of these two trends has led to increased attention to the labor market outcomes of military spouses. Mostly, this research has focused on wives (see Cooke and Speirs 2005 for a notable exception). Although this research is beginning to tell us a great deal about employment outcomes among military spouses, much less is known about the long-term trajectories of those whose careers have been linked to military service by marriage.

The life-course perspective, with its emphasis on linked lives and social ties, is well suited as an organizing framework for understanding the labor market trajectories and outcomes of military spouses. Spouses are not merely two individuals living in close proximity (in fact, military personnel often live apart from their spouses for extended periods of time), but they constitute a unit in which decisions are made jointly that have consequences for all members of a family (Elder and Caspi 1990). The nature of military life often puts military spouses in a position to exert little power in making family decisions. Their life courses are partly dictated by the needs and demands of the military, and the limitations of military life often constrain labor market opportunities for military spouses. As civilian society shifts to increasing female participation in the workforce and expansion of dual-career households, military spouses (typically wives but increasingly husbands) face a context in which their careers are always secondary to their spouses' military careers. Civilian spouses may still face gendered norms and expectations, but they are increasingly able to jointly make work decisions that they consider best for the family as a whole (Drobnic and Blossfeld 2004). Military spouses have much less power to play an equal role in such decisions. One exception may be military spouses who are also in the armed forces. There is an increasing number of dual-military career couples, but very little is known about how they jointly make career-related decisions or how being a dual-military career couple affects relative earnings during and after military service (however, see Smith 2010 for a notable exception). The research to date has almost exclusively focused on military spouses who are seeking employment in the civilian labor market.

Compared with the volume of research on veterans' labor force outcomes, there has been limited research on military spouses, especially on the consequences of their spouses' service for their work lives. The available evidence is remarkably consistent in finding that the majority of military spouses are employed, although they have difficulty finding jobs; employment is correlated with satisfaction with a military lifestyle although military spouses have lower wages and work fewer hours than comparable civilian peers (Bourg 2003; Cooke and Speirs 2005; Grossman 1981; Harrell et al. 2004; Hosek et al. 2002; Payne, Warner, and Little 1992; Schwartz, Wood, and Griffith 1991; Wardynski 2000).

EXPLANATIONS FOR MILITARY SPOUSE OUTCOMES

Prior research documents lower labor force participation, fewer hours worked, and reduced earnings among military spouses, typically the wives of active-duty military personnel (Cooke and Speirs 2005; Gill and Haurin 1998; Grossman 1981; Hosek et al. 2002; Payne, Warner, and Little 1992; Schwartz, Wood, and Griffith 1991; Wardynski 2000). Scholars have documented different patterns of employment and earnings among military wives and civilian women, and this literature is beginning to tackle questions about why these differences arise. In their primarily quantitative analysis, Hosek, Offner, and Sorensen (2005) offered several explanations to account for military spouses' lower earnings. Military spouses are almost invariably "tied migrants," whose moves are dictated by the other spouse (see Bailey, Chapter 9 of this volume), whereas civilian peers may move only when it is advantageous for their employment or earnings. Military bases are often in locales with limited employment opportunities (Booth 2003; Booth, Falk, Segal, and Segal 2000). Employers may not invest in military spouse employees because they are perceived to be migratory. Frequent moves may imply military spouses do not spend as long as their peers searching for ideal employment, and they may settle for lower-paying, less desirable work early on (i.e., in the economists parlance, they may develop lower reservation wages). Alternatively, military spouses may be self-selected and have different "tastes" for work that result in lower wages, hours worked, and labor force participation. That is, knowing that military life holds such challenges, civilian women who marry military men may prefer a more "traditional" lifestyle, with a male breadwinner and a female homemaker.

Military benefits may disincentivize work; housing and basic needs are provided to service members and their families, and the availability of military medical facilities may incentivize childbearing over paid employment. Some spouses are expected to perform social duties and volunteer work for the military community, restricting their availability for paid employment (Segal 1986). Spouses of recent active-duty personnel have also faced unprecedented levels of deployment, which often leaves them home alone with children and likely exacts a toll on their availability for paid employment (Angrist and Johnson 2000).

Finally, women in military families tend to get married and have children younger than their civilian peers (Lundquist and Smith 2005). Lundquist and Smith (2005) suggest that this is due in part to the family-friendly policies and benefits developed to support a volunteer military. The higher and earlier fertility patterns among military spouses are likely to further constrain their opportunities to pursue work and schooling. These demographic barriers are complicated by the current military operating environment. Repeated and lengthy deployments also contribute to reduced work and pay among military spouses, and the effects are most negative for families with a child under 6 years of age (Savych 2008). Spouses tend to reduce work hours before, during, and after deployments. With many soldiers facing a fourth and sometimes fifth year-long tour of duty, the cumulative labor market disadvantage for spouses is likely to be substantial.

SETTING A NEW RESEARCH AGENDA ON MILITARY SERVICE AND LABOR MARKET OUTCOMES

Veterans

Because of the constantly changing context in which individuals serve in the military, we need ongoing descriptive portraits of how veterans fare once they leave military service. We need analyses that move beyond the snapshot-in-time approach and provide richer longitudinal portraits of the post-service trajectory in employment and earnings. Teachman's body of research (Teachman 2004, 2005; Teachman and Tedrow 2004, 2007), which analyzes trajectories of veteran outcomes across several cohorts who served during different historical periods, serves as a good example of a research program that takes variation across period and cohort seriously in the study of the long-term consequences of military service. Current research focusing on the later-life consequences of military service among older populations (Settersten 2006; Wing et al. 2009) illustrates that there are both durable and transitory impacts of military service on the life course.

Much like the call for sociological research to better articulate and examine mechanisms generating inequality (Reskin 2003), we need much more research that investigates the mechanisms behind observed differences between veterans and non-veterans in employment, earnings, and occupational trajectories. We need sharper tests of the various theoretical perspectives long offered in the literature and more detailed studies to narrow in on specific causal mechanisms undergirding variation in outcomes by veteran status. This focus can also advance scholarship outside narrow substantive questions about military service. Sharper tests of potential mechanisms inform our understandings about how and why military service affects peoples' lives, help us craft better and more effective policies for veterans, and contribute to more general social scientific theories to the extent that the military is similar to other institutions (e.g., schools, prisons) that engage people early in the life course and generate or mitigate life-course inequality.

As highlighted earlier, one area of inquiry likely to produce insights is a shift in the scholarly gaze to the role of employer behaviors and perceptions in producing observed veteran/non-veteran differences in employment and earnings. There is an apparent disconnect between some theoretical perspectives offered to explain veterans' outcomes and the empirical evidence on questions about the "returns to service." In particular, limited empirical evidence directly evaluates the "signaling" hypothesis. Some recent research has attempted to fill this void. Below, I discuss some of the findings from this line of inquiry.

Because employers make hiring and pay decisions based partly on prior military experience, they are essential to understanding the returns to military service. Recent scholarship focuses on one aspect of the transition from military to civilian employment, namely the way employers evaluate resumes from equally qualified job seekers who vary in terms of their military experience.

Evidence of military service may indicate to employers an applicant's interpersonal skills, motivation, discipline, and work ethic, as these skills are crucial for success in the disciplined and hierarchical structure of the military. In an era in which these kinds of soft skills are highly valued (Moss and Tilly 1996), signals of such skills may result in preferential hiring by employers. Yet prior research on the returns to service is poorly equipped to identify how employer treatment contributes to observed differences in the labor market outcomes of veterans and non-veterans.

In two recent studies, Kleykamp (2009a,b) uses an experimental approach, employing an audit of hiring practices in two labor markets. In these studies, fictitious job seekers are used to assess how employers respond to two or more equally qualified job applicants. Characteristics of interest to the study are varied—in this case, one applicant has recently served in the military, whereas the other applicant has similar experience in civilian settings. Two studies have been conducted; one in New York City tested employer treatment of male job seekers, and one in a large Midwestern metropolitan area tested responses to female job seekers.

In New York City, when faced with comparable male applicants, employers tended to treat veterans and non-veterans similarly only when the veteran had work experience that was highly transferable to the civilian market. In contrast, veterans who had served in the combat arms generated little interest among civilian employers advertising openings. Race played a moderating role; among veterans with transferable skills, Black veterans generated the most employer interest, whereas Black veterans without transferable skills generated *no* employer interest. Specifically, after sending in 131 resumes, not a single employer called back the Black veteran presenting experience in the armor branch (Kleykamp 2009a).

A more recent study replicated this approach in a large Midwestern metropolitan area with a few key differences in study design, most notably by using female rather than male veterans (Kleykamp 2009b). This study also used matched triplets, rather than pairs, with triplets differing on military experience (one veteran, two non-veterans) and educational attainment (with the veteran and one civilian having only a high school diploma and one civilian being a recent college graduate), but not military occupation. Tests were conducted for both White and Black "teams." The results suggest a hierarchy of employer preference for female job seekers, with military veterans at the top, high school graduates following, and recent college graduates at the bottom. Because these were entry-level jobs that did not require a college degree, we suspect employers may be hesitant about hiring recent college graduates, who may be perceived as overqualified for the modal job tested, but this remains an empirical question. Pairwise contrasts suggest only the military-college contrast was statistically significant at traditional levels (p < 0.05) for both the Black and White teams.

The experimental approach used in these two studies complements prior empirical work because it can identify the causal effect of military experience as a signal to employers. Hiring audits show how employers behave in response to a signal, but can't tell us what employers think the signal means. More research on key actors, including employers actively engaged in hiring employees, would be useful in understanding *why* veteran/non-veteran differences exist and persist over time.

Although recent scholarship has sought to specifically test the utility of the "military service as signal" perspective in explaining veteran advantages and disadvantages in hiring, these studies are not without problems. Notably, they lack generalizability. Experiments are limited in their scope, and in-depth interviews only provide information from relatively small samples. However, existing data collection efforts at the organization level might fruitfully incorporate a few select questions related to veterans or military experience among their workforce.

Employers play a key role in the initial transition from soldier to worker, but so too do veterans themselves. To complement research focusing on employer attitudes and behaviors, research on veterans' labor market outcomes must delve deeper to understand what soon-to-be and recent veterans do in the job search process. The veteran's job search strategy is a micro-level research site likely to generate important insights about why veterans experience the outcomes they do. We have little empirical evidence about the structural impediments to gaining a civilian job, such as access to job information in desired relocation areas or the ways in which veterans present themselves as job candidates. We know little about the expectations veterans have, realistic or perhaps inflated, for their own civilian employment. We know earlier cohorts of veterans faced longer job search times than their peers (Mare, Winship, and Kubitschek 1984); this may stem partly from veterans having to readjust and level their expectations about their first post-military employment. The evidence from employer audit studies, although tentative, suggests a possible hiring advantage for veterans. If true, unemployment among veterans cannot simply be attributed to employer discrimination or bias. We should look further at employer "demand" for veterans, but also at the "supply" influences of veterans seeking civilian work. Such studies might include systematic evaluations of career transition services and programs in the various branches. They could also include more detail from military exit surveys to capture information on the job search process and the employment expectations of soon-to-be veterans and then follow people through the military-to-civilian transition.

The increase in educational benefits in the new GI Bill provides an opportunity to reinvigorate detailed studies of how post-service education influences later employment outcomes. Again, this effort would involve in-depth and longitudinal data collection on veterans' use of educational benefits, as well as documenting the consequences of not utilizing rightfully earned benefits. This is particularly salient given that utilization rates are surprisingly low.

A key theoretical explanation for the "returns" to military service relates to the social capital building function of military service. Service may connect individuals from different parts of the country, with different past experiences, by offering access to new social networks. Knowing how important social networks are in finding work, especially the role of "weak ties," future research should examine how military service alters social networks and whether the network connections developed during service offer benefits in seeking work. Is there meaningful social contact that helps facilitate professional networks upon leaving the military? These networks may connect veterans to nonmilitary places of work, as well as to military contractors (because they increasingly work side-by-side with service personnel).

Finally, the current context of military service differs in important ways for this generation of veterans. Unlike prior cohorts, today's veterans are all volunteers; unlike the early veterans of the All-Volunteer Force, today's veterans have served during wartime. Substantial numbers have endured deployments and been exposed to combat. In addition to differences in the personal experiences of military service, the societal context of reception of veterans differs from that of earlier wars in ways that are not well understood. Because employers and the public at large play an important, often invisible, role in the transition between military and civilian life, future research should be attentive to the ways that the context of service and the context of reception for veterans influence their life-course trajectories.

Spouses

Nearly all of the research approaches introduced for veterans apply, perhaps in slightly altered form, to research on military spouses. The "just the facts" analyses of how veterans' employment and earnings differ from their civilian peers have and will continue to offer insights into what it is that needs to be explained. However, there are comparatively fewer studies documenting the differences between military and civilian spouses' employment and earnings. Some of the key insights about the role of military service among racial-ethnic minorities could be replicated with an eye toward whether similar "bridging" processes translate to the experiences of spouses. We know little to nothing about the long-term consequences of being a "trailing spouse." Important questions remain about whether and to what extent the damage to military spouse employment is compensated over time, as appears to be the case with veterans, or whether the negative effects keep military spouse earnings below those of their peers during a lifetime. Spouses might offer another area in which to test the transformative influence of military life on a host of outcomes. For example, does the "bridging hypothesis" hold among military spouses? Scholars using the military population as a kind of natural experiment (e.g., Lundquist and Smith 2005) are capitalizing on the institutional features of military life to examine broader questions of interest to social scientists. In this way, military spouses might offer another kind of natural experiment for creative researchers.

Prior research has demonstrated the key role selection into the military plays in the analysis of post-military outcomes. Yet we know little about the selection process into a "military" marriage. Do those individuals who choose to be in relationships with military members differ along important lines (e.g., more traditional orientation) that may influence later work outcomes? On the structural side, how does the selectivity of duty locations influence outcomes? Spouses have little control over where they live, and the institution selects for them a duty station based on the service member's occupation, rank, and unit. More research using longitudinal data is needed to understand how poor labor markets around many military installations set employment contexts, how much discrimination there may be against military spouses (who are perceived by employers to be temporary workers), and how much service-related migration disrupts occupational and earnings trajectories.

Finally, research in this area may benefit by incorporating insights from a "household economics" perspective into the study of retention and spouse employment. Although economic theory *assumes* couples make decisions based on joint well-being, it would be useful to explicitly evaluate the extent to which reality matches theoretical assumptions and heuristics. Economic models assume true market conditions in which individuals are free to act as they decide. Yet the nature of military service that subjects members, and thus their families, to state mandates complicates the application of free-market theories. A household-economics perspective in tandem with the life-course concept of linked lives recognizes the centrality of spouse employment considerations in making joint decisions about household economic well-being, including retention in the military and in the marriage. Do couples consider both spouse and service member labor market outcomes jointly in making decisions about staying in or leaving the military? If the trajectories of military spouses remain flat and below their peers, there may in fact be an accumulation of disadvantage whereby spouses' labor market opportunities continue to erode, further limiting their bargaining power within the marriage. How might the negative effect of military service on spouse outcomes disadvantage spouses in influencing these decisions? To what extent do these processes differ among spouses when both serve in the armed forces? On the one hand, both service members face constraints related to finding key jobs co-located in the same area, but dual-military couples have the benefit of being members of an institution with a vested interest in retaining both members of a couple, unlike dual-career spouses in different industries or occupations.

Key Role of Data

A common theme underlying these challenges to researchers is the need for more and better data. The call for data is often the first and loudest cry from researchers, but it is also the one least likely to be taken up. Key improvements in data collection in large-scale national surveys, a greater openness of Department of Defense data management, particularly the Defense Manpower Data Center (DMDC), to working with researchers interested in military studies, and more focused in-depth qualitative studies would go far toward addressing some of the suggestions offered above. Current nationally representative data ask only limited questions about military service, with few indicators of the timing of that service, the length of service, and the nature of the experience. The inclusion of a few additional questions, especially on the occupational specialty during service, would aid researchers seeking to unpack how military service alters human capital development through employment.

8 The Best Years of Our Lives
Military Service and Family Relationships—A Life-Course Perspective

Daniel Burland and Jennifer Hickes Lundquist

Our title makes reference to the classic 1946 film, a dramatization of veteran families, life course, and historical moment. The film demonstrates a persistent tendency of popular culture to view veteran readjustment as a social problem, and to view veterans and their families as a vulnerable population. The historical moment of the film is the massive demobilization that followed World War II. It focuses on the return of three veterans to the same hometown. Family ties, old and new, ultimately save them from various self-destructive tendencies, such as self-pity, escapism, and hopelessness.

The pairing of this problem (homecoming) with its "natural" solution (family) was prefigured in Sociology. Willard W. Waller's *The Veteran Comes Back* (1944) was a contemporary best-seller, warning that veterans who were not carefully reintegrated into society might become a threat to it. Waller's advocacy emphasized the reintegration of the veteran into the stabilizing institution of the family. *The Best Years of Our Lives* (1946, William Wyler, director) echoes Waller by holding up the family as the institution most capable of facilitating the veteran's return to civilian society. As we discuss in greater detail below, the "protagonist" in the film is actually a representative cross-section of "normal" (i.e. White and male) returning veterans, and is thus reminiscent of the social science of the day. Waller and Wyler seemingly concurred: the returning veteran is a problem, and the veteran's family is the solution. Waller believed that no effort should be spared in reintegrating the veteran back into the stable and stabilizing institution of family. Our intent is to understand not only this process of homecoming, but the possibly more current and relevant issue of how military *families* as a whole are "reintegrated" back into society.

We use the phrase "veteran family" to refer to any family that includes at least one member who has served in the armed forces. We readily acknowledge the diversity of ethnicities, orientations, socioeconomic backgrounds, and family structures encompassed by the word "family." We also acknowledge the immense breadth of experiences that all count as "service in the military." Furthermore, we realize the fundamental differences among families formed before, during, or after the qualifying member's military service. We thus concede from the outset that there is no such thing as a "veteran family," just as there can be no monolithic "military family" or "civilian family." Yet we maintain that there are consistent and significant trends among veteran families that signal the importance of designating the veteran family as a subfield of study in its own right.

Despite the small body of literature on families associated with the military, our analysis of the field uncovers several preliminary themes that we will detail in greater depth later in this chapter. We conclude that the projected long-term impact of military service on families is generally positive, particularly for ethnic families who might otherwise have had less access to socioeconomic opportunity. We further note that any such advantage of military service for families may operate more strongly for children than for spouses. This has varied by era, nature of service, and degree of familial exposure to service, of course, but can generally be said to be true. The one major exception to this truth is the more rare case of combat exposure. Combat veterans experience significantly negative impacts on long-term well-being that reverberate through the family life course (see MacLean, Chapter 10 of this volume).

A review of the literature makes it clear that, in terms of familial impacts, there are two primary types of military families: those who "do time" in the military alongside the soldier and thus are themselves embedded in the institutional context for some amount of time and those who form afterward, experiencing the military vicariously through the veteran family member. Our review points to the importance of considering the veteran family through the experience of children, who, as actors in the early developmental stages of the life course, may be the most likely to embody the long-term influence of the military-industrial apparatus. But ultimately our chapter raises more questions than can be currently answered about veteran families, pointing to the largely unexplored field of life-course Sociology.

Although one of the chief tasks of this chapter is to analyze the work that has been done so far in this area, we do not provide a traditional literature review. A traditional approach might consist of two parts: a survey and analysis of the extant literature and suggestions for further study. The nature of the concept "veteran family," its vastness and fluidity, combined with the fact that relatively few scholars have chosen to specialize in the study of this substantive field, puts a limit on the utility of such a traditional approach. In a word, there is a regrettable mismatch between resources and task that has resulted in the field not being covered in any way approaching its entirety. It is a substantive field that exists at the intersection of Military Sociology, a famously understaffed specialty within Sociology, and Sociology of Families, a subfield so large and influential within the discipline that it determines in large part what Sociology means in the public imagination. "Sociology of Families," by whatever name, is a staple course offering of most Sociology departments. In contrast, "Military Sociology" is clearly only a specialty course. It is a lopsided Venn diagram that connects the two, and there are relatively few scholars who have chosen to make a career in the narrow connective space that joins a niche specialty to its larger counterpart. Moreover, among scholars of military families, fewer still specialize in veteran families.

It is in acknowledgment of both the substantive and institutional peculiarities of the field that we undertake a literature review of a less traditional nature, in two parts. First, we ask what the field would look like if it were thoroughly covered. In this section, we propose a taxonomy that identifies all the potential areas for study within the subfield of veteran families. How vast is the field? What are its logical parameters? In part two, we ask what the scholarly subfield actually does look like. Where has the scholarly attention been focused so far? Starting from the principle that analysis always points both ways, we ask what the mismatch between the potential area for study of veteran families, on the one hand, and the area that has so far been studied, on the other, tells us both about the substantive field and about the logic and ethical principles that have underpinned Sociology's approach to the subject.

THE BASIC PARAMETERS OF THE SUBSTANTIVE FIELD

Temporal Connection

The key variable tested by *The Best Years of Our Lives* is that of the moment of family inception relative to the period of service of the qualifying member of the veteran family: one veteran is married before the war; the next, during; and the third, after. Although the film addresses the professional, psychological, and even physical difficulties of homecoming, its emphasis is on family. The film is sophisticated in that it takes into account class differences between veterans, but it is mainly concerned with how the veteran's family is connected to the military through the veteran. The depth of this connection is measured in a way that will be familiar to any sociologist concerned with the life-course concept of sequencing (Call and Teachman 1996; Rindfuss, Swicegood, and Rosenfeld 1987). What, the film asks, did military service replace in the life of the veteran? Is the veteran returning home to children who now scarcely recognize him? Did the veteran spend his marrying years in the service? The veterans are returning from war to civilian life, but also to family life. The "common sense" assumption is that military service is a disruption in the lives of service members that negatively affects their family ties.

By definition, all veterans were once uniformed service members; similarly, many veteran families were once military families. What happens to a veteran is influenced by what happened to that veteran when he or she was still in uniform. Did the veteran experience combat? Was he or she deployed? Did he or she sustain wounds? Did these wounds result in permanent damage requiring continued medical care? It makes sense to think of veteran families in a similar way, as ex-military families. The military subjects its dependent families to particularly strong pressures, both planned and unplanned. A partial list of such pressures includes defining and regulating the family through the imposition and enforcement of socially conservative family law; protecting and providing for this family through a generous social welfare system that includes such substantial benefits as access to Department of Defense schools, tax-free housing and food subsidies, and free health care; excluding nonnormative families entirely both from regulation (apart from prohibiting outright the existence of such families in most historical periods) and from the system of benefits offered to married heterosexual couples and their children; and moving families on average every three years (Segal and Segal 2004). Obviously, such pressures will shape both family structure and family dynamics.

After adapting to the intrusive regulation and generous (but contingent) provisions of the military, how does a family reintegrate into civilian society after the benefits and regulation suddenly cease? This process of adaptation and subsequent reintegration, however difficult, is to be expected, but an important minority of veteran families will experience trauma on a greater scale. This trauma might consist of the disability or death of the service member, an event that usually entails, among other things, receipt of sustained and contingent benefits from the Department of Defense or its proxy, the Department of Veterans Affairs. A veteran family is often created by the demilitarization of a military family, but this demilitarization is rarely total.

Variation by Type of Military Service

Not all military service is alike. It varies along many dimensions, including longevity, branch, rank, function, activity, location, and volition. It is not our intention to perform a survey of the military population here. It has been done expertly elsewhere (Segal and Segal 2004). It is perhaps enough to note in passing that the demands that might be placed upon service members vary immensely according to the qualities of the incoming recruit, the contractual obligation of the enlistment, historical moment, and dumb luck. A term of service might be relatively uneventful or characterized by repeated deployments to a war or to various wars. Officers and enlisted personnel perform radically different roles, often side-by-side. The military is large enough to need both scout-snipers and dental hygienists, but even individuals within the same occupational specialty can have profoundly different experiences, depending on other factors. Thus, the returning veteran brings to the family a complex mix of positive and negative experiences accrued during military service, and the contents of this package of good and bad will vary dramatically according to the nature of the service of that veteran.

Volition as a characteristic of military service is worthy of special mention. Not all soldiers are volunteers. Sometimes, this is quite obvious; in the 20th century, conscription was in effect during World Wars I and II, as well as from 1948 to 1973. However, selective implementation, exemptions granted, outright fraud, "volunteering" in anticipation of being drafted, and even genuine volunteering altered the application of this supposedly simple "blanket" policy in practice. Arguably, the role of volition in filling the ranks of the military has become more, rather than less, complicated since the end of "universal" conscription. In the course of the wars in Iraq and Afghanistan, we have witnessed the mobilization of the Reserves, the implementation of both targeted and more generalized "stop-loss" policies, involuntary Individual Ready Reserve recalls, and holds on retirements. Certainly, new enlistees agree to be subject to these emergency policies; this agreement is a standard part of a service contract. Yet it is undeniable that veterans recalled to duty after already having served a complete term of active-duty service probably return for this additional term with less willingness than they initially brought to the military. The high rate of Individual Ready Reserve recall no-shows attests to this fact. The importance of volition for veteran families is its paramount significance to the frequency, duration, and often the *meaning* of the separation of the service member from his or her family.

To emphasize this point, we call attention to the fact that the standing military of the United States has never been enough by itself to wage prolonged, major war. In times of war, it makes claims on the civilian or near-civilian population (see Kelty and Segal, Chapter 2 of this volume). It is augmented by conscription, involuntary retention or recall of active-duty soldiers, activation of the Guard or Reserves, or some combination of these three means. It is well known that the military expanded by the use of conscription during the Vietnam War, leaving the Reserves and the Guard stateside. In this way, the military was able to make full use of its historically preferred demographic: young adult males. The military reached these men early in the life course, usually before marriage, and, as a result, the postwar divorce rate among Vietnam veterans is lower than among their older (and thus more likely to be married) World War II counterparts (Pavalko and Elder 1990). Conscription was, of course, used extensively during World War II as well, but the high military participation rate during this conflict required the military to draft from an older, less desirable segment of the civilian population, many of whom had already established families. The military is currently making extensive use of its Guard and Reserve components. It remains to be seen how this use will affect the families of these reservists, who are, on average, older than their active-duty counterparts and, accordingly, more heavily invested in an ongoing civilian life course. The military is designed to accommodate deployments as career milestones, not as interruptions; however, the civilian world can be unforgiving of an unplanned and open-ended career interruption. From a life-course perspective, such disruption can have long-term consequences (Elder, Shanahan, and Clipp 1994). How is the traditionally optimal life-course sequence of education, entry into the labor force, and subsequent marriage (Call and Teachman 1991; Hogan 1978) disrupted for these part-time soldiers and their existing or potential families when "one weekend a month" becomes an eighteen-month deployment?

Variation by Demographic Profile

Families, whether civilian, military, or veteran, vary by race, class, ethnicity, geographical origin, marital status, and sexual orientation. Moreover, women's experiences in families often differ dramatically from those of men, and, as Campbell (Chapter 3 of this volume) has shown, women's experiences in military families are important to consider in their own right, as are women's own increasingly common experiences of military service. In all areas of life, outcomes correlate significantly, though not perfectly, with demographic characteristics. The study of veteran families is in large part the study of outcomes, so it follows that our interest in diversity is abiding. We do not find it necessary to survey the diversity of the military in this chapter, mostly because it has received thorough treatment elsewhere in this volume (see the chapters in this volume by Kelty and Segal, Campbell, Lutz, Brown, Bennett and McDonald). Yet there are two salient points to be made about diversity in the context of military families. First, the military is not a cross-section of society. It is overwhelmingly male. Nor are race, ethnicity, regional origin, and class proportionally represented relative to the civilian population. Moreover, the nature of this mismatch has not been constant over time. Desegregation (1948), the end of conscription (1973), and the admittance of women to the service academies (1976) are among the main policy changes that have affected the demographics of the military radically. Simply put, the military used to be much whiter and much more male, and not so long ago either.

The three heroes of *The Best Years of Our Lives* are all heterosexual White males. The director and writers of the film presumably wanted to show "average" soldiers (though from a variety of class backgrounds). Before 1948, the average soldier was heterosexual, White, and male. The military was separated into "colored" (African American) and racially unmarked units, although as Lutz (Chapter 4 of this volume) notes, there were also units composed exclusively of Puerto Ricans and Filipinos. Women service members also served by law in a distinct, second-class, auxiliary military. It might be argued that the White male soldier remains the "normal" soldier today (for example, see Kirby et al. 2000 and Gifford 2005a), not by law, but perhaps by *habitus*. However, the fact remains that official racial segregation has been dismantled and that the demographics of the military have altered accordingly. This occasionally puts us in a difficult position. For the most part, initial life-course research was focused on "normal soldiers" (i.e. White, male) who participated in American wars during the first half of the 20th century. This is not racism or, more accurately, it is a reflection of racism before the fact, because it was inescapably true that typical soldiers were White and male, according to the customs of the time and by law, as noted above. In addition, sociologists who have carried out secondary analyses were often confronted by the invisibility of demographically "marked" service members in available datasets. The historical comparison that a commitment to continuity demands is complicated by the fact that a "normal" soldier and his or her family of today is ever more dissimilar demographically from a "normal" soldier and his or her family of 1945.

Types of Lasting Effects of Military Service on Families

"We take care of our own," and "The needs of the Army [or Navy, etc.]": service members come to expect one or the other of these terms to be used by leadership whenever major policy decisions are announced and explained to the rank and file. Like many banal-sounding military clichés, they are in fact both rich in meaning and powerful in effect. They represent two life-transforming logics in the lives of the service member, subsequent veteran, and the family of that veteran. The military does take "care of its own," providing medical care, life insurance, steady pay, housing, food, and regular promotion to its constituency. Some (but not all) veteran families continue to be "taken care of" by the military even after the qualifying member of the service has been discharged. Benefits provided by the Department of Veterans Affairs include home loans, the GI Bill, retirement pensions, vocational rehabilitation, disability pensions, medical care for service-related chronic health problems, and survivor's benefits. Similarly, "the needs of the Army" can weigh heavily on a family long after the formal term of service of the qualifying member has come to an end. Disability and mutilation; long-term health problems caused by exposure to radiation, carcinogenic chemicals, and experimental vaccines; post-traumatic stress disorder (PTSD) and depression can all shape and even dominate the family structure, spousal obligations, and life of a veteran.

"We take care of our own" and "The needs of the Army [or Navy, etc.]" represent the binary logic of the military "total institution": the one ends only where the other begins. It is certain that not all families experience the best of what the military has to offer. It is equally certain that not all families experience the worst effects of war and military service. The benefits received and harm endured by a military family during its term of service shape the subsequent reality of that family in the civilian world. A military family that is greatly harmed in the course of service (for example, through the death or disability of a family member) is likely to remain connected to the military (as the military comforts and compensates the aggrieved family). This family is thus less likely to reintegrate fully into civilian society. Conversely, a military family that experiences an uneventful term of service is likely to be more empowered to make a clean break with its military past or to exercise more agency with regard to how members take up benefits and continue to interact with the military through the Department of Veterans Affairs.

The preceding discussion suggests that the study of "veteran families" might differ fundamentally from that of "military families" in two ways. First, there is a larger temporal perspective built into the study of the former: veteran families have potentially existed through multiple periods of a service member's life and through major changes in it. Second, the military by necessity acts forcefully in shaping, controlling, and (some might add) protecting its constituent families. As a result, all military families are deeply affected by the fact of being military. In contrast, not all veteran families are affected by the fact of having once been connected to the military. Some veteran families form after the veteran has already separated from the service. In such a case, only the veteran (and not the family he or she joins) will undergo a demilitarization process. Some families that do form during the course of the service of the qualifying service member might emerge from the military relatively unscathed, and the military past of the family might survive only as a fond memory. Yet some families suffer greatly for having been connected to the military, no matter how distantly, and thereafter remain subject in part to its controls by virtue of being obliged to engage with its powerful long-term presence vis-à-vis a demanding compensatory apparatus or through lasting emotional or physical effects. The study of veteran families is in large part the study of how and why families remain connected to the military experience after the service member's formal separation.

THE STATE OF THE FIELD AND FUTURE RESEARCH DIRECTIONS

The literature on military and family focuses almost exclusively on current families in the military, not on veteran families, whereas the existing veteran life-course literature is focused mostly on individuals, not on families. Nevertheless, the outcomes studied in both of these bodies of research have implications for veteran families even if they are not necessarily addressed by the authors. In the foregoing section, we review relevant themes from these two separate literatures and assess what, if applied to veteran families, they might predict for long-term family outcomes. We also point to the areas where more research is needed.

Temporal Connection and Family Formation

Current military families are more directly impacted by military service in the All-Volunteer Force than in previous eras. Prior to the era of the All-Volunteer Force, the average soldier was young, unmarried, and served for a short term. Hence, there was an old adage: "if the Army wanted you to have a wife it would have issued you one." In this context, the most common impact of the military on family was indirect, working through the veteran on family members who came into the picture *after* discharge. Today, the majority of the active-duty force is married (Military Family Resource Center 2000). Marriage is more prevalent and occurs at earlier life stages for military members than for civilian members (Lundquist 2004; Teachman 2007b). In addition, half of service members have become parents, a transition that most likely took place during the first term of service (Burland and Lundquist 2009). This is because members are staying in the military longer than in the past and also because military members tend to get married and have children younger than in civilian society (Lundquist and Smith 2005). Early marriage is consequential for long-term marital stability and family stress (Amato 2010; Booth and Edwards 1985). Families that are formed early in adulthood have higher rates of internal conflict and eventual dissolution. Understanding whether this relationship holds for veteran families by tracking their stability over time is an important question, because unlike other young civilians who marry or have children early, veterans often have comparatively higher socioeconomic status and access to a range of benefits.

There is also evidence that overall completed family size is larger in the military than the national average (Military Family Resource Center 2000). In fact, the All-Volunteer Force military population of dependents and spouses is increasingly dwarfing the population of soldiers in the military. As a result, more research is needed on the processes by which military spouses and dependent children are increasingly "doing time in the service" and what this means for their lives in the long term (see Bailey, Chapter 9 of this volume). Research by Moody (2005) begins with the reasonable premise that the social costs of war are borne by a network that begins with the combatant, extends to the combatant's family, and then expands further to the family's close connections. How these costs are diffused remains an unanswered question, but what seems certain is that the military family is the best first place to look for any porousness in the border between the military and civilian worlds. To the extent that military and civilian lives are linked, this linkage is most evident in the active-duty military family, although it remains in the veteran family as well. Studies suggest that the timing of the creation of this family-military linkage results in either harm or benefit to individual families in a patterned way. The evidence from the military life-course literature is that the "redirection" benefit of military service has a greater impact on veterans who served at younger ages, before forming families and starting careers (Elder 1987; Elder, Modell, and Parke 1993; Wright et al. 2005). Veterans who entered military service at older ages experienced more life-course disruption that was potentially detrimental to subsequent family life. By implication, it may also be that families created after service are more positively benefited than families that form before or during service. This family formation timing comparison has scarcely been studied and is something that merits further research.

Economic Costs and Benefits by Demographic Profile

Regardless of when family formation occurred, one way in which some veteran families may benefit is through the potentially elevated educational and earnings potential of former service members (see Bennett and McDonald, Chapter 6 of this volume, and Kleykamp, Chapter 7 of this volume). Higher socioeconomic status has enormous implications for family well-being, such as marital stability, lower stress, and increased intergenerational wealth and mobility (Edin 2000; Elder et al. 1992; White 1990). Generally, noncombat veterans who come from lower socioeconomic status backgrounds are advantaged economically by service (MacLean and Elder 2007).[1] This has been referred variously as the "bridging effect" and the "knifing off" effect. This was particularly true for World War II–era veterans, and was largely driven by the GI Bill, which lifted significant numbers of families into the American middle class. The GI Bill enabled an entire generation of men to go college, while also allowing many to purchase homes for the first time (Bound and Turner 2002; MacLean 2005; Martindale and Poston 1979). Benefits of the GI Bill for veterans were not strictly economic, but also social and psychological in nature. Mettler (2002) found that World War II veterans, who as a group benefited substantially from the GI Bill, had significantly increased civic and community involvement. Whereas educational advancement is less uniformly characteristic of the Vietnam and All-Volunteer Force eras of service (Teachman 2005, 2007), for veterans from disadvantaged ethnic and/or socioeconomic backgrounds from these more recent eras, future earnings potential is still higher (Angrist 1998; Cohany 1992; Xie 1992). Recent research by Kleykamp (2006) has determined that persons from disadvantaged classes who have college aspirations enlist at a higher than average rate. This research points out the currency of the perception among a significant segment of poor youth that the military is a viable route to educational achievement, which may smooth the transition to adulthood and subsequent entry into the middle class (Kelty, Kleykamp, and Segal 2010; see also Bennett and McDonald, Chapter 6 of this volume). Additionally, for African American men who served during Vietnam or the All-Volunteer Force eras, violence and offending rates are lower (Bouffard 2005). This bridging effect of service also seems to translate into a higher likelihood of marrying for some African American veterans (Usdansky, London, and Wilmoth 2009), indicating that military service promotes family formation, even after exit from the service.[2]

It is important to mention that the military compensation package of benefits has a monetary value far exceeding the cash value of income that soldiers receive. In fact, cash pay and allowances make up only 48% of total compensation, which means that when total compensation for service personnel is figured in, they compare quite well to civilians, matching the top 80th percentile of civilians in compensation (Department of Defense 2008b). The soldier's deferred benefits, such as retirement pension, for example, have important long-term implications for economic well-being that are not often considered in the preceding analyses. Those veterans serving for twenty years (about 15% of enlistees and 40% of officers) can retire from the military as early as their late 30s, which affords them the opportunity to secure a second civilian career while at the same time receiving an immediate and inflation-protected lifetime annuity from the military (see Street and Hoffman, Chapter 11 of this volume). This is an important area in which the socioeconomic studies of veterans and their families should be extended, especially in light of the foundering national Social Security system for civilians.

Overall, the implications of higher socioeconomic attainment for some veterans suggest that there should be a ripple effect for families through the life course and that military service is an engine driving processes of cumulative inequality in the population. We might expect that disadvantaged and/or minority families are better off economically when the parent is a veteran. Therefore, important research questions should examine how the children of veterans compare to the children of non-veterans across a variety of important life indicators—educational attainment, earnings, wealth, family formation patterns, and health, for starters. Given the recently increased military presence of mothers, attention should also be given to whether these patterns vary by the gender of the parent in service, and if they are multiplied in the case of joint-service marriages. Finally, given the potential for service-connected injury and disability among veterans and the availability of Veterans Administration benefits that aim to offset the economic disadvantage they can entail, it is important to investigate how veteran and disability statuses jointly affect experiences of poverty and material hardship for veterans and their family members (Heflin, Wilmoth, and London 2012; London, Heflin, and Wilmoth 2011).

Outcomes for Marital Stability

The evidence for whether military service might be associated with greater long-term marital stability is contradictory. Among current active-duty service members, most research shows that, contrary to popular thought, divorce rates are not elevated in the military. As with other trends, there appears to be a marital stability premium for soldiers from disadvantaged backgrounds who would otherwise have been more vulnerable to marital dissolution in the civilian world (Lundquist 2006; Teachman and Tedrow 2008). However, based on limited research, this advantage does not appear to persist beyond the active-duty period, even though veteran status also affords greater long-term financial stability to these groups.

The general trend among men, even those who experience deployment, seems to be that military service is neutrally associated with eventual divorce (Angrist and Johnson 2000; Karney and Crown 2007; Laufer et al. 1981). However, some recent research suggests that, among men, veterans are significantly more likely than non-veterans to report extramarital sex and to have ever divorced, noting the strong, independent association of extramarital sex with divorce (London, Allen, and Wilmoth forthcoming). Some research suggests that female active-duty soldiers have higher divorce rates than male active-duty soldiers (Angrist and Johnson 2000; Karney and Crown 2007; Lundquist and Smith 2005). Unambiguously, combat experience uniformly impacts marriages and families negatively. Divorce rates are higher among both combat soldiers and veterans (Gimbel and Booth 1994; Ruger et al. 2002; see Call and Teachman 1996 for one exception), and the bulk of qualitative research indicates that military families often experience high levels of conflict and stress after combat deployments (Karney and Crown 2007).

Soldiers who have seen combat are more prone to disability and emotional distress, such as PTSD (see MacLean, Chapter 10 of this volume). These "hidden wounds" (Hendin and Haas 1984) increase marital and family stress. The extent to which these factors are relevant for a large generation of families depends, in part, on the historical era and the numbers of soldiers fighting in war zones. Although combat soldiers have always been a minority compared to those serving in support roles, the changing nature of warfare in recent engagements has blurred the line between frontline soldiers and others. The rapid advancement of war-zone transportation and medical technology means that more soldiers survive combat. Perhaps as a result, one in five recent veterans suffers from PTSD or depression (Tanielian and Jaycox 2008), which are linked with family conflict, violence, and substance abuse (Cosgrove, Brady, and Peck 1995; Harkness 1993; Hendrix and Anelli 1993; RAND Corporation 2008).

Outcomes for Veteran Children

The life-course literature emphasizes how early-life conditions often play a major role in shaping individual trajectories across the life course, although there is ample evidence suggesting that these effects can still be modified and offset by institutions and events later in life (Laub and Sampson 2003). Life events occurring during childhood can often have the most lasting and long-term impacts on individuals. Given that increasing numbers of children are born before or during the period of military service, many are embedded with their families within the military institution rather than only experiencing the military's influence as it is filtered through their parent(s) in the years following service. Thus, many children come into direct contact with this "total institution" (Goffman 1961) at a very young, impressionable age and can themselves be thought of, in many ways, as veteran children.

The most common image in the media and, indeed, in the popular imagination is the child waving a tearful goodbye to a parent shipping out for deployment to a war zone. Parental deployment introduces stress into the family in three distinct stages: the anticipatory stress that comes upon first learning of an upcoming deployment; the absence of the parent while at war; and the reintegration of the parent back into a family role, assuming he or she survives the experience. Hill (1949) documented how families coped with each of these transitional stages during World War II in his seminal book *Families under Stress: Adjustment to the War Crisis of Separation and Reunion*. The longer-term impact on children of having a parent who has engaged in war is less frequently considered. Some research has documented an intergenerational impact of combat trauma on children's well-being. For example, offspring of veterans with PTSD are more likely to suffer secondary traumatization (Cosgrove, Brady, and Peck 1995) and to exhibit behavioral problems even many years later (Jordan et al. 1992). In addition, the chance of parental death is substantially elevated for military children. Loss and bereavement carry their own set of implications for long-term child development, effects that can be highly variable depending on the age of the child (Worden 1996).

Less devastating but more universal in the child's experience of military service is frequent parent absence due to deployment, even during peacetime. Children of parents deployed during the Persian Gulf War experienced more stress and depression than other military children, most acutely in younger children (the majority of children in the military are under age 11) and boys (Jensen et al. 1996). Military families also move often, at a rate of every three to four years, depending on the branch of service. Civilian studies show that children who relocate often suffer in school achievement (Pribesh and Downey 1999); however, the effects have been shown to be much more negligible for military children (Marchant and Medway 1987; Weber and Weber 2005). This may be because structures have been put in place by the military to mitigate potentially negative effects of frequent moves (see Bailey, Chapter 9 of this volume).

There are potentially unique and positive effects for children who are directly exposed to the service, particularly those who live on base and whose parents serve for longer than just one term. However, such positive effects have received relatively little attention in the literature. As with veterans who benefit most from service, the children who likely have the largest long-term payoff for parental veteran status are racial-ethnic minority children. The explicit racial-ethnic integration of military bases means that many minority children who might otherwise be living in segregated, poor, and disadvantaged neighborhoods are removed from such conditions (Crockett 2000). The life-course literature has found that childhood living conditions have potentially long-term impacts on health and well-being (Kuh, Power, Blane, and Bartley 1997). Even off-base neighborhoods in cities and towns that host military bases are distinctively less segregated than nonmilitary base cities (Farley and Frey 1994), which is attributable to the military's historic policy of demanding racial integration in off-base rental housing and businesses frequented by its personnel (Hershfield 1985; see also Lutz, Chapter 4 of this volume).

The military's comprehensive and free health care offered through the *TRICARE for Life* system means that service member dependents have access to excellent and comprehensive preventative medical and dental care. In this type of environment, it is no surprise that infant mortality rates are lower among women soldiers and military spouses, mitigating even the longstanding but little-understood racial disparity in preterm births and infant mortality in the United States (Barfield et al. 1996; Lundquist et al. 2010). It is estimated that 30 to 45% of junior enlisted members would have no access to public or employer-provided health care coverage had they been working in the civilian sector (Department of Defense 2008b). Thus, health care access continues even following military service for many veteran families, constituting a direct way that veteran status potentially impacts the future well-being of families. For one, families of any service member who die during service receive lifetime health insurance from the Department of Veterans Affairs. Second, retired military families continue to receive free health care, and this is the case regardless of whether the veteran dies or divorces (until dependents marry or spouses remarry).

Importantly, and something all but ignored by social scientists, is the early-childhood exposure of White military children to neighbors and schoolmates of color. Perhaps as a consequence of the military's racially integrated environment, African Americans make up a larger proportion of the military population than they do in the national population and interracial families form much more commonly in the military environment (Farley 1999; Jacobson and Heaton 2003). Therefore, racial majority groups come into more frequent and sustained contact with minority peers and superiors, a condition that predicts more inclusive attitudes of racial majorities toward racial "others" (Amir 1969; Sigelman and Welch 1993). There is little question that this degree of interracial integration, unheard of in most American civilian contexts, will have a long-term impact on children's racial attitudes and beliefs.

The same is potentially true of children who have the opportunity to live abroad during part of a parent's military service. Although international military bases can be relatively insular (this varies by country and era of service), deployed families are nevertheless exposed to significantly different cultural norms and languages for an extended period of time. The bicultural benefits and cognitive advantages of early exposure to language are significant (Armstrong and Rogers 1997). There has been some sociological study of the long-term effects of this phenomenon, which refers variously to military children as "third culture kids," "transnational culture kids," or "global nomads" (Ender 1996, 2002; Useem 1993). These studies are an important foundation, but they have not pursued specific developmental outcomes and rely on self-identified veteran children. More systematic collection of data about this population is necessary.

Finally, an important way in which parents' military service can have a direct impact on the long-term development of their children involves cases in which military children grow up to pursue their own careers in the military. Studies have shown that the probability of enlisting and making a career out of military service is highly elevated among youth whose parents also served (Faris 1981, 1984; Kilburn and Klerman 1999). This relationship raises provocative questions about the linked biographies of parent and child across differing historical eras of military service. Little is known about how this process of intergenerational transfer from parent to child occurs. For example, is it merely a network diffusion effect, as suggested by Bailey (Chapter 9 of this volume), who documents that military enlistments are also higher in geographical areas with a stronger military presence, or is it a direct consequence of parental influence and socialization? Important factors to consider include how this relationship may vary in relation to the gender of both the parent and child, and by the racial-ethnic and social class origins of the family. Furthermore, how might the nature of the parent's military experience mediate the intergenerational transference of military employment? If the parent died in uniform, for instance, is the opposite type of transfer more likely to occur? In such a family, would children exhibit a heightened likelihood of joining war resistance movements or pacifist organizations? All of these topics are open questions for future research on intergenerational transmission of the military experience.

Outcomes for Veteran Spouses

Spouses of service personnel may experience more negative effects as "veteran wives" than their children. For spouses, partnering with the veteran in the years following military service, rather than during service, may be optimal with regard to longer-term outcomes. Although frequent relocations are hard on children, the military system builds continuity into the military school system in an attempt to compensate. Spouses have no such continuity in their employment (or educational careers for that matter). As a result, military spouses find it difficult to maintain steady employment or to attain career mobility (see Kleykamp, Chapter 7 of this volume).

Many military bases are located in areas with few job opportunities for civilians (Booth et al. 2000; see also Bailey, Chapter 9 of this volume). On average, military spouses earn less and are more often unemployed and looking for work than civilian women (Hosek et al. 2002; Payne, Warner, and Little 1992). Unless spouses are also serving in the military, which is the case in 10% of military marriages, the geographic structure of the military career necessarily deprioritizes any spouse's career. Because the military is still majority male (86%), military couples often find themselves replicating the traditional marriages of yesterday, with a higher incidence of stay-at-home mothers and working fathers. Evidence suggests that normative expectations for soldiers' wives, particularly those married to officers, still retain a nontrivial degree of gender traditionalism from earlier eras.

In 1998, the military officially decreed that officer promotion could no longer be affected by the actions of spouses; however, expectations for appropriate spousal roles still operate informally (Harrell 2001). Most officers are men; most military spouses are women. Officers' wives are asked to perform a variety of uncompensated work, such as entertaining and providing social and support systems for the families of more junior personnel (Harrell 2000a,b). Soldiers' wives of all ranks are generally expected to invest in their husbands' careers; they are the primary caretakers of the children when their spouses are deployed, and they are encouraged to participate in military culture integration classes and various military life support groups (Harrell 2000a,b). Although the military's efforts to foster a sense of familial solidarity may help children feel more centered and integrated (for example, base schools mandate parental involvement and superiors often make personal visits to check in on enlisted families in their units), military spouses may find such involvement invasive.

For these reasons, focusing on the life-course outcomes of veteran spouses, who are mostly women, as well as veteran children, is an important point of contrast for future research on veteran families. As an "unseen member of the family" (Wertsch 1991), military authority subjects military families to a high degree of scrutiny, including, for example, intervention in instances of adultery and the aggressive intervention of social services (Burland and Lundquist 2009). The effects of the military on different family members may be heterogeneous, which is a topic that has received very little attention in the literature.

What does this suggest for military spouses in their later life stages? Economically, it means that they are not building up the necessary human capital and job experience that would help to protect them in the event of divorce. Given that divorce affects one out of every two marriages, particularly among couples of lower educational attainment (86% of the military are enlisted personnel, who need only a high school diploma to join), this is an important consideration for life-course studies. Divorce is linked to a substantial reduction in women's economic well-being (Hoffman and Duncan 1988), and this extends to their children, who are more often in their mother's custody. It also means that military spouses may feel trapped or overly dependent on their marriage and the military for their well-being. Implications for how this may impact the balance of interpersonal power in veteran families in the long term, as well as the consequences for women's self-esteem trajectory across the life course are important areas to be researched. Furthermore, the more recent role of male (non-service) spouses and the question of whether gender normative notions of spousal relations may interact differently with issues of career autonomy and power are a virtual lacuna in the literature.

There are also profound, often lifelong consequences for the families of combat veterans who become disabled as a result of their military service. This falls most heavily on the military spouse. Just as the soldier's spouse is unofficially relied upon by the Department of Defense to support the military's aims, spouses of disabled veterans take on a major role where Veterans Administration health services leave off. A recent study found that the majority of caregivers (usually wives) spend about ten hours a week caring for a wounded veteran for an average of nineteen months, and, as a result, suffer significant economic penalties in lost time at work and in schooling (Christensen et al. 2009). Importantly, the study found that 43% of caregivers expected to be providing care for the long term. The multiplying economic and emotional effects of intensive caregiving responsibilities carried out across the life course, and possibly even into old age, constitute a critical way in which military service quite literally becomes a lifelong obligation.

CONCLUSION

Our review of the literature suggests that veteran families present compelling initial evidence for furthering our understanding of the life course. Our review also uncovers many unanswered and unasked questions, particularly concerning nontraditional families. It is clear that the military offers substantial support to families willing to adhere to the "traditional" married-with-children, breadwinner-homemaker model (Burland and Lundquist 2009), and as a result, this type of family is overrepresented in the military relative to the civilian world. Even so, nontraditional families are present in the military, although they receive less official support, as well as less scholarly attention. Is there a long-term negative effect of veteran status for women veterans and their families compared to male veterans and their families? If so, is that because women are more likely than men to be in dual-service marriages? Generally, how does the compounded effect of having two veteran adults in the household impact families in the long term? Another important question that is rarely explored involves how military status affects the life course of lesbian, gay, bisexual, and transgender veterans, whose service can sometimes facilitate and sometimes interrupt relationship formation (see Brown, Chapter 5 of this volume).

The questions raised in this chapter also point to the need for new sources of data that measure important markers of former military experience in the family within the context of later-life outcomes. Rather than asking individuals only about their own past military experience, surveys must cast a wider net, asking respondents about the military experience of their parents, and possibly even their siblings and children. Clearly, we need to know far more than only whether a family member was a veteran in order to gauge the full impact of what it means to be a "veteran family."

Ideal measures would include length and era of service, military rank and occupation, whether service occurred during a war, and combat exposure. Measures of length of separations due to deployments, as well as when they occurred, could be particularly useful for understanding spouses' and children's outcomes. Survey questions must also attend to the family members' own exposures to the institution: did they experience the military directly as children or as spouses during the family member's service? Or was their exposure indirect, taking place only after the family member had already left the service? In the former case, it is crucial to collect information on age and length of exposure, and whether and for how long they might have lived on base, attended military schools, or lived abroad.

"We take care of our own," claims the military. We are right to test that claim. Because the military subjects demographically different populations to the same policies, we can and should document how all soldiers in the aggregate benefit or suffer from these policies, as well as studying heterogeneity in the effects of policies across different demographic subpopulations. The contractual nature of these benefits means that they are all connected to sacrifice on the part of the recruit and his or her family. Who meets "the needs of the military"? Which groups sacrifice the most for the least benefit? This logic of complexity demonstrates our sociological commitment to understanding how various events and conditions affect different groups differently. Although distinct population segments among veteran families remain unstudied, it is nonetheless a significant contribution of the sociological subfield focusing on veteran families that it has brought the critical themes of diversity and variable outcomes to the military discourse of equality.

It is not just the recruit who enters into a contract with the military; the family of that recruit enters into a long-term relationship with the military as well. It is well established that military families (those that conform to the military's narrow and exclusionary definition of family) are shaped, supported, controlled, and protected by the institution they serve. So powerful is this connection between the military and the service member's family that the family does not necessarily "get out of the contract" even in the case of death or divorce. As another example, the effects of a service member's serious injury (including PTSD) on his or her family are long term. The military and its proxy, the Department of Veterans Affairs, attempt to regulate this relationship of give and take between family and military. The two currencies of the ongoing engagement are compensation (paid to the family—"We take care of our own") and sacrifice (paid to the military by the family—"the needs of the military").

Benefits paid to surviving family members of a fallen soldier constitute the most conspicuous exchange of benefits for sacrifice. The substantial benefits (usually hundreds of thousands of dollars, followed by a lifetime pension) ensure that the family of the fallen soldier will be connected to the military in a profound and lasting way. The civilian family will even be subject to ongoing regulation by the military, because the military requires that widows and widowers remain unmarried to receive full benefits. The families that have been most damaged by their connection to the military are eligible for the most generous post-service benefits, but are also subject to the greatest ongoing control. This is the deliberate policy of the military, and who could object to matching benefit to sacrifice? Yet the logic of reciprocity is not sufficient to connect the complexity of the military to the complexity of family. Is a pension really adequate compensation for the total loss of a needed family member? Should the government be paying a widow or widower not to remarry? The logic of reciprocity requires that family members continue to sacrifice in order to receive ongoing benefits. The generous package of benefits, along with its attendant requirements, defines the meaning both of the death of one young person and the life of another.

Veteran families are families in which at least one member served in the military. There can be no veteran families without veterans. Yet once the connection between military and family is created, the veteran becomes expendable to the ongoing relationship between his or her family and the total institution he or she served. In fact, the disappearance of the veteran (through incapacitation or death) from family life may result in that family-military relationship being strengthened as the military steps in to fill the void left by the fallen soldier. In this light, can we accept Waller's (1944) claim that the veteran must be reintegrated into the stable and stabilizing institution of family? Is reintegration into the family a prerequisite to reintegration into civilian society? We cannot accept Waller's premise because the evidence shows us that the family context to which the veteran returns is not a civilian space. Instead, it is a militarized space, subject to continued regulation by the total institution it supposedly left behind. The military refuses to relinquish all control over the veteran families for which it offers to provide so generously. Can veteran families ever be fully reintegrated into civilian society? Perhaps the more relevant question is, Do they want to reintegrate back into a world that may have less to offer them in terms of benefits than the military they are ostensibly leaving behind? The military has a hard time relinquishing control over the families it has had under its control, but veteran families seem to be anxious to maintain the connection themselves, even at the cost of a little freedom. The most famous public policy programs for veterans (the GI Bill, home loans, vocational rehabilitation, and disability compensation) are all ostensibly designed to compensate the veteran fairly for losses incurred during service and to move that veteran quickly and efficiently on the path to normal civilian life. Yet somehow the complexity of life eludes the simple and confident logic of the military. Benefits do not always match perfectly with sacrifices made, and some veteran families experience poverty and material hardship even with access to such benefits (Heflin, Wilmoth, and London 2012; London, Heflin, and Wilmoth 2011). Even after a family has formally separated from the service, it often remains stuck in a variety of long-term engagements with the military that influence the life course of veterans and their families in ways that cannot be predicted or controlled by military policy, but certainly should be understood by Sociology.

NOTES

1. The evidence for improved future income earnings for men from less marginalized backgrounds is more mixed, but generally appears to be neutral (Angrist and Krueger 1994).
2. For female veterans the evidence is less sanguine. Although there is an earnings premium for women of the Vietnam era, this is not found for the All-Volunteer Force era (Prokos and Padavic 2000). In fact, for White women, there may be a penalty (Cooney et al. 2003).

9 Military Employment and Spatial Mobility across the Life Course

Amy Kate Bailey

People who join the U.S. military enter an institution in motion. They are required to relocate for basic training, education specific to their military occupational assignments, and postings to military bases across the county and around the globe. This typically means a long-distance move every two to three years. In earlier generations, this level of spatial mobility primarily affected active-duty service members, who tended to be unmarried men. However, in the All-Volunteer Force era, this rapid migration tempo increasingly impacts spouses and children as well. Additionally, a nascent body of work suggests that those who have a history of U.S. military employment—veterans—exhibit migration patterns across their working lives and into retirement that differentiate them from the civilian population.

This chapter focuses on issues related to the spatial mobility of active-duty military personnel, veterans, and their family members. Although much evidence about the spatial patterns of active-duty members of the armed forces exists, I am aware of no systematic effort to synthesize this work and review its major findings. Additionally, the question of how the experience of institutionally driven spatial mobility affects these individuals and their families following separation has received little scholarly attention. This chapter will, therefore, not merely summarize our current knowledge; it will also suggest an agenda for future inquiry.

Whereas this chapter primarily focuses on issues related to military employment and spatial location since the transition to the All-Volunteer Force, a substantial body of research addresses this nexus during earlier eras. For example, Brown (Chapter 5 of this volume) discusses how the massive mobilization during World War II moved large numbers of men, and some women, through urban port cities, which facilitated their exposure to existing urban sexual subcultures and enticed many to remain in those locations upon the end of the war. Such patterns of World War II–related mobility and resettlement facilitated the establishment and expansion of gay ghettoes in major American cities. Additionally, mass suburbanization following World War II was facilitated by Veterans Administration home loans (Glenn 1973; Skocpol 1997), although Black veterans were unable to suburbanize as rapidly as were their White counterparts due to both racist implementation of the GI Bill (Katznelson 2005; see also Bennett and McDonald, Chapter 6 of this volume) and prejudicial banking and real estate practices (Massey and Denton 1993). During the Selective Service draft era, interstate migration for military service comprised a large segment of all young adult male migration (Miller 1969), in patterns that correlated with armed forces personnel concentrations and local economic conditions (Vaidyanathan 1969). For female spouses in the early part of the All-Volunteer Force era, there is evidence that their husbands' frequent military service-related moves depressed their labor force attachment and current wages, which contributed to an increased likelihood of having a birth close to the time of a move and higher fertility overall (Gill, Haurin, and Phillips 1994).

Because the current work is designed to provide guideposts for broader life-course and population studies, I focus on long-term or semipermanent changes in geographic residence in the American context. I will not cover the vast literature on the effects of deployment and the subsequent reintegration of active-duty personnel. Family separation and the risk of combat exposure are real and significant issues, and certainly lie at the intersection of personal biography and historical accident. The psychological correlates, economic outcomes, as well as other effects of temporary occupational relocation are critically important, and they are covered well by Figley (1993), Rentz et al. (2007), and Booth et al. (2007). Much literature also exists on broader collective effects of institutionally driven migration, particularly the impacts of U.S. military bases on foreign host countries. Again, these questions are beyond the scope of this chapter. Readers are referred to Berry (1989), Okazawa-Rey (1997), Rimmer (1997), Sturdevant and Stoltzfus (1992), and Vine (2004) for a diversity of perspectives on a variety of effects of American bases on foreign communities.

I will identify major findings from the literature related to spatial mobility for active-duty personnel, their family members, and veterans across the life course, describing potential implications of the aggregated patterns identified by existing research. This chapter will then highlight gaps in our knowledge, based either on questions that have not yet been systematically pursued or on shortcomings of the existing body of literature. Based on the discussion of what we do not yet know, I will outline a series of questions and methodological approaches for fruitful research in the future.

ACTIVE-DUTY MILITARY PERSONNEL

Active-duty military personnel have higher rates of spatial mobility than do their civilian counterparts (Miller 1969; Segal and Segal 2004). Among cohorts whose military service was completed before the onset of the All-Volunteer Force, this mobility was primarily experienced by individuals in late adolescence and early adulthood, few of whom were married or had children. However, in the All-Volunteer Force context, longer terms of enlistment, typically lasting well into young adulthood, mean that military service persists into time frames when family formation is well underway. Demographic shifts among active-duty personnel also mean that high rates of institutionally linked spatial mobility are now focused among population groups disproportionately represented in the armed forces: Southerners, African Americans, and Whites from blue-collar backgrounds (Oi 1996; Segal and Segal 2004). The positive and negative correlates of repeat migration—for both active-duty personnel and their family members—are concentrated among the individuals who fit these profiles and the communities they originate in and ultimately inhabit.

Spatial Origins: Where Do Military Personnel Come From?

American states and communities are not represented in the armed forces in the same proportions that they are among the civilian population. That is to say, some states send more than their "fair share" of young adults into the military, whereas others have relatively few former residents in uniform. Southern states tend to be overrepresented among active-duty personnel, as do rural states in the West. In general, the Northeast and Midwest supply a smaller percentage of military personnel than would be expected on the basis of population size. Rural communities also provide a disproportionate share of military staff. Although only one in five American adults lives in a rural community, an estimated 45% of armed forces personnel are from rural areas, as are 26% of casualties that have occurred during the current U.S. military operations in Iraq and Afghanistan (Helseth 2007; O'Hare and Bishop 2007; Tyson 2005). Figure 9.1 depicts the rate of military enlistment by state in 2008, calculated as the number of new accessions divided by the total population of young adults aged 18 to 30 years.[1] It shows that states with the highest enlistment rates are concentrated in the South and West. Indeed, with the exceptions of Maine and Missouri—two states with large rural populations—all fifteen of the states with the highest rates of enlistment are in the Southern and Western regions.

In addition to disparities based on state of residence and rural status, the spatial concentration of recruits likely results from variation in adolescent exposure to someone with military experience and the effects of such personal connection on the propensity to enlist in the military (Brown and Rana 2005). The social context in which adolescents decide to join the armed forces, then, has implications for the distribution of geographic origins of military personnel. For example, young men whose fathers had military careers are more likely to enlist than are the sons of other men (Faris 1981). The same is true for adolescents from communities with a larger military presence, as measured by the share of active-duty military

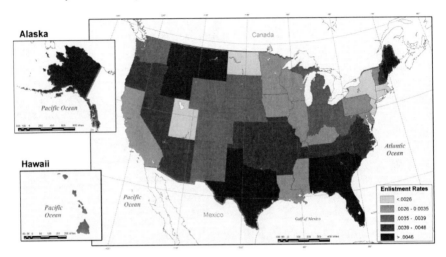

Figure 9.1   Young adult enlistment rates by state, 2008.

personnel among a county's workers, although the effect of military presence varies by race and ethnicity (Kleykamp 2006). Higher enlistment rates among young adults from the South may be related to the concentration of military installations in Southern states, or to the large share of veterans who live in that region. Evidence further suggests that the targeted location of recruiters and recruitment programs also may influence the spatial distribution of new military accessions. For example, the concentration of Junior Reserve Officer Training Corps (JROTC) programs in inner-city high schools (Coumbe, Kotakis, and Gammell 2008), combined with the higher enlistment rates among students who participate in JROTC programs (Pema and Mehay 2009), likely means that specific urban areas are also disproportionately represented among those in uniform.

Many of these geographic disparities in "sending communities" also appear to be linked to the economic prospects of the young adults who live there. In all regions, communities with declining economic profiles send more people into the armed forces, and places where nonmilitary opportunities are plentiful typically send fewer (Brown 1985). The economic logic associated with spatial variation in enlistment rates is supported by temporal fluctuations in recruitment patterns, as well as prior life-course research on adolescent migration expectations. Elder, King, and Conger (1996) find that adolescents who perceive limited job opportunities in their home communities express greater willingness to live far from family as adults. Additionally, both the number and qualifications of new military applicants are generally tied to broader economic conditions, including the young adult unemployment rate and the comparability of civilian and military pay rates (Asch, Heaton, and Savych 2009; Dale and Gilroy 1984).

Spatial Mobility and Geography during Active Duty

An individual remaining in uniform for the average term of service—currently six years—can expect to live in three or four different communities during that period. These distinct residences will likely be in different states or perhaps overseas as the active-duty service member transitions through basic and advanced individual training to additional "permanent" base locations. Those planning on remaining in the armed forces longer than six years will experience additional moves. For families, especially during deployment of the active-duty service member, a move by left-behind spouses and children to be closer to other family members may result in distinctly different moves being experienced by family members at a given point in time.

Characteristics of Active-Duty Migration Behavior

Military personnel move more frequently, and typically move longer distances when they relocate, than is true of civilians (Segal and Segal 2004). This rapid migration tempo may affect which individuals remain in the military over time, because among enlisted personnel, as well as their spouses, satisfaction with the frequency of relocation is a key indicator of their overall level of satisfaction with military life (Bowen 1989). The limited body of research addressing outcomes of repeated long-distance migration for military personnel identifies negative effects on mental health and social functioning. For example, large pluralities of soldiers who have recently relocated report that their moves resulted in economic hardships and stress related to housing insecurity or inadequate time to prepare for a move (Booth et al. 2007). In the extreme, younger soldiers appear to be at elevated risk of committing suicide in the wake of occupational relocation (Rothberg 1991). However, because military enlistment in the All-Volunteer Force is freely chosen and the degree of spatial mobility is often a known and expected feature of military life, it may be anticipated that short-term negative effects often associated with migration are attenuated for members of the armed forces and their families with increased time in residence or experience with moving.

The military also plays a role in redistributing young adults throughout the country, by virtue of the concentration of training facilities and bases in specific Southern and Western states (Barnes and Roseman 1981; Office of the Deputy Under Secretary of Defense—Installations and Environment 2008). For example, 775 young adults from Montana joined the military in 2008 (Department of Defense 2008a). Assuming equivalent numbers from other years and that these Montanans each remain in the military for the average six-year term of service, we can expect 4,650 men and women from Montana to be in the active forces at any given time. However, only about 3,000 military jobs were located in Montana in 2008 (U.S. Census Bureau 2009). Arithmetically, even if we assume that all of the military personnel stationed in Montana are from that state—a clearly erroneous assumption—the remaining 1,650 young Montanans on active duty must have moved out of that state, which represents roughly one-third of all military personnel from Big Sky Country or 1% of the population of all Montanans aged 18 to 29 in 2008.

Following separation from the military, unmarried personnel are likely to move back in with their parents, reflecting that for many, the relocation associated with being in the armed forces is viewed as temporary (DaVanzo and Goldscheider 1990; White and Lacy 1997). This might be the case more so today because an elongated transition to adulthood involving longer durations of co-residence with parents is becoming increasingly normative (Settersten and Ray 2010). However, even a limited stay in a different state, region of the country, or perhaps a foreign country can have profound effects on a range of psychosocial outcomes, particularly when experienced during young adulthood (Ender 2002). Experiencing a diverse group of colleagues from geographically dispersed origins, learning new cuisines and folkways, and perhaps even acquiring a new language can be transformative. Gaining in-depth knowledge of specific communities in which military bases are located, and learning how to quickly relocate and establish networks in a new community, may also affect residential preferences and migration patterns later in life.

What Do We Know about Military Base Communities?

To the extent that service in the armed forces determines the geographic location of military personnel and their families, the characteristics of base communities matter. Localities that house military bases differ from other areas on a number of important dimensions, which may have positive or negative influences on various life-course trajectories and outcomes. For example, neighborhoods located on post, as well as in the surrounding neighborhoods, tend to be among the most racially integrated in the country (DeFina and Hannon 2009; Farley and Frey 1994). However, residential neighborhoods that house large military populations are also quite likely to be located near environmentally toxic sites (Heitgerd and Lee 2003).

As Table 9.1 demonstrates, counties that house large military bases also have social, economic, and demographic profiles that vary substantially from those of the broader United States. Active-duty military personnel— and their family members—typically live in communities that are younger and have a larger percentage of veterans than is true of the nation as a whole. Additionally, although these communities tend to have higher-than-average proportions of adults with high school diplomas, local areas that host Army and Marine Corps bases have lower-than-average rates of college graduates. To the degree that these contextual differences shape young adults' and children's expectations and experiences, they similarly shape life-course development.

Table 9.1   Comparing Social, Economic, and Demographic Characteristics of the U.S. to Those of Communities with Large Military Presence, 2006–2008

	Percent High School Graduates	Percent College Graduates	Percent Veterans	Percent Labor Force in Military	Median Age	Percent Black
Total U.S. Population	84.5%	27.4%	10.1%	4.9%	36.7 years	12.3%
Island County, Washington (Naval Air Station Whidbey Island—Navy)	94.4%	28.1%	22.8%	20.1%	40.3 years	1.5%
Cumberland County, North Carolina (Fort Bragg—Army)	88.8%	21.6%	23.0%	17.2%	32.9 years	35.3%
El Paso County, Colorado (Air Force Academy and Peterson and Schriever Air Force Bases)	91.9%	31.6%	18.8%	6.9%	34.3 years	6.2%
Onslow County, North Carolina (Camp Lejeune—Marine Corps)	88.1%	17.5%	26.2%	38.6%	25.7 years	16.8%

Source: Census Bureau's American Fact Finder website, http://factfinder.census.gov/home/staff/main.html?_lang=en, accessed on 2 December 2009 and 19 May 2010.

LINKED LIVES: TRAILING FAMILY MEMBERS

These migration patterns and base community characteristics increasingly affect not only military personnel themselves, but also their spouses and children. The effect of repeat migration on the family members of active-duty personnel became an issue of increasing concern among social scientists and military leaders following the transition to the All-Volunteer Force in 1973. Research identifies negative consequences of repeat migration on family life and the labor market consequences associated with being a "trailing spouse" in a military family (see Burland and Lundquist, Chapter 8 of this volume, and Kleykamp, Chapter 7 of this volume).

Trailing Spouses

The transition to the All-Volunteer Force—and subsequent increase in the share of married personnel on active duty—coincided with rapid increases in women's labor force participation, creating fertile ground for labor market researchers. Civilian spouses of active-duty military personnel are, by definition, the trailing partners in migration decisions, and often cycle through communities in which military bases are the major employer. Nearly four decades of evidence now documents that military wives experience lower rates of labor force participation, higher rates of unemployment, and lower returns to human capital than do married civilian women (Grossman 1981; Hayghe 1986; Payne, Warner, and Little 1992). For female spouses, this may translate into higher fertility (Gill, Haurin, and Phillips 1994). Labor market penalties for trailing spouses also result in poorer occupational outcomes for civilian husbands (Cooke and Speirs 2005; Little and Hisnanick 2007).

These effects result in large part from labor market consequences of migration itself as spouses have reduced opportunities for building tenure with a specific employer and must invest more time in both the job search process and unpaid family labor associated with relocation. Additionally, the co-location of thousands of military families affects both the supply and demand aspects of labor market composition. The monopsonistic effects of concentrated military employment depress wages throughout the local labor market (Booth 2003); moreover, trailing spouses tend to be younger women lacking college degrees—workers whose labor market outcomes would likely be subpar even in robust economic environments. Although various factors contribute to their labor market experiences, these trailing spouses overwhelmingly perceive that the military has negatively influenced their labor market outcomes (Castaneda and Harrell 2008), which may affect their level of satisfaction with military life.

Children in Military Families

The early literature on children in military families tended to focus on the negative effects of frequent migration on children's outcomes, although the number of career military personnel was a small and highly selected group, suggesting that those results may not be generalizable to the All-Volunteer Force context. Today, roughly 1.2 million children have at least one parent on active duty in a branch of the armed forces (Kelley, Finkel, and Ashby 2003), which means that repeat migration associated with parental military employment is a feature of childhood for a growing number of American children, and also that a sufficient number of these children exist to provide substantial opportunities for research on their outcomes.

There are reasons to believe that migratory children whose parents are in the military may not have the same, typically negative, academic and behavioral outcomes experienced by the children of civilians who migrate, or that the negative effects of repeat mobility may not be as extreme. In light of the early age of accession for most military personnel, and average tenure of roughly six years, their children may be quite young—perhaps not even school-aged—when military-related migration occurs. Military migration is likely experienced by school-aged children most often when their parent(s) opt for longer military careers.

For older children, moving entails a major disruption, including the acquisition of new peers and adjustment to a new school and community. However, frequent moves are normalized in military culture, so they may be accepted more readily than among civilian families. Because the military has created a culture of migrants, peer groups are more fluid and may be more accepting of newcomers than is true outside of the military. Relocation services often exist within base communities, and to the extent that they are sufficient and effective, may mitigate the negative outcomes typically associated with moving. Indeed, adults who grew up in highly mobile military families provide mixed accounts. Reflecting the current empirical literature, these "military brats" report that their families' frequent migrations were both a source of stress and an opportunity for developing broader perspectives of the world (Ender 2002).

Additionally, because the curriculum in military schools is fairly standardized, the risk of academic failure may be minimized. Children who move within the Department of Defense educational system remain within a single organizational entity, as compared to children from civilian families in the public school system who likely experience substantial curricular variation and disjunction when moving between school districts and states. Parents may also act to mitigate the negative educational and social effects of repeated migration. For example, many military families choose to home school their children. Military parents have also developed a grassroots network of organizations and mutual support groups to provide military children with social opportunities and parent-instructors with curricular and legal resources. To the extent that children respond poorly to repeated moves and are unable to conform to behavioral expectations within the military, parental dissatisfaction with military life may affect their decision to separate from the armed forces (Booth et al. 2007).

In general, the effects of repeated migration on military children are mediated by the quality of family functioning and by parents' mental health status and coping skills (Kelley, Finkel, and Ashby 2003). However, whether the overall effects of institutionally linked geographic mobility are positive or negative remains in question and the specific mechanisms at play—the recency of a move or overall rate of mobility—remain unclear. In one of the most comprehensive studies of the early All-Volunteer Force era, Marchant and Medway (1987) found few relationships between migration and children's social or academic outcomes. However, research by Kelley, Finkel, and Ashby (2003) suggested that recent moves are associated with lower levels of children's social integration, net of maternal mental health and overall family functioning. Some research finds that adolescents who have made a large number of moves tend to exhibit fewer behavioral issues than is true among lower-migration military youth, a finding they attribute to the development of resilience (Weber and Weber 2005). Alternatively, military personnel whose children experience serious academic or behavioral problems associated with migration may opt to leave the military long before those children reach adolescence. Overall, the evidence regarding the effects of frequent migration on children in highly mobile military families is mixed and there is a substantial need for more research.

VETERANS

A relatively broad literature identifies the places where veterans live, thanks in large part to the inclusion of a question about veteran status in the decennial United States Census since 1940.[2] Draft-era evidence suggests that newly discharged veterans were likely to remain in the states where they had been stationed (Vaidyanathan 1969). The propensity to remain in base communities continues among military retirees, with veterans likely to cluster in counties that house a military base (Jackson and Day 1993). As Table 9.1 demonstrates, it is likely that base communities retain a broad cross-section of veterans, regardless of whether they retired after a career in the military or left the armed forces after a shorter enlistment period. Although young adults on active duty tend to be concentrated in metropolitan areas with smaller total core populations, upon separation from the military, they tend to move to larger population centers (Plane, Henrie, and Perry 2005).

In a pattern reflecting that observed among new enlistees, veterans are not equally distributed among states or regions in the United States. Although the largest proportional concentrations of all veterans are found in the Midwest and South, Southern and Western states have the largest shares of younger veterans—those from the Vietnam or All-Volunteer Force eras (Richardson and Waldrop 2003). Veterans appear to have been on the vanguard of selecting Sun Belt retirement destinations, particularly in base communities, and these states have the largest numeric concentrations of veterans (Barnes and Roseman 1981; Cowper and Corcoran 1989). However, those older veterans who do not migrate in retirement tend to have fewer resources and greater health care needs. As they "age in place," they are more reliant on Veterans Administration provision of health care, which is a factor that could result in an unequal burden being placed on some state budgets (Cowper and Longino 1992), as well as a qualitatively different retirement experience that is linked to their migration behavior.

The scant existing evidence suggests continuing effects of military service on veterans' migration propensity across the life course. Much research on veterans' spatial mobility before retirement appears in the medical and social services literature, focusing on issues related to providing service to a vulnerable population receiving publicly funded care. Veterans who rely on the Veterans Administration for health care are more likely to settle closer to Veterans Administration facilities when they move (McCarthy et al. 2007). However, it appears that all veterans have higher rates of migration across the life course than is true of similar non-veterans (Bailey 2011; Cowper et al. 2000). Conforming to the predictions of migration theory, individuals who have moved once are more apt to make repeat moves—either returning home or as "onward migrants," moving to new places.

Federal policies may also influence veterans' spatial trajectories, including their distribution within metropolitan areas and participation in broader internal migration streams. For example, although access to Veterans Administration home loans persists as a key route to home ownership for veterans, little research has focused on its implications for their spatial distribution since the middle of the 20th century. Among the broader U.S. population, we find interregional migration to geographic areas with "high tech" military research-and-development and production capabilities (Markusen, Hall, Campbell, and Detrick 1991). Whether veterans comprise a disproportionate share of these migration streams is unknown. Additionally, veterans of the All-Volunteer Force era appear to be at greater risk of homelessness upon reentry into civilian life than was true of veterans from earlier cohorts. Homelessness itself, as well as extended spells of homelessness, is particularly pronounced among White veterans of the All-Volunteer Force, which is a result, in part, of socioeconomic selection of persons from disadvantaged backgrounds into military service (Gamache, Rosenheck, and Tessler 2001; Rosenheck, Frisman, and Chung 1994; Tessler, Rosenheck, and Amache 2003).

FUTURE DIRECTIONS

Many unanswered questions remain regarding the spatial patterning of former military personnel—including whether veterans persist in their residence in racially integrated communities, whether intergenerational effects exist for children who were raised in highly mobile families, and how the long-term career trajectories of trailing civilian spouses are affected. Additionally, in light of the increased demographic diversity of the armed forces, and therefore the new veteran population (Wilmoth and London 2011), it is unclear whether identified patterns of migration and residential choice will continue to hold for veterans who are women, and how they might cleave along lines of race, ethnicity, sexual orientation, or social class.

Although we know that veterans maintain a higher rate of migration across the life course, it is unclear how many return to their communities of origin or move to new destinations—a process known as "onward migration." Comparing broader patterns of veterans' return and onward migration to that of non-veterans would help elucidate whether service in the armed forces facilitates spatial mobility similar to that linked to completing a college education. It is also unknown whether differences exist in the life-course stage at which onward migration or return migration might occur. The answers to these questions have implications for the labor force characteristics and age structures of communities that send disproportionately high numbers of young adults into the military, as well as for communities that attract large numbers of veterans. As such, future research into this area may uncover impacts of veterans' migration on the civilian populations within sending and receiving communities.

A relatively large share of research on the spatial and geographic implications of military service on the life course has focused on effects for another group of civilians: trailing family members. However, surprisingly few studies examine the psychological and social correlates of repeated institutionally driven migration on armed forces personnel. A better understanding of the ways in which armed forces personnel are affected by institutionally driven migration may facilitate staff retention, improve job performance, and enhance troop morale.

The mixed findings on migration effects among children in military families may result from methodological issues and the resulting selectivity of the population of children and families being studied. We know that a civilian spouse's satisfaction with the "military lifestyle," and particularly with the frequency of geographic location, affects his or her overall level of satisfaction with the military (Burrell et al. 2006), and spousal satisfaction is in turn a key factor in decisions of military staff to reenlist (Gill and Haurin 1998). It is likely that the effects of repeat migration on children may have a similar level of influence on family decisions. Because current findings that identify positive correlates—or reduced negative outcomes—for children who have experienced higher-order mobility are based on cross-sectional research, they likely disproportionately select children and families who are more able to tolerate the social dislocation associated with repeat migration. Additionally, much of the extant research relies on small sample sizes, with respondents collected from a limited number of observation sites using nonrandom selection processes.

The research on the effects of military-linked migration on families is also challenged by the "chicken and egg" question it faces. In short, most correlates of migration are mediated by family functioning and the mental health of key family members. However, these factors are themselves affected by migration (McKain 1973), so reliance on cross-sectional analyses conflates selection and causation in ways that do not allow researchers to crisply address these questions. Longitudinal research in this area, involving pre- and postmigration assessments of social integration, mental health, and family functioning measures, would help better assess the ways in which being a trailing family member in military migration may be beneficial or damaging.

Research on migration outcomes among children whose parents are in the military also offers unique opportunities for scholars. Because the curriculum at military-linked schools is largely standardized, students transitioning between military bases do not face the dual challenges of simultaneously adjusting to a new social situation and a new course of study. Exploiting this factor should allow the isolation of academic effects of geographic mobility from those of curricular mismatch. Additionally, because school records for children in Department of Defense schools are easily transferred within the same institution, the academic performance of highly mobile children in this system are likely to be more complete, and yield a more comprehensive picture of the acute and chronic correlates of changing schools than is possible for many repeat-migrant children in the civilian population. Finally, because the Department of Defense provides financial subsidies to civilian school districts in base communities that are disproportionately impacted by the high rate of population churning among their students, comparing student outcomes in these schools to those of students in other school districts with similar levels of residential instability—such as high-minority urban districts—could help to disaggregate the effects of resource deprivation from those inherent in residentially unstable communities.

What life-course labor market effects exist for trailing spouses? We know much about the labor force participation of the civilian men and women married to active-duty personnel, but the cumulative effects on their work lives once their spouses have left the military is uncertain. It is likely that unstable work histories and depressed occupational returns to human capital common among spouses of military personnel disadvantage these (primarily) women well into the life course, long after their spouses have joined the veteran population. This reduced labor market attachment may influence not only future earnings and occupational status, but also their ability to establish and vest independent pension benefits, including Social Security. In light of the high rates of divorce observed among military families—particularly the growing number of families with a member who has experienced combat (Ruger, Wilson, and Waddoups 2002)—the (mostly) women who shoulder this burden may be at particular risk of poverty in mid- and later life.[3] Evidence that ever-married men who have served in the military are more likely to have engaged in extramarital affairs and that veteran status and marital infidelity are jointly associated with the likelihood of divorce further highlights this risk for trailing spouses (London, Allen, and Wilmoth forthcoming).

Researchers would also do well to focus on the possible macro-level effects of institutionally linked spatial mobility. An important line of questions could interrogate the impact of community disparities in the rate of young adults being sent into the military. For example, preliminary research suggests that the U.S. military campaigns in Iraq and Afghanistan resulted in a disproportionately heavy casualty burden on rural America (Curtis and Payne 2010). The armed forces' reliance on reserve components to "round out" troop strength in wartime has also drained rural communities of medical personnel (Helseth 2007). Even in the absence of sustained overseas conflict, the disproportionate share of (predominantly male) small town and rural youth who join the military may affect labor force composition, local marriage markets, and population age structures in these communities. A more nuanced understanding of the ways in which individual opportunity presented by the military interacts with effects on local sending communities is needed.

An additional area of future research should focus on consequences for communities that absorb large numbers of migrating veterans. As the demographic profile of the active-duty military force diversifies, and to the degree that veterans' aggregated characteristics differ from those of the communities that they move into, veterans' migration may serve to redistribute demographic groups within the United States, affecting the racial composition of both sending and receiving communities. Given that veterans and their family members will have been exposed to highly integrated residential communities during their period of active-duty service, their preferences for living in racially segregated conditions common in American cities may have declined. It is unknown whether veterans live in more racially and ethnically integrated communities, on average, than is true for civilians without military experience. Given the elevated rates of interracial marriage among armed forces personnel (Jacobson and Heaton 2003), one of the spouses in these couples will likely be a minority in the neighborhood they subsequently live in, and their children may increase its share of biracial young people. Additionally, to the degree that the human capital profiles of veterans and non-veterans differ (Bailey 2008), the presence of large concentrations of veterans may alter labor force composition, and ultimately the industries and jobs that can be supported.

Geographic variation in rates of enlistment, coupled with disparities in settlement patterns among veterans, suggest that civilian populations may also be affected by the spatial population dynamics linked to the military. Future research, then, would do well to interrogate the ways in which the trajectories of individuals with and without military experience differ, as well as possible interactions between the two in communities with high rates of enlistment and veteran settlement.

CONCLUSION

Active-duty military personnel migrate more frequently than do civilians, and members of the armed forces move longer distances when they relocate. This elevated rate of mobility appears to persist across the life course, with veterans more likely to move than non-veterans. In the context of the All-Volunteer Force, this accelerated pattern of spatial mobility affects not only service personnel, but often their spouses and children. Research on the effects of residential mobility on children of military personnel yields mixed results. Evidence unequivocally demonstrates that civilian spouses of armed forces personnel experience negative labor market outcomes linked to migration. Many questions on the individual and collective effects of this institutionally linked spatial mobility remain unanswered.

In the All-Volunteer Force era, these questions have implications not only for the individuals and families who are directly affected, but for broader patterns of social inequality. Today's military barracks are largely occupied by African Americans, young adults from Southern states and rural areas, and those without a college degree—and for many of these young people, joining the armed forces represents an intentional effort at upward socio-economic mobility. To the degree that the geographic mobility required of active-duty personnel is damaging to them or their families, the effect of the military will be to concentrate these negative outcomes on members of disadvantaged groups. This hampers the ability of the military, as an influential social institution, to be an engine of social change in regard to promoting social equality. It could also exacerbate rather than alleviate inequality if the negative effects of increased mobility associated with military service outweigh the benefits of military service (e.g., access to training, GI Bill, and other benefits). Until we fully understand the individual, familial, and collective dynamics associated with this rapid tempo of relocation, the military, as an institution, will be unable to adequately and effectively respond to the needs of its employees, and relations between the military and civil society will be diminished.

NOTES

1. Note that military staffing policy currently allows new enlistments up to age 42. However, given the relatively small number of these middle-aged adults who join the armed forces for the first time, I use a more restricted population base in the denominator.
2. See, however, documentation identifying problems with this measure in both 1940 and 1950, available from the Minnesota Population Center at http://usa.ipums.org/usa-action/variables/VETSTAT#description_tab (accessed 17 July 2012) . Scholars generally agree that measures of veteran status derived from the U.S. Census are valid only from 1960 onward.
3. However, see Call and Teachman (1991), Pavalko and Elder (1990), and Karney, Loughran, and Pollard (forthcoming) for evidence that service in the military, and even combat exposure, may have varying effects on marriage stability for different cohorts.

10 A Matter of Life and Death
Military Service and Health

Alair MacLean

A substantial amount of evidence documents that service members who fight in wars are more likely than those who do not to suffer injury and death (Gawande 2004), as well as enduring physical and mental health problems (Institute of Medicine 2008a). However, in part due to positive health selection among those entering the military, at some points in the life course, veterans may have health that is better or no worse than that of non-veterans (London and Wilmoth 2006; Wilmoth, London, and Parker 2010). Despite a sociological tradition of studying health variation across different segments of the population that stretches back to the 19th century (Durkheim 1951), relatively few scholars have examined how military service affects health within a life-course perspective.

In this chapter, I draw on two related sociological traditions—cumulative inequality theory and the life-course perspective—to shed light on the empirical contributions of previous work regarding the relationships between military service and health.[1] First, I describe cumulative inequality theory and its implications for the study of health disparities. Then I describe the life-course concept of turning point, with particular reference to military service. Finally, I apply these perspectives to the large body of existing research that addresses service members' health prior to, during, and after the period of active-duty military service, but does not explicitly use life-course concepts and perspectives.

By focusing on how early-life factors shape later-life transitions, trajectories, and outcomes, the life-course perspective enables a dynamic analysis of military service and health that takes into account both positive health selection into the military and the consequences of military service for health (see Wilmoth and London, Chapter 1 of this volume). In fact, it is impossible to consider the consequences of military service for health without taking health selection into the military into account (see Wolf, Wing, and Lopoo, Chapter 13 of this volume). Previous studies make it clear that researchers need to be cautious about concluding that military service contributes to better health or serves as a positive turning point given that selection into military service is strongly influenced by sociodemographic characteristics and health status in early life. With respect to health during service, scholars have produced findings suggesting that military service may exacerbate preexisting early-life disadvantages and health-related inequalities, particularly if service involves combat exposure. With respect to health after service, findings suggest that military service may affect health in ways that are consistent with both the cumulative inequality and the turning point accounts, or with neither of these accounts, depending on particular historical and individual circumstances.

CUMULATIVE INEQUALITY

The chapter draws on cumulative inequality theory, which expands the theory of cumulative advantage first elaborated by Merton, who developed the theory, which he labeled the "Matthew Effect," to explain why some scientists receive more credit than others for similar or collaborative work. He argued that scientists receive more credit if they complete a particular work when they are already prominent (Merton 1968). Over the past forty years, researchers and theorists have argued that the same process applies to both advantages and disadvantages in a range of contexts (Dannefer 1987, 2003; DiPrete and Eirich 2006; O'Rand 1996). According to this theory, people accumulate advantages if they start from positions of advantage and accumulate disadvantages if they start from positions of disadvantage. Thus, individuals experience more positive or negative outcomes in a variety of domains, including health, depending on their positions within the social structure. Importantly, both between- and within-cohort inequalities influence the process of accumulating advantage and disadvantage across the life course.

Individuals are most likely to gain advantages or disadvantages when they undergo important developmental events during the transition to adulthood, such as when they finish school, enter the labor force, get married, or have children (Ferraro, Shippee, and Schafer 2009; Shanahan 2000). Enlisting in the military is another event that can potentially shape the accumulation of advantage and disadvantage. The timing and sequence of these various events during the demographically dense period of early adulthood (Rindfuss 1991) set the stage for the accumulation of health-related resources, such as education, income, and social network ties that impact health outcomes across the life course. Whereas early-life events set the stage for increasing heterogeneity in a cohort as inequalities accumulate over time, in order to understand the extent to which cumulative inequality shapes health outcomes, it is important to follow a cohort as it ages. However, studies that focus on older people may understate cumulative inequality due to selective mortality. Given that more disadvantaged groups tend to have higher age-specific mortality rates, the people who remain in an older cohort may differ from the people who were part of the group in earlier years. The remaining members may, therefore, look more similar to each other and less unequal than would the original members of the cohort (Ferraro, Shippee, and Schafer 2009).

Many previous researchers have implicitly evaluated cumulative inequality by examining health disparities among civilians (Willson, Shuey, and Elder 2007). In studies of civilians, scholars have documented a social and economic gradient in health, showing that higher social standing is correlated with better health. If people are more educated, for example, they tend to live longer and have fewer illnesses (Elo 2009). An emergent body of sociological research focuses on socioeconomic status as a fundamental cause of health disparities (Chang and Lauderdale 2009; Link and Phelan 2010; Warren and Hernandez 2007). Researchers who have examined workers in civilian occupations have concluded that those with lower social standing experience greater stress than those with higher standing, and that this stress contributes to health inequalities (Marmot et al. 1991). This research shows that disadvantage in one realm—socioeconomic attainment—is associated with disadvantage in another—health. However, cumulative inequality theory has been applied infrequently to study how military service is associated with health (London and Wilmoth 2006; Nayback 2008). In addition, the extant research rarely acknowledges that the civilian population contains a mix of non-veterans who never served in the military and veterans who served in the military at an earlier point in the life course. Some scholars have therefore argued that military service is a "hidden variable" that warrants more systematic and careful attention than it has thus far received in various research literatures (Elder and Clipp 1988b; Settersten 2006; Spiro, Schnurr, and Aldwin 1997).

TURNING POINTS

Whereas the theory of cumulative inequality focuses on how inequality increases over time, scholars have described how various life-course transitions can result in turning points that produce discontinuities in the life course. Positive turning points lead to better-than-expected trajectories and outcomes, and negative turning points can initiate or compound existing disadvantages that contribute to worse-than-expected trajectories and outcomes (Elder, Gimbel, and Ivie 1991; Ferraro, Shippee, and Schafer 2009; Sampson and Laub 1996). Some criminologists, for example, have shown that relatively more privileged teens suffer a greater negative effect from being arrested than less privileged teens. They attribute this result to "disadvantage saturation," which suggests that disadvantaged people stop accumulating adverse consequences once they pass a certain level of disadvantage (Hannon 2003), but an equally plausible interpretation is that arrest represents a negative turning point for more privileged adolescents and contributes to processes of long-term cumulative disadvantage for less privileged youth. Youths from both more and less advantaged social positions are affected by arrest, but the consequences of arrest and its capacity to redirect the life course are more immediately visible among more advantaged youth.

Events, transitions, and experiences that serve as positive turning points help to interrupt the disadvantage accumulation process. If people experience an event as a turning point, their lives are transformed, and they follow different trajectories than they would have otherwise. Research suggests military service can serve as a positive turning point, particularly in the lives of young men from disadvantaged backgrounds (see Bennett and McDonald, Chapter 6 of this volume, and Kleykamp, Chapter 7 of this volume). Among veterans who grew up in disadvantaged families or neighborhoods, military service provides a chance to obtain educational benefits, employment training, and access to health care. Disadvantaged youth benefit from the fact that military service "knifes off" their previous experience (Brotz and Wilson 1946), providing them a "bridging environment" where they can learn skills that they would not have acquired as civilians (Browning, Lopreato, and Poston 1973).

There are various mechanisms by which military service can come to represent a positive turning point or improve the health of the men and women who serve. For instance, service encourages service members to exercise and be physically active. Service may also improve health by providing members with food that is healthier than that eaten by civilians (Mission: Readiness 2010). In many eras, veterans have also had access to government funding to increase their educational attainment (Stanley 2003; see also Bennett and McDonald, Chapter 6 of this volume). Given that education is associated with better health (Elo 2009), the armed forces may also foster improved health by enabling current and former members to increase their education. Military service may also enhance access to high-quality health care through the military and, for some, the Department of Veterans Affairs' Veterans Health Administration (Wilmoth and London 2011; see also Street and Hoffman, Chapter 11 of this volume). Other veterans have access to *TRICARE for Life*, the health care provided to people who retire from the military, usually after twenty years of service. Scholars have shown that the Veterans Administration provides care that is better, on average, than that provided by civilian providers (Asch et al. 2004). Thus, some segments of the veteran population may have different health outcomes due to more consistent access to health care (for a discussion of how veterans move to gain access to health care, see Bailey, Chapter 9 of this volume). Taken together, these observations suggest that military service could be a positive turning point that affects socioeconomic attainment, as well as health and other health-related life-course domains (London and Wilmoth 2006).

Of course, not all people who serve in the military experience it as a positive turning point. Military service can represent a negative turning point for those who acquire training-related injuries, experience military sexual trauma (Frayne et al. 2006; Suris and Lind 2008; Turner et al. 2004), experience combat-related physical injuries or post-traumatic stress disorder (PTSD) (Institute of Medicine 2008a; Tanielian and Jaycox 2008), or receive blue or dishonorable discharge because they are gay, bisexual, or lesbian (see Brown, Chapter 5 of this volume). Like positive turning points, negative turning points redirect the life course. Given the many risks associated with combat, and the ways that deployment can disrupt established life-course trajectories in ways that have implications for later-life health, there is substantial potential for military service to produce negative turning points for some individuals in some historical contexts.

Researchers may have difficulty assessing the positive and negative effects of military service because these effects might be, to some extent, co-occurring and countervailing in the lives of veterans. Also, there are both positive and negative selection effects that need to be taken into account; the military draws more from some social strata than others, but also has relatively stringent physical, mental, and moral standards for admission and rejects potential recruits who are overweight, in poor health, or have apparent moral shortcomings (National Research Council 2006). Thus, there is a need to take account of both positive and negative health and social selection into the military when trying to assess the consequences of military service, for better or worse.

CONCEPTUALIZING THE RELATIONSHIP BETWEEN MILITARY SERVICE AND HEALTH

Together, cumulative inequality theory and the life-course perspective provide a framework for understanding how military service could influence health trajectories and outcomes at different ages and stages of development (see Wilmoth and London, Chaper 1 of this volume). Specifically, they highlight how military service could be associated with health in one of three ways. First, individuals are selected into military service on the basis of various sociodemographic and health characteristics, some of which should be positively related to health outcomes (e.g., health screening) and others of which may be negatively related to health outcomes (e.g., childhood economic disadvantage). Thus, any health differences between active-duty personnel, veterans, and civilians might be due to differences in early-life characteristics that shaped the inclination and ability to serve in the armed forces (see Wolf, Wing, and Lopoo, Chapter 13 of this volume).

Second, military service could negatively impact health outcomes due to combat- and training-related injuries, exposure to hazardous environmental conditions (e.g., Agent Orange), or the development of detrimental health behaviors (e.g., smoking, alcohol consumption, drug abuse). However, military service could also positively impact health outcomes if it encourages the development of healthy habits (e.g., exercise) or if it provides social distinction and prestige that affects a sense of mastery and self-esteem among those who have served. It could have characteristics that make it similar to civilian occupations (Marmot et al. 1991), which independently affect health at least partly because they incorporate more or less stressful circumstances. In either the negative or the positive case, active-duty personnel and veterans may experience particular health trajectories because of specific military-related experiences.

Third, military service could indirectly shape health outcomes across the life course by influencing various health-related factors, such as education, income, social networks, and access to health care. Extant research suggests military service is correlated with, and thus serves as a proxy for, other health-related measures of social standing. Thus, persons with a history of military service may have different health trajectories and outcomes than non-veterans because of the ways that military service experiences affect subsequent life-course trajectories and outcomes across multiple health-related domains, such as educational attainment, employment, marriage and family, and residential location (see chapters in this volume by Bennett and McDonald, Kleykamp, Burland and Lundquist, and Bailey).

In addition to distinguishing among health factors present before, during, and after military service, it is also relevant to keep in mind that the influence of military service on health may vary by the social locations of individuals, particularly in terms of race, ethnicity, class, gender, and sexual orientation. Women may, for example, be affected by their service differently than men. Over the last forty years, women have become a larger proportion of active-duty and veteran populations. In 1972, they represented 2% of military personnel; thirty years later, they represented 15% (Segal and Segal 2004). Female soldiers have borne the brunt of military sexual trauma, including rape and sexual harassment, which they experience at much greater rates than do male soldiers (Frayne et al. 2006; Suris and Lind 2008; Turner et al. 2004), and their later mental and physical health may be negatively affected by such trauma (Goldzweig et al. 2006). Yet few previous scholars have evaluated whether race, ethnicity, class, and gender moderate the relationship between military service and health (but see London and Wilmoth 2006; Wilmoth, London, and Parker 2011). In addition, researchers have not examined these characteristics within an intersectional framework that allows for the possibility that these characteristics have effects that are not just additive, but interactive. According to the intersectional perspective, Black women, for example, may be affected by events in ways that do not simply reflect the impacts of race and gender, but rather the interaction between those two characteristics (McCall 2005). Given the limitations of the extant research, readers should keep in mind that much of our understanding of the relationship between military service and health is based primarily on White men who served during particular historical circumstances.

BEFORE SERVICE: HEALTH AND SOCIOECONOMIC SELECTION

In this section, I summarize research regarding whether service members differ from each other and from civilians in terms of their pre-service health-related characteristics and health. Such differences might influence estimates of how military service affects post-service health. Researchers could estimate associations between military service and health that are biased because people choose and are chosen to serve in the armed forces based on preexisting socioeconomic and health-related characteristics, as well as early-life health status and conditions. Biased estimates could result if some current and former military personnel are selected before they serve for better or worse health trajectories and outcomes in later life than civilians. Indeed, people are selected to serve in the military and to be deployed to combat on the basis of their health and correlated characteristics (National Research Council 2006), which could result in the effects of service and combat being either over- or understated. Scholars have shown that there may be relevant pre-service differences between service members and civilians (described below), which could either mask or amplify the extent to which military service contributes to cumulative inequality or serves as a turning point in people's lives.

Service members, for example, are chosen for their good health, which could lead to overestimates of positive effects or underestimates of negative effects of service. The military rejects potential recruits who are overweight or have other indicators of poor health (National Research Council 2006). Before their service, therefore, military personnel are less likely to be in poor health than are civilians. Yet researchers most often evaluate whether service members have worse or better health than civilians using data collected after service has ended. Analyzing these data, they are able to observe that military personnel have relatively good health, and conclude that service improves health. Alternatively, even if service negatively affects health, they may see no association between service and health, and conclude that service has no effect. In practice, many scholars have observed, using various data sources and analytic approaches, that military service negatively affects health trajectories and outcomes (Elder, Shanahan, and Clipp 1997; London and Wilmoth 2006; Wilmoth, London, and Parker 2010, 2011), although they may underestimate the extent of this negative effect. To assess the extent of bias, they can pursue one of three strategies. First, they can acknowledge the limitations of the data with regard to health selection. Second, they can measure whether the health of service members changes as a consequence of serving in the armed forces, by measuring health both before and after service. Third, they can correct for selection with statistical techniques, such as regressions that include background control variables or use of instrumental variables that the researchers believe directly affect service, but do not directly affect health (Dobkin and Shabani 2009; see also Wolf, Wing, and Lopoo, Chapter 13 of this volume). Given the range of factors that are arguably health related, identifying suitable instruments has proven to be extremely challenging.

Scholars confront a related problem, the "healthy warrior" effect, which could lead them to underestimate the negative effects of combat. Before sending people into combat, the armed forces screen for health conditions. Previous researchers have referred to this as the "healthy warrior" or "healthy deployer" effect (Armed Forces Health Surveillance Center 2007a). Due to this selection effect, researchers could conclude that combat improves or at least does not negatively affect the health of troops; however, recent research suggests that the declines in later-life health are steepest among male veterans who experienced wartime service (Wilmoth, London, and Parker 2010). Ideally, researchers should correct statistically for the health of military personnel before combat. At the very least, they should consider statistical estimates of the negative effects of combat to be a lower bound.

Scholars must also deal with the opposite problem when considering how the association between military service and health is affected by service members' average socioeconomic characteristics, which may lead service members to suffer worse health than civilians. In the contemporary all-volunteer period and for much of the draft era, people were more likely to enlist in the military if their families or they had lower socioeconomic attainment (Kleykamp 2006; Segal, Burns, Falk, Silver, and Sharda 1998; Teachman, Call, and Segal 1993b), which is independently and negatively correlated with health (Chang and Lauderdale 2009; Elo 2009; Link and Phelan 2010; Warren and Hernandez 2007). Young adults have tended not to enlist in the military, for example, if they have the academic capabilities and aspirations that make it likely they will go to college (MacLean 2005). Veterans have tended to be less likely to have attained higher education than non-veterans. Many scholars have shown that educational attainment is associated with health disparities; more educated people tend to have better health, live longer, have fewer health conditions, and rate their health more favorably than less educated people (Elo 2009). Thus, veterans may have worse health than non-veterans not because they served in the military, but because they came from socioeconomically disadvantaged backgrounds and have fewer years of schooling. If this is the case, education could be an omitted variable, and a negative association between military service and health could be spurious. Researchers should therefore examine the association between service and health while controlling for education and other socioeconomic characteristics. However, in doing so, it is important to distinguish between measures of parental socioeconomic status and the respondent's own socioeconomic status, including distinguishing between educational attainment prior to the onset and after the completion of military service. Carefully measuring education in relation to the timing of military service enables the researcher to disentangle the educational effects that operate through selection into military service from the educational effects that are a consequence of military service.

Researchers confront another possible problem in assessing how service affects health because studies are often based on retrospective reports, which may be affected by current status. In most surveys, veterans or service members report their military experiences retrospectively and their health status contemporaneously. People may report more negative experiences in the past if they are suffering from poor health in the present. One study, for example, found that veterans who were trying to get help from the Veterans Administration were more likely to report combat exposure than those who were not seeking such assistance (Frueh et al. 2005). However, another study found that veterans reported combat experiences in a national survey that were corroborated by archival sources (Dohrenwend et al. 2006). Scholars should therefore consider the possibility of retrospective reporting bias, but not dismiss analyses solely on those grounds.

DURING SERVICE

Potential Mechanisms

Regardless of pre-service characteristics, military personnel can experience several service-connected outcomes that they would not encounter in most lines of civilian work. In the following section, therefore, I summarize previous research regarding how military service affects the health of people while they are serving in the armed forces, particularly as it relates to physical injury, mental illness, and death. I will begin by briefly reviewing the different mechanisms that potentially can explain how military service directly affects health. All of these explanations focus on how some military personnel have different experiences than others while serving in the armed forces, and different experiences than civilians who have never served in the military. Researchers have, for the most part, evaluated whether military personnel suffer worse health if they served during wartime and experienced combat. However, armed forces personnel serve in different ranks, branches, and military occupations, and for different durations. They may serve, for example, in the Army or the Navy, in the enlisted or the officer ranks, in different occupational specialties, or for a single enlistment period or a twenty-year career. Yet relatively few scholars have evaluated whether military personnel have different health outcomes because of these diverse experiences (Edwards 2008; Keehn 1978), at least in part because of data constraints (see Teachman, Chapter 14 of the volume).

Researchers have primarily examined variation in health among service members in relation to three different mechanisms: environmental exposures, health behaviors, and combat. Veterans of different wars, for example, may have been differentially affected by the environment, particularly by contact with chemicals. During the Vietnam War, soldiers were exposed to Agent Orange, the popular name for the chemical that was sprayed on the ground to remove plants that could hide enemy fighters. Vietnam veterans have attributed some of their later illnesses to this exposure during their active-duty wartime service (Scott 1992). During the first Gulf War, service members were also exposed to environmental toxins. Analysts have debated whether veterans of that war suffer from a group of symptoms that they labeled Gulf War Syndrome (Brown et al. 2000). Some researchers have shown that veterans who deployed have more symptoms of illness than veterans who did not deploy to the Gulf. However, others have argued that these symptoms do not stem from one underlying syndrome (Institute of Medicine 2006).

Military personnel may have relatively poor health because they are more likely than civilians to engage in poor health behaviors, such as smoking and drinking. During some eras, for example, the armed forces enabled smoking by providing troops with cigarettes. Previous researchers have examined the extent to which people start or increase smoking cigarettes when they enter the armed forces. Some analysts have shown that veterans are more likely than non-veterans to smoke, which may lead them to have worse health (Bedard and Deschênes 2006; Dobkin and Shabani 2009). However, recently, the military has begun a campaign to encourage service members not to start smoking and to convince those who already smoke to stop (Department of Defense 2011d). There is also some evidence that service members are more likely to use alcohol and drugs than civilians. They are more likely, for example, to develop problems with alcohol and also more likely to abuse drugs if they were deployed to war zones (Shipherd, Stafford, and Tanner 2005; Wright, Carter, and Cullen 2005). Active-duty service members may initiate the use of these substances to self-medicate, or as a means of treating distress or the symptoms of mental illnesses brought about by the strains of separation, training, or combat.

The health consequences of combat exposure have received the lion's share of attention in the research literature in part because veterans with service-connected injuries and disabilities, as well as their family members, are highly relevant populations for policy makers. Making adequate provisions for wounded warriors and their family members is a national priority that is widely supported by the public. If they are exposed to combat, service members may be wounded in action, suffer negative long-term mental health consequences, or die. The needs of wounded or traumatized veterans, as well as the deaths of service members, have specific consequences for those whose lives are linked to them; both circumstances have the potential to transform lives.

Physical Injuries

During the first eight years of the wars in Afghanistan and Iraq, service members who were wounded in action accounted for 2% of those who were deployed, which represents approximately 37,000 troops. Among the wounded, half returned to active duty within two days. For those who did not, the implication is that their wounds were more serious (Department of Defense 2009a,b). If people select into service, or are assigned to different military roles on the basis of civilian socioeconomic status, these injuries may exacerbate existing health disparities or contribute to cumulative inequality among veterans and their family members, who are often called upon to care for them. Alternatively, the "healthy warrior" effect may mask the long-term effects of these injuries, which could result in researchers underestimating the extent to which these service-related injuries serve as negative turning points in the life course.

In both peacetime and wartime, service members can be injured in accidents, during training, or as a result of military sexual assault, as well as in combat (Sanders et al. 2005). Such injuries present a conceptual problem for scholars attempting to assess the effects of service on health. Although military personnel who suffer combat wounds do so because they served in the armed forces, people can be injured in accidents even if they do not serve in the military. The context, cause, and, perhaps, severity of seemingly similar injuries vary in ways that are often not captured in available data sources. Service members may also suffer accidents not because they are in the military, but because they are relatively young. Until the age of 60, people are at greater risk of being injured in accidents when they are younger than when they are older (Massie and Campbell 1993). Thus, in assessing the impact of military service on noncombat injuries, researchers should compare soldiers to similar civilians.

Scholars have recently begun to focus on the long-term impacts on military personnel of traumatic brain injuries experienced in combat (Institute of Medicine 2008b). People suffer such injuries after collisions, accidents, or blasts that injure their heads. Some civilian workers are more likely to suffer such injuries at work than are others, particularly those who work as police officers, mine workers, or football players. Troops have always suffered such injuries during wartime; however, even during peacetime, they have experienced these injuries during training or if they have accidents. During the peacetime era of the late 1990s, for example, military personnel were most likely to suffer brain injuries because of accidents. During the more recent war years, they have been more likely to experience brain injuries due to hostile action or combat (Armed Forces Health Surveillance Center 2007b). Researchers have paid increasing attention to brain injuries during the current wars in Iraq and Afghanistan for two reasons (Institute of Medicine 2008b). First, in those conflicts, troops have been particularly vulnerable to blast injuries from improvised explosive devices. Second, they are more likely to survive such incidents than they were in past wars because military medical practices have improved. In attempting to gauge the needs of survivors of traumatic brain injuries, analysts have mostly had to rely on findings from work assessing the impact of such injuries on civilians, such as people who play football or survive car accidents. From this related research, they have reasonably extrapolated that wartime injuries will have physical consequences, such as headaches, and psychological consequences, such as depression (Institute of Medicine 2008b).

Mental Health

In addition to physical consequences, service members may also suffer mental health problems as a consequence of their participation in the armed services. Such problems are particularly prevalent among those who were exposed to combat. In 2007, service members most commonly sought treatment for three mental health diagnoses: depression, post-traumatic stress disorder (PTSD), and substance abuse (Armed Forces Health Surveillance Center 2008). Although many researchers have evaluated the mental health of current and former military personnel, apparently no scholars have examined these issues using a life-course approach.

Psychiatrists formally adopted the term PTSD to describe the symptoms presented by Vietnam veterans who had experienced combat, and first included it in the Diagnostic and Statistical Manual of Mental Disorders published by the American Psychiatric Association in 1980 (Kulka et al. 1990). Before the Vietnam War, physicians diagnosed such soldiers as suffering from such conditions as "irritable heart," "shell-shock," or "battle fatigue" (Dean 1997; Shay 2002). Currently, physicians diagnose PTSD when a person has experienced a traumatic event that leads to "reexperiencing" the event through flashbacks or nightmares, and has physical symptoms, such as jumpiness and insomnia. The term has been applied broadly to describe how people respond to different traumatic events, including combat, rape, and molestation (Institute of Medicine 2008a).

As with people who survive other traumas, military personnel can experience immediate- or delayed-onset PTSD and short-term, long-term, or intermittent symptoms. Some service members begin showing symptoms immediately after they experience a traumatic event, whereas others begin to suffer months or even years later. One study, for example, showed that when soldiers were assessed as soon as they returned from Iraq, the rates of PTSD appeared relatively low, approximately 1 to 5%. When they were assessed six months later, the rates were higher, approximately 3 to 8% (Bliese et al. 2007).

It is important to note that for those who serve in the military during peacetime, there can be positive mental health outcomes associated with military service. Wyman, Lemmon, and Teachman (2010) demonstrate that active-duty veterans who served during the peacetime years of the All-Volunteer Force era have significantly lower levels of depression than non-veterans and Reserve-duty veterans. This mental health advantage is greatest right after discharge and gradually disappears thereafter such that, within ten years of discharge, active-duty veterans have depression levels that are similar to non-veterans. This suggests that, during peacetime, the military may provide an environment that reduces the likelihood of depression, perhaps by providing structure to daily routines, extended social networks, stable employment, enhanced self-esteem, and predictable advancement.

Deaths

As shown in Figure 10.1, between 1980 and 2008, the leading cause of death among active-duty service members was either accidents or combat, depending on the time period. During peacetime, service members died

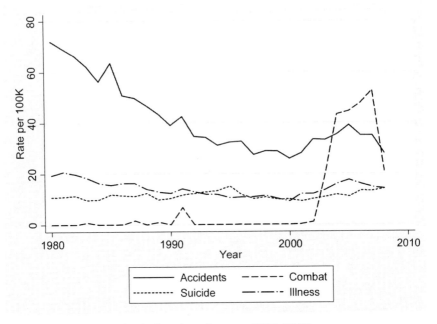

Figure 10.1 Military deaths by selected causes, 1980–2008.

most commonly from training and nontraining accidents. During the recent war years, service personnel became more likely to die in combat. Throughout the period, they have also died from illnesses and suicide. The death of a service member obviously ends that individual's life, but it can have substantial and potentially life-altering consequences for surviving parents, spouses, and children whose lives are linked to that service member.

One cause of death unique to military service is death from hostile fire. Compared to service members who served during the 20th century, service members today are relatively more likely to be wounded, but less likely to be killed (Buzzell and Preston 2007; Gawande 2004). As shown in Table 10.1, over 115,000 American troops were killed during World War I, more than 400,000 died during World War II, 36,000 died in the Korean War, and 58,000 were killed in the Vietnam Conflict (Department of Defense 2011a). The numbers of people killed in the more recent wars in Iraq and Afghanistan are much smaller. Less than 400 were killed in the first Persian Gulf War; as of the end of 2011, over 4,400 had died in the Persian Gulf region during Operation Iraqi Freedom and Operation New Dawn, and slightly more than 1,700 had died in Afghanistan during Operation Enduring Freedom (Department of Defense 2011a,b,c). Over the past hundred years, the odds of being wounded versus dying among American service personnel have increased from 1.75 during World War I to 8.69 in Operation Enduring Freedom. The increasing odds of surviving with combat-related injuries have implications not only for service members, but also the family members who serve as caregivers to wounded warriors.

Table 10.1 Total Number of Persons Serving, Died, and Wounded, by War

War	Number Serving	Total Deaths	Total Wounded, Not Mortal	Odds of Being Wounded versus Dying
World War I	4,734,991	116,516	204,002	1.75
World War II	16,112,566	405,399	670,846	1.65
Korean War	5,720,000	36,574	103,284	2.82
Vietnam Conflict	8,744,000	58,220	303,644	5.22
Persian Gulf War	2,225,000	383	467	1.22
Operation Iraqi Freedom	—	4,407	31,921	7.24
Operation New Dawn	—	66	305	4.62
Operation Enduring Freedom (Afghanistan only)	—	1,744	15,157	8.69

Source: Department of Defense (2011 a, b, c).
Note: Odds are based on calculations done by J.W. Wilmoth. Number serving for Operations Iraqi Freedom, New Dawn, and Enduring Freedom are not publicly available. Data for 18th- and 19th-century wars are available at http://siadapp.dmdc.osd.mil/personnel/CASUALTY/ WCPRINCIPAL.pdf. Number of deaths in the Korean War including non-theater deaths is equal to 54,246.

Some researchers suggest that socioeconomic disadvantage has been associated with war-related mortality, although the same may not be true of the current wars. They argue that the men who were killed in action differed from the general population in terms of race and class. Most analysts focus on the American troops who died in Vietnam (Barnett, Stanley, and Shore 1992; Zeitlin, Lutterman, and Russell 1973); however, one paper evaluates the characteristics of the American troops who were killed in Korea (Mayer and Hoult 1955). These studies suggest that U.S. servicemen were more likely to be killed if they came from neighborhoods or families that had fewer socioeconomic resources when compared to the rest of the population. Servicemen could have differed in these ways because the men who entered the military differed from the rest of the population or because the troops who were sent into combat differed from the troops who were not. More recently, scholars have begun to evaluate the characteristics of the service members who have died in Iraq and Afghanistan, suggesting that racial-ethnic minority service members have not been disproportionately likely to be killed in combat. They have shown that Blacks are underrepresented among these deaths (Buzzell and Preston 2007; Gifford 2005a). Officers have also been less likely to be killed than have enlisted service members (Buzzell and Preston 2007).

Although military personnel are at risk of dying in combat or in service-related accidents, scholars have long focused on the extent to which military service is associated with suicide. In the 19th century, Emile Durkheim evaluated rates of suicide among the members of different social groups and found that French soldiers committed suicide at a higher rate than the general population. He argued that the greater rate of suicide among soldiers stemmed from the way they were trained. According to his argument, the armed forces train soldiers to see themselves as part of a group and not as individuals. Thus, soldiers value their own lives less highly than do civilians and are, accordingly, more likely to commit suicide (Durkheim 1951). Contemporary researchers, who are more likely to attribute suicide to depression and other mental health problems, have recently begun to evaluate suicide among troops serving in the wars in Iraq and Afghanistan. During this era, service members have been more likely than civilians to commit suicide. In 2004, the suicide rate among civilians was 10.9 per 100,000. Between 1997 and 2006, the average suicide rate among soldiers deployed to war zones was 12.2 per 100,000 and appears to be increasing (Mental Health Advisory Team 2008). Therefore, military personnel continue to exhibit an elevated risk of suicide-related mortality, although the reasons for this elevated risk are not yet fully understood.

AFTER SERVICE

In this section, I summarize what researchers have found regarding how veterans differ from non-veterans in terms of their health after service. Because most people who enter the armed forces serve for relatively short durations, they spend most of the adult life course as veterans. Given that most health research that focuses on the "civilian" population does not distinguish between those with and without histories of military service, much of what we know about civilians might be applicable to veterans, especially among cohorts in which high proportions served. However, there may also be substantive differences.

Similar to research on health differences during military service, scholars who have focused on veteran status and health have paid particular attention to physical health, mental well-being, and mortality. Most have evaluated how veterans are affected immediately after their service, in the short-term. However, some have examined whether veterans are affected years later, in the medium and long term. They have implicitly assessed whether veterans and non-veterans differ in how they grow old. As with analysts exploring the effects of military service on the health of active-duty personnel, these researchers tend to evaluate whether veterans are negatively affected by experiencing combat either because service produced negative turning points in their lives or contributed to cumulative disadvantage, although they do not necessarily explicitly reference the life-course perspective. These researchers have been less likely to assess the possibilities that veterans may differ from each other in terms of health because they served in different branches, ranks, and occupations. Taken together, the findings suggest that veterans are affected by military service in ways that are sometimes consistent with the theory of cumulative inequality, sometimes with the concept of turning points, and sometimes with neither.

Although most researchers have focused on how health is affected by combat, some have tried to identify how serving in the military affects health regardless of whether veterans were exposed to combat. These investigations allow for the possibility that military service might be beneficial for health or serve as a positive turning point because it connects veterans to educational, health care, and other social and economic benefits. They also allow for a focus on women, who do not generally experience combat, even though the lines between combat and noncombat roles for women are increasingly blurred in contemporary conflicts. If they serve during peacetime, for example, service members are unlikely to be exposed to some of the most health-damaging risks or experiences. Even during wartime, some military personnel do not see combat. For example, according to one estimate, less than one-third of active-duty enlisted people deployed to Iraq and Afghanistan between 2001 and 2006, whereas two-thirds did not deploy during these years (Shen et al. 2009). Given that there is substantial heterogeneity in military service experiences, some scholars have investigated whether veterans have different levels of post-service physical and mental health problems than non-veterans, on average. Sometimes, because of data constraints, these studies do not take combat exposure into account; sometimes, they are able to differentiate noncombat and combat veterans.

Illness, Poor Health, and Disability

Medical researchers have shown that service members and veterans who deployed to war zones are more likely than those who did not to suffer a variety of medical diagnoses, including chronic fatigue, gastrointestinal diseases, skin disorders, and chronic pain (Institute of Medicine 2008a). People who deployed are also more likely than those who did not to report being generally ill (Institute of Medicine 2008a) and to have worse self-rated health (Armed Forces Health Surveillance Center 2009). Recent research indicates that at age 40, Reserve-duty service veterans and non-veterans who passed the military service entrance exam have better self-rated health than non-veterans who did not take the service exam. However, veterans who served on active duty have poorer self-rated health, even after controlling for a range of covariates, including socioeconomic status and health behaviors (Teachman 2010). These results suggest that military service during the All-Volunteer Force era is associated with poor mid-life health (Teachman 2010). During the recent wars, troops have been more likely to rate their health as poor or fair when they returned relative to when they left for Iraq and Afghanistan (Armed Forces Health Surveillance Center 2009). However, this self-rated health assessment may vary by rank, because previous studies have shown that service members report better health if they served in higher ranks in the military (Keehn 1978). Net of education and income, officers rate their health better than do comparable enlisted personnel, which suggests that military rank may affect health directly (MacLean and Edwards 2010).

In contrast to the scholars focusing on combat veterans, social science researchers have shown that the impact on health of military service is not clear when veterans are not differentiated according to rank or combat exposure. They have shown, for example, that Vietnam War veterans appear to have worse health than non-veterans. Such veterans are more likely to rate their health as fair or poor, have physical limitations, and be anxious or depressed (Dobkin and Shabani 2009). When they corrected for nonrandom selection into the armed forces using an instrumental variable approach (see Wolf, Wing, and Lopoo, Chapter 13 of this volume), they found the significantly worse health of veterans observed in the OLS regression models were not significant in the two-stage least squares models. However, they conclude that the two-stage least squares models "that use the Vietnam draft lottery as an instrument for military give us estimates too imprecise to be informative" (Dobkin and Shabani 2009: 79). Thus, the question of whether selection accounts for the veteran status difference in health outcomes in this cohort remains unresolved.

There is evidence based on data from the general population that military service has enduring effects on health and disability that affect veterans and their families. Veterans who served during wartime, particularly World War II and the Korean War, experience steeper later-life health declines than non-veterans (Wilmoth, London, and Parker 2010). In addition, combat veterans experience greater rates of disability and unemployment across the life course (MacLean 2010). Veterans also have higher rates of limitations and disabilities than non-veterans (Wilmoth, London, and Parker 2011). Although the higher rates of functional limitation and disability among veterans have implications for family care providers, these higher levels of disability also may influence the economic well-being of veteran families. Recent research indicates that households containing disabled veterans experience an increased risk of poverty and material hardship (Heflin, Wilmoth, and London 2012; London, Heflin, and Wilmoth 2011). Therefore, it is important to keep in mind the implications of veterans' health concerns for those whose lives are linked to veterans, including spouses, children, parents, and other extended family members.

Mental Health

Researchers have shown that veterans have symptoms of PTSD years or even decades after their service has ended. Service members can suffer PTSD for short or long periods of time. They can also suffer symptoms that stop and start again. For these reasons, analysts often distinguish between the lifetime and current prevalence of the disorder, and estimates vary depending on the instrument that is used to measure it. According to one estimate, 8% of the U.S. population suffers from PTSD. Combat exposure is believed to be the cause of approximately one-third of these cases (Institute of Medicine 2008a). Among veterans of the wars in Iraq and Afghanistan, nearly one-fifth report symptoms of one or more mental health diagnoses (Tanielian and Jaycox 2008).

Previous research has found that the effects of combat exposure on mental health are moderated by social support. Veterans are less likely to have PTSD, for example, if they have stronger social networks (Fontana, Rosenheck, and Horvath 1997). Generally, they are less likely to develop the disorder if they have people with whom they can talk and more likely to have the disorder if they are socially isolated. However, this association may reflect reverse causality, with mental health or illness affecting social networks rather than the reverse (Ren et al. 1999). Veterans with PTSD may have weaker networks than comparable veterans without the disorder because the symptoms of the disorder could drive away friends and relatives.

Post-Service Mortality

In addition to examining the physical and mental health consequences of combat and service, scholars have also evaluated post-service mortality, reaching different conclusions depending on which types of veterans are studied. Veterans are more likely to die from external causes (such as accidents, suicides, or homicides, as opposed to internal causes like diseases, such as cancer or cardiovascular disease) if they deployed to war zones, and the risk is highest in the years immediately after service (Boehmer et al. 2004). Scholars have found that veterans are more likely to commit suicide if they are mentally ill. Vietnam veterans, for example, were more likely to have attempted suicide if they had psychiatric disorders (Fontana and Rosenheck 1995). As described above, veterans are more likely to have psychiatric disorders, such as PTSD and depression, if they saw combat. These findings suggest that veterans may be more likely to commit suicide if they served in war zones, which is consistent with findings from the recent wars in Iraq and Afghanistan (Mental Health Advisory Team 2008).

To assess the impact of combat on later mortality, some researchers have prospectively followed veterans over time. According to this longitudinal research, World War II veterans died when they were younger if they were exposed to combat (Elder et al. 2009). Vietnam veterans died when they were younger if they had PTSD. They also died at younger ages if they served in Vietnam than if they served in other locations (Boscarino 2006). Most analysts conclude that veterans who survive wars subsequently die when they are younger because such service increases the odds of death from external rather than internal causes (Boehmer et al. 2004; Boscarino 2006). Combat veterans die at greater rates from external causes than do other veterans, particularly in the first five years after they return (Boehmer et al. 2004). Because these veterans die when they are younger, scholars need to exercise caution in concluding that veterans have better or the same health as non-veterans among older people (for a discussion of mortality selection as it relates to research on military service and the life course, see Wolf, Wing, and Lopoo, Chapter 13 of this volume).

Other researchers have evaluated the effects of service on mortality by focusing retrospectively on veterans in the aggregate. They have shown that mortality rates are higher among cohorts with more veterans who were eligible to serve in World War II and Korea (Bedard and Deschênes 2006). They have also shown that mortality rates were higher among men who were born on days that made it more likely they would be selected in the draft lottery for the Vietnam War (Hearst, Newman, and Hulley 1986).

Some research indicates that the social gradient in health that has been documented among civilians likely exists in the military, which may be consistent with cumulative inequality theory. They have shown, for example, that veterans who served in the enlisted ranks die at younger ages than do former officers (Edwards 2008). In part, these officers live longer because they are more educated and earn more money relative to enlisted service members (MacLean and Edwards 2010).

Researchers have also shown that the effects of service on mortality may be moderated by race and the age at which people entered the military. The findings of these studies are mixed. People were more likely to die at younger ages if they entered the military at younger ages during the Civil War (Pizarro, Silver, and Prause 2006). However, they were more likely to die at younger ages if they entered the military during the Vietnam War when they were older. Among veterans who served primarily during World War II, the Korean War, and the Cold War era, some evidence is consistent with the life-course-as-positive-turning-point hypothesis (for African Americans) and some evidence is consistent with the life-course-disruption hypothesis (for those who enlisted at later ages) (London and Wilmoth 2006).

CONCLUSION

This chapter draws on the life-course perspective and cumulative inequality theory to provide a framework for considering how military service is related to health, and how the relationship between military service and health depends on the circumstances of service and the characteristics of service members. Service members experience increased risk of illness, injury, and death, both during and after service, particularly if they served in combat or were deployed to war zones. Military service may also contribute to cumulative inequality with respect to health, although it can serve as a turning point that alters life-course trajectories. Whether and how such processes contribute to the widening or narrowing of health disparities at the population level is a topic that requires additional research.

Another issue that requires additional research concerns the extent to which the health consequences of military service endure. Some researchers have demonstrated that the effects of service on health are strong in the short term, but the evidence about the long-term effects of military service is more mixed. Some studies indicate that the effects of military service dissipate with age, as veterans die or adapt to negative circumstances, whereas other studies find strong effects of military service on men's later-life health trajectories and mortality. If additional research supports the notion that the effects of military service dissipate with age, then the effects of service could be consistent with the fluctuations drawn in life satisfaction charts (Clausen 1998), which show that negative and positive events affect lives in the short but not in the long term. However, if military service operates like other early-life institutional influences, such as college or incarceration, then it might have long-term effects on health across the life course (see Wilmoth and London, Chapter 1 of this volume).

Military service involving combat may exacerbate existing inequalities or create new ones. However, few scholars have evaluated whether service also contributes to cumulative inequality in physical health outcomes in the broader population. Nor, with few exceptions (Teachman 2010), have they extensively examined whether the military gradient in health extends to mental health outcomes with nationally representative data. Another area that has received relatively little attention is the impact of veterans' health on the lives of their family members, although some studies on this topic are available in the extant literature (Beckham, Lytle, and Feldman 1996; Calhoun, Beckham, and Bosworth 2002; Dekel et al. 2005; Renshaw, Allen, Rhoades, and Blais 2011). Efforts are underway to develop better measurement tools for the assessment of well-being among the spouses of veterans with PTSD (Hayes et al. 2010), to better understand the experiences of caregivers of veterans with traumatic brain injuries (Phelan et al. 2011), and to develop and evaluate the adequacy of policies and programs that aim to meet the needs of families of veterans with specific service-connected health problems (Murdoch, van Ryn, Hodges, and Cowper 2005; Sheets and Mahoney-Gleason 2010). These and related topics represent promising avenues for future research on how military service affects the lives of veterans and those to whom their lives are linked.

Consistent with the view of military service as a turning point, researchers have shown that the effects of service are moderated by race and age at entry into the military. Scholars have yet to fully assess whether military service may provide a turning point across other health outcomes for both noncombat and combat veterans. Furthermore, relatively little is known about the extent to which military service is a positive or negative turning point in the lives of female service members or gay, lesbian, or bisexual service members, who have served under very different constraints than heterosexually identified service members (see Brown, Chapter 5 of this volume).

Most researchers have focused on how military service affects health in the short term, neglecting, for the most part, to examine effects in the long term, or as veterans grow old. There are numerous national longitudinal surveys that include measures of veteran status that could be used to examine these issues. However, these studies often contain limited information about relevant military service experiences, such as combat exposure, service-related injuries, branch, rank, and occupational specialty. In addition, the findings of these studies are at risk of being biased by unobserved heterogeneity due to post-service mortality differences between veterans and non-veterans (see Wolf, Wing and Lopoo, Chapter 13 of this volume). At older ages, the veterans most affected by combat may have already died, leaving veterans who are less affected and perhaps more robust. Such selection may cause analysts to underestimate the negative effects of service, in general, and combat exposure, in particular. However, veterans may also recover from the negative effects of combat as they age, which would be difficult to determine with data that only captures the veteran many years after separation from service. Future research could evaluate these alternative possibilities directly, assuming there is adequate longitudinal data to measure the relevant concepts across the life course (see Teachman, Chapter 14 of this volume).

If there were adequate data, researchers could begin to more fully disentangle the effects of age and cohort on health among veterans. Today, veterans constitute a relatively large share of people 65 years and older, nearly 25%. These older veterans served during the draft era that encompassed the Vietnam War and earlier wars. Over the next twenty years, veterans will constitute a much smaller share of the older population, only 10%. Many of these older veterans will have served in the early peacetime years of the All-Volunteer Force (Wilmoth and London 2011). This shift in the composition of the older veteran population is likely to have a substantial impact on variation in later-life health by veteran status and the associated health care needs of older veterans.

These cohorts will be followed by those who served at the beginning of the 21st century in Operation Iraqi Freedom, Operation New Dawn, and Operation Enduring Freedom. These troops are experiencing unique challenges due to the shifting nature of enemy engagement and the increased reliance on Reserves in these recent wars. When they become veterans, they may be negatively affected by physical disability and traumatic brain injury associated with exposure to improvised explosive devices, in addition to combat-related PTSD. Yet it is important to keep in mind that more than two-thirds of active-duty service members did not deploy to combat zones between 2001 and 2006 (Shen et al. 2009). When these noncombat personnel become veterans, they may have health that is better or no worse than comparable non-veterans. How the experiences of these veterans will affect the society to which they return has yet to be assessed, and will depend to a considerable degree on the circumstances they face upon their reentry to the civilian labor market and family life. It is crucial that we use state-of-the-art methods to track the experiences of these military service personnel as they return to civilian life in order to understand the impact of this service on their own health trajectories and outcomes, as well as on the well-being of their family members.

NOTES

1. Preparation of this chapter was supported by a grant from the National Institute on Aging (R03 AG 029275).

11 Military Service, Social Policy, and Later-Life Financial and Health Security

Debra Street and Jessica Hoffman

As evidence presented in every chapter of this volume attests, participation in the military can exert influence throughout the life course, altering individuals' life chances and choices in myriad ways (see Wilmoth and London, Chapter 1 of this volume). Military service influences educational attainment, family formation, employment experiences, migration, and health for those who served and their families/dependents, although the strength and direction of the influence is shaped by unique circumstances associated with particular eras of service during young and middle adulthood[1]. Active-duty service members, veterans, and their families have access to a host of educational, financial, housing, medical, and other supportive benefits offered by the Department of Defense and the Department of Veterans Affairs. Such benefits are available exclusively to individuals whose records of military service qualify them, or their dependents and survivors, for the array of benefits designed to honor and compensate them for the risks associated with military service. Given this, these benefits have immediate, middle-range, and long-term impacts on various life-course trajectories that unfold as people age.

Although military benefits may have important effects on life-course trajectories and outcomes that depend on experiences during and after military service, many older veterans (and their beneficiaries) are *dually entitled* to a range of benefits important for financial and health security[2] in later life. By *dual entitlement*, we mean that certain older veterans are qualified to receive benefits both from military service-related programs (such as military retirement pay and health insurance, or health care, rehabilitative, education, and housing benefits from the Veterans Administration), as well as benefits from civilian programs (such as Social Security and Medicare, including pensions, health insurance, and disability insurance). Dual entitlement to both military service-related and civilian benefits accords some, but not all, veterans an additional layer of support and a more secure safety net for the uncertainties of later life.

Length and branch of service, military occupation, rank, combat exposure, and active- duty versus Reserve status are but a few of the service-related variables that influence entitlement to particular types of military benefits and, inevitably, at least some later-life outcomes. Variations in the particulars of military service underscore a range of possible differences among individuals with diverse service experiences and between individuals who have served (hereafter veterans) and non-veterans. We consider financial and health security implications for typical elderly veterans whose service is routine—that is, without major service-related disabilities—at the intersection of military benefits and policies designed for civilians' later lives. Obviously, not all elderly veterans fit the profile of experiencing either typical or routine military service. Some elderly veterans separate from military service with considerable impairments from service-related disabilities; others, such as lesbian, gay, bisexual, and transgender (LGBT) service members, experience disadvantages both in benefits and service conditions during their entire periods of enlistment. However, in this chapter we mainly focus on the interplay between routine military and civilian benefits that are intended to provide for financial and health security in later life.

During a lifetime, the benefits and risks associated with military service distinguish financial and health security outcomes for retired veterans from veterans with shorter military careers and their non-veteran counterparts, although as Teachman (Chapter 14 of this volume) notes, research that makes such comparisons across veteran and non-veteran groups is rare. In addition to intergroup differences between veterans and non-veterans, differential exposure to service-related risks and benefits contributes to intra-cohort variation in retirement experiences among veterans. Intra-cohort variation emerges as service-related risks and benefits intersect with varying individual (e.g., gender, race and ethnic background, family status, sexual identity, and social class background) and service-related characteristics (e.g., rank, length and branch of service, combat exposure, occupational category, service era, and other variable dimensions of military service) (Wilmoth and London 2011).

This chapter provides a framework for considering how policies associated with routine military service are embedded within the broader context of social policies designed to shape later-life outcomes for civilian populations. As such, we highlight intersections between military programs and civilian social policies that shape differences in prospects for later-life financial and health security. A brief discussion of the general contours of later-life financial and health security is followed by details of programs designed mainly for civilians and programs devised specifically for military service members, veterans, and their dependents. The policy infrastructure provides context for understanding distinctive later-life outcomes. In particular, we consider how *dual entitlement* to military benefits and social policies designed for the civilian population may contribute to better financial and health security for many aging veterans and their families. We conclude the chapter by highlighting avenues for future research to unpack the complexities of policy interactions on later-life experiences for veterans with different service histories, family statuses, and service-related needs.

MILITARY SERVICE AND LATER-LIFE OUTCOMES: CONFOUNDING FACTORS

Understanding how exactly the risks and benefits of military service undermine or augment particular later-life outcomes that distinguish veterans from non-veterans, as well as veterans with different service profiles or from different service eras, is complicated. As several chapter authors have observed, exposure to risks and benefits associated with military service involve complex sets of selection issues (see Wolf, Wing, and Lopoo, Chapter 13 of this volume) that make straightforward interpretation of the service relatedness of later-life outcomes a challenging, complex, and evolving enterprise. First, early-adulthood transitions that funnel individuals into adult trajectories, distinguishing veterans from non-veterans, must be considered—who serves in the first place, and why? Selection into military service, whether due to individual preference for a military career or because various service branches only permit individuals with particular desired characteristics, yields a uniformed service that differs compositionally from the adult non-veteran population. Selection out of the pool eligible for service because of health problems or other characteristics that the military considers disqualifying has a similar effect.

Second, once in the military, a different set of selection processes kicks in—who exits military service, why, and when? Differences in the timing and reasons for returning to civilian life between non-career veterans (who serve relatively short stints) and career veterans (who serve long enough to receive retirement benefits) are other factors that complicate understanding service-related influences on later-life outcomes. Third, who survives into later life, and how does that vary with military service experience? Both non-career and career veterans may experience service-related morbidity and mortality profiles that are distinctive, and may distinguish surviving elderly veterans in unique (and as yet incompletely understood) ways from the elderly non-veteran population (see MacLean, Chapter 10 of this volume). This is another potential source of selection bias that bedevils comprehensive understanding of the predictors of later-life outcomes.

Analyses comparing veterans of different eras and non-veterans typically depend on cross-sectional snapshots that do not (and usually cannot) account very well for selection processes in earlier adulthood or differential survival into later-life samples. All three of the selection problems outlined above occur within a single cohort of individuals; they reflect interacting influences of individual choices, structural locations, institutional arrangements encountered, and secular historical influences that contribute to cumulative (in)equality over individual lifetimes.

Myriad factors shape health and financial security for elderly Americans. Military service is clearly one of them, as it is a signature experience that shapes the life-course outcomes of individuals and families who serve, and which, to date, has received relatively limited attention in the research literature on later-life outcomes. In fact, military service, especially war-time service, is largely a "hidden" variable underlying knowledge about aging (Settersten 2006). Wilmoth and London (2011) document increasing diversity of military veterans in the early 21st century, encompassing gender, race, ethnicity, and conditions of service. Meeting the needs of aging Americans requires recognition of the increasing diversity of the general population, including how the unique conditions of different cohorts' levels and types of military service—whether mainly peacetime service or enlistments dominated by conflicts, such as Vietnam and Operation Iraqi Freedom/Operation Enduring Freedom—can engender different kinds of later-life service-related needs among veterans and distinguish veterans from non-veterans within a given cohort in important ways.

The circumstances of service during particular eras of peace or times of conflict, such as World War II, the Korean War, the Cold War, Vietnam, the Gulf War, and Operation Iraqi Freedom/Operation Enduring Freedom, each have their own effects on veterans' later-life experiences. In different historical periods, the potential and intensity of combat exposure, specific benefit packages, and secular conditions surrounding military service differ, underscoring the link between individual experiences and historical circumstances. The broader social context matters both during veterans' period of service and for their life chances and trajectories post-service, whether in terms of public support for military operations; policies developed to meet evolving needs of service members, veterans, and their families; availability of employment and educational opportunities; and the influence of civilian social policies. The contextual landscape of American society within which military institutions are embedded adds another layer of complexity to understanding how and under which conditions earlier military service, compared to an entirely civilian life course, influences distinctive profiles of financial and health security in later life.

FINANCIAL AND HEALTH SECURITY IN LATER LIFE

Financial security in later life depends on reliable access to resources: dependable streams of income, whether through entitlement to pensions and retirement benefits, the consumption of savings and returns on investments, or wealth. Retirement only became an institutionalized part of the American life course following the passage of the Social Security Act of 1935, when the public pension system was developed to provide secure income in old age. Social Security is the foundation of the American pension regime, which also encompasses occupational pensions and individual retirement savings. Civilian pension regimes help to regulate labor markets because their benefit structures entice workers to remain in or retire from paid work, guaranteeing later-life income for individuals (and often, their dependents and survivors) once employment ends. Retirement pay for career veterans operates with patterns of incentives and income guarantees broadly similar to the civilian pension system. Because the institution of retirement depends on adequate income to sustain consumption in old age, pension regimes that shape the timing and experience of labor market exit and determine the stability and generosity of retirement income are critical components to later-life well-being for all but the wealthiest older individuals.

Income

Although Social Security is the largest single source of income for most retired Americans (Social Security Administration 2010), its benefits were never intended to be the sole source of later-life income. Having access to occupational pension benefits or individual savings and wealth usually makes the difference between having adequate income to meet needs versus experiencing financial insecurity in old age (Harrington Meyer and Herd 2007; Street and Desai 2011; Street and Wilmoth 2001). As indicated above, inequalities in later-life outcomes, like sources of income and wealth, are systematically linked to inequalities that are experienced earlier and accumulate across the life course. These include inequalities associated with gender and family status (Harrington Meyer and Herd 2007; Hartmann and English 2009; Street and Wilmoth 2001), sexuality (Cahill and South, 2002; see also Brown, Chapter 5 of this volume), race and ethnicity (Social Security Administration 2010), occupational sector, income level, and union status (U.S. Bureau of Labor Statistics 2010). Military service is another obvious factor that may be systematically associated with income inequality in later life.

Particulars of military service and civilian employment provide foundations for later-life financial security. For example, career veterans receive deferred compensation after separation from service (in lay terms, "military pensions" or "military retirement pay") that is roughly analogous to civilian occupational pensions. However, retired veterans often collect military retirement pay at much younger ages than typically found with civilian pensions. Once discharged, the career veteran can also accrue additional pension entitlement and retirement savings through a second career in civilian employment, while simultaneously receiving military retirement pay (Congressional Research Service 2010). Non-career veterans, who enlist for shorter terms, do not have the added benefit of military retirement pay that career veterans receive. Beyond pensions, service-disabled active-duty members and veterans may also be eligible for a range of disability-related income and services—ranging from Social Security disability payments (even while receiving military pay), to Veterans Administration and military disability allowances and specialized health care, to subsidies for assisted living and supportive housing—that enhance their later-life security (U.S. Department of Veterans Affairs 2011b). Although there are notable holes in the service-disability safety net—veterans from rural areas,

LGBT claimants, or those caught up in bureaucratic delays of establishing claims—for other veterans, dual entitlement to a matrix of military/veteran benefits plus civilian benefits creates a more robust safety net.

Wealth

Alongside federal tax benefits that subsidize and create incentives for individual saving and investment for retirement income, social policies also shape the acquisition of wealth. Research on the effects of military service on wealth accumulation across the life course is scant, and findings are somewhat equivocal (Fitzgerald 2006), perhaps due to typical data limitations that plague comprehensive examinations on the impact of military service to later-life outcomes. Although wealth is much more unequally distributed than income (Social Security Administration 2010), even individuals with little access to other forms of wealth often own homes in the United States. Recognizing that home ownership is a pathway to wealth accumulation, several government policies and programs encourage Americans to purchase rather than rent homes (Conley and Gifford 2006), and generous federal and state tax incentives offset the costs of home ownership (Hacker 2005; Howard 1997; Street 2007a). Unlike those who have never served, veterans can also tap into Veterans Administration mortgage programs that help military families purchase homes, and more recently, into programs that adapt housing to meet specialized physical needs (U.S. Department of Veterans Affairs 2011b).

Household wealth is concentrated almost entirely in the value of homes, which is the single largest asset for average Americans. This can be especially important in later life, when elderly Americans' homes are potential nest eggs that can be leveraged to fund consumption during retirement years (Eschtruth, Sun, and Webb 2006; Rosnick and Baker 2010). Steadily escalating real estate values from the 1990s through 2008 in most markets created opportunities for individuals who were contemplating retirement or had recently retired to convert housing assets into cash for consumption, buying a smaller home and putting leftover cash in the bank or in more liquid investments. For other older homeowners, new financial products, like reverse mortgages, enabled them to extract equity from their homes while aging in place (Eschtruth, Sun, and Webb 2006; Rosnick and Baker 2010). Although not a very liquid form of wealth, housing equity for some older homeowners is an additional buffer against financial insecurity in old age. Housing is another policy area where military service creates dual entitlement, both to specialized Veterans Administration housing benefits and to general programs that are also available to non-veterans, like tax breaks for home ownership.

Health

Health security is another area of concern in later life. In general, age-related and chronic health conditions increase the need for routine access to affordable medical care as people grow older. Unlike most other modern countries that have some form of universal entitlement to health insurance, the United States relies on a patchwork of employment-based and public health insurance programs, as well as a medical safety net of mandated providers of last resort (e.g., emergency rooms), with millions of Americans lacking health insurance altogether. Age-based, nearly universal entitlement to publicly provided health insurance under Medicare distinguishes elderly Americans from younger Americans, who have no guaranteed entitlement to health insurance. In fact, one of the only groups of working-aged adults with health care rights is the active-duty military. Unlike the health insecurity experienced by many younger Americans, Medicare entitlement provides a measure of health security for older Americans.[3] Career veterans can maintain health security through eligibility for the *TRICARE for Life* program, which provides health insurance coverage to veterans and their families. Consequently, health is another policy area where dual entitlement can increase health security for veterans in later life, although only career veterans, not veterans with shorter enlistments, are typically eligible. It is the specific program details in civilian and, especially, military/veteran policies that determine dual eligibility and influence later-life financial and health security for individuals and their families.

CIVILIAN RETIREMENT AND HEALTH POLICIES

Franklin Roosevelt's New Deal created the first truly national social welfare programs, with Social Security and Old Age Assistance designed explicitly to provide income in later life. Social Security is a contributory social insurance program that provides lifetime pensions for retired workers aged 65 and older and their dependents (the retirement age is now 67 for anyone born after 1959, and early retirement with actuarially reduced benefits has been permitted since the 1970s). Workers who make Federal Insurance Contributions Act (FICA) payroll contributions for enough covered quarters of qualified employment are entitled to Social Security benefits. Over time, Social Security has been adapted to address changing risks and needs, including extensions of benefits for dependent and surviving spouses, benefits for ex-spouses, and provision of disability benefits. Dependents and survivors of workers in heterosexual common-law marriages are also eligible for Social Security benefits, provided that the union was established in a state that recognizes common-law marriages. However, even where same-sex marriages are legal, same-sex couples are not entitled to dependent or survivor benefits under Social Security because their marriages are not recognized by the federal government. Such lack of legal recognition excludes many married and long-term partnered LGBT individuals from important financial benefits that can sometimes be cornerstones of financial security in later life.

What distinguishes federal programs, like Social Security (and military retirement pay), from other types of retirement income is their security—benefits last for a lifetime, are not dependent on investment returns (like private plans), and are inflation-proofed to help retirees maintain their standard of living as they draw down their savings (Street 2007b). Although male and female veterans are entitled to receive the same benefits, the security of federal benefits comes at the cost of discriminating against LGBT individuals in terms of benefits for dependents in domestic partnerships (see Brown, Chapter 5 of this volume). Increasingly, private sector employers and state and local governments are far more progressive than federal programs in offering health and income benefits for same-sex couples. Some private sector and state/local government employers provide coverage by incorporating unmarried domestic partners in long-established relationships or same-sex spouses as beneficiaries on their partners' employment-based benefits, just like their heterosexual counterparts. For example, in 2010, about 31% of civilian employers offered defined benefit pension plans with survivor benefits. Documenting benefits for unmarried domestic partners for the first time, the 2011 National Compensation Survey showed that about 14% of civilian employers provided survivor benefits for unmarried domestic partners (U.S. Bureau of Labor Statistics 2011c).

Although Social Security was designed mainly to meet the needs of the general civilian population, veterans also earn entitlement to Social Security retirement benefits in two ways. First, veterans who return to civilian life after military service often work in jobs in which they pay FICA taxes and accrue quarters of Social Security eligibility through employment, just like their non-veteran counterparts. Second, even during military service, Social Security eligibility credits accrue. The interface between Social Security and military services is evolving. Current members of the military services (since 2001) make payroll contributions to establish eligibility for future Social Security benefits. Older veterans earned Social Security credits without making FICA contributions. For active-duty service members (since 1957) and reservists (since 1988), military earnings for active-duty service have counted toward the Social Security earnings calculation. Military personnel serving between 1957 and 2001 earned additional credits toward Social Security without having FICA taxes withheld to pay for credits. From 1940 to 1957, noncontributory Social Security earnings of $160 per month were credited to service members. From 1957 to 1977, service members received an additional $300 earnings credit for each calendar quarter they received active-duty basic pay, and from 1978 to 2001, received an additional $100 in Social Security earnings credit for each $300 in active-duty basic pay, up to a maximum of $1,200 per year (U.S. Department of Veterans Affairs 2011b). Veterans are entitled to both Social Security retirement and Social Security disability benefits.

In 1965, Medicare, a centerpiece of President Lyndon Johnson's War on Poverty, created a new entitlement to health insurance for Americans 65 years and older. Medicare is a federal health insurance program that originally provided coverage for acute care hospital stays (Part A) and physician visits (Part B) to elderly individuals, because so many could not afford private health insurance. In 2003, enactment of Medicare Part D expanded the program to include prescription drug coverage. Despite its essential role in health insurance entitlement for elderly Americans, Medicare does not cover all medical costs—there have always been substantial deductibles, co-pays and coinsurances, and gaps in essential coverage that had to be paid out of pocket. Out-of-pocket health care expenses are higher for elderly Americans than for all other age groups. Consequently, health security in old age requires covering out-of-pocket costs with resources beyond Medicare, whether through Medicaid (public insurance for the impoverished), commercial Medigap health insurance (private insurance for those individuals who can afford premiums), retiree health insurance benefits from employment (becoming more rare and insecure), or wealth. Non-veteran elders need extra resources to bridge significant gaps in Medicare coverage for expensive and medically necessary health care, rendering Medicare entitlement alone insufficient to create robust health security. For elderly career veterans, Medicare enrollment plus TRICARE is another form of dual entitlement. The combination provides comprehensive health insurance coverage similar to, and often better than, non-veterans' coverage, even with high-quality private Medigap policies.

MILITARY BENEFITS

Historically, soldiers and sailors were among the earliest American pensioners, and the military has worked to maintain the health of its service members, care for its wounded, and provide for the families of fallen soldiers. For service to the nation, veterans receive an array of benefits from the government—housing, medical care, income—that are not provided to non-veterans. Among the first social policy benefits recorded in America were disability pensions to soldiers in Virginia (1624) and the Plymouth Colony (1636), land grants to soldiers serving in various conflicts, and sometimes dependents' benefits, with the last surviving widow of a Revolutionary War soldier receiving a survivor's pension payment in 1906 (Jensen 2003). In 1820, service pensions for Continental Army or Navy veterans, conditioned on financial need but not disability, were implemented (Jensen 2003). Predating the 20th-century development of the modern welfare state, with its pension regime of Social Security and employment-based pensions, the federal government provided extensive pension benefits to Union Civil War veterans and their dependents. At the peak, Union veteran pensions were estimated to account for one-third of the entire federal budget (Skocpol 1992). Historically, as now, both military service and cohort membership made a difference in life chances and, by extension, later-life financial security arising from social benefits provided to veterans (Jensen 2003; Segal 1989).

Veterans who served during World War II, the Korean War, and the Vietnam era were subject to conscription, in contrast to the late-20th and 21st-century All-Volunteer Force that evolved once the draft ended in 1973. Even under conscription, service members and veterans encountered cohort-specific differences in military compensation and benefit packages. For example, the GI Bill transformed the life chances of many thousands of World War II veterans who pursued higher education by means of its generous educational benefits. As a result of the GI Bill, better-educated veterans returned to non-veteran roles (Segal 1989), which had consequences for those veterans' lives and for the lives of those who were linked to them (Mettler 2005). However, the value of service-related education benefits has not remained constant. It has declined substantially for later cohorts of veterans; Cold War–era veterans only retroactively received educational benefits after the reinstatement of the program in 1966, and even then the level of benefits veterans received under the post–Korean War program was lower than the original World War II GI Bill (MacLean 2005; see also Bennett and McDonald, Chapter 6 of this volume).

Each military cohort's later-life experiences are shaped by numerous unique factors. These include members' backgrounds and personal characteristics, the specific characteristics of their military service, the secular conditions in the broader economy encountered after their period of service ends, and the benefits accrued during active-duty service and to which veterans are entitled upon discharge or retirement. Veterans of the Continental Army received land grants (Jensen 2003); similarly, contemporary active-duty service members obtain housing benefits as part of their compensation package, and veterans are eligible for Veterans Administration loans that assist with home purchases (U.S. Department of Veterans Affairs 2011b). Both historical land grants and more recent mortgage assistance enhance the capacity for individual wealth acquisition across the life course.

Military pay and benefits are tied to policies in place during specific periods of service. For example, service members who enlisted prior to 1980 received retirement pay based on a calculation involving rank, active-duty pay, and years of service, similar to the way pension benefits for non-veterans would have been calculated under traditional defined benefit occupational pensions (Congressional Research Service 2010). Unlike non-veterans, whose pensions were paid at particular ages of pension eligibility (typically ages in the mid-fifties or older) regardless of the age when they actually retired from paid work, active-duty career veterans of that era could receive retirement pay immediately upon retirement after twenty years of service, which for some could be as early as age 38. This difference in the timing of retirement benefits is substantial—with military retirement benefits paid upon separation from the military, often to relatively youthful veterans, contrasted with civilian occupational pension and retirement payments typically available only at much older ages for non-veterans. Members of the Reserves who accumulate twenty years or more of service can also receive military retirement pay when they reach age 60, acquiring entitlement to military retirement pay, Social Security, and (if offered) civilian employment-based pensions simultaneously. In contrast, the non-career veteran status of former service members with relatively short enlistments creates retirement income profiles that are more similar to non-veterans than to career veterans—that is, no military retirement pay and receipt of civilian pension and Social Security benefits when they withdraw from paid work in later life.

There are strings attached to receiving military retirement pay at such early ages—mainly the possibility, however remote, that a military retiree might be called back to active duty. Still, receiving a secure retirement benefit at a relatively young age during middle adulthood, or earning entitlement to military retirement pay while working full time in civilian employment during service in the Reserves, is a form of dual entitlement that contributes to financial security in later life. Two guaranteed income streams for some veterans, instead of the typical one for non-veterans, augment career veterans' earnings from civilian employment after separation from the military. Not all military retirees work in civilian employment post-discharge, although many do. Neither do all veterans serve long enough to receive military retirement benefits; unless they are disabled, most non-career veterans embark earlier on careers in the civilian workforce, but without the additional safety net of military retirement pay. Unless they receive compensation for a service-related disability, non-career veterans' adult employment and retirement income profiles look very similar to their non-veteran counterparts who have only ever worked in civilian employment.

Especially for veterans whose military occupational training enhances human capital valued by private employers or whose military service gives them an employment advantage in the defense sector or in preferred hiring pools for public sector employment (see Kelty and Segal, Chapter 2 of this volume), decades-long civilian careers following military discharge can garner substantial additional wages and build entitlement to another source of retirement income if the individual works for an employer offering pensions or retirement savings plans. For some career veterans, prospects for financial security are enhanced by a third layer of retirement income: dual entitlement to Social Security and military retirement pay, plus accrual of additional retirement income associated with civilian employment (Congressional Research Service 2010).

Military retirement pay is similar to civilian noncontributory defined benefit pensions; pay for individuals who joined prior to 1980 was available after twenty years of service at 50% of base pay—with a 2.5% annual top-up (up to 75%) for additional years of service. Although formulas for calculating retirement pay have changed somewhat over the years, military pensions are among the dwindling number of defined benefit plans linked to occupations (Congressional Research Service 2010). Serving for a minimum of twenty years is almost the only way to qualify for military retirement pay.[4] This type of "cliff" vesting puts non-career service members at a disadvantage for earning eligibility toward eventual pension entitlement (Congressional Research Service 2010). Civilians wait a maximum of six years to "vest," which provides nonforfeitable rights to employer contributions in occupational pensions, even if they leave that employment. Pension rights for military veterans are all or nothing—fully vested and entitled to retirement pay after twenty years of honorable service or no military retirement pay at all for shorter enlistments.

Another retirement benefit available to career veterans is TRICARE, which provides "wrap around" coverage for all Medicare-eligible TRICARE beneficiaries who are enrolled in Medicare Parts A and B. TRICARE is a secondary payer, which operates somewhat like the most comprehensive private Medigap policies that minimize out-of-pocket expenses for coinsurance and deductibles that Medicare does not cover. There are no premiums associated with TRICARE, although veterans, like non-veterans, must pay Medicare Part B premiums to maintain Medicare Part B coverage. TRICARE also offers additional health services not covered by Medicare, at no cost to the beneficiary (TRICARE 2010). For career veterans, there should be no unexpected costs for later-life health care unless they use services covered neither by Medicare nor TRICARE. Career veterans who retire can also obtain medical care at military base health care facilities on a space-available basis (active-duty members and their dependents get priority). Obviously, among eligible veterans, dual eligibility for civilian (Medicare) and military health benefits (TRICARE/VA/base hospital and pharmacy privileges) contributes substantially to health security in later life and may improve financial security as well.

LATER-LIFE OUTCOMES AND MILITARY SERVICE

Within the research literature on the life course, scholars have emphasized that the accumulation of disadvantage can explain many patterns of heterogeneity that exist among individuals across a range of statuses and outcomes, and that inequalities tend to increase with age (Dannefer 1987, 2003; O'Rand 1996). Many individual characteristics that are earlier life-course precursors to later-life inequality—gender, minority status, educational attainment, disability status, among others—are well documented for elderly Americans in the general population. However, for elderly veterans, the precise contours of the influence of those individual characteristics on heterogeneity in later-life outcomes are not yet well understood. For studying outcomes associated with life-course processes and exposures, *cumulative inequality* provides a promising theoretical framework. Not only does cumulative inequality demand consideration of the relative influences of both constrained agency and differential structural location on individual trajectories and outcomes, cumulative inequality also requires attention to the potential for advantages in one life domain to be at least somewhat independent from disadvantage in another (Ferraro, Shippee, and Schafer 2009).

Beyond the influence of individual characteristics, later-life inequalities arise from differential exposure and experiences during different eras of military service. Military service—none at all versus short or long duration—is a transformative mechanism for individuals with otherwise similar characteristics and starting points entering adulthood (see Kelty and Segal, Chapter 2 of this volume, and Bennett and McDonald, Chapter 6 of this volume). So too is service members' discharge status—whether healthy and able to work on the return to civilian life or disabled due to service-related experiences. Both veteran and non-veteran retirees can benefit from all social policies designed for the general population, from Social Security and Medicare to tax shelters for retirement savings and federal income tax deductions for mortgage interest and property tax on homes. Such entitlements are citizens' rights, with universal eligibility for civilian benefits regardless of need. However, only veterans are *dually entitled* to the additional layer of federal benefits associated with routine military service. Military benefits, typically available to non-career and career veterans, provide indirect pathways toward financial and health security later in life through access to educational benefits and occupational training and entitlement to Veterans Administration mortgages that help service members acquire wealth through home ownership. Only career veterans have full access to the generous military benefits that most directly influence later-life financial and health security—retirement pay and health coverage. Non-career veterans who have either not served long enough to establish eligibility or who have not met other standards for benefit eligibility usually have limited or no access to these benefits. This restricts the scope and value of dual entitlement benefits for non-career veterans, which may create a later-life financial and health profile more similar to non-veterans than to their career veteran counterparts, as shown later in this chapter in Table 11.1.

Direct and indirect routine service-related benefits for veterans parallel employee benefits available to many non-veterans working in private sector jobs. Although the details vary, in some ways, military retirement pay is similar to occupational pensions and retirement savings accrued in civilian employment. TRICARE is not very different from employer-provided retirement health insurance, except that it extends beyond the period of "employment" rather than only commencing at retirement. Despite surface similarities, there are important differences between service-related and civilian benefits obtained through employment. First, federal benefits for veterans are much more secure than civilian employment-based benefits, which are offered under conditions decided by, and at the discretion of, employers. Defined benefit retirement plans and health insurance coverage that corporations once routinely offered retirees in benefit-rich occupations are increasingly rare (Hacker 2005; Weller, Wenger, and Gould 2004), making the retirement pay and TRICARE benefits offered to career veterans even more advantageous. Second, military benefits tend to offer more comprehensive coverage and "kick in" for veterans at younger, sometimes much younger, ages than do pensions or employment-based retiree health insurance for non-veterans. This seems appropriate, because one of the goals of military retirement and health benefits policies is to compensate men and women for the sacrifices they make to serve their country. However, the requirement of career-long service to establish eligibility for many benefits limits the value of military benefits for non-career veterans. Consequently, one might expect that career veterans would be more advantaged in terms of later-life outcomes than non-career veterans or non-veterans.

To illustrate our point, we provide an empirical example. Table 11.1 shows descriptive statistics based on analyses of pooled data from the 2008, 2009, and 2010 American Community Survey. These nationally representative data permit us to compare later-life outcomes for nonemployed veterans and non-veterans aged 65 to 70 years at the time of the survey. This cohort is the most recently retired group for whom current national data are available, and it is distinctive in several other ways. First, birth cohorts in the late Depression and World War II period were relatively small and entered adulthood during an extended period of economic expansion, which contributed to their relatively greater labor market opportunities than were experienced by the larger prior and subsequent birth cohorts (Carlson 2008). Second, entry into military service among members of this cohort, which largely predated the All-Volunteer Force era, was more broadly distributed across the socioeconomic spectrum than for later cohorts, although much less diverse by gender, race, and ethnicity than younger cohorts (Segal and Segal 2004; Wilmoth and London 2011; see also Lutz, Chapter 4 of this volume). For this reason, data shown in Table 11.1 are for men only and not distinguished by race or ethnicity. Selecting data for individuals in this age range who are not working for pay at the time of the survey permits us to look at broad outcomes associated with military service that culminate in distinctive patterns of later-life health and financial security experienced in early retirement. Focusing on a single cohort of retirees at a specific time also provides an implicit way to hold constant certain other background characteristics, such as birth cohort, era of military service, period effects in early retirement years, and secular influences in the broader economy that also create differences in health and income security for older individuals.

We can distinguish between non-career and career veterans based on a combination of potential years of service and entitlement to military health insurance, TRICARE. Total income is pretax income from all sources; median and average Social Security income, retirement income, and "other"[5] income are also presented in Table 11.1, along with the percentage of each group receiving any nonzero income from those sources. Homeowners—those who occupy a dwelling they own outright or on which they

Table 11.1 Men Aged 65–70 Years, Not in the Labor Force, by Military Service (N=145,594)

	Entire Sample	Non-Veterans	Non-career Veterans	Career Veterans
Income				
Total Income				
Average	$33,928	$32,121	$35,340	$53,780
Median	$23,276	$20,734	$25,817	$46,791
% Receiving	97%	96%	98%	100%
SS Income				
Average	$14,460	$14,192	$14,909	$14,733
Median	$14,941	$14,584	$15,500	$14,888
% Receiving	89%	88%	92%	96%
Retirement Income				
Average	$23,472	$23,198	$22,549	$32,099
Median	$16,600	$15,653	$16,262	$26,332
% Receiving	48%	44%	53%	90%
Housing				
Home Ownership	83%	81%	86%	92%
Average Value	$263,957	$268,944	$257,168	$243,665
Health Insurance				
Medicare	97%	97%	98%	100%
TRICARE	6%	—	8%	100%
Veterans Administration	12%	—	29%	46%
Employer-Provided	38%	36%	44%	33%
Medigap Coverage	31%	31%	32%	19%
Medicaid	15%	18%	11%	8%
N	145,594	91,638	49,358	4,598

Source: Author's analysis of the American Community Survey, 2008–2010.
Notes: Data are weighted using person replicate weights provided in the American Community Survey dataset. We only present data for two groups of veterans: non-career (relatively short enlistments) and career (20+ year enlistments) veterans whose categorization was completely unambiguous. Omitted from presentation are individuals who served in the military, but who we cannot definitively categorize as either career or non-career veterans (N=9,968). Supplemental analysis indicates the excluded are "mid-length" service veterans whose profiles are more similar to non-career than career veterans. Medigap coverage includes wrap-around insurance benefits for Medicare gaps provided through a privately purchased insurance policy.

pay a mortgage—estimated the current value of their homes for the American Community Survey, which provides one indicator of wealth accumulation. Table 11.1 also includes measures for health insurance coverage. Any respondent who was currently or ever enrolled in Veterans Administration health care services is counted as having Veterans Administration coverage. TRICARE denotes veterans' coverage under the health program of the United States military or another military health program. The measure for "Medigap Coverage" includes individually purchased Medigap policies. Employer-provided insurance indicates whether, at the time of the interview, an individual had health insurance coverage through a former employer or union, and the Medicaid category reflects coverage under the means-tested state-federal program for the poor.

The second, third, and fourth columns of Table 11.1 show summary data (percentages and averages, with medians shown beneath average amounts) disaggregated by military service experience (i.e., non-veterans, non-career veterans, and career veterans). Most retirees in the analytic sample (62.9%) were non-veterans with no record of service in any branch of the armed forces. Among the remainder, 33.9% were non-career veterans whose eras of service covered fewer years than required to establish routine eligibility for military retirement pay. Only 3.1% of individuals in the sample were designated career veterans, retired men who reported service encompassing at least twenty-one years and who also reported having TRICARE coverage.

Documenting routine sources of later-life income and wealth (using home ownership as a proxy) provides a general sense of the financial security for this recent cohort of 65- to 70-year-old American male retirees, considered both as a whole and by differences in military service. Comparison of average total income to median total income indicates that the average of the entire sample is skewed by a small subset of very high-income respondents. Those outlier high incomes contribute to an average total of $33,928, whereas the overall median total income is only $23,276. Comparing averages across groups is one way to assess relative financial security; however, considering average income in isolation paints an unrealistically optimistic income picture for recent retirees, because average total income is nearly 70% higher than median total income for the sample. Non-veterans had the lowest average and median total incomes, and were the most socioeconomically diverse group. Non-career veterans' total income, however measured, was higher than for non-veterans, whereas career veterans' total income was the highest of all.

The vast majority of retirees have income from Social Security. On average, non-veterans received about $14,200 in Social Security benefits in the prior twelve months, compared to somewhat higher average amounts for the two veteran groups. A far bigger difference is observed with respect to the percent receiving, as well as the amounts of retirement income across the three groups. About 44% of non-veterans receive nonzero amounts, averaging $23,198 annually for those receiving any retirement income. Of non-veterans 56% received no retirement income from sources other than Social Security. A higher percentage, over 53% of non-career veterans received at least some retirement income, although average annual amounts around $22,500 are slightly lower than for non-veterans. By far, the most advantaged group is made up of career veterans. Many more receive retirement income (90%) and they receive substantially higher average amounts, approximately $32,100 over the prior twelve months.

Beyond regular income, another component of financial security is access to wealth. As noted previously, the single largest asset for elderly Americans is their own home. Although home ownership is a rather crude proxy for individual wealth, there is no other measure available in the American Community Survey. Most retirees are homeowners (83%), and their estimated home value averaged approximately $264,000. Similar to the socioeconomic diversity reflected in non–Social Security sources of income, the average value of homes owned by individuals varies widely, from exceedingly modest dwellings to multimillion dollar estates. About two-thirds of American households of all ages owned their homes in 2010 (U.S. Census Bureau 2011), a figure substantially lower than for the retiree sample. About 81% of non-veterans, 86% of non-career veterans, and 92% of career veterans were homeowners, although civilian homes had the highest average value and career veterans the least. The patterns in house value may reflect greater propensities to move among veterans, residence in communities where military bases are most frequently located and housing prices may be lower, regulations associated with qualification for Veterans Administration mortgages that effectively cap housing values, or it may reflect much wider distributions of wealth in the general population of retirees than among veterans alone. The higher percentages of home ownership among career and non-career veterans may reflect veterans' ability to tap into Veterans Administration mortgage programs, as well as other service-connected home ownership initiatives that are entirely unavailable to non-veterans.

Finally, the health insurance measures shown in Table 11.1 are broad indicators of health security—intended to capture the extent and breadth of coverage that would guarantee an individual secure and routine access to health care, without financial barriers. Coverage is dominated by Medicare (97%); around 6% report Veterans Administration coverage, which is available only to veterans. Military health care, TRICARE, is available to all veterans who have retired, but it is not routinely available to non-career veterans. Compared to non-veterans, non-career veterans have higher rates of employer-provided retiree health insurance. This likely reflects an indirect pathway from military service to entitlement to better benefits in later life. Military service may give ex-members priority for public sector employment, and public sector employment offers more comprehensive and secure employment-based fringe benefits (both pensions and health insurance) than private sector employment. Among non-veterans and non-career veterans, Medigap coverage is more prevalent (31% and 32%, respectively) than among career military veterans (19%), whose more comprehensive health coverage under TRICARE and Veterans Administration systems reduces the need for Medigap policies. Non-veterans are more than twice as likely to use Medicaid compared to career veterans.

The data provided in Table 11.1 show that a relatively small group of career veterans enter the early retirement years (from 65 to 70) as beneficiaries of a dual stream of high-quality federal retirement and health benefits alongside civilian benefits, enhancing financial and health security in later life. Although the extent of coverage and value of benefits distinguishes career veterans from their non-veteran and non-career veteran counterparts, additional research is needed to determine the contribution that dual entitlement to military benefits makes, while also taking into account potentially confounding factors like social class and education.

SERVICE-CONNECTED DISABILITY AND OTHER SPECIALIZED PROGRAMS

Despite these routine areas of entitlement in which military compensation and programs parallel benefits in the private sector and civilian entitlement programs, not all military benefits cover all veterans, and not all military benefits have counterpart programs in private sector employment or civilian social policies. This is especially true for the many specialized Veterans Administration programs that are predicated on need rather than entitlement, with eligibility established by assessed level of service-related disability (Wilmoth and London 2011; for more detailed elaboration of Veterans Administration benefits, see U.S. Department of Veterans Affairs 2011b). For veterans with combat-related injuries and service-related disabilities, financial and health security in later life looks very different than it does for veterans who separate from service in good health or for non-veterans who have not been exposed to the most debilitating physical and psychological privations of military service and combat. Further, because non-career veterans rarely have full access to the range of health care services provided by the Veterans Administration and are not eligible for benefits like TRICARE and retirement pay that are available to career service members, most veterans have to rely on other private and public sources of health care and retirement income.

For veterans with service-related disabilities, specialized Veterans Administration programs have been designed to try to meet their needs. Access to health care benefits provided through the Veterans Administration is determined, in large part, by the veterans' disability rating score. Veterans with severe combat-related injuries and high levels of disability have priority access to Veterans Administration services. However, recent research (Hynes et al. 2007) shows that not all veterans who are dually entitled to use Medicare and Veterans Administration care seek help at the

Veterans Administration. Among 1.47 million veterans in a study of outpatient use, 18% only used the Veterans Administration, 36% only used Medicare, and 46% used both Veterans Administration health care and Medicare. Among veterans who were inpatients, nearly 70% used Medicare only, whereas patients with higher Veterans Administration priority were, unsurprisingly, more likely to rely on Veterans Administration health care. Whereas the Veterans Administration provides an important safety net, for individuals who live far from Veterans Administration facilities or reside in urban environments and have other health insurance, different health services are often used (Hynes et al. 2007).

The Veterans Administration provides cash compensation to veterans with service-connected disabilities and their survivors and also offers means-tested pensions to impoverished veterans with wartime service. Additional Veterans Administration benefits include discounted life insurance, housing adaptation, and burial allowances (Congressional Research Service 2006). A recent innovation to Veterans Administration policy includes benefits for caregivers of veterans with severe disabilities, including entitlement to respite care (U.S. Department of Veterans Affairs 2011b)—an example of how military benefits have value beyond those experienced directly by the service member, and can enhance the lives and well-being of others whose lives are linked to individuals serving in the military. However, recent research indicates that working-aged households containing a disabled veteran experience an increased risk of poverty and material hardship (Heflin, Wilmoth, and London 2012; London, Heflin, and Wilmoth 2011), which calls into question whether the benefits received by disabled veterans and their families are providing a sufficient safety net. Such evidence of increased poverty and hardship among working-age veterans with disabilities may be indicative of disadvantage that can accumulate across the life course and contribute to later-life health and financial insecurity.

Beyond Veterans Administration benefits that provide critical benefits for veterans with service-related disabilities, several other military benefits that are more broadly available may also contribute in small but important ways to the financial and health security of older veterans. Access to services on military bases, such as commissaries and base exchanges, and Morale, Welfare, and Recreation office services, can help aging veterans stretch their financial resources and tap into valuable services. For retirees who live close enough to military bases, some can receive health care at military medical facilities (on a space available basis) and fill prescriptions at base pharmacies, another enhancement for health security.

DISCUSSION

As individuals serve in the military, they simultaneously build *dual entitlement* to civilian benefits, such as Social Security and Medicare, in addition to any service-related military health and retirement benefits they may become entitled to receive. Veterans also have opportunities to build wealth through service-related incentives to buy homes using Veterans Administration mortgage loan guarantees, in addition to tax subsidies all Americans can use to increase home ownership. In some ways, military benefits parallel benefits offered to private sector employees, with the important exception of specialized packages available to service members who are injured or disabled during their enlistments. Service-related benefits associated with routine military service are a form of dual entitlement that provides enhanced potential for later-life financial security to eligible veterans. Such dual entitlement provides the small number of career veterans with particularly greater possibilities for later-life financial and health security. The later-life benefits of military service for non-career veterans, who are the largest group of veterans, is far less clear because they seldom receive either retirement pay or TRICARE. Some non-career veterans may be able to translate extra education or military occupational training into good civilian sector jobs, or leverage Veterans Administration home ownership into individual wealth. However, most indicators suggest that later-life financial and health prospects for non-career military, at least those with no service-related disabilities, are more similar to non-veterans than to dually entitled career veterans. Whether non-career military service contributes to positive turning points with respect to later-life financial and health security for men and women from disadvantaged backgrounds is a question that remains virtually unexplored in the literature (see Bennett and McDonald, Chapter 6 of this volume).

Of course, veterans' benefits exist at least in part so that the military services can compete with potential private sector employers to attract appropriate enlistees, to retain talented and essential service members in military service, and to compensate for some of the risks that accompany military service, especially during armed conflict (Segal 1989; Segal and Segal 2004; Wilmoth and London 2011). As such, service-related benefits share with employer-provided benefits an element of labor market management—employers' efforts to incentivize the best talent to join and remain with the organization, and to separate or retire when downsizing is necessary or when skills essential to the organization's mission erode. However, a clear distinction between employment-based compensation and benefits and military service-related remuneration is the moral imperative implicit in military benefit packages—that willingness to risk one's life for one's country should be met with specialized compensation that acknowledges the public value of the sacrifices that military service can entail (Segal 1989). Exposure to risks earlier in the life course distinguishes veterans from non-veterans in several life domains, including health and mortality (London and Wilmoth 2006; Wilmoth, London, and Parker 2010, 2011; see also MacLean, Chapter 10 of this volume). However, later-life survivors of military service represent a select group of retirees (see Wolf, Wing, and Lopoo, Chapter 13 of this volume), whose life-course trajectories are characterized by an accumulation of inequalities, including disadvantage due to service-related disabilities for some, and advantages associated with dual entitlement to both service-related benefits and benefits from civilian social policies for others. This unequal accumulation is likely to play out differently for different groups, not only for veterans and non-veterans, but also for veterans with different characteristics (gender, race, ethnicity, sexuality) and tenures in service. Although we have presented evidence in this chapter about financial and health security from the experiences of a single cohort under conditions of routine service, the looming cohorts of retiring veterans with very different service profiles will doubtless change the landscape of later-life financial and health security for service members of different eras.

In this chapter, we have identified how dual entitlement to federal benefits, military and civilian, makes some veterans eligible for multiple sources of income and benefits that can establish them as a group of Americans likely to enjoy financial and health security in later life. However, non-career veterans who do not serve long enough to establish eligibility for military benefits enter later life on similar financial and health security footings as their non-veteran counterparts—entitled to Social Security and Medicare, but depending on increasingly contingent employment-based health and income benefits to achieve a measure of financial and health security for themselves and their families.

Despite recognition that military benefits and social policies interact to create predictable profiles for later-life financial and health security for non-career veterans, career veterans, and non-veterans, the empirical contours of the different groups' outcomes have yet to be firmly established. From the perspective of the impact of military service, more research is needed to fully understand the contribution that timing in military service—the duration of enlistment, the era of service, and age at discharge—make for later-life outcomes. Barely touched on in this chapter are the many ways that others' lives linked to veterans—spouses, partners, children, survivors, and caregivers—all are affected by the intersections between military benefits, on the one hand, and civilian social policies on the other. How those linked lives are affected by the interplay between military benefits and other social policies is fertile ground for future research. Because so much of the life-course literature identifies military service as making a distinctive contribution to altered life trajectories, documenting and understanding the similarities and differences in income, wealth, and health among veterans and their families with different service histories and demographic profiles, and between veterans and non-veterans, are other areas ripe for research. So, too, is documenting and understanding the precursors of material hardship and poverty among veterans, and the unique confluence of demographic, service, and social influences on the post-service lives of military personnel who have served during Operation Iraqi Freedom/Operation Enduring Freedom.

Cross-sectional and longitudinal datasets with sufficient detail to fully unpack the factors associated with later-life financial and health security of different groups of veterans with different individual and service characteristics are rare. Rarer still are datasets with adequately detailed measures of military occupation, rank, length and branch of service, combat exposure, and disability, which would enable us to understand veterans' circumstances, that also include sufficient data on civilian populations to sustain comparisons at similar parts of the life course (see Teachman, Chaper 14 of this volume). The need for detailed longitudinal data with more nuanced measures to permit important comparisons seems obvious for researchers determined to distinguish the effects of military service for elderly American veterans from the civilian influences that shape later lives.

NOTES

1. We appreciate helpful comments from Jeralynn Cossman and Robert Wagmiller.
2. We use the phrase "financial security" to indicate secure access to adequate income and the phrase "health security" to reflect routine access to appropriate health care with few financial barriers. See MacLean (Chapter 10 of this volume) for a discussion of military service and health across the life course.
3. A small pool of nonelderly Americans are covered by Medicare, with eligibility established either though receiving Social Security disability benefits or having end-stage renal disease.
4. Aside from a few "early" retirement programs designed to reduce the size of the armed forces or early retirement due to disability (Congressional Research Service 2010).
5. The "other" income category is a residual category that includes any earnings from the following sources: welfare payments, investment earnings, Supplemental Security Income, or compensation from any sources not included in the other income variables measured in the American Community Survey.

12 United States Military Services' Sponsorship of Life-Course Research
Past, Present, and Future

Paul A. Gade and Brandis Ruise

This brief chapter reviews the history of military-sponsored life-course research and provides examples of how the intellectual constructs of the life-course perspective can be used to analyze and understand the "human dimension" of military operations and functions. [1] Using core life-course principles and concepts—lifelong development, historical time and place, timing in lives, linked lives, human agency, transitions and trajectories—that are described more fully in the introductory chapter (see Wilmoth and London, Chapter 1 of this volume), we discuss how the life-course perspective might be applied to help improve life outcomes for military service members and their families. Throughout the chapter, we suggest military-relevant questions that seem well suited to life-course analyses, explanations, and, perhaps, preventive and clinical counseling practices for those who are likely to experience or already have experienced combat. By highlighting these connections, we aim to make the case that it is not only within the scope of the mission of the U.S. military services to fund and develop practices that are informed by life-course research, but that it is imperative they do so.

MILITARY FUNDING HISTORY FOR LIFE-COURSE RESEARCH

The U.S. Department of Veterans Affairs has funded research from the life-course perspective assessing the effects of military service on lifelong individual development (Spiro, Schnurr, and Aldwin 1997). At the direction of the U.S. Congress, the Veterans Administration funded the well-known National Vietnam Veterans Readjustment Study (Kulka et al. 1990), and many of the findings from that study are still being discussed and disputed. However, direct financial support from the military services for life-course research *per se* has been quite modest. In fact, the only funding has come from the U.S. Army, and almost all of that from the U.S. Army Research Institute for the Behavioral and Social Sciences.

Researchers at the U.S. Army Research Institute have had a longstanding interest in conducting and supporting research on military service and

244 Paul A. Gade and Brandis Ruise

the life course. In 1991, researchers from the U.S. Army Research Institute and several university collaborators published a special issue of *Military Psychology* on military service and the life-course perspective. At that time, within the military services and the Department of Defense, we saw a growing and deepening interest in the long-term behavioral effects of military service experiences on service members. We believed that the political climate represented a turning point for research on military personnel that begged for a substantial investment by the U.S. military services in the development of the life-course perspective and empirical research (Gade 1991). We thought that research using the life-course perspective might provide a longer view of the variables that affect enlistment and a better understanding of the impact of military service experiences on post-service lives. In that special issue of *Military Psychology*, we pointed out the inadequacies of the then-current theory and methods, which were based almost exclusively on predictive models, for providing explanations of the mechanisms by which past life experiences influence enlistment behavior and how life experiences in the military services affect subsequent life choices and well-being. We suggested that the life-course perspective was just what military personnel researchers needed to frame their research questions and provide explanations about enlistment, service experiences, and the post-service behaviors in which many from the Department of Defense and the Army, in particular, seemed most interested.

Arguably, the military funding environment for life-course research today is similar to that prevailing in 1991, despite the fact that research based on the life-course perspective has developed substantially over the past two decades. In order to develop a better understanding of current and past funding environments for military-sponsored life-course research, it is important to anchor the discussion of those environments in their historical times and places. Therefore, we initiate this discussion with a brief historical narrative of life-course research funding within the U.S. Army. We do so with the hope that this history will provide a background that life-course theorists and researchers can use when developing future life-course research proposals that the Army and other military services will find useful and competitively fundable. This historical narrative begins with a discussion of a very important survey motivated by the Army's need to understand how Army service impacts significant aspects of Soldiers'[2] lives both during and after their service.

The 1985 Army Experience Survey Sets the Stage

In late 1984, the Secretary of the Army, John O. Marsh, Jr., directed the U.S. Army Research Institute to conduct a major survey of service members who left the Army after one term, quit before completing their enlistment requirement, or who had recently retired from the Army. Secretary Marsh believed there was much to be learned from these veterans that would help with future Army recruiting and improve our understanding of the impact of service on the post-service lives of Army veterans. The survey assessed how those who had served felt about their Army experience and how that experience affected their post-service employment, their satisfaction with service, and their likelihood of recommending the Army as a place to prepare young people for life and careers after high school.

The U.S. Army Research Institute contracted with WESTAT, Inc., a well-known Washington, D.C.–area survey firm, to conduct the inquiry (WESTAT 1986). The survey results held several surprises for the Army, not the least of which was that Army jobs did not provide training in specific job skills that could transfer to subsequent civilian employment, although they did help Soldiers develop general work skills that apparently served them well in their post-service work environments. These results were significant enough to be reported to and commented on by the President of the United States, which we believe had a significant influence on the Army's subsequent funding of life-course research. We also believe that it influenced the approval of a postdoctoral fellowship with Glen H. Elder, Jr. for one of the authors (Paul Gade) in 1990–1991.

The U.S. Army Funds Life-Course Research

Shortly after completing the Army Experience Survey in 1986, Dr. Gary Bowen—one of the WESTAT researchers who had worked closely with the U.S. Army Research Institute in developing and conducting the survey—left WESTAT to assume an academic position in the School of Social Work at the University of North Carolina-Chapel Hill. At Chapel Hill, Gary became familiar with the life-course research being done by Glen Elder in the Sociology Department. Through his work as a key researcher on the Army Experience Survey, Gary knew about the Army's and my (Paul Gade's) interest in the social and psychological antecedents and consequences of military enlistment for veterans' lives. As a result, after being introduced by Gary to Glen and his life-course approach, Glen and I shared ideas over the next four years about the effects of military service. Encouraged by these discussions, I applied and received approval for a one-year Secretary of the Army Research and Study Fellowship beginning in the fall of 1990. This was to be a postdoctoral research and study fellowship with Glen to explore the long-term effects of military service on veterans using the life-course perspective. As part of the fellowship, I also planned to work with Jay Teachman at the University of Maryland and Vaughn Call at the University of Wisconsin.

That one-year fellowship resulted in a special issue of the journal *Military Psychology* dedicated to military service and the life-course perspective, for which I served as the special issue editor (Gade 1991). As part of that special issue, one of the studies completed under the auspices of that postdoctoral fellowship, a *post hoc* life-course analysis of the Army

Experience Survey data provided support for the "bridging hypothesis," which states that military service acts as a bridge to adult life, especially for disadvantaged youth (Browning, Lopreato, and Poston 1973; see also Kelty and Segal, Chapter 2 of this volume, and Bennett and McDonald, Chapter 6 of this volume). Two papers in that special issue (Elder, Gimbel, and Ivie 1991; Hastings 1991) stressed the lifelong effects of World War II–era military service on veterans, who were well aware of those impacts. Call and Teachman (1991) presented data that called into serious question the popular myth that Vietnam veterans have had unhappier marriages than their non-veteran counterparts. We also showed how important the timing of military service was for a variety of post-service outcomes (Gade, Lakhani, and Kimmel 1991).

In addition to research published in the special issue, there were several other spinoffs from that fellowship year. In one case, the U.S. Army Research Institute funded a two-year National Research Council Postdoctoral Fellowship for Dr. Jennifer Keene, who had recently completed her doctorate with John Modell, a historian from Carnegie Mellon University. Glen Elder, who had worked on life-course research projects with John Modell, recommended Jennifer to the U.S. Army Research Institute for the National Research Council Fellowship. This relationship turned out to be quite productive, resulting in Jennifer's first book, a historical time and place perspective on the American men who served in World War I, describing the impact of that service on their lives and those of others (Keene 2001). That work clearly showed how the service experience of Soldiers during World War I set the stage for the passage of the GI Bill, which is one of the most important pieces of legislation affecting veterans' lives from World War II to the present.

Another important outcome from the fellowship was the encouragement it provided Glen Elder to successfully apply to the U.S. Army Research Institute's Research and Advanced Concepts Office for contracts that ran from 1993 to 1997. This funding allowed him to study the long-term effects of military service on Soldiers and publish several important papers on military service and the life course (Elder 1994; Elder, Shanahan, and Clipp 1994; Lee, Vaillant, Torrey, and Elder 1996).

Several other life-course research efforts were funded by the U.S. Army Research Institute in addition to those undertaken by Glen Elder and Jennifer Keene. One of these was an effort by Dr. Irene Frieze, a psychologist at the University of Pittsburgh, who, assisted by graduate students, used the life-course perspective to examine the long-term effects of Vietnam-era military service on several post-service quality-of-life measures for middle-aged veterans. Theirs was a convenience sample of 374 men from an Ivy League school who had served in Vietnam (Bookwala, Frieze, and Grote 1994). The major results showed that those who had served in Vietnam were less satisfied in mid-life with their careers, finances, and life in general than were their non-service counterparts or those who had served outside

Vietnam. However, the Vietnam veterans were more satisfied with their male friendships than were those who served outside of Vietnam. These findings are especially interesting, because the servicemen in this research were from high socioeconomic status backgrounds and graduates of an elite university.

Other research, although not funded by the U.S. Army Research Institute, was inspired by the work emerging from these early initiatives. For example, Dr. Michael Parker, who was then a Lieutenant Colonel in the U.S. Army and a social worker and is now a professor of social work at the University of Alabama and an associate professor with the Division of Geriatric Medicine and Palliative Care at the University of Alabama in Birmingham, says his work was inspired conceptually by the *Military Psychology* special issue in 1991. A life-course perspective helped frame his research with military families when he was a National Institute of Aging Postdoctoral Fellow at the University of Michigan and his later work as a Hartford Foundation Geriatric Scholar at the University of Alabama. He and his colleagues conducted several studies funded in part by the U.S. Army, the Hartford Foundation, and the National Institute on Aging. These studies applied life-course principles to help Army social workers better understand Soldier and family wellness, as well as some of the challenges (e.g., elder care) associated with the aging process (Parker, Call, and Barko 1999; Parker, Call, Toseland, Vaitkus, Roff, and Martin 2002; Parker, Fuller, Koenig, Vaitkus, Bellis, Barko, Eitzen, and Call 2001; Parker et al. 2001). Later, Parker and other colleagues formed a special interest group within the Gerontological Society of America that focused on aging veteran issues within a life-course framework, and he applied a life-course perspective to a federally funded longitudinal study of over 1,000 community dwelling seniors (Parker, Roff, Klemmack, Koenig, Baker, and Allman 2003).

To date, one of the most important life-course research projects that the U.S. Army Research Institute has funded is the current and continuing work of Glen Elder and his associates at the University of North Carolina-Chapel Hill and the Carolina Population Research Center. They are using data from the National Longitudinal Study of Adolescent Health (Add Health), combined with detailed administrative and ability/aptitude measurement data from the Defense Manpower Data Center (DMDC), to investigate the pathways to higher education and skills acquired through service in the All-Volunteer Force (Elder, Wang, Spence, Adkins, and Brown 2010). This research, ongoing since 2007 and supported by two contract efforts, is designed to document these pathways and their benefits for current military personnel and veterans. Combining previously unavailable, detailed historical administrative military service data and ability/aptitude measures from the Department of Defense with comprehensive Add Health survey data enabled these researchers to examine the antecedents, consequences, and trajectories of modern military service through the lens of the life-course perspective in ways that had not previously been possible.

LIFE-COURSE RESEARCH AND THE HUMAN DIMENSION

In this age of technological warfare, the Department of Defense and the military services are beginning to recognize that human beings are the most important and cost-effective performance components of military operations and weapon systems. As a knowledgeable former defense official put it, "Weapons are not the most important ingredient in winning wars. People come first, ideas are second, and hardware is only third" (Sprey 2011: 101). Recently, the U.S. military services have discovered, or more correctly rediscovered, the human dimension, a much-discussed, albeit ill-defined, concept in the U.S. military services, especially in the U.S. Army. For example, General William Wallace, the previous Commanding General of the Army's Training and Doctrine Command (TRADOC), indirectly defined the human dimension concept for the Army in a foreword he wrote: "I want this concept to serve as a point of departure for wide-ranging discussion, research, and investigations into what impacts the performance, reliability, flexibility, endurance, and adaptability of an Army made up of Soldiers, their families, civilians, and contractors" (Army Capabilities Integration Center 2008: i). As one can see, this covers almost everything associated with U.S. military-related human behavior, both at the individual and group levels.

A life-course approach to research and operational issues seems to be an ideal research platform for exploring the human dimension. Knowing more about the effects of military service during the active-duty period, as well as how military service shapes service members' short- and long-term trajectories and outcomes in multiple domains, has the potential to help the military services understand the human dimension of service and design the most beneficial policies and programs. Thus, in this section of the chapter, we refocus on the core principles of the life-course perspective because we believe they are useful for organizing research and structuring policy as well. To do this, we identify each principle of the life-course perspective and highlight connections that demonstrate the relevance of this research to the military services' focus on the human dimension. Then, referencing the reviews of the literature provided in this volume, we summarize what we consider to be important future research issues that can and should be addressed by life-course researchers investigating the impact of military service.

So as not to raise expectations too high, we must warn the reader that when we presented an earlier draft of the information below to the TRADOC Army Capabilities Integration Center (ARCIC) in 2007 in response to their request for help in developing their human dimension concept, it seemed to fall on deaf ears. None of what we presented about potential contributions of life-course research to either the conceptualization of, or the research base focused on the human dimension was incorporated in their 2008 final concept paper report (ARCIC 2008)—but then none of the information in any of the other topic papers was used either. Fortunately, the ARCIC report is neither the Army's nor the military's final word on the human dimension concept. There is still opportunity for rethinking.

The Army's interest in lifelong learning and development fits nicely with the first life-course principle, *lifelong development*. Researchers and military leaders are encouraged to consider the longer-term impacts of the developmental processes of training and operational experiences, as well as their short-term, more immediate performance outcomes. These effects can be far reaching and may include recruiting and retention, in addition to transitions into civilian life after military service. A focus on lifelong development highlights the need for longitudinal data collection (see Teachman, Chapter 14 of this volume).

The second life-course principle, *historical time and place*, reminds us that to understand fully the impact of recent wars on our Soldiers, we need to understand the similarities and differences that previous wars have had on individual lives and to test aspects of the life-course perspective that have developed from research with veterans of those earlier periods of service (see Burland and Lundquist, Chapter 8 of this volume, and Kleykamp, Chapter 7 of this volume). We also need to focus on geographic mobility and the influences of place on development (see Bailey, Chapter 9 of this volume). In general, this life-course principle suggests the need for a focus on variation both within and across cohorts of service members whose active duty occurred during particular military eras (Wilmoth, London, and Parker 2010; see also Wilmoth and London, Chapter 1 of this volume).

The third life-course principle, *timing in lives*, underscores the finding that those who entered military service at younger ages during previous wars were more likely to benefit from the experience than were those who entered later in life (Elder, Gimbel, and Ivie 1991). Wartime service often disrupted lives that were well established, but the training and educational opportunities that service provided often benefited those who entered service before establishing themselves in jobs or marriages. These should be important considerations for the military services, individuals contemplating military service, and those conducting research with Reserve component service members who have been involuntarily activated. Life-course researchers need to pay more attention to the timing and sequencing of events in the lives of Soldiers.

The military services are well aware that service members are highly dependent on and attached to one another, and they encourage this cohesiveness. Increasingly, during the era of the All-Volunteer Force, Soldiers, more often with spouses and children, stay in the military for careers. As a result, we need to put greater focus on both military and veteran families (see Burland and Lundquist, Chapter 8 of this volume), and the bidirectional influences of the military on diverse family members and family members on Soldiers. Finally, as Bailey (Chapter 9 of this volume) reminds us, some places have more veterans than others, as do some families, a situation that creates opportunities for intergenerational, familial, and community-mediated influences on the propensity to enter the military and attitudes toward the military. These interdependencies fit well with the fourth principle of the life-course perspective, *linked lives,* which highlights the influence of the social context in which individuals operate and the great power of this context in regulating the behavior of individuals. Militaries around the world stress the importance and positive impact of cohesion on performance, especially in combat, and yet ignore its importance for understanding the negative behavior of Soldiers, such as that seen at Abu Ghraib. Understanding the "dark side" of linked lives should also be part of our research agenda.

Human agency, the fifth life-course principle, reminds us that service members, like everyone else, construct their lives through the decisions and choices they make within the constraints of the structures and historical events that they experience. Choices made when enlisting, such as branch of service or occupational specialty, significantly affect the nature of a person's military experience and likely their post-military life as well. As Street and Hoffman (Chapter 11 of this volume) note, the decision whether to pursue a military career has implications for service members' old-age financial and health security, as well as that of their family members. Similarly, choices in other domains of life will influence the military service experiences of Soldiers.

Trajectories and transitions are also important theoretical constructs that we need to incorporate in our military life-course research. As discussed in several chapters in this volume, the various dynamic pathways that are important to military personnel, as well as to civilians, include education, career, marriage, raising children, and health. In addition to transitions that civilians also experience, examples of major life transitions that are important for military life-course researchers to consider include entry to military service, initial training, overseas duty, command assignment, attendance at special schools, and, especially, combat duty.

Transitions that are pivotal events in one's life are referred to as *turning points,* which can either be abrupt changes in direction, such as those precipitated by a combat assignment, or more gradual effects, such as those triggered by using the GI Bill for education. They can also be positive or negative in valence and direction. As discussed by Bennett and McDonald (Chapter 6 of this volume) with respect to education and employment and MacLean (Chapter 10 of this volume) with respect to health, there is evidence that military service can offset early-life disadvantage and thereby redirect the life course in some historical periods. However, combat-related injuries and other military experiences can lead to negative turning points. Examples of military-related turning points are major deployments, wars, and selection for Special Forces training—and the act of entering or leaving military service. Advancement within the military services, especially the officer corps in each service, is cohort driven. Progress in getting particular jobs, schooling, and promotion is always gauged by one's entry-level cohort.

Being behind your cohort or "year group" in getting the right assignments or schooling often detracts from future promotions, assignments, and even retirement. Such trajectories during the active-duty period can significantly shape what happens during the veteran period.

MILITARY LIFE COURSE NOW AND IN THE FUTURE

The chapters in this volume provide a comprehensive summary of what we know about military service across the life course. Yet there is much that remains unknown, and there is a great need for additional life-course research on the effects of military service. Examples of some of the primary insights that emerge from the life-course perspective on military service include the notion that the effects of military service on people's lives largely depend on the age at which they served, the nature of their military service, and the social-historical context of their birth cohort. Military service can be a bridge to a better economic life and a more stable family for those who begin service before they have established careers and marriages, whereas it can be very disruptive for those entering military service after careers and marriages have been well established. Understanding this issue is especially important when senior officials consider Reserve call-ups. Life-course research has also shown that serving in the military tends to have positive effects on the socioeconomic achievement and marital stability of non-Whites, and more generally, on the educationally and economically disadvantaged. Serving as an officer seems to have positive economic and marital stability effects for everyone. Combat experience, especially directly experiencing the deaths of others, often leads to chronic post-traumatic stress disorder (PTSD) symptoms, both mild and severe, which can have lifelong negative effects on health and earnings. Although social support tends to ameliorate these effects, there are likely consequences for the lives of those supportive persons to whom Soldiers with PTSD are linked and these need to be addressed by life-course based research and policy as well.

Much of the life-course perspective is built on findings from older cohorts, especially those who served during World War II. We need to verify and extend the principles of the life-course perspective to modern Soldier populations, so we can gain a better understanding of the effects of the changing nature of military service on the lives of service personnel. Jay Teachman's chapter (Chapter 14 of this volume) outlines the kinds of data that are needed for sound and truly longitudinal research on service members' careers. Such data are mandatory to document the effects of service on those who serve until retirement, those who serve for shorter periods, and those who serve in the Reserve components. In order to move the field forward, Drs. David Segal and Meredith Kleykamp at the University of Maryland, along with some of the authors of the chapters in this volume and others, are developing an ambitious longitudinal research program to generate the sorts of data on modern military service members that we currently lack. These data will be essential in order for us to develop better understandings of the effects of military service across the life course.

There are many areas in which we need additional research. We need a better understanding of the lifelong effects of military training on veterans and families in relation to economic well-being, but also in relation to quality of life. Recent evidence documenting the joint effects of veteran and disability statuses on poverty and material hardship provide important foundations for such additional research (Heflin, Wilmoth, and London 2012; London, Heflin, and Wilmoth 2011). We also need to understand better how the basic principles of the life-course perspective interact to produce the varied effects that military service can have on the important life outcomes of education, health (both mental and physical), socioeconomic achievement, and marital/family stability. As the chapters in this volume by Bennett and McDonald, Kleykamp, Burland and Lundquist, and Bailey attest, many questions remain open or underresearched. We also need additional research that addresses questions about the factors that influence adaptive and maladaptive transitions into the military, and from the military to civilian life. Perhaps one of the most interesting research applications of the life-course perspective lies in study of the long-term effects of deploying Reserve component Soldiers for peacekeeping and stability operations. The activation and deployment of Reserve component Soldiers lends itself well to a life-course analysis. Such deployments strongly resemble the mobilization of civilians during previous wars in terms of its potential effects on the lives of Soldiers and their families. Studying such deployments provides a context and an opportunity to verify and extend earlier research findings related to service-generated life-course disruptions.

CONCLUSION

In summary, life-course research focusing on the impacts of military service on people's lives is firmly based on several decades of foundational work, but much remains to be learned. To date, the funding for life-course research by the military services has been minimal. Although the life-course perspective offers a strong rationale, as well as methods, for studying the human dimension of military service, it has yet to capture the imagination of those military leaders who could and probably should fund it. The human dimension concept that has seized the minds of many military leaders seems to offer an excellent entrée for life-course researchers. The consortium of life-course researchers involved in the production of this volume and also collaborating with David Segal, Meredith Kleykamp, and others at the University of Maryland may be able to use the human dimension as a springboard to promote awareness of the life course among key military and political leaders. Unfortunately, this effort comes at a time when all budgets are likely to be slashed to the bone. As a result, military life-course research may have to wait some time for a better level of funding from the military services and, perhaps, in the meantime develop alternative strategies for maintaining the burgeoning group of life-course researchers interested in military service as an important and potentially transformative social institution. Perhaps the historical narrative of research funding within the U.S. Army that we provided at the outset of this chapter will be of some use to researchers in devising ways to keep life-course research in the military services viable during the looming lean times.

NOTES

1. The views, opinions, and/or findings contained in this article are solely those of the authors and should not be construed as an official Department of the Army or Department of Defense position, policy, or decision unless so designated by other official documentation. This work was supported in part by the U.S. Army Research Institute for the Behavioral and Social Sciences under contract number W5J9CQ-11-C-0040.
2. We capitalize the word "Soldier" because it has become a U.S. Army tradition, which was begun by a previous Chief of Staff of the U.S. Army as a way of honoring our Soldiers' service and stressing their important role in our national defense.

13 Methodological Problems in Determining the Consequences of Military Service

Douglas A. Wolf, Coady Wing, and Leonard M. Lopoo

Given the wars in Iraq and Afghanistan, there is considerable interest in understanding the consequences of military service for a variety of outcomes. This interest is not new. In the past, researchers have studied the effects of service on later-life mortality (e.g., Hearst, Newman, and Hulley 1986; London and Wilmoth 2006; McDonagh 1946; see also MacLean, Chapter 10 of this volume), marital behavior (e.g., Call and Teachman 1996; Laufer and Gallops 1985; Pavalko and Elder 1990; see also Burland and Lundquist, Chapter 8 of this volume), and economic well-being (e.g., Angrist 1990, 1991, Angrist and Krueger 1994; see also Kleykamp, Chapter 7 of this volume), as well as on other outcomes. Although researchers have made important advances in our understanding of the consequences of military service in a variety of contexts, these studies are generally plagued by one or more methodological problems. Many of those same methodological problems would, as well, confront researchers attempting to advance the agenda for future research on military service (see Teachman, Chapter 14 of this volume).

Studies of the consequences of military service, particularly those that seek to locate their investigations within the life-course perspective, encounter methodological problems that occur throughout applied social science research. One such problem is that of measurement: the nature and content of "military service" varies considerably over time, particularly in the distinction between periods of combat and periods of peacetime, but it also varies among those serving at any given time, for example, according to the branch of service, age at entry, duration of service, rank, and occupational specialty. Missing data, especially selectively missing data, is another widespread measurement problem, and one that is ubiquitous in social science research.

Another set of methodological problems concerns the role of time: given the centrality of lifelong developmental change in life-course research (Settersten 2003), longitudinal or multiperiod data are important for comparing outcomes between veterans and non-veterans. However, this in turn forces the researcher to cope with the tradeoffs between prospective studies, which may take years to execute and give rise to potential sample attrition problems, and the use of retrospective data, which, by necessity, can be collected from survivors only and may be greatly contaminated by recall errors. Temporal change also leads to a more technical methodological problem, namely the proper representation of change (i.e., transitions) versus level (i.e., point-in-time values) for key outcomes in the developmental trajectories of interest.

A third problem confronting those doing research on the consequences of military service is that of the proper unit of analysis: although it is true that individuals serve in the military, an individual's observed pattern of service reflects a complex decision-making process in which the influence of, and possibly the choices made by others may also play a role. For example, the past and current military service activities of parents or older siblings may influence one's own decisions, but may also play a role in decisions made by others, higher in the military chain of command, concerning one's unit assignment, exposure to combat, and other elements of military experience. These considerations are, in turn, tied to the emphases in life-course research on "agency" and on "linked lives" (Dannefer and Kelley-Moore 2009; see also Teachman, Chapter 14 of this volume, and Wilmoth and London, Chapter 1 of this volume). Here again, the unit-of-analysis problem has a technical manifestation, namely a number of concerns related to model specification, such as the statistical independence of outcomes among members of a given family or even unrelated individuals whose actions take place in a common spatial or social context.

Still another class of methodological problems, which present particular challenges to those studying the consequences of military service, fall under the general heading of "selection," a term that arises in many analytic contexts. In some cases, it is treated as a threat to "internal validity" (Shadish, Cook, and Campbell 2002) and in others as a source of bias in sample representativeness, and, therefore, inferential validity (Heckman 1979). In all such cases, the existence of selection problems stands in the way of attributing causality to any observed differences in outcomes between those who have and have not served in the military. It is to this final topic, selection, that we devote our attention in this chapter.

THE RELEVANCE OF SELECTION TO RESEARCH ON MILITARY SERVICE

Our discussion is mostly conceptual, but we believe that selective entry and exit from the military and the heterogeneous effects of military service are central to many of the topics examined in the other chapters of this book. The first section of the book is concerned with changes in the demographic composition of the armed forces over historical time. Compositional shifts reflect, at least in part, changes in institutional factors that encourage and discourage military service over time. For instance, Lutz (Chapter 4 of this volume) describes the racial and ethnic composition of the armed forces in different wars and examines some of the key historical events that led to the integration of the U.S. armed forces. These changes are one source of the selection problems associated with answering questions about the effects of military service. Careful research on the reasons for changes in demographic composition is essential for studying the causal effects of service on specific groups. The chapter by Street and Hoffman (Chapter 11 of this volume), which discusses military retirement and health benefits, also provides important contextual information that may help researchers better understand selection processes.

Methodological issues are also central to the second section of the book, which examines effects of military service on the life-course outcomes of veterans and their families. Efforts to understand the ways that military service leads to different educational outcomes and earnings levels are clearly complicated by the possibility that people who serve in the military may have ended up with different earnings and education levels even in the absence of service. In particular, Kleykamp (Chapter 7 of this volume) confronts several of the issues we consider here. We agree with her conclusion that progress on questions about how and why military service affects the labor market outcomes of military spouses will require better data and research designs that can help untangle complicated selection processes. Teachman (Chapter 14 of this volume) also highlights the need for new types of data to support future research on the effects of military service.

We begin by pointing out an important distinction, namely the difference between the effects of former military service (i.e., effects among veterans) and the effects of any military service (i.e., effects on those currently serving as well as veterans). In either case, there is an implied comparison between those with military service and those who never have been, or never will be, members of the military. Most social science research on the consequences of military service compares veterans (i.e., persons formerly in the military) and non-veterans. However, the effects of military service can be more broadly construed and can include effects that are relevant for those still serving. One possible consequence of current military service is premature death due to combat or training accidents. Military personnel who die during service are removed from the population of those among whom the later consequences of veteran status might be studied. The distinction between effects manifested among veterans and effects manifested in the larger population that includes those currently serving, while obvious, is often left implicit by researchers in this area. Most research focuses on effects among veterans, probably reflecting the nature of data available for research purposes: in nearly all cases, the samples used are drawn from the civilian population only. The usual focus on veterans also makes sense from a program evaluation perspective, inasmuch as the "treatment"—military service—is not complete until one returns to the civilian population. Accordingly, we focus on this type of data and on the problems it presents.

METHODS FOR ADDRESSING SAMPLE SELECTION

This chapter addresses several selection issues present in many studies of military service. We divide the myriad forms of selection into three broad classes: (1) initial selection into the military, which may reflect both self-selection and institutional selection; (2) later selection back into the civilian population among those who ever serve; and (3) selection on prior mortality, also sometimes called "left censoring," which includes deaths that occur after the completion of military service but prior to the start date for a given dataset. The first of these problems has received the most attention in past literature.

The first of our analytic categories, selective entry into military service, encompasses a number of both the demand- and supply-side factors that make military service nonrandom. Personal characteristics, such as a family history of military service or a desire for the discipline military service provides, might make one more likely to enlist in the military. To the extent that these characteristics are observable in data, one can control for them in models that estimate the impact of military service. However, it is often the case that these factors are either unobserved or unknown. Failure to control for them could potentially bias estimates of the impact of military service. At the same time, the military itself has established a variety of criteria that makes service nonrandom. For instance, recruits must meet minimum health and physical standards and earn a qualifying score on a test of cognitive ability. If health or cognitive ability is correlated with the outcome of interest, then any comparison of average outcomes between veterans and non-veterans that fails to control for them will suffer from omitted variable bias. It is also noteworthy that many of the criteria have changed over time. Thus, one should not only expect to see heterogeneity across veterans and non-veterans within a birth cohort, but should also expect to find heterogeneity among veterans over time.

The second type of selection we consider—selection back into the civilian population—is in many ways the reverse of the first. As already mentioned, some military personnel die in combat or from other service-related causes, and therefore never return to civilian life. Among the majority of personnel who survive, some fraction will elect to remain in the military for many years. The decision to continue to serve, which presumably reflects perceptions of the relative benefits of the military and civilian sectors of the economy, may bias comparisons between veterans and non-veterans throughout a cohort's life cycle. This type of selection has received very little attention in the social science literature and may be particularly significant among recent cohorts because relatively high percentages of those serving during the era of the All-Volunteer Force are pursuing careers in the military.

Finally, we discuss a third type of selection, namely the selective loss from the civilian population of veterans prior to data collection, which is a problem of particular relevance to studies of the older population. For example, the National Long Term Care Survey (NLTCS), which recorded health and disability information for samples of people 65 and older on six occasions from 1982 through 2004, includes an indicator of veteran status. Yet many in the population of veterans who would otherwise have been in the 65-and-older group in 1982 did not live long enough to be included in the sample. Differential survivorship of veterans and non-veterans during the years between time of service and the time of data collection might produce biased or misleading inferences about the consequences of military service.

With these three types of selection defined, the goals of the remainder of this chapter are twofold. First, we elaborate on the three forms of selection mentioned above. Importantly, these issues surface in most investigations of military service regardless of the outcome. Second, we report on some methodological advances that have been, or might be, used to tackle the problems that selection creates. We detail the advantages of the methods, as well as potential problems with using these techniques. We focus on the post–World War II period, which encompasses a range of both peacetime and wartime military service experiences. All three of the categories of selection that we discuss can be thought of as variations on a common theme: the problem of having a valid comparison group. Because that problem is widespread in the applied social sciences, the methodological issues discussed in this chapter may have implications for a broader set of substantive investigations.

THE DECISION TO JOIN THE MILITARY

To motivate our discussion of selection into the military, it is useful to consider a simple model of the process of entry into the armed forces. For example, one might assume that upon graduation from high school, young men and women are faced with the choice of (1) acquiring additional education, (2) entering the civilian labor market, or (3) enlisting in the military (see Bennett and McDonald, Chapter 6 of this volume for a discussion of these pathways to adulthood). Additional life-course behaviors, such as marriage and childbearing, may also be relevant at this age, but we will disregard these potential aspects of the transition to adulthood. A more complex depiction of the choice problem is possible; for example, some may enlist in the military as a vehicle for financing higher education at a later date, whereas others may commence officer training while in college, entering into a contractual agreement for a period of military service after graduation. However, the simpler three-way discrete-choice problem specified above has proven useful in a number of empirical studies.

This discrete-choice framework is predicated on the idea that individuals have at least some degree of autonomy in choosing schooling, employment, or military service, and that their actions in these domains will be governed by perceived self-interest. Given the three mutually exclusive early-life choices available in this framework, any factors that influence the perceived net attractiveness of any one of them is expected to alter the relative frequency with which all three are selected. The list of such factors is quite long and includes "internal" factors, such as mental and physical health as well as psychological and physiological traits, cognitive skills and aptitudes, attitudes towards risk, material aspirations, and other forms of preferences or motivations. It also includes any number of "external" factors, including proximity to and costs of various institutions of higher education, labor market conditions, familial and peer influences, and military recruiting efforts and inducements, as well as a variety of period-specific factors, including patterns of military deployment and conflict at the time of one's peak susceptibility to service.

Particularly relevant to the decision about whether to enlist are the legal and regulatory structures that define the obligation—if any—to serve in the military during specific historical time periods. From 1948 to 1973, the prospect of compulsory military service, enforced through the draft, was a major factor shaping the opportunities and choices made by those who were subject to its provisions (i.e., generally men aged 19 to 26). From 1951 to 1969, it was possible to use one's student status to obtain a deferment from the draft's provisions (Frusciano 1980). At various times during this period, additional categories of deferment or exemption from the military draft were defined, for example, on the basis of paternity or the provision of support to a dependent. Among those subject to the draft during this period, the risks of being called were not uniform. For example, under Executive Order 11119 of September 10, 1963, local draft boards were required to select men in the following order: delinquents, volunteers, single men (aged 19 to 26, oldest first), and then married men without children (Selective Service System 2008).

A major change to the draft was the institution of a lottery system based on randomization during the Vietnam War, from 1969 to 1973.[1] Three such lotteries were carried out. The first, on December 1, 1969, pertained to men born between 1944 and 1950. Men born in 1951 were drafted in 1971, whereas those born in 1952 were subject to a lottery in 1972. In the first lottery, birth dates were selected randomly and assigned a random sequence number (RSN). The first date drawn, September 14, was given RSN 1 meaning that all men born on September 14 in any year from 1944 to 1950, inclusive, were assigned RSN 1. Dates were drawn until each day had been assigned a RSN. Induction for the drafted men proceeded by RSN. Those with RSN 1–30 were called in January of 1970. Those with

RSN 1–60 were called in February of 1970 and so on. In each draft year, a ceiling was set for the highest RSN to be drafted. In 1970, that number was 195. In 1971, the ceiling was 125, and in 1972, the ceiling was 95. In 1973, the draft was abolished and replaced by the "All-Volunteer" military that remains in place today.

A number of empirical studies have employed some form of the schooling-work-military choice model outlined above and have identified numerous predictors of entry into the armed forces during given historical periods (Bachman et al. 2000; Elder et al. 2010; Gibson, Griepentrog, and Marsh 2007; Griffith and Perry 1993; Johnson and Kaplan 1991; Kilburn and Klerman 1999; Kleykamp 2006; Legree et al. 2000). We are especially interested in discovering predictors of entry into military service that are not expected to influence potential consequences of military service, a point to which we return below.

ANALYTIC FRAMEWORK: CONSTANT VERSUS HETEROGENEOUS EFFECTS

The analytic framework we envision for estimating the effect of military service is regression-based, in which some outcome variable—Y_i, which might be a measure of health, disability, wage, earnings, labor supply, marital status, or even vital status—is related to a binary indicator of veteran status (V_i), as well as a disturbance term, ε:[2]

$$Y_i = \beta_0 + \beta_1 V_i + \varepsilon_i. \quad (1)$$

Equation (1) depicts veteran status as an undifferentiated category, which is plainly an oversimplification. The model ignores several dimensions along which the effects of military service might vary, including the branch in which service was performed, the duration of service, exposure to combat, rank attained, and occupational specialty. Although it is important to recognize the potential for heterogeneity in the experience of military service and its consequences, those dimensions are typically unrecorded in the data available to researchers. Nevertheless, it is important to remember that the standard model presented in equation (1) pools different types of veterans into a single group.

If veteran status were randomly assigned, then determining the impact of military service on the outcome would be relatively straightforward. One could simply compare the average of Y among those who served in the military to the average of Y for those who did not, and the difference between these averages—which, in the context of equation (1) is equal to the β_1 coefficient—would provide an estimate of the effect of having served in the military.

It is precisely the fact that military service is not randomly assigned that creates many of the problems discussed in this chapter. Because individuals usually self-select into the military or are subject to nonrandom selection criteria that vary over historical time, we expect to find systematic correlates of military service that are not represented in the model. For example, in their study of mortality, Hearst, Newman, and Hulley (1986) expressed concern that veterans may be disproportionately drawn from low socioeconomic status families that have higher mortality rates than more affluent families. Using equation (1) in this application, failure to control for the socioeconomic status of the respondent's family of origin in the model would distort the estimated impact of military service: the effect of military service will be conflated with the influence of socioeconomic status.

Although socioeconomic status can be potentially controlled for in these models, one can often conceive of a range of unobservable (to the analyst) factors that are correlated with both service and the outcome of interest that could generate biased estimates of the effect of military service. One indication of the potential seriousness of this omitted variables problem is illustrated in Figure 13.1. This figure shows the percentage of those screened for induction into military service that were rejected on the basis of a physical exam during the 1950 to 1971 period. Any number of attributes—extremes of stature, physical abnormalities (e.g., flat feet), health conditions (e.g., arrhythmia), hearing or vision problems, and others—may produce such a rejection. What is particularly striking about Figure 13.1 is how high the rates of rejection shown are, as well as the substantial year-to-year variability in the rejection

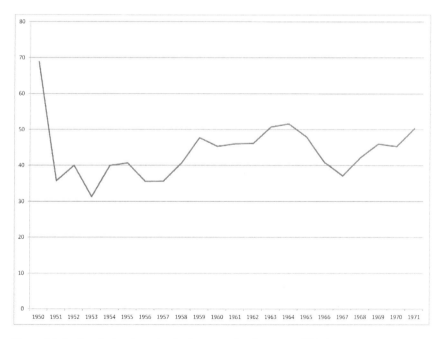

Figure 13.1   Pre-induction physical exam rejection rates (%), by year.

rate. The specific conditions that lead to rejection, or to nonrejection, with respect to eligibility for service are nearly always unrecorded in the data used to study the consequence of service. In general, the consequence of omitting these, or any other relevant variables, may be to create the appearance of an effect of military service that includes, to some unknown extent, differences that would have been present even had those who actually served in the military chosen not to do so.

Implicit in the model described by equation (1) is the notion that the treatment effect of military service is appropriately described as being constant (i.e., that the effect of military service is the same for everyone who serves). Recent research in the fields of statistics and econometrics offers an alternative model of the relationship between military service and an outcome Y (Angrist and Imbens, 1994). This new work recognizes that the effect of military service may vary across individuals. Consider equation (2):

$$Y_i = \gamma_0 + \gamma_{1i} V_i + \varepsilon_i. \quad (2)$$

In this model, the γ_{1i} is a person-specific effect of military service. Just as with the standard constant effects model in equation (1), any omitted factors that are correlated with veteran status and the outcome remain problematic in the heterogeneous effects model in equation (2). However, the new model raises an additional concern: the person-specific effects themselves may be correlated with the decision to enlist in the military. One way to make sense of this concern is to imagine that individuals may select into the military differentially based on their expected gain from service. In other words, people have some understanding of the benefits of military service; hence, one should expect to find that the people most likely to serve voluntarily are those who have the greatest gains by serving.

The presence of heterogeneous treatment effects changes the interpretation of standard regression models. In particular, attention shifts from an all-encompassing "effect" of military service to various "averages" of the person-specific effects. The broadest possible average effect is called the "average treatment effect" and it represents an estimate of the difference in mean outcomes that would occur if the entire population were treated versus untreated[3]. In the context of military service one might think of this overall average effect as the difference in the mean value of Y that would be observed in a country if it had no military service compared to a same country if everyone served in the military. Such a comparison may have limited relevance for the United States, where the size of the military has varied over time, but has seldom come anywhere near the extremes of complete service or complete non-service; it might make more sense in countries with much more extreme levels of service, such as Israel, Switzerland, and Japan. In some cases, researchers might be more interested in average effects among narrower sub-populations like the people who decide to serve because of specific changes in recruitment policies.

The heterogeneous treatment effects model is probably more realistic than the constant effects model, but it forces researchers to think carefully about the target population of interest and it can make it difficult to compare effect estimates across studies that rely on different empirical strategies. If one is interested in estimating heterogeneous effects of military service, identification of the entire distribution of person-specific effects can become unrealistic because there are no policies or enforcement tools that are capable of shifting the entire population into or out of military service.

In the next section of the paper, we discuss some of the means through which economic, sociological, and institutional factors can affect individual enlistment decisions. We argue that explicit analysis of who joins the military and why they join is essential to interpreting the estimates of the effects of military service that are produced by a particular study. Much of our discussion also applies—with appropriate modifications—to selection problems that arise because of selective exits from the military and selective mortality associated with military service.

Instrumental Variables: Theory

When attempting to remove the influence of pre-military service differences in models of the consequences of military service, researchers frequently employ a model that utilizes an instrumental variable (IV). An IV is one that is correlated with the endogenous variable—in our case, military service—but that is unrelated to all of the other factors that contribute to Y. For the IV estimator to operate properly, therefore, the IV should be related to Y, but only through V (which in this case is veteran status), a principle known as the "exclusion restriction."

The most common way to estimate an IV model is called two-stage least squares (2SLS). The method is easiest to understand as a two-step procedure, although it can technically be implemented in a single step. In the first stage, one regresses the endogenous variable on the IV. Using the coefficient estimates from this model, one next predicts veteran status, $\hat{V}$, for each i. Because $\hat{V}$ is derived from a model with the IV, the identification of the slope coefficient in the first stage is not dependent on variation in Y generated from any of the omitted or erroneously measured variables. In the second stage, one substitutes $\hat{V}$ for V in a model of the outcome Y, such as in equation (1), and this model produces consistent estimates of β_1.

When standard IV methods are applied to a model with heterogeneous treatment effects, as in equation (2), the estimated parameters will not—in general—correspond to the overall average treatment effect. In most applications of instrumental variable methods to the context of military service, the estimated effects correspond to the average treatment effect among people who are *induced* to serve in the military because of variation in the instrumental variable. This parameter is often called the Local or Complier Average Treatment Effect (Angrist and Imbens 1994; Angrist and Pishke 2009). Most instruments will affect the decisions of a relatively small group of people and this is important to keep in mind when interpreting specific studies.

IV estimation is not without costs. Compared to ordinary least squares, the standard error for the slope estimates are larger for 2SLS models by a factor that is inversely related to the strength of the correlation between the instrument and the endogenous variable (Kennedy 1998). Thus, researchers prefer instruments that are highly correlated with the endogenous variable, a property referred to as the "relevance" condition.

Instrumental Variables: Application

There are no foolproof tests to determine the validity of an instrumental variable. One often has to craft a reasonable explanation for why the instrument meets the exclusion restriction and relevance condition. It can be quite challenging to convince a skeptical reader that one has found one or more variables that meet these criteria for purposes of isolating the causal effects of military service on a given outcome. Here, we review a number of variables that have been, or might be, used in this way. We organize the variables into a three-part hierarchy, beginning with those that are the most problematic—that is, the least convincing—and ending with those that appear to be the strongest.

Arguably Exogenous Factors

This list includes any number of factors that vary across individuals within cohorts, or between cohorts over time, and that alter the net incentives to volunteer for the military, take actions that reduce one's vulnerability to involuntary service, or pursue other options, such as paid employment or additional schooling. The literature addressing who serves in the military offers some clues to the identity of such variables. For example, Kilburn and Klerman (1999) found that "recruiter density" (military recruiters per capita), measured at the state level, influenced enlistment activity, whereas Kleykamp (2006) found a similar result for county-level military employment. Geographic moves made by the parents of a high school student predict later enlistment (Johnson and Kaplan 1991). Dale and Gilroy's (1984) analysis of aggregate data (at the national level) showed that civilian unemployment rates predict military enlistment; they also found significant effects of variation in policy variables, such as military pay and educational benefits. Somewhat farther afield, Currie and Moretti (2003) used the number of two- and four-year colleges in an individual's county of residence as an instrument for educational attainment; the same variable could exert an indirect influence on the decision to volunteer for military service. Other potential instruments include the cost of college, the availability of student aid, and the wage gap between college and high school graduates. In general, the challenge facing the researcher is to make a convincing argument that any of these variables influence going into the military, but not the outcome of interest, such as later wages, employment, marriage, health, or wealth.

Also relevant here are institutional features, particularly the draft, provisions of which were reviewed above. Historically, men were frequently exempted from military service or were granted deferments for a variety of reasons, including college enrollment or being the parent of a minor child. During the pre-lottery draft era, there may have been geographic variation in the behavior of local draft boards. In general, we would expect that variation over time in the provisions of the draft might help identify between-cohort variation in the propensity to serve in the military, but that this source of exogenous variation provides little or no leverage for identifying within-cohort variations in those propensities.

Policy Changes That Create a "Natural Experiment"

Several researchers have taken advantage of the random nature of the draft lottery instituted during the Vietnam Conflict (e.g., Angrist 1990, 1991; Angrist, Imbens, and Rubin 1996) to generate an estimate of the impact of military service on health and labor market outcomes using a 2SLS model. Given the random nature of the risk of being drafted through the lottery, researchers have used birth dates or lottery status as an instrument for veteran status, arguing that one's draft status through the lottery meets both the exclusion restriction and relevance condition. If the effect of military service is constant for a particular outcome—that is, equation (1) is a reasonable representation of the phenomenon being modeled—then one only needs a single instrument and the lottery draft should work reasonably well.

However, in their seminal work on the topic, Angrist, Imbens, and Rubin (1996) argue that veteran status likely has heterogeneous effects for many outcomes. Using the draft lottery from the Vietnam era as an illustration, they explain that if there are heterogeneous effects of military service and that people select into the military based on their expected gain from service, then the lottery instrument can only estimate the effect of military service for those induced to serve by the draft, but who would not have served otherwise, a group they call "compliers."

To elaborate, consider two groups of men: a group that had their random sequence number (RSN) called during the Vietnam draft lottery and another that did not. If there had been no draft, some proportion of the members in each group would have served voluntarily. Because the draft lottery was random, that proportion should be the same for both groups. Furthermore, within this heterogeneous effects framework, we assume that those who volunteered to serve expected to receive the greatest gain from service. Now, imagine within the group that had their RSN called through the draft, a subset served only because they were drafted. These men are the so-called compliers. Angrist, Imbens, and Rubin (1996) argue that a 2SLS model that uses the drafted versus not-drafted distinction as an instrument can only estimate the average marginal effect for the group of compliers, an effect they call the local average treatment effect, or LATE.

Again, if the effects of military service were constant, as in equation (1), then the 2SLS estimate for compliers would suffice for all men, including those who volunteered. In contrast, the assumption of the heterogeneous effects model, represented by equation (2), is that the compliers had less incentive to join the military than the volunteers. Therefore, the estimated effect of military service must have been less beneficial for the compliers than the volunteers. To get the entire set of marginal effects for the volunteers and those who would not serve even if drafted (i.e., the effect of military service for all people) requires strong theory and many different types of instruments—a daunting proposition at minimum.

Intentional Randomization for Research Purposes

In the post-draft era, the different branches of the military compete for scarce labor resources with each other and with civilian firms. The military's demand for people with advanced technical skills has also increased over time. To cope with these pressures, various branches of the military have designed enlistment and reenlistment bonus programs, as well as programs that provide more generous in-kind benefits, such as educational subsidies. In conjunction with researchers at the RAND Corporation, the Department of Defense has conducted two large, nationwide social experiments designed to evaluate alternative enlistment programs.

From July 1982 to June 1984, the Army studied the effects of three different enlistment bonus programs designed to encourage enlistment among people with above-average scores on aptitude tests who were willing to enroll in specific skill categories. The study had three treatment arms. In the first treatment, enlistees who earned above-average aptitude scores and chose high-demand skill categories received $5,000 cash bonuses. In the second treatment, people earning above-average scores and enlisting in high-demand skill categories for four-year terms of service received $8,000 cash bonuses. In the third treatment people with above-average scores who enlisted in high-demand skill categories received $8,000 cash bonuses for four-year terms of service or $4,000 bonuses for three-year terms. The three enlistment bonus programs were randomly assigned across Army recruitment centers in covariate-balanced geographical regions of the country. The design and analysis of the first enlistment bonus experiment are described in Polich, Dertouzos, and Press (1986). Both of the expanded bonus programs led to a (small) increase in the total number of high-skill people who enlisted in the Army. They also increased the average term of service among high-skill recruits. A second randomized study of the effects of recruitment incentives was undertaken from 1989 to 1990 (Buddin 1991). This second study found that a particular package of skill-targeted enlistment bonuses increased the number of high-skill enlistments by about 3% relative to the existing Army College Fund program, and that the program had a negligible effect on the average length of service agreement selected by high-skill recruits. These treatments might serve as instruments in future work, much as the draft lottery did during the Vietnam era, and allow researchers to estimate treatment effects for those induced to join by the programs.

"REVERSE" SELECTION FROM THE MILITARY TO THE CIVILIAN POPULATION

Although a large majority of those who enter the military remain in it for only a short period—two to four years—many remain for longer periods, and some end up as careerists, spending twenty or more years in the uniformed services. Thus, as a cohort ages and passes through the years of peak labor force participation, a gradually shrinking proportion of the cohort remains in the military. Figure 13.2 illustrates this phenomenon: the figure plots the percentage of men in selected single-year birth cohorts that remain on active duty, by age, for ages 20 through 50 years.[4] Between-cohort variation in the proportion serving during their early 20s

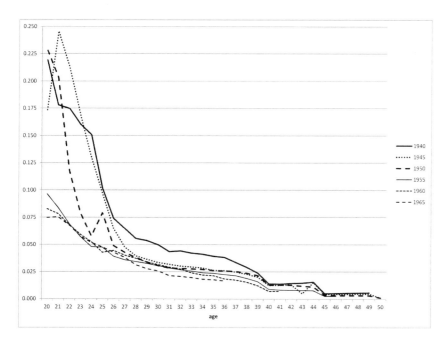

Figure 13.2   Proportion of birth cohort currently serving in military, by age.

is pronounced, especially between cohorts reaching age 20 before and after the end of the draft. Among all cohorts shown, the percentage serving falls below 5% by age 30, declining gradually thereafter.

Several studies have analyzed retention in the armed forces, focusing mainly on the effectiveness of financial inducements to reenlist (Daula and Moffitt 1995) or on other economic factors, such as civilian unemployment levels (Goldberg 1985). In an interesting example of symmetry of responses, Mehay and Hogan (1998) found financial incentives to voluntarily leave the military during a time of downsizing (1992) to be effective, paralleling the efficiency of reenlistment bonuses as a retention tool. These models of military retention are, by extension, models of accession to the civilian population.

Nearly all studies of educational attainment, labor force behavior, earnings, income inequality, and other economic and sociodemographic outcomes use data from samples of the civilian population only, and pay little or no attention to the absence from those data sources of military personnel. However, research on differences between veterans and non-veterans in any of these outcomes must take care to consider the representativeness of their veteran subsamples—that is, those formerly in the military—in comparison to the entire respective cohorts, including those who have not yet returned to the civilian population.

The military retention literature reviewed above is based on samples taken exclusively from military populations, whereas the literature on the consequences of military service uses data sampled from the civilian population. Any attempt to assess potential selection bias associated with the use of exclusively civilian samples would seem to require data that represent both the civilian and military populations. With such data one might estimate a two-equation "selection" model, with one equation differentiating individuals as members of the military versus the civilian population, and the other representing some consequence of past military service conditional on membership in the civilian population. As in any such model of selection, a key issue is whether the random component of the selection equation (i.e., unmeasured factors that influence one's presence in the civilian population) is correlated with the random component in the outcome equation. Different arguments supporting the existence of such positive or negative correlations could presumably be made for different outcomes.

At any rate, data drawn from both the civilian and military populations are quite rare; one exception is the decennial census, although the census is hampered by both its purely cross-sectional nature and its sparse coverage of relevant covariates. The American Community Survey, collected annually by the Census Bureau, is another promising exception given its inclusion of a wider range of covariates than the decennial census. There may also be some potential for addressing this issue through the pooling of service records with data from samples of the civilian population. In the absence of such data, researchers have little choice but to limit their analyses to ages beyond 30 years or so, after which the proportion of a cohort that remains in the military is quite low, and hope that any remaining biases inherent in comparisons of veterans and non-veterans are acceptably small.

SELECTION ON PRIOR MORTALITY

The type of selection just considered implies a need to wait until well into a cohort's life cycle to make comparisons between veterans and non-veterans, in order to maximize the comparability of the two groups. Yet doing so is likely to exacerbate a different sort of selection problem, namely the problem of selective loss of veterans from the sample prior to follow-up. This problem has received very little attention in the literature on consequences of military service. One exception is Angrist and Chen (2011), who analyze wage and schooling consequences of Vietnam-era military service for a narrow cohort of men—those born between 1948 and 1952—in 2000, when they were 48 to 52 years old. Given that nearly thirty years had elapsed between the Vietnam-era service and the timing of the outcome in this study, post-military selective mortality might affect the composition of the sample, and, therefore, bias any estimates of the effects of veteran status on the outcomes of interest. Angrist and Chen (2011) address this possibility, comparing expected to actual numbers of draft-eligible men in their 2000 sample; these comparisons lead them to conclude that excess civilian mortality has not had a substantial effect on sample composition in 2000. Although this conclusion may be warranted, it need not hold for other cohorts, or for other outcomes, or for the same cohort at a point later in its life cycle.

In general, researchers studying the consequences of military service at ages well after the timing of such service should be mindful of the possibility of differential survivorship between veterans and non-veterans prior to data collection. If the outcome of interest—health or economic status, for example—is likely to be related to mortality, as many such outcomes are, then the possibility for selection bias again arises. This phenomenon could, in principle, be handled using another variant on the previously mentioned "selection" model: here, one equation would represent survivorship from some baseline year to the year[s] in which the outcome is measured (e.g., 2000, in the Angrist and Chen paper mentioned above), and the other would, again, represent the effect of veteran status on some outcome given survivorship to that point. This would produce an odd form of the usual selection model, namely one in which the "treatment"—veteran status— appears in both the "selection" and the "outcome" equations.

Even in the unlikely event that there were no unmeasured variables producing selection bias, pre-sample mortality could still undermine the conclusions drawn from a comparison of veterans and non-veterans, if—as the life-course perspective reminds us—the consequences of military service play out over the life cycle and are manifested in different ways at different points in the life cycle. For example, the health trajectories of veterans may be better (or worse) than those of non-veterans relatively early in the life cycle (for example, during the 30s and 40s) but, due to delayed responses or cumulative processes, be worse (or better) at later ages, for example in the 50s and 60s or at older ages. These sorts of "crossover" phenomena are often found in demographic research and have been recently documented with respect to men's health in longitudinal research comparing veterans and non-veterans, as well as veterans with different service experiences (Wilmoth, London, and Parker 2010). As a variation on this possibility, a comparative study of veterans and non-veterans at older ages may fail to find any differences along some outcome dimension, yet there could have been large differences between the two groups for that very outcome at younger ages.

Pre-sample mortality seems like a particularly germane problem in studies of mortality differentials between veterans and non-veterans. For example, one study that used data from the Health and Retirement Study (HRS) found that military service was associated with an elevated likelihood of death over the ten-year period 1992–2002 (London and Wilmoth 2006). Liu, Engel, Kang, and Cowan (2005), who focused only on the 70+ portion of the HRS sample (which was originally called the AHEAD study), similarly found that veterans were more likely than non-veterans to die over the 1993 to 1995 interval and concluded that these findings imply a mortality crossover of veterans' and non-veterans' mortality schedules prior to age 70. However, they did not attempt to empirically demonstrate the validity of this claim.

We provide some simple, but suggestive, evidence on pre-sample selection, using the demographic technique of intercensal survivorship ratios (Hill 1999; Preston, Hill, and Drevenstedt 1998; United Nations 1983). Our application of this technique uses individual-level data from 1% samples of the 1960 and 1990 U.S. Census (Ruggles et al. 2010). In particular, we estimate the thirty-year survival probability for men in two groups, veterans (v) and non-veterans (n) by age (a) in 1960, using the relationship:

$$S_j = \frac{N_{j, a + 30, 1990}}{N_{j, a, 1960}} \text{, for } j = v, n \qquad (3)$$

The intercensal survivorship ratio technique requires that the population studied be closed to migration, a condition we approximate by limiting our analysis to native-born men. Men are classified as veterans in the 1960 census data if they were serving in the military at the time, or had previously served in the military. Our coding of "veteran" in the 1990 census data attempts to isolate men whose military service is likely to have begun by 1960, in order to ensure that the populations enumerated in the numerator and denominator of (3) are comparable. For example, our tabulation of the census data classifies 33,162 men aged 25 to 29 in 1960 as veterans and 29,743 men aged 55 to 59 as veterans in 1990, producing an estimated survival ratio of 0.897. By defining our "treatment" group as men who were already veterans by 1960, and considering their survival to 1990, we produce estimates of pre-sample mortality particularly relevant to the HRS sample.

Estimated survival ratios for veterans and non-veterans in six age groups are shown in Figure 13.3. For four of the 1960 age groups (25–29, 30–34, 35–39, and 40–44 years) veterans have higher chances of surviving to 1990 than non-veterans, whereas for the 50–54 age group in 1960, the situation is reversed. The thirty-year survival ratios for men 45–49 years old in 1960 are virtually identical for veterans and non-veterans. For only three age groups—those 25–29, 40–44, and 50–54 years in 1960—are the survival ratios of veterans and non-veterans significantly different from one another. Nevertheless, there is a clear impression of favorable survival experience of veterans compared to non-veterans for those younger than 45 in 1960, and a reversal of that advantage, suggestive of a "crossover," among men in their 50s in 1960. These results contrast sharply with the findings presented in Bedard and Deschênes (2006), who find that mortality rates among veterans are nearly 27% higher than among non-veterans, on average, during the 1968 to 2000 period. Their analysis pertains to men born from 1920 to 1939, which coincides almost perfectly with our 30–39 age group. There are several important differences between the Bedard-Deschênes study and

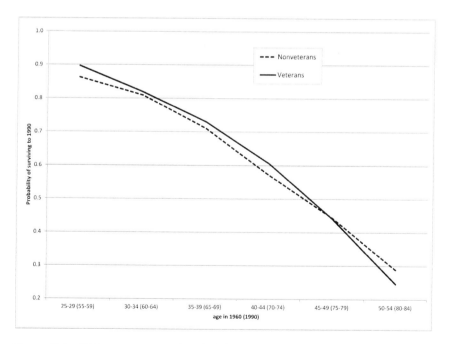

Figure 13.3 Thirty-year survival probabilities of veterans and non-veterans by age in 1960.

ours: they compare a direct measure of mortality experience, the annual death rate, while we compare an indirect measure, the thirty-year survivorship ratio; they also study a later time period, although one that overlaps substantially with ours. Nevertheless, the conclusions supported by the two analyses are quite different, suggesting the fruitfulness of further investigation of these patterns.

The results shown in Figure 13.3 pertain to six nonoverlapping birth cohorts and represent mortality experiences that precede each cohort's recruitment into, for example, the Health and Retirement Study. Our 25–29 age group (in 1960) corresponds to the older half of the original HRS sample (which was age 51–61 in 1992), whereas our 40–54 age groups overlap reasonably well with the original AHEAD sample (which was age 70 and older in 1993). In general, it appears that upon recruitment into the HRS sample, the veteran and non-veteran groups represented their respective birth cohorts to differing degrees, and it seems that some (and possibly a great deal) of the consequences of military service for these groups had occurred earlier in their lives. Researchers should, therefore, exercise caution when drawing conclusions from data that come from late in the life course, when the experience that defines the groups being compared is not directly observed because it occurred early in life.

DISCUSSION

Policy makers, academics, individuals who serve, as well as family members of those who serve, all have an interest in understanding the consequences of military service. As we have explained in this chapter, estimating these consequences is extraordinarily difficult due in large part to a variety of selection issues. We have addressed only a few of the potential problems one confronts when trying to answer questions related to the effects of military service: nonrandom initial selection into the military, nonrandom exit from military service, and selective mortality. We have also described how these selection issues might affect estimates of the consequences of military service.

The nonrandom selection of individuals into the military has received the most attention by scholars to date. As a result, our understanding of the techniques used to address omitted variable bias has evolved over time. These findings highlight the importance of strong theory, as well as a comprehensive understanding of the phenomenon. We have also learned that tackling this issue is more complex than researchers initially believed: one needs many instruments that operate to induce different segments of the population into service.

The other two types of selection discussed here, selection out of the military and selective mortality, have received very little research attention and surely merit more. Advances in methodological techniques, as well as more comprehensive data collection, would improve our ability to address these issues (see Teachman, Chapter 14 of this volume).

We would be remiss if we did not call attention to the fact that in most applications, multiple forms of selection are present. Researchers who work in this area typically only consider one selection issue at a time. However, others likely exist. Furthermore, one might imagine that attempts to improve one selection issue might exacerbate the problems created by other selection problems. For example, if one chooses to observe an outcome among those aged 50 or older to allow those in military service the time necessary to reenter the civilian population, thereby overcoming the selective exit issue we described earlier, one likely increases the chances that differential mortality will affect the results.

The problems addressed in this chapter appear, in various guises, in a wide variety of social science and policy research settings. Selection into a group of analytic interest with respect to unobserved characteristics—for example, selective entry among civilian entrants to the armed forces, or selective reentry into the civilian population among those in the military, the two cases we considered—is frequently recognized in applied research, and an array of established tools are available with which to try to eliminate suspected selection bias. The left-censoring problem—selection on prior mortality—that we have discussed is less often noticed, yet is present in numerous contexts, especially those that address late-life consequences of early-life experiences or exposures. Two examples of this problem, both of which are active areas of research, are the influence of early-life circumstances on late-life health and the effect of childbearing on later health and well-being.

Several studies have examined the effects of childhood health or socioeconomic status on late-life health using samples drawn from the older population; examples include Palloni et al. (2005), who study older Puerto Ricans, and Banks, Oldfield, and Smith (2011), who compare English and American older adults. However, there is also substantial evidence that adverse health and socioeconomic conditions in childhood are associated with increased mortality rates in adulthood (Elo and Preston 1992; Golobardes, Lynch, and Smith 2004). Similarly, research has investigated the effects of fertility patterns on a number of later-life outcomes, such as the timing of retirement (Hank 2004), household wealth (Scholz and Seshadri 2009), and chronic disease (Henretta 2007); in all the studies cited, the data come from samples drawn from the older population. Yet other research has demonstrated that women's mortality rates differ by parity (for a review see Hurt, Ronsmans, and Thomas 2006).

In both areas of research just described, differential mortality that occurs after exposure to the risk factor of interest—poor health during childhood or early childbearing—but prior to the collection of data on late-life outcomes, produces analytic problems analogous to those we discussed in the context of exposure to military service. First, the pre-sample selective mortality changes the prevalence of exposure to the risk factor among the population of older survivors relative to the prevalence of the risk factor earlier in life. Second, survivors to late life who were exposed to the risk factor differ along unmeasured dimensions from those who were not exposed to the risk factor; moreover, the nature of the unmeasured differences between exposure groups changes over the life cycle due to differential mortality selection. Finally, the causal impacts of the exposure to the risk factor may change over the life course, further undermining the external validity of conclusions based on analyses of data collected from those who survive to older ages.

At minimum, therefore, we encourage researchers in the field to consider these potential problems and interpret their results accordingly. Addressing the various types of selection covered in this chapter is a challenging task, but it is essential to moving knowledge forward in this research area. In addition, the work in this area is likely to provide a model for dealing with selection that can contribute to other areas of inquiry.

NOTES

1. See Angrist (1991) and Selective Service System (2009) for a history of the Vietnam era draft.
2. In most applications, one would also control for a variety of background factors, which might be represented by the vector X. We remove this additional set of factors to simplify the exposition.
3. It is also standard in such models to assume that such a large scale up would not lead to any spillover or general equilibrium effects.
4. We are grateful to Woody Carlson for providing the data used to generate Figure 13.2; for details on these data see Carlson and Andress (2009).

14 Setting an Agenda for Future Research on Military Service and the Life Course

Jay D. Teachman

Research on military service has a long and rich history. Indeed, the roots of quantitative Sociology can be traced to research sponsored by the military during World War II. *The American Soldier* (Stouffer et al. 1949a,b) represents a watershed in empirical Sociology that continues to shape social scientific thought today (Williams 1989, 2006). Methodological innovations, such as Guttman scaling, and theoretical foundations, such as relative deprivation, trace their heritage to *The American Soldier*. Subsequent research has continued to document the important role that the military plays in national and international relations, as well being a laboratory to study professional and occupational structures (Siebold 2001). Yet despite this research heritage, fifty years after the publication of *The American Soldier*, we know surprisingly little about the ways that military service is linked to the lives of the men and women who have served their country.

Over the last seventy years, at least 1.5 million military personnel have been on active duty during each year, affecting 10 to 70% of relevant birth cohorts (Segal and Segal 2004). The peak participation figures are for birth cohorts affected by war (World War II, Korea, Vietnam), but military service is common even for peacetime birth cohorts. For example, Pettit and Western (2004) estimate that 17% of Black men and 14% of White men born from 1965 to 1969 have served in the military. If men experiencing incarceration are excluded, nearly one in four Black men in this cohort has served in the military. Thus, military service is not an anomaly or an isolated event in the transition to adulthood, even during the All-Volunteer Force era; it is a common event that occurs at ages during which many men (and increasingly women) are making decisions about education, participating in the labor force, forming intimate relationships, and starting families (see Kelty and Segal, Chapter 2 of this volume). An often-ignored fact is that the military remains the single largest employer of young men in the U.S. (Angrist 1998), and therefore continues to be an important institutional influence in the lives of many young adults, particularly those from disadvantaged backgrounds (see Bennett and McDonald, Chapter 6 of this volume).

The previous chapters in this volume have synthesized what we currently know about various aspects of military service in American men's and women's lives. In this chapter, I provide a sketch of what we do not know and identify the important unanswered questions that should drive future research. Finally, I outline the sorts of data that are necessary to answer the important questions facing life-course researchers. Throughout this chapter, I use four principles of the life course to organize the discussion: (1) human agency, (2) the importance of time and place, (3) linked lives, and (4) cumulative, lifelong development (MacLean and Elder 2007; for a more detailed description of the life-course perspective, see also Mortimer and Shanahan 2003).

Human agency speaks to the notion that people choose between military service, education, and civilian labor market employment. Time and place are important contextualizing parameters. Military service is not uniformly experienced by all men and women. All service occurs in a context shaped by local, national, and international forces that determine the nature of service and how that service is evaluated. The notion of linked lives attunes us to the fact that individuals do not live in isolation from each other. People live their lives in rich, often overlapping social networks. Finally, military service can have effects that last a lifetime. Current military service certainly highlights differences between military personnel and civilians. Yet the effects of military service can appear many decades after service occurs, making comparisons between veterans and non-veterans across the life course an important consideration. Overall, these life-course principles can serve as a guide for conceptualizing the relationship between military service and the life course (see Wilmoth and London, Chapter 1 of this volume), organizing past research, identifying overlooked research questions, providing insights into needed data, and defining the necessary boundaries of new data collection efforts that will move the field forward in the future.

WHAT IS NOT KNOWN ABOUT THE LIFE COURSE AND MILITARY SERVICE?

Earlier chapters in this volume outline the literature linking military service to the life course. Given its transformative potential and importance in the lives of young men and women, it is not surprising that military service has been linked to a wide range of outcomes, including marriage, divorce, and cohabitation; socioeconomic attainment; and health (see Kelty and Segal, Burland and Lundquist, Bennett and McDonald, Kleykamp, and MacLean in this volume). In this context, I suggest that it is important to note that variation and changes in the civilian environment facing veterans and non-veterans are as important to consider as variation and changes in the military environment that act upon active-duty service members and veterans. Thus, alterations in civilian opportunities for educational and economic success are likely to be as important for determining crime and delinquency as changes in the selectivity of the military and the nature of military service itself.

In addition, the literature linking marriage, divorce, and cohabitation to military service is limited in several fashions. First, it is difficult to obtain consistent data on these important family life-course statuses across different historical eras. Event history data that include the dates of important transitions for nationally representative samples have become available only recently. Second, the mechanisms linking military service to these family life-course events remain unclear. Whereas active-duty service appears to spur marriage, at least for more recent cohorts, the mechanisms by which this effect occurs remain opaque and crudely measured at best. Third, little is known about the extent to which military service affects marriage, divorce, and cohabitation after the period of active-duty service ends. Teachman (2007b) reports that rates of marriage for men who served in the military are higher than for non-veterans, but these results may be due to the selectivity of military service (Usdansky, London, and Wilmoth 2009; see also Burland and Lundquist, Chapter 8 of this volume). Fourth, although we have begun to accumulate information about a select number of family-related transitions, other family events, such as childbearing, childrearing, and kin relationships, remain severely underresearched.

Even though much has been learned, the literature linking socioeconomic attainment and military service is also limited in many ways. First, there remains a lack of comparable data that can be used to examine the consequences of military service across different eras. This makes it difficult to understand why changes in the consequences of military service may have occurred over time. Second, the number of socioeconomic outcomes that have been investigated is limited. Income and education are most commonly considered, but outcomes such as occupation, wealth accumulation, home ownership, poverty, and material hardship are scarcely discussed (but see Fitzgerald 2006; Heflin, Wilmoth, and London 2012; London, Heflin, and Wilmoth 2011; Teachman and Tedrow 2004). Third, trajectories of socioeconomic attainment, and the interrelationships between various components of attainment across the life course, have largely been ignored. Only recently have researchers begun to move beyond static indicators of income and education. Fourth, research on socioeconomic attainment continues to struggle with appropriate controls for selectivity and precise specification of the mechanisms through which military service impacts post-service accomplishments (see Bennett and McDonald, Chapter 6 of this volume, and Kleykamp, Chapter 7 of this volume).

Finally, a significant gap in the health literature exists, in that there is very little research that addresses the health implications of noncombat military service (see MacLean, Chapter 10 of this volume). Although we know that veterans who experience combat have more negative health outcomes than noncombat veterans, we do not know how noncombat veterans compare to the general population. On the one hand, the screening process that selects veterans into the service suggests that they should be healthier than non-veterans. On the other hand, poor health habits (e.g., use of tobacco and alcohol) learned in the military may operate to negate any positive selectivity effect. The existing literature also fails to fully consider how variations in military service affect health. For example, are the health-related effects of military service different for officers versus enlisted men, for different military occupational specialties, or for different terms of service? In addition, with the exception of tobacco and alcohol use, there is little indication in the literature of the mechanisms through which military service affects health. For instance, variations in life-course patterns of education, income, and occupational attainment associated with military service may impact health outcomes.

A BROADER PERSPECTIVE ON WHAT IS MISSING

For the most part, research on the determinants and consequences of military service is fragmented and focused on a limited set of outcomes. Many of these limitations are related to the data sources available (a point to which I return later). Most databases that are mined for information about the covariates of military service were not designed with this task in mind. As a consequence, researchers are often constrained in the questions that they can ask. Important questions that need to be asked are left unanswered due to the lack of adequate information. As a consequence, we still know little about the characteristics of men and women that lead them to enlist in the military and how these characteristics may have changed over time. Although we know that enlistments are tied to competing opportunities in the civilian labor market and rates of pay available in the military (Orvis and Asch 2001), as well as a number of sociodemographic background characteristics (Bachman et al. 2000; Segal, Bachman, Freedman-Doan, and O'Malley 1999; Teachman, Call, and Segal 1993b), we know little about how aspirations to join the military are formed, how these aspirations change across adolescence and young adulthood, and how they are linked to aspirations for competing activities, such as the pursuit of additional schooling and entering the civilian labor market (see Kelty and Segal, Chapter 2 of this volume, and Bennett and McDonald, Chapter 6 of this volume). We know even less about the interplay between individual patterns of life-course development and contextual factors, including opportunities and constraints, such as geography (see Bailey, Chapter 9 of this volume) and birth cohort, which might affect the propensity to serve.

Continuing with this theme, we also lack information about the interface between potential enlistees and the military recruitment system. There are two parties to this interface: the potential enlistee and the military. On the one hand, we need to ask how potential enlistees view the military, the different branches of the military, and the enlistment process. On the other hand, we also need to ask about historical changes in the recruitment standards (physical, moral, educational, and mental) used by the military services to screen applicants. On a related note, it is essential to consider variation and changes in opportunities for educational and economic success in the civilian environment. Thus, the selectivity of men and women into the military is the result of the interplay that occurs between the potential enlistee and the military within the context of the civilian environment. Anything short of a full understanding of this process means that issues surrounding selectivity will plague attempts to understand the relationship between military service and the life-course trajectories of veterans (see Wolf, Wing, and Lopoo, Chapter 13 of this volume).

Data limitations in research are also generated by changes in the nature of military service itself. For example, in the latter part of the All-Volunteer Force era, there have been substantial increases in the number of women and Hispanics who have elected to serve, but there is only limited information about the enlistment decisions driving these increases. What are the individual and macro-level conditions that have driven these increases? In addition, there is very little information about the interface between military service and the life-course trajectories of women and Hispanics. Although a handful of articles have begun to tackle the issue of enlistment (Elder et al. 2010; Segal, Segal, Bachman, Freedman-Doan, and O'Malley 1998) and the family (see Burland and Lundquist, Chapter 8 of this volume), as well as the income consequences of military service for women (Cooney, Segal, Segal, and Falk 2003; Prokos and Padavic 2000), the results remain sparse. Even less information is available about Hispanics in the military (Segal and Segal 2004; Segal, Thanner, and Segal 2007; see also Lutz, Chapter 4 of this volume). These limitations result from the recent increase in the presence of women and Hispanics in the military and the lack of data about military service in the latter part of the All-Volunteer Force era.

Gays and lesbians represent another overlooked group of military veterans (see Brown, Chapter 5 of this volume). Although gays and lesbians have always served in the U.S. military, from 1993 until 2011, they served under a "Don't Ask, Don't Tell" policy that has likely increased their representation. Gates (2004) suggests that from 1950 to 1990, the rate of participation in the military was higher for heterosexual than for gay men. However, since 1990, there has been no difference in the participation rates of gay and straight men. As the number of women in the military has increased, the much higher participation rate of lesbian compared to heterosexual women has remained. Despite their presence in the military, we still know essentially nothing about the ways in which military service intersects the life-course development of gay men and lesbians (see Brown, Chapter 5 of this volume). The recent repeal of the Don't Ask, Don't Tell policy will provide a unique and time-sensitive opportunity to study the impact of a policy change on the lives of gay, bisexual, and lesbian service members.

Aside from issues of selectivity and the obvious lack of information about military service for women, Hispanics, and other minority groups, there are a number of gaps in our knowledge of the consequences of military service. The list is obviously long, and I only attempt to illustrate some of the more obvious gaps in knowledge. I start by mentioning research on attitudes, values, and goal orientation. Elder (1986) has shown that veterans often cite military service as a turning point in their lives (see also Elder, Gimbel, and Ivie 1991; Ivie, Gimbel, and Elder 1991). Although this research demonstrates that veterans believe that military service affects their lives and their outlook on life, there is no baseline against which to make comparisons (that is, attitudes and values prior to military service are not measured). Moreover, comparisons to more recent cohorts of veterans are lacking. With human agency being a central concept of the life-course perspective, it is crucial to understand the role of attitudes and values in determining behavior and the ways in which these attitudes and values are shaped by major life-course experiences, such as military service.

Another overlooked area of research relates to the social networks and information chains possessed by men and women, and how they are altered by military service. Because the life-course perspective emphasizes linked lives, information about social networks is essential. Elder and Clipp (1988a,b) provide interesting clues about the influence of military service on social networks. Given that military service removes individuals from relatively dense networks in their early adult lives and places them in radically different environments, it possesses the potential to disrupt existing social networks and establish new social ties that affect lives in multiple ways. Because social networks have been linked to outcomes as varied as health (Smith and Christakis 2008), education (Lin 1999), job searches (Granovetter 1995), and migration (Massey 1990), it is important to understand how military service alters the linkages that men and women accumulate over time. By expanding social networks into the related body of literature on social capital, an even greater range of outcomes becomes evident (Portes 1998).

Related to the modification and formation of social networks and social capital are possible linkages between military service and community integration. Sociological theories, in general, and the life-course perspective, in particular, posit strong effects of context, as measured by both time and place (Sampson, Morenoff, and Gannon-Rowley 2002). There is considerable evidence that military service influences geographic mobility (see Bailey, Chapter 9 of this volume), although researchers do not often attend to the spatial and mobility aspects of military service in their studies or how they influence community engagement. To the extent that military service is linked to individuals' embeddedness in communities, participation in the ongoing activities of communities, and beliefs about community action, it can affect a range of life-course outcomes. Future research needs to consider mobility and multiple components of community context, including the presence of, and engagement with, schools, churches, civic forums, business leagues, and various interest groups (including veterans groups).

Although past research has begun to outline some of the family-related outcomes of military service, such as marriage and divorce (see Burland and Lundquist, Chapter 8 of this volume), there are other components of the family life course that have received very little attention. The relationships between military service and basic demographic processes, such as fertility, migration, and mortality, have received virtually no attention (but see Cowper and Corcoran 1989; Cowper et al. 2000; London and Wilmoth 2006; Lundquist and Smith 2005). Additional demographically relevant life-course processes, such as retirement, intergenerational relationships, infant mortality, and physical and mental disability, have also received relatively little attention from researchers interested in the effects of military service.

In addition to various topical areas that have failed to receive needed attention, there are broader-scale gaps that occur in the extant literature. There are several potential components of these gaps. First, much research on military service has tended to view service as unidimensional. That is, all types of military service are considered to be indistinguishable. In part, this assumption results from data limitations (i.e., researchers are often only able to determine whether a respondent is or is not a veteran). Yet military service is not experienced uniformly. It differs along many dimensions, including branch of service, length of service, rank obtained, training received, military occupation performed, number and types of deployments, risk of combat, active-duty and veteran benefits available, and historical period. We have little knowledge about the impact of these variations in military service on the life course, although there are some examples of how such diversity in service affects life-course outcomes. Elder (1986, 1987), as well as Dechter and Elder (2004), demonstrate that, among older cohorts, officers generally fared better than their enlisted compatriots. A handful of economically oriented papers (Bryant and Wilhite 1990; Goldberg and Warner 1987; Mangum and Ball 1987, 1989) have shown that training received in the military affects subsequent civilian wages. Sampson and Laub (1996) indicate that, among World War II veterans, those who were deployed overseas generally experienced more positive effects of service. Teachman (2007a) shows that the effect of All-Volunteer Force–era service on education varies according to branch of service and length of service. Teachman and Tedrow (2008) also demonstrate that the negative influence of military service during the All-Volunteer Force era on marital disruption is limited to service in the Army. MacLean and Edwards (2010) found that male officers have better self-rated health than enlisted men, which is due in part to longer duration of service, whereas Wilmoth, London, and Parker (2010) demonstrate differences in later-life health trajectories among cohorts of men who served during the various periods of war and peace during the middle of the 20th century.

For the most part, existing research has also failed to consider the cumulative and interrelated effects of military service. A central component of the life course is that change and effect are cumulative (Dannefer 2003). Yet most research on military service focuses on a single outcome, often at a single point in time. A full understanding of the effects of military service requires an understanding of life-course trajectories as they unfold over multiple domains. For example, to understand the impact of military service on health demands an understanding of how service is related to important determinants of health, such as education, income, occupation, and marital status (see Wilmoth and London, Chapter 1 of this volume). Moreover, it is not sufficient to simply include these variables as controls in a model predicting health status. It is necessary to theorize and estimate the connections that military service has with these determinants of health across the life course.

A related concern is the need to substantially increase our ability to identify the mechanisms through which military service affects life-course outcomes. Here, we need a clear distinction between current military service and veteran status. Active-duty military service is demanding and comes with a set of costs and benefits that make it a very unique occupation. Indeed, it is a total institution that structures the lives of young men and women while they are serving, and also shapes the lives of family linked to the service member and, thereby, the military. Research cited above and in the chapters in this volume notes the strong association between current military service and a variety of outcomes, such as income, marriage, divorce, and health. What remains in many cases is for research to better identify why these strong associations occur. For example, beyond selectivity, why is current military service tied to health outcomes? What are the relative roles played by easy access to health care and standards for health and physical fitness versus the ready availability of tobacco and alcohol products and performance of often hazardous occupations?

But researchers must also recognize that military service is a critical, but usually short period of time in the life course. Most individuals spend only a few years serving their country. Perhaps more important, therefore, are questions tied to the long-term consequences of military service. Why should military service affect health forty years after a service member has been discharged? What are the pathways by which military service may lead to different disease outcomes, to different patterns of disability, or to different trajectories of physical and mental decline? These questions are only examples of the sorts of questions that we must ask, and then answer, if we are to comprehend the ways in which military service structures the life course. It is not sufficient to simply note that the lives of veterans are different forty years after service. It is necessary that we be able to point to the mechanisms that lead to different trajectories.

I end this section by noting that the effects of military service may not be proportionate across time. By this I mean that military service may produce results that vary according to stage in the life course. For example, Teachman (2007b; Teachman and Tedrow 2008) shows that the effects of military service on marriage and divorce are largely restricted to the period of time respondents serve on active duty. After discharge from the military, there is little difference in family formation and dissolution patterns between veterans and civilians. In other instances, an effect of military service may not appear immediately. It may be the case, for instance, that the negative health effects of excessive tobacco use among veterans will not appear for decades after active-duty service. Patterns of effects across the life course may be quite complex, which enhances the importance and value of considering life-course trajectories. What may appear to be a null effect of military service at one point in the life course may be very different at earlier or later points in time.

Researchers should also be aware of variations in the effects of military service that might occur according to selected background characteristics (see Bennett and McDonald, Chapter 6 of this volume, and Kleykamp, Chapter 7 of this volume). The "bridging environment" hypothesis, whereby racial-ethnic minority group members are more likely to benefit from military service, is a classic example of this notion (Browning, Lopreato, and Poston 1973). Another example is provided by Sampson and Laub (1996), who find that military service during World War II was more likely to have positive effects on the life-course trajectories of disadvantaged men (i.e., men with criminal backgrounds or men from deprived socioeconomic households). Sampson and Laub attribute their findings to the linked lives notion found in theories of the life course. In particular, they note that military service "knifes off" past experiences, including immersion in poor social networks. Military service provides everyone with a more or less clean start in which prior differences are largely deemphasized.

DATA LIMITATIONS AND NEEDS

As I noted earlier, data limitations have hindered researchers as they seek to answer important questions about the nature of the relationship between military service and the life course. Before outlining some data needs in greater detail, let me present a few general characteristics necessary for data linking military service with the life course.

First, such data should be longitudinal (i.e., information on the same individuals across multiple points in time). Cross-sectional data are very difficult to use because they cannot be employed to construct trajectories of change across various dimensions of the life course. This problem can be alleviated somewhat by asking retrospective questions about life-course events and processes, but problems of recall and validity quickly become an issue (Smith 1984; Williams et al. 2001). It is often difficult for individuals to accurately recall the dates at which some events occurred (e.g., dates at which jobs started and ended, dates for the beginnings and endings of illnesses or disabilities), and perhaps even more difficult to recall information about their attitudes, values, and intentions at some point in the past. At older ages, such studies also miss the life-course histories of individuals who do not survive to the date the study was conducted (see Wolf, Wing, and Lopoo, Chapter 13 of this volume). Thus, the best way to gather information for a life-course investigation of the consequences of military service is in a prospective, longitudinal study.

Of course, longitudinal studies are not without their limitations. They are expensive, time-consuming, and only able to provide information on the life course through the oldest age covered in the last round of data collection. However, the ability to obtain information about multiple dimensions of the life course as it unravels is invaluable. The longitudinal nature of such data also makes it easier to assign causal ordering to a series of life-course events by allowing analysts to place them in sequence. Finally, longitudinal data pay attention to time and place by allowing the effects of military service to vary across the life course. As indicated earlier, the effects of military service may wane or grow as time passes. Longitudinal data collection will capture these shifts in the relationship between military service and various outcomes at different points in the life course.

Second, longitudinal data should contain information about both civilians (non-veteran and veteran) and active-duty members of the military. A great deal of research has been sponsored by the various branches of the military concerning service members. These data can be invaluable for making policy for active-duty service members, and, in certain cases, when there are clear benchmarks for the civilian population, they can provide information about the impact of military service on some outcomes. For example, Kang and Bullman (1996) show that mortality rates among all military personnel who served in the Persian Gulf from 1990 to 1991 were higher than for their civilian counterparts by comparing military deaths to standardized death ratios for the civilian population. Other possibilities exist, such as matching studies in which veterans are randomly matched to several civilian controls, although these have limited applicability beyond more narrowly defined projects aimed at a researching a single outcome.

For the most part, therefore, such military-only data are of limited value to researchers interested in the life-course implications of military service because they do not contain relevant information about civilians across a wide range of outcomes. Similarly, information obtained on civilians only cannot provide detail about the implications of current military service for the life course. Indeed, the focus of many research projects on the "civilian, non-institutionalized population" has considerably weakened our ability to understand the life-course trajectories of a substantial fraction of the population. Of course, some information about military service can be obtained in samples of the civilian population by asking questions about prior military service, but such questions are often limited to ascertaining whether the respondent was a veteran and often neglect to collect information about the timing, duration, and other characteristics of service. For example, the 2000 census contained questions about military service in the long form, which was sent to one out of every six households. Respondents were asked whether they had ever served on active duty (or were currently serving on active duty), the rough historical period during which service occurred (within five- to fifteen-year bands), and whether service lasted two or more years. No other information about military service was obtained and the dating of such service was so broad that it is difficult to place it in an ordering of life-course events. Beginning with the 2010 census, the long form was replaced by the American Community Survey, which collects more detailed information on military service status, period of service in relation to specific historical eras, and service-connected disability ratings.

Third, data collection should ideally begin prior to the ages at which military service customarily begins (before age 16). By collecting data on individuals before they enlist in the military, we can better model selectivity. There are several *post hoc* procedures that have been used to model the effects of selectivity, but the best means to correct for selectivity is to measure explicitly those factors that distinguish veterans from non-veterans; in the final analysis, selectivity is nothing more than an omitted variable problem (see Wolf, Wing, and Lopoo, Chapter 13 of this volume). The ability to measure selectivity requires data that precede entrance into the military, which in turn demands that we understand and are able to measure the factors that we believe to be linked to selectivity (Teachman, Call, and Segal 1993b). Thus, we must develop good models of military service before we attempt to measure those factors that will allow us to obtain cleaner estimates of the effects of military service itself. Models of selectivity also need to take into account the fact that selectivity may differ according to the outcomes being considered. For example, factors that tap selectivity with respect to educational attainment may be different from those that measure selectivity with respect to health. Indeed, it may be impossible to develop a single model for selectivity, with the result that multiple models may be required.

A promising data source for examining selectivity is the National Longitudinal Study of Adolescent Health (Add Health). Begun in 1994, Add Health now consists of four waves of data, with the latest round collected in 2008. Beginning with grades 7 to 12, respondents in Add Health have been followed through ages 24 to 32. Thus, Add Health now captures the ages at which most young men and women enter the military. One strength of the Add Health data for developing models of military service is the wide range of data collected. For example, the Add Health survey contains information on family socioeconomic status, physical and mental health, various biomarkers, attitudes, friendship networks, school and community characteristics, use of alcohol and drugs, criminal activities, family formation behaviors, and many other variables. In addition, the data collected in Add Health changes over time to match the life-course stage at which respondents find themselves. Currently, Add Health only collects information about dates of service, branch, and rank. Yet this database has provided insights about current enlistment patterns showing that young men who enlist generally come from disadvantaged backgrounds, with limited connections to others and a history of fighting (Elder et al. 2010). As additional rounds of Add Health data are collected, the database will also gain traction as a source of information about the consequences of military service, especially if additional information about the nature of service (e.g., military occupation, training, duty stations) is obtained. As discussed by Gade and Ruise (Chapter 12 of this volume), Glen Elder and his collaborators at the University of North Carolina-Chapel Hill have received funding from the Army Research Institute to augment Add Health with detailed administrative and ability/aptitude measurement data from the Defense Manpower Data Center (DMDC).

Data that allow for the estimation of good selectivity models will also allow a stratified approach to sampling that will yield sufficient numbers of individuals who enter the military. Although about 10 to 12% of recent cohorts of young men and women have entered into the military, which makes the military the largest single employer of young persons, a simple random selection likely will not yield a sufficiently large sample of eventual service members to conduct efficient statistical tests unless the original sample size is quite large. This problem is exacerbated when one recognizes that sample sizes involving respondents in the military should be sufficient to address differences in life-course outcomes that are thought to occur according to differences in military service. Stratified samples will also help ensure that sufficient numbers of women and minorities are captured to model the relationship between military service and their life-course trajectories.

Fourth, data collection should not ignore the possibility that selectivity is not fixed at the point of entry into the military. Rather, selectivity may be transitory. That is, the confounding factors that distinguish between veterans and non-veterans may not remain stable over time. The life course is dynamic, as are the factors determining various life-course outcomes. Consequently, different factors may account for selectivity at different parts of the life course. For example, what leads young men and women to enlist at age 18 may be different from what leads them to enlist at age 25. Older men and women are more likely to have had their decision to enlist molded by experience in the civilian labor market, intimate relationships such as cohabitation and marriage, and postsecondary schooling. Thus, it may be a mistake to assume that selection into the military is based on a constant set of background and personality factors.

Fifth, perhaps it goes without saying, but data collection must continue to survey sample members who enter into the military. Currently, most longitudinal data collection efforts fail to follow respondents once they enter the military. Not only does this practice increase the likelihood that these individuals will not be tracked once they return to civilian life, it means that we have little information about the nature of military service itself (except for questions that may be asked retrospectively). This information is best collected at the time that military service occurs, not afterward. Concurrent data collection also makes it possible to link current service to a number of important life-course transitions that are closely linked to the ages at which military service typically occurs (e.g., marriage, child-bearing, schooling, first home purchase). On a related note, it is important that longitudinal data collection efforts ensure that active-duty and veteran subjects have follow-up rates that are similar to the rate for non-veterans. Selective attrition on the basis of military service status, due either to subjects being lost to follow-up or mortality, can seriously compromise the validity of comparisons across groups over time.

Sixth, to the extent possible, longitudinal data expands the need for contextual information. Individuals live their lives in time and place and therefore are affected by their surroundings. Members of the military move often and live in communities that are often distinctive in the proportion of service members they include. Military service may also affect the migration histories of veterans long after they have left the military, resulting in different community characteristics that confront them (see Bailey, Chapter 9 of this volume). There may also be strong interactions between veteran status and the characteristics of communities. Because they possess different characteristics and enjoy unique benefits (e.g., GI Bill, Veterans Administration health care), veterans may react differently than non-veterans to the community contexts within which they find themselves (Gifford 2005b).

Seventh, because lives are linked, data collection efforts need to pay attention to the networks within which service members, veterans, and civilians are embedded. On the one hand, this means that respondents must be asked about the nature and extent of ties to others. On the other hand, it also means spouses, partners, children, friends, co-workers, and others to whom service members are linked should be interviewed as appropriate for particular studies (Carrington, Scott, and Wasserman 2005). This is a costly endeavor and may require that such information be collected for a subsample of military respondents, or all military respondents and a random subsample of nonmilitary respondents. Such information will help researchers decipher the linkages that are broken and created by military service and how these linkages are tied to life-course trajectories. What are the network opportunities and constraints faced by the men and women who serve in the military, and how do they maneuver in this landscape? In particular, are there instances in which removal from past networks are more likely to yield positive outcomes, as suggested by the "knifing off" perspective? Or are there instances in which the construction of new networks might engender positive outcomes, as indicated by the "bridging hypothesis"? It is likely that both the structure of and change in networks help generate stability and change in other life-course trajectories and outcomes. Thus, the changing, dynamic nature of networks and their influence also demand that information about network connectivity be collected on an ongoing basis. Moreover, to the extent that networks reflect social capital, overlapping networks of support and information should be important. This suggests a need for data about how networks may operate to set the context within which other covariates impact life-course trajectories.

Eighth, more than ever, longitudinal data need to consider Reserve and active-duty service, as well as movement between the two. During much of the All-Volunteer Force era, Reserve-duty service was radically different from active-duty service. With the advent of wars in Iraq and Afghanistan, the line between active-duty and Reserve service has blurred. Other than the short period surrounding the first Gulf War, All-Volunteer Force–era service in the Reserves prior to 2001 was generally limited to weekend meetings and two weeks of annual training. For the most part, Reserves lived in a civilian world; they held civilian jobs, lived in civilian neighborhoods (often far from large concentrations of military personnel), did not enjoy benefits of active-duty service (e.g., base housing, base shopping, health care), and were unlikely to be deployed. Since 2001, that situation has changed, with Reserves being subject to long deployments, often multiple times. The result is that life-course disruptions associated with such deployments may be even more substantial for Reserve members who were not planning on such substantial interruptions to their civilian lives. The consequences for those whose lives are linked to deployed Reserve members may also be more substantial.

Ninth, we need much better information about the nature of military service. Experiences vary across branches and ranks, as well as along many other measurable dimensions. Understanding the distinction between membership in the Reserves and active-duty service is one example of the need for better data. Yet again, we need better models of the nature of military service so that we can measure what we believe to be important. Some characteristics of service are clearly important to consider. One of these is exposure to combat. At a minimum, the duration and intensity of combat experiences need to be measured, as well as any physical and mental wounds that resulted from such experiences. Other important characteristics include length of service (to measure potential disruption of life-course trajectories), military training and occupation (to measure transferability to civilian jobs), number and duration of transfers between duty stations (even if temporary), type of discharge, and rank obtained. Also important to consider would be more subjective measures of military service. It may be valuable to know how service members view their time in the military, such as whether they believe their time was well spent or whether the military helped them mature in any facet of their lives. Minorities could be asked for their views on whether the military lessens their likelihood of experiencing discrimination.

The fact that military service is experienced differently by various service members also indicates the need to consider the relationship between characteristics of service members and different types of service. For example, the growing number of women serving in the military makes it essential to consider how gender may moderate the impact of various types of service on life-course outcomes. Do women react the same way that men do to their time in the military? Are gender roles minimized during military service and are service members evaluated differently by civilians depending on gender? Similar questions revolve around other important markers of placement in our social system, such as race, ethnicity, and sexual orientation.

Tenth, although the vast majority of research concerning the military has been quantitative in nature, qualitative data collection efforts are in order. For example, the Veterans History Project, an oral history of veterans' experiences, is already beginning to provide insights into the meaning of military service in the lives of men (LaVerda, Vessey, and Waters 2006). Other research has used qualitative research to investigate concepts that are difficult to measure and assess topics that are subject to differing interpretations and meanings, such as boundary ambiguity in families (Faber et al. 2008). It is becoming increasingly obvious that merging quantitative and qualitative approaches to the same problem can yield information that would otherwise be missed (Axinn and Pearce 2006). Qualitative research can open up new research questions and suggest new approaches to old problems. In many instances, qualitative work directs subsequent quantitative work by developing new hypotheses and data collection efforts. The synergy between the two approaches is likely to be maximized in a longitudinal data collection effort in which lessons learned during one round of data collection can inform subsequent data collection efforts. Indeed, the value of both approaches has been clearly defined within the broader notion of life-course research (Giele and Elder 1998). Accordingly, any data collection effort should seek to join both quantitative and qualitative approaches.

CONCLUSION

Military service is an important component of the life course for men and women. However, we still have little understanding of what such service means for outcomes as diverse as education, employment, family life, socioeconomic attainment, health, or values and attitudes. What we do know about the effects of military service is sometimes limited in time and place, and often fails to test important causal mechanisms. The chapters in this volume have outlined what we know about important elements of the relationship between military service and various components of the life course. In outlining what we know, the amount that remains to be discovered becomes evident. The body of literature concerning military service and the life course is growing, but still remains nascent.

In describing data needs, I have paid attention to the ideal characteristics of a data collection effort. I have presented ten characteristics of data on military service that should guide future efforts. Achieving progress on each of these data characteristics may be difficult, as such a collection effort would require considerable time, effort, and money. Additionally, it is important to consider the fact that some individuals may not believe military service merits the attention implied by these investments. Yet the ability to understand an institution that touches a significant proportion of our citizens' lives argues for more data and more research. Public policy revolving around service members and their families is increasingly an issue of concern. Moreover, the long wars being waged in Iraq and Afghanistan suggest that issues related to military service will require increasing attention in terms of both policy and financial resources. Without a clear understanding of the mechanisms by which military service is linked to various life-course trajectories and outcomes, we risk making important policy and funding decisions blindly.

From a theoretical perspective, the suggested data collection effort promises to yield information on life-course trajectories in general, as well as on the consequences of military service for the life course. Military service is intimately linked to the overall life-course patterns of both men and women. Obtaining a better understanding of the factors that shape these trajectories will help us to sharpen our theoretical models concerning human development throughout the life span, as well as to develop public policies. As a demanding and resourceful institution that intersects the life course of young men and women at a critical point in their lives, and has implications for the lives of those who are linked to these young men and women, military service holds the potential to significantly shape the subsequent life-course trajectories of veterans and their significant others. How veteran status plays out in the intermeshed lives of service members, and their families and communities, can provide a blueprint for the ways in which historical and social context influence individual choice and experience.

References

Abbott, Andrew. 2005. "The Historicality of Individuals." *Social Science History* 29 (1): 1–13.

Adler-Baeder, Francesca, Joe F. Pittman, and Lisa Taylor. 2005. "The Prevalence of Marital Transitions in Military Families." *Journal of Divorce and Remarriage* 44 (1–2): 91–106.

Allsup, Vernon Carl. 1982. "The American G.I. Forum: Origins and Evolution." Mexican American Monographs, No. 6. Austin: University of Texas Press.

Altschuler, Glenn C., and Stuart M. Blumin. 2009. *The GI Bill: A New Deal for Veterans*. New York: Oxford University Press.

Alwin, Duane F. 2012a. "Integrating Varieties of Life Course Concepts." *Journals of Gerontology: Social Sciences* 67B (2): 206–220.

Alwin, Duane F. 2012b. "Words Have Consequences." *Journals of Gerontology: Social Sciences* 67B (2): 232–234.

Amato, Paul. 2010. "Research on Divorce: Continuing Trends and New Developments." *Journal of Marriage and Family* 72 (3): 650–666.

American Veterans for Equal Rights (AVER). 2009. "Another Base Murder: Gay Sailor Killed at Camp Pendleton." Retrieved December 21, 2009, http://www.aver.us/aver/index.php?option=com_content&view=article&id=66:august-provost-1&catid=28:press-releases&Itemid=42.

Amir, Yehuda. 1969. "Contact Hypothesis in Ethnic Relations." *Psychological Bulletin* 71 (5) (May): 319–342.

Anderson, Joseph L. 2007. "The Vacant Chair on the Farm: Soldier Husbands, Farm Wives, and the Iowa Home Front, 1861–1865." *Annals of Iowa* 66 (3&4): 241–265.

Angrist, Joshua D. 1990. "Lifetime Earnings and the Vietnam Era Draft Lottery—Evidence from Social Security Administrative Records." *American Economic Review* 80 (3): 313–336.

Angrist, Joshua D. 1991. "The Draft Lottery and Voluntary Enlistment in the Vietnam Era." *Journal of the American Statistical Association* 86 (415): 584–595.

Angrist, Joshua D. 1993. "The Effect of Veterans Benefits on Education and Earnings." *Industrial & Labor Relations Review* 46 (4): 637–652.

Angrist, Joshua D. 1998. "Estimating the Labor Market Impact of Voluntary Military Service Using Social Security Data on Military Applicants." *Econometrica* 66 (2): 249–288.

Angrist, Joshua D., and Stacey H. Chen. 2011. "Schooling and the Vietnam-Era GI Bill: Evidence from the Draft Lottery." *American Economic Journal: Applied Economics* 3: 96–118.

Angrist, Joshua D., Guido W. Imbens, and Donald B. Rubin. 1996. "Identification of Causal Effects Using Instrumental Variables." *Journal of the American Statistical Association* 91 (434): 444–455.

Angrist, Joshua D., and John H. Johnson. 2000. "Effects of Work-Related Absences on Families: Evidence from the Gulf War." *Industrial & Labor Relations Review* 54 (1): 41–58.

Angrist, Joshua D., and Alan B. Krueger. 1994. "Why Do World War II Veterans Earn More Than Nonveterans." *Journal of Labor Economics* 12 (1): 74–97.

Angrist, Joshua D., and Jörn-Steffen Pischke. 2009. *Mostly Harmless Econometrics: An Empiricists Companion.* Princeton: Princeton University Press.

Antonucci, T. C., and H. Akiyama. 1995. "Convoys of Social Relationship: Family and Friendships within a Life Span Context." In *Handbook of Aging and the Family,* edited by R. Blieszner and V. H. Bedford, pp. 355–371. Westport, CT: Greenwood Press.

Aoki, Andrew, and Okiyoski Takeda. 2009. *Asian American Politics.* Cambridge, MA: Policy Press.

Armed Forces Health Surveillance Center. 2007a. "Healthy Deployers: Nature and Trends of Health Care Utilization during the Year prior to Deployment to OEF/OIF, Active Components, U.S. Armed Forces, January 2002–December 2006." *Medical Surveillance Monthly Report* 14 (3) (June): 2–5.

Armed Forces Health Surveillance Center. 2007b. "Traumatic Brain Injury among Members of Active Components, U.S. Armed Forces, 1997–2006." *Medical Surveillance Monthly Report* 14 (5) (August): 2–69.

Armed Forces Health Surveillance Center. 2008. "Absolute and Relative Morbidity Burdens Attributable to Various Illnesses and Injuries, U.S. Armed Forces, 2007." *Medical Surveillance Monthly Report* 15 (3) (April): 15–20. http://www.dtic.mil/cgi-bin/GetTRDoc?Location=U2&doc=GetTRDoc.pdf&AD=ADA496191.

Armed Forces Health Surveillance Center. 2009. "Update: Deployment Health Assessments, U.S. Armed Forces, December 2008." *Medical Surveillance Monthly Report* 16 (1) (January): 12–16. http://www.dtic.mil/cgi-bin/GetTRDoc?AD=ADA495050&Location=U2&doc=GetTRDoc.pdf.

Armor, David J. 1996. "Race and Gender in the US Military." *Armed Forces & Society* 23 (1): 7–27.

Armstrong, Penelope W., and Jerry D. Rogers. 1997. "Basic Skills Revisited: The Effects of Foreign Language Instruction on Reading, Math, and Language Arts." *Learning Languages* 2 (3) (Spring): 20–31.

Army Capabilities Integration Center (ARCIC). 2008. "The U.S. Army Concept for the Human Dimension in Full Spectrum Operations 2015–2024." June 11. Fort Monroe, VA: U.S. Army Training and Doctrine Command. http://www-tradoc.army.mil/tpubs/pams/p525-3-7.pdf.

Asch, Beth J., Christopher Buck, Jacob Alex Klerman, Meredith A. Kleykamp, and David S. Loughran. 2009. *Military Enlistment of Hispanic Youth: Obstacles and Opportunities.* Santa Monica, CA: RAND.

Asch, Beth J., Paul Heaton, and Bogdan Savych. 2009. "Recruiting Minorities: What Explains Recent Trends in the Army and Navy?" Santa Monica, CA: RAND. Retrieved November 11, 2011, http://www.rand.org/pubs/monographs/2009/RAND_MG861.pdf.

Asch, Steven M., Elizabeth A. McGlynn, Mary M. Hogan, Rodney A. Hayward, Paul G. Shekelle, Lisa Rubenstein, Joan Keesey, John Adams, and Eve A. Kerr. 2004. "Comparison of Quality of Care for Patients in the Veterans Health Administration and Patients in a National Sample." *Annals of Internal Medicine* 141 (12): 938–945.

Atiyeh, Bishara S., S. W. A. Gunn, and S. N. Hayek. 2007. "Military and Civilian Burn Injuries during Armed Conflicts." *Annals of Burn and Fire Disasters* 20 (4): 203–215. http://www.medbc.com/annals/review/vol_20/num_4/text/vol20n4p203.htm.

Attie, Jeanie. 1998. *Patriotic Toil: Northern Women and the American Civil War.* Ithaca, NY: Cornell University Press.

Axinn, William G., and Lisa D. Pearce. 2006. *Mixed Method Data Collection Strategies.* New York: Cambridge University Press.

Bachman, Jerald G., David R. Segal, Peter Freedman-Doan, and Patrick M. O'Malley. 2000. "Who Chooses Military Service? Correlates of Propensity and Enlistment in the US Armed Forces." *Military Psychology* 12 (1): 1–30.

Bahde, Thomas. 2009. "'I Never Wood Git Tired of Wrighting to You': Home and Family in the Civil War Letters of Joseph and Currency Van Nattan." *Journal of Illinois History* 12 (Summer): 129–154.

Bailey, Amy Kate. 2008. "The Changing Composition of the Veteran Population: Human Capital Characteristics of Black and White Men, 1940–2000." In *The Effect of Veteran Status on Spatial and Socioeconomic Mobility: Outcomes for Black and White Men in the Late 20th Century*, pp. 46–73. Unpublished dissertation.

Bailey, Amy Kate. 2011. "Race, Place and Veteran Status: Migration among Black and White Men, 1940–2000." *Population Research and Policy Review* 30 (5): 701–728.

Banks, James, Zoe Oldfield, and James P. Smith. 2011. "Childhood Health and Differences in Late-Life Health Outcomes between England and the United States." NBER Working Paper Series, 17096. Retrieved September 27, 2011, http://www.nber.org/papers/w17096.

Barfield, Wanda, P. H. Wise, F. P. Rust, J. B. Gould, and S. L. Gortmaker. 1996. "Racial Disparities in Outcomes of Military and Civilian Births in California." *Archives of Pediatric and Adolescent Medicine* 150 (10): 1062–1067.

Barley, Stephen R. 1998. "Military Downsizing and the Career Prospects of Youths." *Annals of the American Academy of Political and Social Science* 559: 141–157.

Barnes, C. Taylor, and Curtis C. Roseman. 1981. "The Effect of Military Retirement on Population Redistribution." *Texas Business Review* 55 (3) (May/June): 100–104.

Barnett, Arnold, Timothy Stanley, and Michael Shore. 1992. "America's Vietnam Casualties: Victims of a Class War?" *Operations Research* 40 (5) (September–October): 856–866.

Batalova, Jeanne. 2008. "Immigrants in the US Armed Forces." Migration Policy Institute. Retrieved August 21, 2008, http://www.migrationinformation.org/USfocus/display.cfm?id=683.

Batalova, Jeanne, and Michael Fix. 2006. "New Estimates of Unauthorized Youth Eligible for Legal Status under the DREAM Act." Migration Policy Institute. Retrieved July 30, 2012, http://www.migrationpolicy.org/pubs/Backgrounder1_Dream_Act.pdf.

Baum, Sandy, and Jennifer Ma. 2009. *Trends in College Pricing 2009.* New York, New York: The College Board.

Beauchamp, Dennis, Jim Skinner, and Perry Wiggins. 2003. *LGBT Persons in Chicago: Growing Older. A Survey of Needs and Perceptions.* Chicago: Chicago Task Force on LGBT Aging.

Beckham, J. C., B. L. Lytle, and M. E. Feldman. 1996. "Caregiver Burden in Partners of Vietnam War Veterans with Posttraumatic Stress Disorder." *Journal of Counseling and Clinical Psychology* 64: 1068–1072.

Bedard, Kelly, and Olivier Deschênes. 2006. "The Long-Term Impact of Military Service on Health: Evidence from World War II and Korean War Veterans." *American Economic Review* 96 (1): 176–194.

Bedwell, Michael. 2009. "Anthony Woods: Courage and Conviction." Gay Military Signal. Retrieved December 21, 2009, http://www.gaymilitarysignal.com/0912Woods.html.

Belkin, Aaron. 2003. "Don't Ask, Don't Tell: Is the Gay Ban Based on Military Necessity?" *Parameters* 33 (July 1): 108–119.

Belkin, Aaron. 2008. "'Don't Ask, Don't Tell'—Does the Gay Ban Undermine the Military's Reputation?" *Armed Forces & Society* 34 (2): 276–291.

Belkin, Aaron, and Geoffrey Bateman. 2003. *Don't Ask, Don't Tell: Debating the Gay Ban in the Military*. Boulder, CO: Lynne Rienner Publishers.

Belkin, Aaron, and Melissa Sheridan Embser-Herbert. 2002. "A Modest Proposal—Privacy as a Flawed Rationale for the Exclusion of Gays and Lesbians from the US Military." *International Security* 27 (2): 178–197.

Benjamin, S. 2007. "Don't Ask, Don't Translate." *New York Times*. Retrieved September 14, 2011, http://www.nytimes.com/2007/06/08/opinion/08benjamin.html?_r=2&scp=1&sq=stephen%20benjamin%20don%27t%20ask&st=cse.

Bennett, Michael J. 1996. *When Dreams Come True: The GI Bill and the Making of Modern America*. Washington, DC: Brassey's Inc.

Bennett, Pamela R., and Amy Lutz. 2009. "How African American Is the Net Black Advantage? Differences in College Attendance among Immigrant Blacks, Native Blacks, and Whites." *Sociology of Education* 82 (1): 70–99.

Bennett, Pamela R., and Yu Xie. 2003. "Revisiting Racial Differences in College Attendance: The Role of Historically Black Colleges and Universities." *American Sociological Review* 68 (4): 567–580.

Berger, Mark C., and Barry T. Hirsch. 1983. "The Civilian Earnings Experience of Vietnam-Era Veterans." *Journal of Human Resources* 18 (4): 455–479.

Berger, Mark C., and Barry T. Hirsch. 1985. "Veteran Status as a Screening Device during the Vietnam Era." *Social Science Quarterly* 66 (1): 79–89.

Berkman, L., K. Ertel, and M. Glymour. 2011. "Aging and Social Intervention: Life Course Perspectives." In *Handbook of Aging and the Social Sciences*, edited by R. Binstock and L. George, pp. 337–351. 7th ed. San Diego, CA: Academic Press.

Berlin, Gordon, Frank F. Furstenberg Jr., and Mary C. Waters. 2010. "Introducing the Issue." *The Future of Children* 20 (1): 3–18.

Berry Jr., William E. 1989. *U.S. Bases in the Philippines: The Evolution of the Special Relationship*. Boulder, CO: Westview Press.

Bérubé, Alla. 1990. *Coming Out under Fire: The History of Gay Men and Women in World War Two*. New York: The Free Press.

Binkin, Martin, Mark J. Eitelberg, Alvin J. Schexnider, and Marvin M. Smith. 1982. *Blacks and the Military*. Washington, DC: The Brookings Institute.

Blau, Peter, and O. D. Duncan. 1967. *The American Occupational Structure*. New York: Wiley.

Bliese, Paul D., Kathleen M. Wright, Amy B. Adler, Jeffrey L. Thomas, and Charles W. Hoge. 2007. "Timing of Postcombat Mental Health Assessments." *Psychological Services* 4 (3): 141–148.

Blomme, Deirdre, and Bruce Western. 2011. "Cohort Change and Racial Differences in Educational and Income Mobility." *Social Forces* 90 (2): 375–395.

Boehmer, Tegan K. C., Dana Flanders, Michael A. McGeehin, Coleen Boyle, and Drue H. Barrett. 2004. "Postservice Mortality in Vietnam Veterans—30-Year Follow-Up." *Archives of Internal Medicine* 164 (17): 1908–1916.

Bonczar, Thomas P. 2003. "Prevalence of Imprisonment in the U.S. Population, 1974–2001." Bureau of Justice Statistics Special Report. Washington, DC: U.S. Dept of Justice.

Bookwala, Jamila, Irene Frieze, and Nancy Grote. 1994. "The Long-Term Effects of Military Service on Quality of Life—the Vietnam Experience." *Journal of Applied Social Psychology* 24 (6): 529–545. ISI:A1994PA23800004.

Booth, Alan, and John N. Edwards. 1985. "Age at Marriage and Marital Instability." *Journal of Marriage and Family* 47 (1): 67–75.

Booth, Bradford. 2003. "Contextual Effects of Military Presence on Women's Earnings." *Armed Forces & Society* 30 (1): 25–51.

Booth, Bradford, William W. Falk, David R. Segal, and Mady Wechsler Segal. 2000. "The Impact of Military Presence in Local Labor Markets on the Employment of Women." *Gender & Society* 14 (2): 318–332.

Booth, Bradford, and David R. Segal. 2005. "Bringing in the Soldiers Back In: Implications of Inclusion of Military Personnel for Labor Market Research on Race, Class, and Gender." *Race, Gender & Class* 12 (1): 34–57.

Booth, Bradford H., Mady Wechsler Segal, D. Bruce Bell, with James A. Martin, Morten G. Ender, David E. Rohall, and John Nelson. 2007. *What We Know about Army Families: 2007 Update*. Fairfax, VA: ICF International. Prepared for U.S. Army Family and Morale, Welfare and Recreation Command.

Bordieri, James E., and David E. Drehmer. 1984. "Vietnam Veterans—Fighting the Employment War." *Journal of Applied Social Psychology* 14 (4): 341–347.

Borjas, George J., and Finis Welch. 1986. "The Postservice Earnings of Military Retirees." In *Army Manpower Economics*, edited by Curtis L. Gilroy. Boulder, CO: Westview Press.

Boscarino, Joseph A. 2006. "Posttraumatic Stress Disorder and Mortality among US Army Veterans 30 Years after Military Service." *Annals of Epidemiology* 16 (4): 248–256.

Boston Evening Gazette. 1861. "Boston Evening Gazette." In *Northern Editorials on Secession*, Vol. 2, edited by Howard Cecil Perkins and American Historical Association, p. 1073. New York: D. Appleton-Century Co.

Boucher, Ronald L. 1973. "The Colonial Militia as a Social Institution: Salem, Massachusetts 1764–1775." *Military Affairs* 37 (4) (December): 125–130.

Bouffard, Leana Allen. 2005. "The Military as a Bridging Environment in Criminal Careers: Differential Outcomes of the Military Experience." *Armed Forces & Society* 31 (2): 273–295.

Bound, John, and Sarah Turner. 2002. "Going to War and Going to College: Did World War II and the G.I. Bill Increase Educational Attainment for Returning Veterans?" *Journal of Labor Economics* 20 (4): 784–815.

Bourg, Chris. 2003. "Married to the Military: The Employment and Earnings of Military Wives Compared with Those of Civilian Wives." *Armed Forces & Society* 30 (1): 170–172.

Bowen, Gary L. 1989. "Satisfaction with Family Life in the Military." *Armed Forces & Society* 15 (4): 571–592.

Bowling, Kirby L., Juanita M. Firestone, and Richard J. Harris. 2005. "Analyzing Questions That Cannot Be Asked of Respondents Who Cannot Respond." *Armed Forces & Society* 31 (3): 411–437. ISI:000229024700004.

Bowman, James L., J. Jay Volkert, and J. Victor Hahn. 1973. *Educational Assistance to Veterans: A Comparative Study of Three G.I. Bills. Final Report*. Washington, DC: U.S. Government Printing Office, Superintendent of Documents.

Brock, Darla. 1991. "'Our Hands Are at Your Service': The Story of Confederate Women in Memphis." *West Tennessee Historical Society Papers* 45: 19–34.

Brotz, Howard, and Everett J. Wilson. 1946. "Characteristics of Military Society." *American Journal of Sociology* 51 (5): 371–375. ISI:000205009000003.

Brown, Alexis Girardin. 2000. "The Women Left Behind: Transformation of the Southern Belle, 1840–1880." *The Historian* 62 (4): 759–778.

Brown, Charles. 1985. "Military Enlistments—What Can We Learn from Geographic Variation." *American Economic Review* 75 (1): 228–234.

Brown, Maria T. 2009. "LGBT Aging and Rhetorical Silence." *Sexuality Research & Social Policy* 6 (4): 65–78.

Brown, Phil, Stephen Zavestoski, Sabrina McCormick, Meadow Linder, Joshua Mandelbaum, and Theo Luebke. 2000. "A Gulf of Difference: Disputes over

Gulf War-Related Illnesses." *Journal of Health and Social Behavior* 42 (September): 235–257.

Brown, Ulysses J., and Dharam S. Rana. 2005. "Generalized Exchange and Propensity for Military Service: The Moderating Effect of Prior Military Exposure." *Journal of Applied Statistics* 32 (3): 259–270.

Browning, Harley L., Sally C. Lopreato, and Dudley L. Poston. 1973. "Income and Veteran Status—Variations among Mexican Americans, Blacks and Anglos." *American Sociological Review* 38 (1): 74–85.

Bryant, Karl, and Kristen Schilt. 2008. "Transgender Veterans Survey: Conducted December 13, 2007, to May 1, 2008." White Paper prepared for The Palm Center and the Transgender American Veterans Association. Akron, OH: Transgender American Veterans Association. Retrieved July 30, 2012, http://www.tavausa.org/Transgender%20People%20in%20the%20U.S.%20Military.pdf.

Bryant, Richard R., V. A. Samaranayake, and Al L. Wilhite. 1993. "The Effect of Military Service on the Subsequent Civilian Wage of the Post-Vietnam Veteran." *Quarterly Review of Economics and Finance* 33 (1): 15–31.

Bryant, Richard R., and Al L. Wilhite. 1990. "Military Experience and Training Effects on Civilian Wages." *Applied Economics* 22 (1): 69–81. ISI:A1990CJ09000007.

Buchanan, NiCole T., Isis H. Settles, and Krystle C. Woods. 2008. "Comparing Sexual Harassment Subtypes among Black and White Women by Military Rank: Double Jeopardy, the Jezebel, and the Cult of True Womanhood." *Psychology of Women Quarterly* 32 (4): 347–361. ISI:000263070200001.

Buckley, Gail Lumet. 2001. *American Patriots: The Story of Blacks in the Military from the Revolution to Desert Storm.* New York: Random House.

Buddin, Richard J. 1991. *Enlistment Effects of the 2+2+4 Recruiting Experiment.* Santa Monica, CA: RAND.

Burdeos, Ray L. 2008. *Filipinos in the U.S. Navy & Coast Guard during the Vietnam War.* Bloomington, Indiana: Author House.

Burgess, Lisa. 2008. "$150,000 Bonus Offered for Some Special Forces." *Stars and Stripes.* Retrieved July 30, 2012, http://www.stripes.com/news/150–000-bonus-offered-for-some-special-forces-1.75636.

Burland, Daniel, and Jennifer Hickes Lundquist. 2009. "Family Relationships and the Military." In *Encyclopedia of Human Relationships*, edited by Harry T. Reis and Susan K. Sprecher. Newbury Park, CA: Sage Publications.

Burrell, Lolita M., Gary A. Adams, Doris B. Durand, and Carl A. Castro. 2006. "The Impact of Military Lifestyle Demands on Well-Being, Army, and Family Outcomes." *Armed Forces & Society* 33 (1): 43–58.

Burrelli, David F., and Jody Feder. 2009. "Homosexuals and the U.S. Military: Current Issues." Congressional Research Service, Washington, DC. Retrieved July 30, 2012, http://www.fas.org/sgp/crs/natsec/RL30113.pdf.

Burton, William L. 1988. *Melting Pot Soldiers: The Union's Ethnic Regiments.* Ames: Iowa State University Press.

Bushatz, Amy. 2010. "Troop Divorce Rates Level in 2010." Military.com. Retrieved January 2, 2012, http://www.military.com/news/article/troop-divorce-rates-level-in-2010.html.

Butler, John Sibley. 1993. "Homosexuals and the Military Establishment." *Society* 31 (1) (November/December): 13–21.

Butz, William P., and Barbara Boyle Torrey (2006). "Some Frontiers in Social Science." *Science* 312 (5782): 1898–1900.

Buzzell, Emily, and Samuel H. Preston. 2007. "Mortality of American Troops in the Iraq War." *Population and Development Review* 33 (3): 555–566.

Cahill, Sean, and Ken South. 2002. "Policy Issues Affecting Lesbian, Gay, Bisexual and Transgender People in Retirement." *Generations* 26 (2): 49–54.

Cahill, Sean, Ken South, and Jane Spade. 2000. *Outing Age: Public Policy Issues Affecting Gay, Lesbian, Bisexual, and Transgender Elders.* Washington, DC: Policy Institute of the National Gay and Lesbian Taskforce.

Cain, L. D. 1964. "Life Course and Social Structure." In *Handbook of Modern Sociology,* edited by R. E. L. Feris, pp. 272–309. Chicago: Rand McNally.

Calhoun, P. S., J. C. Beckham, and H. B. Bosworth. 2002. "Caregiver Burden and Psychological Distress in Partners of Veterans with Chronic Posttraumatic Stress Disorder." *Journal of Traumatic Stress* 15: 202–212.

Call, Vaughn R. A., and Jay D. Teachman. 1991. "Military Service and Stability in the Family Course." *Military Psychology* 3 (4): 233–250.

Call, Vaughn R. A., and Jay D. Teachman. 1996. "Life-Course Timing and Sequencing of Marriage and Military Service and Their Effects on Marital Stability." *Journal of Marriage and the Family* 58 (1): 219–226.

Camacho, Paul R., and Paul L. Atwood. 2007. "A Review of the Literature on Veterans Published in *Armed Forces & Society,* 1974–2006." *Armed Forces & Society* 33 (3): 351–381.

Campbell, D'Ann. 1984. *Women at War with America: Private Lives in a Patriotic Era.* Cambridge, MA: Harvard University Press.

Campbell, D'Ann. 1990. "Service Women of World War II." *Armed Forces & Society* 16 (2) (January): 251–270.

Card, Josefina. 1983. *Lives after Vietnam: The Personal Impact of Military Service.* Lexington, MA: Lexington Books.

Carlson, Elwood. 2008. *The Lucky Few: Between the Greatest Generation and the Baby Boom.* New York: Springer.

Carlson, Elwood, and Joel Andress. 2009. "Military Service by Twentieth-Century Generations of American Men." *Armed Forces & Society* 35 (2): 385–400.

Carnevale, Anthony P., and Stephen J. Rose. 2004. "Socioeconomic Status, Race/Ethnicity, and Selective College Admissions." In *America's Untapped Resource: Low-Income Students in Higher Education,* edited by Richard D. Kahlenberg, pp. 101–156. New York: Century Foundation Press.

Carrington, Peter J., John Scott, and Stanley Wasserman. 2005. *Models and Methods in Social Network Analysis.* Cambridge, UK: Cambridge University Press.

Castaneda, Laura Werber, and Margaret Cecchine Harrell. 2008. "Military Spouse Employment: A Grounded Theory Approach to Experiences and Perceptions." *Armed Forces & Society* 34 (3): 389–412.

Catanzarite, Lisa, and Lindsey Trimble. 2008. "Latinos in the United States Labor Market." In *Latinas/os in the United States: Changing the Face of America,* edited by Havidán Rodríguez, Rogelio Sáenz, and Cecilia Menjívar, pp. 149–167. New York: Springer.

Chafe, William Henry. 1972. *The American Woman: Her Changing Social, Economic, and Political Roles, 1920–1970.* New York: Oxford University Press.

Chang, Virginia W., and Diane S. Lauderdale. 2009. "Fundamental Cause Theory, Technological Innovation, and Health Disparities: The Case of Cholesterol in the Era of Statins." *Journal of Health and Social Behavior* 50 (September): 245–260.

Chauncey Jr., George. 1989. "Christian Brotherhood or Sexual Perversion? Homosexual Identities and the Construction of Sexual Boundaries in the World War One Era." In *Hidden from History: Reclaiming the Gay & Lesbian Past,* edited by Martin Duberman, Matha Vicinus, and George Chauncey Jr., pp. 294–317. New York: Meridian.

Chauncey, Jr., George. 1994. *Gay New York: Gender, Urban Culture, and the Making of the Gay Male World 1890–1940.* New York: BasicBooks.

Chesson, Michael B. 1996. "Prison Camps and Prisoners of War." In *The American Civil War: A Handbook of Literature and Research,* edited by Steven E. Woodworth, pp. 466–478. Westport, CT: Greenwood Press.

Christensen, Eric, Candace Hill, Pat Netzer, DeAnn Farr, Elizabeth Schaefer, and Joyce McMahon. 2009. "Economic Impact on Caregivers of the Seriously Wounded, Ill, and Injured." CNA Analysis & Solutions. CRM D0019966.A2, April. http://www.cna.org/documents/D0019966.A2.pdf.

Clausen, John A. 1998. "Life Reviews and Life Stories." In *Methods of Life Course Research: Qualitative and Quantitative Approaches*, edited by Janet Z. Giele and Glen H. Elder Jr., pp. 189–212. Thousand Oaks, CA: Sage Publications.

Clipp, Elizabeth Colerick, and Glen H. Elder Jr. 1996. "The Aging Veteran of World War II: Psychiatric and Life Course Insights." In *Aging and Post-Traumatic Stress Disorder*, edited by Paul E. Ruskin and John A. Talbott, pp. 19–51. Washington, DC: American Psychiatric Press.

Coffin, Howard. 1993. *Full Duty: Vermonters in the Civil War*. Woodstock, VT: Countryman Press.

Coffman, Edward M. 2000. "The Duality of the American Military Tradition: A Commentary." *Journal of Military History* 64 (4): 967–980.

Cohany, Sharon R. 1992. "The Vietnam-Era Cohort: Employment and Earnings." *Monthly Labor Review* 115 (6): 3–15.

Cohen, Jere, David R. Segal, and Lloyd V. Temme. 1986. "The Educational Cost of Military Service in the 1960s." *Journal of Political & Military Sociology* 14 (2): 303–319.

Cohen, Jere, and Lloyd V. Temme. 1986. "Military Service Was an Educational Disadvantage to Vietnam-Era Personnel." *Sociology and Social Research* 70 (3): 206–208. ISI:A1986C864300004.

Cohen, Jere, Rebecca Lynn Warner, and David R. Segal. 1995. "Military Service and Educational Attainment in the All-Volunteer Force." *Social Science Quarterly* 76 (1): 88–104. ISI:A1995RC27600007.

Conant, Eve. 2010. "DADT Protester Lieutenant Choi Is Officially Discharged from Army." *Newsweek*, July 22. http://www.newsweek.com/blogs/the-gaggle/2010/07/22/exclusive-dadt-protestor-lt-choi-is-officially-discharged-from-army.html.

Confer, Clarissa W. 2007. *The Cherokee Nation in the Civil War*. Norman: University of Oklahoma Press.

Congressional Research Service. 2006. "Veterans' Benefits Issues for the 109th Congress." *CRS Report for Congress*, Order Code RL33216. Washington, DC: The Library of Congress.

Congressional Research Service. 2010. "Military Retirement: Background and Recent Developments." *CRS Report for Congress*, Order Code RL34751. Washington, DC: The Library of Congress.

Conley, Dalton, and Brian Gifford. 2006. "Home Ownership, Social Insurance, and the Welfare State." *Sociological Forum* 21 (1) (March): 55–82.

Cooke, Thomas J., and Karen Speirs. 2005. "Migration and Employment among the Civilian Spouses of Military Personnel." *Social Science Quarterly* 86 (2): 343–355.

Cooney Jr., Richard T. 2003. "Moving with the Military: Race, Class, and Gender Differences in the Employment Consequences of Tied Migration." Ph.D. Dissertation, Department of Sociology, University of Maryland, College Park, Maryland.

Cooney Jr., Richard T., Mady Wechsler Segal, David R. Segal, and William W. Falk. 2003. "Racial Differences in the Impact of Military Service on the Socioeconomic Status of Women Veterans." *Armed Forces & Society* 30 (1): 53–85.

Cooper, Richard V. L. 1981. *Military Retirees' Post-Service Earnings and Employment*. Santa Monica, CA: RAND.

Cosgrove, Lisa, Mary E. Brady, and Patricia Peck. 1995. "PTSD and the Family: Secondary Traumatization." In *The Legacy of Vietnam Veterans and Their Families: Survivors of War: Catalysts for Change*, edited by Dennis K. Rhoades,

Michael R. Leaveck, and James C. Hudson, pp. 38–49. Washington, DC: Agent Orange Class Assistance Program.

Coumbe, Arthur Thomas, Paul N. Kotakis, and W. Anne Gammell. 2008. *History of the U.S. Army Cadet Command: Second Ten Years, 1996–2006.* Fort Monroe, VA: U.S. Army Cadet Command.

Cowper, Diane C., and Elizabeth H. Corcoran. 1989. "Older Veterans—Possible Forerunners of Migration: Migration Patterns of the Elderly Veteran Population versus the General Elderly Population, 1960–1980." *Journal of Applied Gerontology* 8 (4) (December): 451–464.

Cowper, Diane C., and Charles F. Longino. 1992. "Veteran Interstate Migration and VA Health Service Use." *Gerontologist* 32 (1): 44–50.

Cowper, Diane C., Charles F. Longino, Joseph D. Kubal, Larry M. Manheim, Stephen J. Dienstfrey, and Jill M. Palmer. 2000. "The Retirement Migration of US Veterans, 1960, 1970, 1980, and 1990." *Journal of Applied Gerontology* 19 (2): 123–137.

Craighill, Margaret D. 1966. "The Women's Army Corps." In *Neuropsychiatry in World War II*, Vol. 1: *Zone of Interior,* edited by Albert J. Glass and Robert J. Bernucci. Government Document D 104.11:N 39. Washington, DC: Government Printing Office.

Crockett, Stephanie A. 2000. "Race and the Census: Interracial Marriages More Common Here Because of Military." *Virginian-Pilot*, August 14, A1.

Crost, Lyn. 1994. *Honor by Fire: Japanese Americans at War in Europe and the Pacific.* Navato, CA: Presidio.

Crystal, Steve, and K. Waehrer. 1996. "Later-Life Economic Inequality in Longitudinal Perspective." *The Journals of Gerontology, Series E: Psychological Sciences and Social Sciences* 51: 307–318.

Culpepper, Marilyn Mayer. 1991. *Trials and Triumphs: The Women of the American Civil War.* East Lansing: Michigan State University Press.

Currie, Janet, and Enrico Moretti. 2003. "Mother's Education and the Intergenerational Transmission of Human Capital: Evidence from College Openings." *Quarterly Journal of Economics* 118 (4): 1495–1532.

Curry, G. David. 1985. *Sunshine Patriots: Punishment and the Vietnam Offender.* South Bend, IN: University of Notre Dame Press.

Curtis, Katherine J., and Collin F. Payne. 2010. "The Differential Impact of Mortality of American Troops in the Iraq War: The Non-Metropolitan Dimension." *Demographic Research* 23 (2): 41–62.

D'Amico, Francine, and Laurie Lee Weinstein (eds.). 1999. *Gender Camouflage: Women and the U.S. Military.* New York: New York University Press.

D'Anton, Micheal A. 1983. "Personnel Officers' Attitudes toward Vietnam Era Veterans." *Journal of Political & Military Sociology* 11 (1): 21–34. ISI:A1983QP61400003.

D'Emilio, John. 1989. "Gay Politics and Community in San Francisco since World War II." In *Hidden from History: Reclaiming the Gay & Lesbian Past*, edited by Martin Duberman, Matha Vicinus, and George Chauncey Jr., pp. 456–473. New York: Meridian.

Dale, Charles, and Curtis L. Gilroy. 1984. "Determinants of Enlistments—A Macroeconomic Time-Series View." *Armed Forces & Society* 10 (2): 192–210.

Dannefer, Dale. 1987. "Aging as Intracohort Differentiation: Accentuation, the Matthew Effect, and the Life Course." *Sociological Forum* 2 (2): 211–236.

Dannefer, Dale. 1988. "Age Structure, the Life Course, and 'Aged Heterogeneity': Prospects for Research and Theory." *Comparative Gerontology* 2: 1–10.

Dannefer, Dale. 2003. "Cumulative Advantage/Disadvantage and the Life Course: Cross-Fertilizing Age and Social Science Theory." *The Journals of Gerontology, Series B: Psychological Sciences and Social Sciences* 58 (6): S327–S337.

Dannefer, Dale. 2012. "Enriching the Tapestry: Expanding the Scope of Life Course Concepts." *The Journals of Gerontology: Social Sciences* 67 (2): 221–225.

Dannefer, Dale, and Jessica A. Kelley-Moore. 2009. "Theorizing the Life Course: New Twists in the Paths." In *Handbook of Theories of Aging*, edited by Vern L. Bengtson, Merril Silverstein, and Norella M. Putney, pp. 389–412. 2nd ed. New York: Springer.

Dannefer, Dale, and Peter Uhlenberg. 1999. "Paths of the Life Course: A Typology." In *Handbook of Theories of Aging*, edited by Vern L. Bengtson and K. W. Schaie, pp. 303–326. New York: Springer.

Dansby, Mickey R., and Dan Landis. 2001. "Intercultural Training in the United States Military." In *Managing Diversity in the Military: Research Perspectives from the Defense Equal Opportunity Management Institute*, edited by Mickey R. Dansby, James B. Stewart, and Schulyer C. Webb, pp. 9–28. New Brunswick, NJ: Transaction Publishers.

Dansby, Mickey R., James B. Stewart, and Schulyer C. Webb (eds.). 2001. *Managing Diversity in the Military: Research Perspectives from the Defense Equal Opportunity Management Institute*. New Brunswick, NJ: Transaction Publishers.

Danzon, Patricia Munch. 1980. *Civilian Earnings of Military Retirees*. Santa Monica, CA: RAND.

Dao, J. 2011. "Bachmann's 'Don't Ask' Position a Legal Possibility." *New York Times*, August 15. http://thecaucus.blogs.nytimes.com/2011/08/15/bachmanns-dont-ask-position-a-legal-possibility/?scp=1&sq=don%27t%20ask,%20don%27t%20tell&st=cse.

Daula, Thomas, and Robert Moffitt. 1995. "Estimating Dynamic Models of Quit Behavior: The Case of Military Reenlistment." *Journal of Labor Economics* 13 (3) (July): 499–523.

DaVanzo, Julie, and Frances Kobrin Goldscheider. 1990. "Coming Home Again: Returns to the Parental Home of Young Adults." *Population Studies* 44 (2) (July): 241–255.

David, Paul A., and Warren C. Sanderson. 1987. "The Emergence of a Two-Child Norm among American Birth-Controllers." *Population and Development Review* 13 (1) (March): 1–41. http://www.jstor.org/stable/1972119.

Davison, Eve H., Anica P. Pless, Marilyn R. Gugliucci, Lynda A. King, Daniel W. King, Dawn M. Salgado, Avron Spiro, and Peter Bachrach. 2006. "Late-Life Emergence of Early-Life Trauma—The Phenomenon of Late-Onset Stress Symptomatology among Aging Combat Veterans." *Research on Aging* 28 (1): 84–114.

Dawson, Sarah Morgan. 1960. *A Confederate Girl's Diary*. Bloomington: Indiana University Press.

Dean, Eric T. 1997. *Shook over Hell: Post-Traumatic Stress, Vietnam, and the Civil War*. Cambridge, MA: Harvard University Press.

DeAngelis, Karin K., and David R. Segal. 2009. "Building and Maintaining a Post-9/11 All-Volunteer Military Force." In *The Impact of 9/11 on Politics and War: The Day That Changed Everything?*, edited by Matthew J. Morgan, pp. 43–60. New York: Palgrave MacMillan.

Dechter, Aimee R., and Glen H. Elder Jr. 2004. "World War II Mobilization in Men's Work Lives: Continuity or Disruption for the Middle Class?" *American Journal of Sociology* 110 (3): 761–793.

DeFina, Robert, and Lance Hannon. 2009. "Diversity, Racial Threat and Metropolitan Housing Segregation." *Social Forces* 88 (1): 373–394.

Dekel, R., H. Goldblatt, M. Keider, Z. Solomon, and M. Polliack. 2005. "Being the Wife of a Veteran with Posttraumatic Stress Disorder." *Journal of Family Issues* 54: 24–36.

DEOMI Research Division. 1990. "Quarterly Statistical Profile of Minorities and Women in the Department of Defense Active Forces, Reserve Forces, and the United States Coast Guard." June. Patrick AFB, FL: Defense Equal Opportunity Management Institute (DEOMI).

DEOMI Research Division. 2000. "Semi-Annual Race/Ethnic/Gender Profile of the Department of Defense Active Forces, Reserve Forces, and the United States Coast Guard." Statistical Series Pamphlet 00–3. Patrick AFB, FL: Defense Equal Opportunity Management Institute.

DEOMI Research Division. 2006. "Annual Demographic Profile of the Department of Defense and U.S. Coast Guard FY 2006." Patrick AFB, FL: Defense Equal Opportunity Management Institute. Retrieved July 30, 2012, http://www.deomi.org/downloadableFiles/Demographics_2006_09.pdf.

Department of Defense. 1989. *Hispanics in America's Defense*. Washington, DC: U.S. Department of Defense.

Department of Defense. 2005. "Population Representation in the Military Services FY 2005: Executive Summary." Washington, DC: U.S. Department of Defense. Retrieved January 10, 2009, http://www.defenselink.mil/prhome/poprep2005/summary/summary.html.

Department of Defense. 2006. "Population Representation in the Military Services, FY2004." Washington, DC: U.S. Department of Defense. Retrieved July 31, 2012, http://prhome.defense.gov/rfm/MPP/ACCESSION%20POLICY/poprep2004/download/2004report.pdf

Department of Defense. 2008a. "Active Duty Military Personnel Strengths by Regional Area and by Country." Washington, DC: U.S. Department of Defense. Retrieved July 30, 2012, http://www.globalsecurity.org/military/library/report/2008/hst0806.pdf.

Department of Defense. 2008b. "Report of the Tenth Quadrennial Review of Military Compensation." July. Washington, DC: U.S. Department of Defense. Retrieved July 18, 2012, http://www.defense.gov/news/QRMCreport.pdf.

Department of Defense. 2009a. "DoD Personnel and Military Casualty Statistics." Washington, DC: U.S. Department of Defense, Statistical Information Analysis Division. Retrieved January 9, 2009, http://siadapp.dmdc.osd.mil/personnel/MMIDHOME.HTM.

Department of Defense. 2009b. "Casualty Summary by Reason Code." Washington, DC: U.S. Department of Defense, Statistical Information Analysis Division. Retrieved February 5, 2009, http://siadapp.dmdc.osd.mil/personnel/CASUALTY/gwot_reason.pdf.

Department of Defense. 2010a. "Today's Military." Washington, DC: U.S. Department of Defense. Retrieved May 6, 2010, http://www.todaysmilitary.com.

Department of Defense. 2010b. "Allowances (Per Diem, Travel, Transportation)." Washington, DC: U.S. Department of Defense, Defense Travel Management Office. Retrieved May 23, 2010, http://www.defensetravel.dod.mil/site/perdiem.cfm.

Department of Defense. 2010c. "Demographics 2010: Profile of the Military Community." Washington DC: U.S. Department of Defense. Retrieved July 30, 2012, http://www.militaryhomefront.dod.mil/12038/Project%20Documents/MilitaryHOMEFRONT/Reports/2010_Demographics_Report.pdf.

Department of Defense. 2011a. "Military Casual Information." Washington, DC: U.S. Department of Defense. Retrieved December 31, 2011, http://siadapp.dmdc.osd.mil/personnel/CASUALTY/castop.htm.

Department of Defense. 2011b. "US Casualty Status." Washington, DC: U.S. Department of Defense. Retrieved December 31, 2011, http://www.defense.gov/news/casualty.pdf.

Department of Defense. 2011c. "Principal Wars in Which the United States Participated: U.S. Military Personnel Serving and Casualties." Washington, DC: U.S.

Department of Defense. Retrieved January 2, 2012, http://siadapp.dmdc.osd.mil/personnel/CASUALTY/WCPRINCIPAL.pdf.

Department of Defense. 2011d. "Quit Tobacco—Make Everyone Proud." January 6. Washington, DC: U.S. Department of Defense. http://www.ucanquit2.org/Default.aspx.

Department of Defense and Office of the Secretary of Defense. 2011e. "Global War on Terrorism—Casualty by Reason (October 7, 2011 through December 5, 2011)." Washington, DC: U.S. Department of Defense. Retrieved January 4, 2010, http://siadapp.dmdc.osd.mil/personnel/CASUALTY/gwot_reason.pdf.

Department of Defense. 2012. "Casualty Statistics for Operation Iraqi Freedom and Operation Enduring Freedom." Washington, DC: U.S. Department of Defense. Retrieved January 3, 2012, http://www.defense.gov/news/casualty.pdf.

Department of Health and Human Services. 2007. "Responsible Fatherhood Spotlight: Fathers in the Military." Fact Sheet. Gaithersburg, MD: U.S. Department of Health and Human Services, Administration for Children and Families' (ACF) Office of Family Assistance (OFA). Retrieved February 22, 2009, http://library.fatherhood.gov/cwig/ws/library/docs/fatherhd/Blob/59210.pdf?w=NATIVE%28%27BASIC+ph+is+%27%27NRFC+Spotlights%27%27+AND+TI+ph+is+%27%27Fathers+in+the+Military%27%27+AND+AUTHORS+ph+like+%27%27National+Responsible+Fatherhood+Clearinghouse%27%27%27%29&upp=0&rpp=-10&order=native%28%27year%2FDescend%27%29&r=1&m=1.

de Tray, Dennis. 1982. "Veteran Status as a Screening Device." *American Economic Review* 72 (1): 133–142.

Diehl, Jackson. 2009. "It's Vietnam, Again: Does That Analysis Stand Up for Every U.S. Intervention?" *The Washington Post.* October 25. Retrieved November 8, 2011, http://www.washingtonpost.com/wp-dyn/content/article/2009/10/23/AR2009102303408.html.

DiPrete, Thomas A., and Gregory M. Eirich. 2006. "Cumulative Advantage as a Mechanism for Inequality: A Review of Theoretical and Empirical Developments." *Annual Review of Sociology* 32: 271–297.

Dobkin, Carlos, and Reza Shabani. 2009. "The Health Effects of Military Service: Evidence from the Vietnam Draft." *Economic Inquiry* 47 (1): 69–80.

Dohrenwend, Bruce P., J. Blake Turner, Nicholas A. Turse, Ben G. Adams, Karestan C. Koenen, and Randall Marshall. 2006. "The Psychological Risks of Vietnam for US Veterans: A Revisit with New Data and Methods." *Science* 313 (5789): 979–982.

Dooley, Thomas A. 1956. *Deliver Us from Evil: The Story of Viet Nam's Flight to Freedom.* New York: Farrar, Straus and Cudahy.

Dorn, Edwin. 1989. *Who Defends America?: Race, Sex, and Class in the Armed Forces.* Washington, DC: Joint Center for Political Studies Press.

Drobnic, Sonja, and Hans-Peter Blossfeld. 2004. "Career Patterns over the Life Course: Gender, Class, and Linked Lives." *Research in Social Stratification and Mobility* 21 (139): 164.

Durkheim, Emile. 1951. *Suicide: A Study in Sociology.* Glencoe, IL: Free Press.

Edin, Kathryn. 2000. "What Do Low-Income Single Mothers Say about Marriage?" *Social Problems* 47 (1) (February): 112–133. http://caliber.ucpress.net/doi/abs/10.1525/sp.2000.47.1.03x0282v.

Edwards, Ryan D. 2008. "Widening Health Inequalities among US Military Retirees since 1974." *Social Science & Medicine* 67 (11): 1657–1668.

Eitelberg, Mark J. 1988. *Manpower for Military Occupations.* Washington, DC: Office of the Assistant Secretary of Defense.

Elder Jr., Glen H. (ed.). 1985. *Life Course Dynamics: Trajectories and Transitions, 1968–1980.* Ithaca, NY: Cornell University Press.

Elder Jr., Glen H. 1986. "Military Times and Turning Points in Men's Lives." *Developmental Psychology* 22 (2): 233–245.

Elder Jr., Glen H. 1987. "War Mobilization and the Life Course: A Cohort of World War II Veterans." *Sociological Forum* 2 (3) (July): 449–472.

Elder Jr., Glen H. 1994. "Time, Human Agency, and Social Change: Perspectives on the Life Course." *Social Psychology Quarterly* 57 (1) (March): 4–15.

Elder Jr., Glen H., and Susan L. Bailey. 1988. "The Timing of Military Service in Men's Lives." In *Social Stress and Family Development*, edited by Joan Aldous and David M. Klein, pp. 157–174. New York: Guilford.

Elder Jr., Glen H., and Avshalom Caspi. 1990. "Studying Lives in a Changing Society: Sociological and Personological Explorations." In *Studying Persons and Lives*, edited by Albert I. Rabin, pp. 201–247. New York: Springer.

Elder Jr., Glen H., and Elizabeth Colerick Clipp. 1988a. "Wartime Losses and Social Bonding—Influences across 40 Years in Men's Lives." *Psychiatry—Interpersonal and Biological Processes* 51 (2): 177–198. ISI:A1988T483300006.

Elder Jr., Glen H., and Elizabeth Colerick Clipp. 1988b. "War Experiences and Social Ties: Influences across 40 Years in Men's Lives." In *Social Change and the Life Course, Volume 1: Social Structures and Human Lives*, edited by Matilda White Riley, pp. 306–327. Beverly Hills, CA: Sage Publications.

Elder Jr., Glen H., and Elizabeth Colerick Clipp. 1989. "Combat Experience and Emotional Health—Impairment and Resilience in Later Life." *Journal of Personality* 57 (2): 311–341.

Elder Jr., Glen H., Elizabeth Colerick Clipp, James Scott Brown, Leslie R. Martin, and Howard W. Friedman. 2009. "The Lifelong Mortality Risks of World War II Experiences." *Research on Aging* 31 (4): 391–412.

Elder Jr., Glen H., Rand D. Conger, E. Michael Foster, and Monika Ardelt. 1992. "Families under Economic Pressure." *Journal of Family Issues* 13 (1) (March): 5–37.

Elder Jr., Glen H., Cynthia Gimbel, and Rachel Lynne Ivie. 1991. "Turning Points in Life: The Case of Military Service and War." *Military Psychology* 3 (4): 215–231.

Elder Jr., Glen H., and Monica Kirkpatrick Johnson. 2002. "Perspectives on Human Development in Context." In *Psychology at the Turn of the Millennium*, Vol. 2: *Social, Developmental, and Clinical Perspectives*, edited by Claes von Hofsten and Lars Bergman, pp. 153–175. East Sussex, UK: Psychology Press Ltd.

Elder Jr., Glen H., Monica K. Johnson, and R. Crosnoe. 2003. "The Emergence and Development of Life Course Theory." In *Handbook of the Life Course*, edited by J. T. Mortimer and M. J. Shanahan, pp. 3–19. New York: Kluwer Academic/Plenum.

Elder Jr., Glen H., Valarie King, and Rand D. Conger. 1996. "Attachment to Place and Migration Prospects: A Developmental Perspective." *Journal of Research on Adolescence* 6 (4): 397–425.

Elder Jr., Glen H., John Modell, and Ross D. Parke. 1993. "Studying Children in a Changing World." In *Children in Time and Place: Developmental and Historical Insights*, edited by Glen H. Elder Jr., John Modell, and Ross D. Parke, pp. 3–22. Cambridge, UK: Cambridge University Press.

Elder Jr., Glen H., and Michael J. Shanahan. 2006. "The Life Course and Human Development." Chapter 12 in *Theoretical Models of Human Development*, Vol 1: *The Handbook of Child Psychology*, edited by Richard E. Lerner, pp. 665–715. 6th ed. New York: Wiley.

Elder Jr., Glen H., Michael J. Shanahan, and Elizabeth Colerick Clipp. 1994. "When War Comes to Men's Lives: Life-Course Patterns in Family, Work, and Health." *Psychology and Aging* 9 (1) (March): 5–16.

Elder Jr., Glen H., Michael J. Shanahan, and Elizabeth Colerick Clipp. 1997. "Linking Combat and Physical Health: The Legacy of World War II in Men's Lives." *American Journal of Psychiatry* 154 (3): 330–336.

Elder Jr., Glen H., Lin Wang, Naomi J. Spence, Daniel E. Adkins, and Tyson H. Brown. 2010. "Pathways to the All-Volunteer Military." *Social Science Quarterly* 91 (2) (June): 455–475.

Ellison, Christopher G. 1992. "Military Background, Racial Orientations, and Political Participation among Black Adult Males." *Social Science Quarterly* 73 (2): 360–378. ISI:A1992JC97500011.

Elo, Irma T. 2009. "Social Class Differentials in Health and Mortality: Patterns and Explanations in Comparative Perspective." *Annual Review of Sociology* 35: 553–572.

Elo, Irma T., and Samuel H. Preston. 1992. "Effects of Early-Life Conditions on Adult Mortality: A Review." *Population Index* 58: 186–212.

Ender, Morten G. 1996. "Growing Up in the Military." In *Strangers at Home: Essays on the Effects of Living Overseas and Coming "Home" to a Strange Land*, edited by Carolyn D. Smith, pp. 125–150. Bayside, NY: Aletheia Publications.

Ender, Morten G. 2002. *Military Brats and Other Global Nomads: Growing Up in Organization Families*. Westport, CT: Praeger.

Entwisle, Doris R., Karl L. Alexander, and Linda S. Olson. 2000. "Early Work Histories of Urban Youth." *American Sociological Review* 65 (2): 279–297.

Erikson, Erik Homburger. 1968. *Identity: Youth and Crisis*. New York: W.W. Norton & Company.

Eschtruth, Andrew D., Wei Sun, and Anthony Webb. 2006. *Will Reverse Mortgages Rescue the Baby Boomers?* Issue Brief No. 54. Boston: Center for Retirement Research at Boston College.

Espiritu, Yen Le. 2003. *Home Bound: Filipino American Lives across Cultures, Communities, and Countries*. Berkeley: University of California Press.

Faber, Anthony J., Elaine Willerton, Shelley R. Clymer, Shelley M. MacDermid, and Howard M. Weiss. 2008. "Ambiguous Absence, Ambiguous Presence: A Qualitative Study of Military Reserve Families in Wartime." *Journal of Family Psychology* 22 (2): 222–230.

Faris, John H. 1981. "The All-Volunteer Force—Recruitment from Military Families." *Armed Forces & Society* 7 (4): 545–559. ISI:A1981MQ37800003.

Faris, John H. 1984. "Economic and Noneconomic Factors of Personnel Recruitment and Retention in the AVF." *Armed Forces & Society* 10 (2) (Winter): 251–275.

Farley, Reynolds. 1999. "Racial Issues: Recent Trends in Residential Patterns and Intermarriage." In *Diversity and Its Discontents*, edited by Neil J. Smelser and Jeffrey C. Alexander, pp. 85–128. Princeton, NJ: Princeton University Press.

Farley, Reynolds, and William H. Frey. 1994. "Changes in the Segregation of Whites from Blacks during the 1980s—Small Steps toward A More Integrated Society." *American Sociological Review* 59 (1): 23–45.

Farmer-Kaiser, Mary. 2004. "'Are They Not in Some Sorts Vagrants?' Gender and the Effects of the Freedmen's Bureau to Combat Vagrancy in the Reconstruction South." *Georgia Historical Quarterly* 88 (1) (Spring): 25–49.

Farmer-Kaiser, Mary. 2007. "'With a Weight of Circumstances Like Millstones about Their Necks': Freedwomen, Federal Relief, and the Benevolent Guardianship of the Freedmen's Bureau." *Virginia Magazine of History and Biography* 115 (3): 412–442.

Faulkner, Carol. 2004. *Women's Radical Reconstruction: The Freedmen's Aid Movement*. Philadelphia: University of Pennsylvania Press.

Faust, Drew Gilpin. 1996. *Mothers of Invention: Women of the Slaveholding South in the American Civil War*. Chapel Hill: University of North Carolina Press.

Faust, Drew Gilpin. 2008. *This Republic of Suffering: Death and the American Civil War*. New York: Alfred A. Knopf.

Feaver, Peter D., and Richard H. Kohn (eds.). 2001. *Soldiers and Civilians: The Civil-Military Gap and American National Security*. Cambridge, MA: MIT Press.

Ferling, John. 1981. "The New-England Soldier—A Study in Changing Perceptions." *American Quarterly* 33 (1): 26–45. ISI:A1981LX86100002.

Ferraro, Kenneth F., Tetyana Pylypiv Shippee, and Markus H. Shafer. 2009. "Cumulative Inequality Theory for Research on Aging and the Life Course." In *Handbook of Theories of Aging*, edited by Vern L. Bengtson, Merril Silverstein, Norella M. Putney, and Daphna Gans, pp. 413–434. 2nd ed. New York: Springer.

Figley, Charles R. 1993. "Coping with Stressors on the Home Front." *Journal of Social Issues* 49 (4): 51–71.

Fischer, Hannah. 2010. "United States Military Casualty Statistics: Operation Iraqi Freedom and Operation Enduring Freedom." RS22452, March 25. Washington, DC: Congressional Research Service. http://www.fas.org/sgp/crs/natsec/RS22452.pdf.

Fitzgerald, Kelly G. 2006. "The Effect of Military Service on Wealth Accumulation." *Research on Aging* 28 (1): 56–83.

Fligstein, Neil D. 1980. "Who Served in the Military, 1940–73." *Armed Forces & Society* 6 (2): 297–312. ISI:A1980JC86300010.

Fontana, Alan, and Robert Rosenheck. 1995. "Attempted Suicide among Vietnam Veterans—A Model of Etiology in a Community Sample." *American Journal of Psychiatry* 152 (1): 102–109.

Fontana, Alan, Robert Rosenheck, and Thomas Horvath. 1997. "Social Support and Psychopathology in the War Zone." *Journal of Nervous and Mental Disease* 185 (11): 675–681.

Frank, Lisa Tendrich (ed.). 2008. *Women in the American Civil War*. Santa Barbara, CA: ABC-CLIO.

Frank, Nathaniel, Victoria Basham, Geoffrey Bateman, Aaron Belkin, Margot Canaday, Alan Okros, and Denise Scott. 2010. "Gays in Foreign Militaries 2010: A Global Primer." Santa Barbara, CA: Palm Center.

Frankel, Noralee. 1999. *Freedom's Women: Black Women and Families in Civil War Era Mississippi*. Bloomington: Indiana University Press.

Frayne, Susan, V. A. Parker, C. L. Christiansen, S. Loveland, M. R. Seaver, Lewis Kazis, and Katherine Skinner. 2006. "Health Status among 28,000 Women Veterans: The VA Women's Health Program Evaluation." *Journal of General Internal Medicine* 21 (Suppl 3): S40–S46.

Fredland, John Eric, and Roger D. Little. 1985. "Socioeconomic Status of World War II Veterans by Race—An Empirical Test of the Bridging Hypothesis." *Social Science Quarterly* 66 (3): 533–551.

Friedman, Matthew J. 1998. "The Matsunaga Vietnam Veterans Project." *The National Center for Post-Traumatic Stress Disorder, PTSD Research Quarterly*, 9 (4): 6–8. Retrieved July 31, 2012, http://www.ptsd.va.gov/professional/newsletters/research-quarterly/V9N4.pdf

Frueh, B. Christopher, Jon D. Elhai, Anouk L. Grubaugh, Jeannine Monnier, Todd B. Kashdan, Julie A. Sauvageot, Mark B. Hamner, B. G. Burkett, and George W. Arana. 2005. "Documented Combat Exposure of US Veterans Seeking Treatment for Combat-Related Post-Traumatic Stress Disorders." *British Journal of Psychiatry* 186: 467–472.

Frusciano, Thomas J. 1980. *Student Deferment and the Selective Service College Qualification Test, 1951–1967*. Princeton, NJ: Educational Testing Service.

Gabaccia, Donna R. 2010. "Is It about Time?" *Social Science History* 34 (1): 1–12. ISI:000275121500001.

Gade, Paul A. 1991. "Preface to the Special Issue." *Military Psychology* 3 (4): 185–186.

Gade, Paul A., Hyder Lakhani, and Melvin Kimmel. 1991. "Military Service: A Good Place to Start?" *Military Psychology* 3 (4): 251–267.

Gallman, J. Matthew. 1990. *Mastering Wartime: A Social History of Philadelphia during the Civil War.* Philadelphia: University of Pennsylvania Press.

Gamache, Gail, Robert Rosenheck, and Richard Tessler. 2001. "The Proportion of Veterans among Homeless Men: A Decade Later." *Social Psychiatry and Psychiatric Epidemiology* 36 (10): 481–485.

Gates, Gary J. 2004. *Gay Men and Lesbians in the U.S. Military: Estimates from Census 2000.* September 28. Washington, DC: The Urban Institute.

Gawande, Atul. 2004. "Casualties of War—Military Care for the Wounded from Iraq and Afghanistan." *New England Journal of Medicine* 351 (24): 2471–2475.

George, Linda K. 2003. "What Life-Course Perspectives Offer the Study of Aging and Health." In *Invitation to the Life Course: Toward New Understandings of Later Life,* edited by Richard A. Settersten Jr., pp. 161–190. Amityville, NY: Baywood Publishing.

George, Linda K. (forthcoming). "Age Structures, Aging, and the Life Course." In *Gerontology: Perspectives and Issues,* edited by Janet M. Wilmoth and Ken Ferraro. 4th ed. New York: Springer.

Gershick, Zsa Zsa. 2005. *Secret Service: Untold Stories of Lesbians in the Military.* Los Angeles: Alyson Books.

Gibson, Jennifer Lee, Brian K. Griepentrog, and Sean M. Marsh. 2007. "Parental Influence on Youth Propensity to Join the Military." *Journal of Vocational Behavior* 70 (3): 525–541.

Giele, Janet Z., and Glen H. Elder Jr. (eds.). 1998. *Methods of Life Course Research: Qualitative and Quantitative Approaches.* Thousand Oaks, CA: Sage Publications.

Giesberg, Judith Ann. 2005. "From Harvest Field to Battlefield: Rural Pennsylvania Women and the U.S. Civil War." *Pennsylvania History* 72 (2) (April): 159–192.

Gifford, Brian. 2005a. "Combat Casualties and Race: What Can We Learn from the 2003–2004 Iraq Conflict?" *Armed Forces & Society* 31 (2): 201–225.

Gifford, Brian. 2005b. "The Spillover Effects of Military Communities on the Need for Health Care Safety-Net Services." WR-299, September. Santa Monica, CA: RAND. http://www.rand.org/pubs/working_papers/WR299/index.html.

Gill, H. Leroy, and Donald R. Haurin. 1998. "Wherever He May Go: How Wives Affect Their Husband's Career Decisions." *Social Science Research* 27 (3): 264–279.

Gill, H. Leroy, Donald R. Haurin, and J. Phillips. 1994. "Mobility and Fertility in the Military." *Social Science Quarterly* 75: 340–353.

Gimbel, Cynthia, and Alan Booth. 1994. "Why Does Military Combat Experience Adversely Affect Marital Relations?" *Journal of Marriage and the Family* 56 (3): 691–703.

Gimbel, Cynthia, and Alan Booth. 1996. "Who Fought in Vietnam?" *Social Forces* 74 (4): 1137–1157.

Ginzberg, Lori D. 1990. *Women and the Work of Benevolence: Morality, Politics, and Class in the Nineteenth-Century United States.* New Haven, CT: Yale University Press.

Glenn, Norval D. 1973. "Suburbanization in the United States since World War II." In *The Urbanization of the Suburbs,* edited by Louis H. Masotti and Jeffrey K. Hadden, pp. 51–78. Beverly Hills, CA: Sage Publications.

Godson, Susan H. 2001. *Serving Proudly: A History of Women in the U.S. Navy.* Annapolis, MD: US Naval Institute Press.

Goffman, Erving. 1959. *The Presentation of Self in Everyday Life.* New York: Doubleday.

Goffman, Erving. 1961. *Asylums: Essays on the Social Situation of Mental Patients and Other Inmates*. New York: Doubleday Anchor.

Goffman, Erving. 1963. *Stigma: Notes on the Management of Spoiled Identity*. New York: Simon & Schuster.

Goldberg, Matthew S. 1985. "New Estimates of the Effect of Unemployment on Enlisted Retention." CRM 85–51, July. Alexandria, VA: Center for Naval Analyses. http://www.cna.org/documents/2785005100.pdf.

Goldberg, Matthew S., and John T. Warner. 1987. "Military Experience, Civilian Experience, and the Earnings of Veterans." *Journal of Human Resources* 22 (1): 62–81.

Goldzweig, Caroline L., Talene M. Balekian, Cony Rolon, Elizabeth M. Yano, and Paul G. Shekelle. 2006. "The State of Women Veterans' Health Research." *Journal of General Internal Medicine* 21: S82–S92.

Golobardes, Bruna, John W. Lynch, and George D. Smith. 2004. "Childhood Socioeconomic Circumstances and Cause-Specific Mortality in Adulthood." *Epidemiologic Reviews* 26: 7–21.

Government Accountability Office. 2009. "Military Personnel: Reserve Component Servicemembers on Average Earn More Income While Activated." GAO-09–688R Reservists' Income Loss, June 23. Washington, DC: GAO. http://www.gao.gov/new.items/d09688r.pdf.

Granovetter, Mark S. 1973. "Strength of Weak Ties." *American Journal of Sociology* 78 (6): 1360–1380.

Granovetter, Mark S. 1995. *Getting a Job: A Study of Contacts and Careers*. Chicago: University of Chicago Press.

Grant, Jaime M. 2010. *Outing Age 2010: Public Policy Issues Affecting Lesbian, Gay, Bisexual, and Transgender Elders*. Washington, DC: National Gay and Lesbian Task Force Policy Institute.

Greenberg, I. M. 1969. "Project 100,000: The Training of Former Rejectees." *The Phi Delta Kappan* 50 (10): 570–574.

Griffith, James D., and Shelley Perry. 1993. "Wanting to Soldier: Enlistment Motivations of Army Reserve Recruits before and after Operation Desert Storm." *Military Psychology* 5 (2): 127–139.

Griswold del Castillo, Richard (ed.). 2008. *World War II and Mexican American Civil Rights*. Austin: University of Texas Press.

Grossman, Allyson Sherman. 1981. "The Employment Situation for Military Wives." *Monthly Labor Review* 104 (2): 60–64.

Gutman, Herbert George. 1976. *The Black Family in Slavery and Freedom, 1750–1925*. New York: Pantheon Books.

Hacker, Jacob S. 2005. *The Great Risk Shift: The Assault on American Jobs, Families, Health Care, and Retirement and How You Can Fight Back*. Oxford, UK: Oxford University Press.

Hampf, M. Michaela. 2004. "'Dykes' or 'Whores': Sexuality and the Women's Army Corps in the United States during World War II." *Women's Studies International Forum* 27 (1): 13–30.

Hank, Karsten. 2004. "Effects of Early Life Family Events on Women's Late Life Labour Market Behavior: An Analysis of the Relationship Between Childbearing and Retirement in Western Germany." *European Sociological Review* 20: 189–198.

Hannon, Lance. 2003. "Poverty, Delinquency, and Educational Attainment: Cumulative Disadvantage or Disadvantage Saturation?" *Sociological Inquiry* 73 (4): 575–594.

Hara, Min. 2000. "Action from a Sergeant's Diary." In *Only What We Could Carry: The Japanese American Internment Experience*, edited by Lawson Fusao Inada and California Historical Society. Berkeley, CA: Heyday Books.

Hareven, Tamara K. (ed.). 1978. *Transitions: The Family and the Life Course in Historical Perspective.* New York: Academic Press.

Harkness, Laurie Leydic. 1993. "Transgenerational Transmission of War-Related Trauma." In *International Handbook of Traumatic Stress Syndromes*, edited by John Preston Wilson and Beverley Raphael, pp. 635–644. New York: Plenum Press.

Harrell, Margaret Cecchine. 2000a. *Invisible Women: Junior Enlisted Army Wives.* Santa Monica, CA: RAND.

Harrell, Margaret Cecchine. 2000b. "Brass Rank and Gold Rings: Class, Race, Gender, and Kinship within the Army Community." Ph.D. dissertation, Department of Anthropology, University of Virginia, Charlottesville, VA.

Harrell, Margaret Cecchine. 2001. "Army Officers' Spouses: Have the White Gloves Been Mothballed?" *Armed Forces & Society* 28 (1): 55–75.

Harrell, Margaret Cecchine, Nelson Lim, Laura Werber Castaneda, and Daniela Golinelli. 2004. *Working around the Military: Challenges to Military Spouse Employment and Education.* Santa Monica, CA: RAND.

Harrington Meyer, Madonna, and Pamela Herd. 2007. *Market Friendly or Family Friendly?: The State and Gender Inequality in Old Age.* New York: Russell Sage Foundation.

Harrison, Bennett and Barry Bluestone. 1988. *The Great U-turn, Corporate Restructuring and the Polarizing of America.* New York: Basic Books.

Hartmann, Heidi, and Ashley English. 2009. "Older Women's Retirement Security: A Primer." *Journal of Women Politics and Policy* 30 (2–3): 109–140.

Hasselbring, Andrew Strieter. 1991. "American Prisoners of War in the Third Reich." Ph.D. dissertation, Temple University, Philadelphia.

Hastings, Thomas J. 1991. "The Stanford-Terman Study Revisited: Postwar Emotional Health of World War II Veterans." *Military Psychology* 3 (4): 201–214.

Hattiangadi, Anita U., Aline O. Quester, SgtMaj USMC Ret. Gary Lee, Diana S. Lien, Ian D. MacLeod, David L. Reese, and Robert W. Shuford. 2005. "Non-Citizens in Today's Military: Final Report." CRM D0011092.A2/Final. Alexandria, VA: Center for Naval Analyses. http://www.cna.org/documents/D0011092.A2.pdf.

Hayes, J., B. Wakefield, E. M. Andresen, J. Scherrer, L. Traylor, P. Wiegmann, T. Denmark, and C. DeSouza. 2010. "Identification of Domains and Measures for an Assessment Battery to Examine the Well-Being of Spouses of OIF/OEF Veterans with Posttraumatic Stress Disorder." *Journal of Rehabilitation Research & Development* 47: 825–840.

Hayghe, Howard V. 1986. "Military and Civilian Wives—Update on the Labor-Force Gap." *Monthly Labor Review* 109 (12): 31–33.

Hearst, Norman, Thomas B. Newman, and Stephen B. Hulley. 1986. "Delayed Effects of the Military Draft on Mortality—A Randomized Natural Experiment." *New England Journal of Medicine* 314 (10): 620–624.

Heckman, James J. 1979. "Sample Selection Bias as a Specification Error." *Econometrica* 47 (1): 153–161.

Heflin, Colleen, Janet M. Wilmoth, and Andrew S. London. 2012. "Veteran Status and Material Hardship: The Moderating Influence of Disability." *Social Service Review* 86 (1): 119–142.

Heitgerd, Janet L., and C. Virginia Lee. 2003. "A New Look at Neighborhoods near National Priorities List Sites." *Social Science & Medicine* 57 (6): 1117–1126.

Heller, Donald E. (ed.). 2002. *Condition of Access: Higher Education for Lower Income Students.* Westport, CT: American Council on Education and Praeger Publishers.

Helseth, Candi. 2007. "War Has Big Impact in Rural Areas." *The Rural Monitor* (Spring). Retrieved July 30, 2012, http://www.raconline.org/newsletter/2007/spring.php.

Hendin, Herbert, and Ann Pollinger Haas. 1984. *Wounds of War: The Psychological Aftermath of Combat in Vietnam.* New York: Basic Books.

Hendricks, Jon. 2012. "Considering Life Course Concepts." *Journals of Gerontology: Social Sciences* 67 (2): 226–231.

Hendrix, Charles C., and Lisa M. Anelli. 1993. "Impact of Vietnam War Service on Veterans' Perceptions of Family Life." *Family Relations* 42 (1) (January): 87–92.

Henretta, John. 1992. "Uniformity and Diversity: Life Course Institutionalization and Late Life Work Exit." *Sociological Quarterly* 33 (2): 265–279.

Henretta, John. 2007. "Early Childbearing, Marital Status, and Women's Health and Mortality after Age 50." *Journal of Health and Social Behavior* 48: 254–266.

Herbert, Melissa S. 2000. *Camouflage Isn't Only for Combat: Gender, Sexuality and Women in the Military.* New York: New York University.

Herbold, Hilary. 1994. "Never a Level Playing Field: Blacks and the GI Bill." *The Journal of Blacks in Higher Education* 6: 104–108.

Herek, Gregory M. 1993. "Sexual Orientation and Military Service—A Social Science Perspective." *American Psychologist* 48 (5): 538–549.

Hershfield, David C. 1985. "Attacking Housing Discrimination: Economic Power of the Military in Desegregating Off-Base Rental Housing." *American Journal of Economics and Sociology* 44 (1) (January): 23–28.

Herszenhorn, David M., and Carl Hulse. 2010. "House Votes to Allow Repeal Of 'Don't Ask, Don't Tell' Law." *New York Times*, May 28.

Hill, Mark E. 1999. "Multivariate Survivorship Analysis Using Two Cross-Sectional Samples." *Demography* 36 (4): 497–503.

Hill, Reuben. 1949. *Families under Stress: Adjustment to the Crises of War Separation and Reunion.* New York: Harper.

Himmelfarb, Naomi, Deborah Yaeger, and Jim Mintz. 2006. "Posttraumatic Stress Disorder in Female Veterans with Military and Civilian Sexual Trauma." *Journal of Traumatic Stress* 19 (6): 837–846.

Hirsch, Barry T., and Stephen L. Mehay. 2003. "Evaluating the Labor Market Performance of Veterans Using a Matched Comparison Group Design." *Journal of Human Resources* 38 (3): 673–700.

Hoffman, Saul D., and Greg J. Duncan. 1988. "What Are the Economic Consequences of Divorce?" *Demography* 25 (4) (November): 641–645.

Hogan, Dennis P. 1978. "The Variable Order of Events in the Life Course." *American Sociological Review* 43 (4) (August): 573–586.

Hogan, Dennis P. 1981. *Transitions and Social Change: The Early Lives of American Man.* New York: Academic.

Holder, Kelly A. 2007. "Exploring the Veteran-Nonveteran Earnings Differential in the 2005 American Community Survey." Paper presented at American Sociological Association annual meeting, August 11–14, New York, New York.

Holm, Tom. 1996. *Strong Hearts, Wounded Souls: Native American Veterans of the Vietnam War.* Austin: University of Texas Press.

Holm, Tom. 2006. "Indian Scout." In *American Icons: An Encyclopedia of the People, Places, and Things That Have Shaped Our Culture,* Vol. 2, edited by Dennis R. Hall and Susan G. Hall. Westport, CT: Greenwood Press.

Holobaugh, Jim, and Keith Hale. 1993. *Torn Allegiances: The Story of a Gay Cadet.* Boston: Alyson Publications.

Holzer, Harry J. 1999. *What Employers Want: Job Prospects for Less-Educated Workers.* New York: Russell Sage Foundation.

Holzer, Harry J., and Sheldon Danziger. 2001. "Are Jobs Available for Disadvantaged Workers in Urban Areas?" In *Urban Inequality: Evidence from Four Cities,* edited by Alice O'Connor, Chris Tilly, and Lawrence D. Bobo, pp. 496–538. New York: Russell Sage Foundation.

Holzer, Harry J., Steven Raphael, and Michael A. Stoll. 2006 "How Do Employer Perceptions of Crime and Incarceration Affect the Employment Prospects of Less-Educated Young Black Men?" In *Black Males Left Behind*, edited by Ronald B. Mincy, pp. 67–85. Washington, DC: The Urban Institute.

Hosek, James, Beth J. Asch, C. Christine Fair, Craig W. Martin, and Michael Mattock. 2002. *Married to the Military: The Employment and Earnings of Military Wives Compared with Those of Civilian Wives*. Santa Monica, CA: RAND.

Howard, Christopher. 1997. *The Hidden Welfare State: Tax Expenditures and Social Policy in the United States*. Princeton, NJ: Princeton University Press.

Howe II, Harold. 1988. *The Forgotten Half: Pathways to Success for America's Youth and Young Families. Final Report*. Washington, DC: William T. Grant Foundation, Commission on Work, Family, and Citizenship.

Humes, Edward. 2006. *Over Here: How the G.I. Bill Transformed the American Dream*. Orlando, FL: Harcourt Books.

Hunter, E. L., Ryan Kelty, Meyer Kestnbaum, and David R. Segal. 2004. "Civil-Military Relations in an Era of Bioterrorism: Crime and War in the Making of Modern Civil-Military Relations." In *Advances in Health Care Management*, Vol. 4: *Bioterrorism Preparedness, Attack and Response*, edited by John Blair, Myron Fottler, Grant Savage, and Leonard H. Friedman, pp. 319–344. San Diego, CA: Elsevier.

Huntington, Samuel. 1957. *The Soldier and the State: The Theory and Politics of Civil-Military Relations*. Cambridge, MA: Belknap Press of Harvard University Press.

Hurt, L. S., C. Ronsmans, and S. L. Thomas. 2006. "The Effect of Number of Births on Women's Mortality: Systematic Review of the Evidence for Women Who Have Completed Their Childbearing." *Population Studies* 60: 55–71.

Hynes, Denise M., Kristin Koelling, Kevin Stroupe, Noreen Arnold, Katherine Mallin, Min-Woong Sohn, Frances Weaver, Larry M. Manheim, and Linda Kok. 2007. "Veterans' Access to and Use of Medicare and Veterans Affairs Health Care." *Medical Care* 45 (3): 214–223.

Ikin, Jillian F., Malcolm R. Sim, Dean P. McKenzie, Keith W. A. Horsley, Eileen J. Wilson, Warren K. Harrex, Michael R. Moore, Paul L. Jelfs, and Scott Henderson. 2009. "Life Satisfaction and Quality in Korean War Veterans Five Decades after the War." *Journal of Epidemiology and Community Health* 63 (5): 359–365. Imbens, Guido W. and Joshua D. Angrist. 1994. "Identification and Estimation of Local Average Treatment Effects." *Econometrica* 62 (2): 467–475.

Inada, Lawson Fusao and California Historical Society. 2000. *Only What We Could Carry: Japanese Americans and the Internment Experience*. Berkeley, CA: Heyday Books.

Inouye, Daniel. 2000. "Journey to Washington." In *Only What We Could Carry: Japanese Americans and the Internment Experience*, edited by Lawson Fusao Inada and California Historical Society. Berkeley, CA: Heyday Books.

Institute of Medicine. 2006. "Gulf War and Health: Volume 4. Health Effects of Serving in the Gulf War." September 12, 2011. http://www.iom.edu/Reports/2006/Gulf-War-and-Health—Volume-4-Health-Effects-of-Serving-in-the-Gulf-War.aspx.

Institute of Medicine. 2008a. "Gulf War and Health: Volume 6. Physiologic, Psychologic, and Psychosocial Effects of Deployment-Related Stress." November 15, 2011. http://www.iom.edu/Reports/2007/Gulf-War-Health-Vol-6-Physiologic-Psychologic-Psychosocial-Effects-Deployment-Related-Stress.aspx.

Institute of Medicine. 2008b. "Gulf War and Health: Volume 7. Long-Term Consequences of Traumatic Brain Injury." December 3, 2011. http://www.iom.edu/Reports/2008/Gulf-War-and-Health-Volume-7-Long-term-Consequences-of-Traumatic-Brain-Injury.aspx.

Ivie, Rachel Lynne. 1992. "Long-Term Effects of Women's Military Service." Doctoral dissertation, University of North Carolina at Chapel Hill.

Ivie, Rachel L., Cynthia Gimbel, and Glen H. Elder Jr. 1991. "Military Experience and Attitudes in Later Life: Contextual Influences across Forty Years." *Journal of Political and Military Sociology* 19 (1) (July): 101–117.

Izumigawa, Stanley. 2000. "One Replacement's Story." In *Only What We Could Carry: Japanese Americans and the Internment Experience*, edited by Lawson Fusao Inada and California Historical Society. Berkeley, CA: Heyday Books.

Jabour, Anya. 2007. *Scarlett's Sisters: Young Women in the Old South*. Chapel Hill: University of North Carolina Press.

Jackson, Charles L., and Frederick A. Day. 1993. "Locational Concentrations of Military Retirees in the United States." *Professional Geographer* 45 (1): 55–65.

Jacobson, Cardell K., and Tim B. Heaton. 2003. "Inter-Group Marriage and United States Military Service." *Journal of Political and Military Sociology* 1 (1): 1–22.

Janowitz, Morris. 1960. *The Professional Soldier: A Social and Political Portrait*. New York: Free Press.

Janowitz, Morris, and Charles C. Moskos Jr. 1974. "Racial Composition in the All-Volunteer Force." *Armed Forces & Society* 1 (1) (October): 109–123.

Jayamaha, Buddhika, Wesley D. Smith, Jeremy Roebuck, Omar Mora, Edward Sandmeier, Yance T. Gray, and Jeremy A. Murphy. 2007. "The War as We Saw It." *The New York Times*, August 19. http://www.nytimes.com/2007/08/19/opinion/19jayamaha.html?_r=2&pagewanted=1.

Jensen, Laura. 2003. *Patriots, Settlers, and the Origins of American Social Policy*. Cambridge, UK: Cambridge University Press.

Jensen, Peter S., David Martin, and Henry Watanabe. 1996. "Children's Response to Parental Separation during Operation Desert Storm." *Journal of the American Academy of Child & Adolescent Psychiatry* 35 (4) (April): 433–441.

Johnson, Robert J., and Howard B. Kaplan. 1991. "Psychosocial Predictors of Enlistment in the All-Voluntary Armed Forces: A Life-Event-History Analysis." *Youth and Society* 22 (3) (March): 291–317.

Johnson, W. Brad, and Robin A. Buhrke. 2006. "Service Delivery in a 'Don't Ask, Don't Tell' World: Ethical Care of Gay, Lesbian, and Bisexual Military Personnel." *Professional Psychology—Research and Practice* 37 (1): 91–98.

Johnston, A. 2007. Equality Illinois News. Winter 2007. Chicago: Equality Illinois. Retrieved June 15, 2011, http://www.eqil.org/PDFs/ieNews_final.pdf.

Jones, Franklin D., and Ronald J. Koshes. 1995. "Homosexuality and the Military." *American Journal of Psychiatry* 152 (1): 16–21. ISI:A1995PZ93400004.

Jordan, B. Kathleen, Charles R. Marmar, John A. Fairbank, William E. Schlenger, Richard A. Kulka, Richard L. Hough, and Daniel S. Weiss. 1992. "Problems in Families of Male Vietnam Veterans with Posttraumatic Stress Disorder." *Journal of Consulting and Clinical Psychology* 60 (6) (December): 916–926.

Jordan, Will J., and Stephen B. Plank. 2000. "Talent Loss among High-Achieving Poor Students." In *Schooling Students Placed at Risk: Research, Policy, and Practice in the Education of Poor and Minority Adolescents*, edited by Mavis G. Sanders, pp. 83–108. Mahwah, NY: Lawrence Erlbaum Associates.

Justice Policy Institute. 2000. "The Punishing Decade: Prison and Jail Estimates at the Millennium." May. Washington DC: Justice Policy Institute. Retrieved July 30, 2012, http://www.justicepolicy.org/images/upload/00-05_rep_punishingdecade_ac.pdf.

Kahlenberg, Richard D. 1996. *The Remedy: Class, Race, and Affirmative Action*. New York: Basic Books.

Kain, John F. 1968. "Housing Segregation, Negro Employment, and Metropolitan Decentralization." *Quarterly Journal of Economics* 82 (2): 175–197.

Kalisch, Philip A., and Beatrice J. Kalisch. 1978. *The Advance of American Nursing*. Boston: Little, Brown.

Kane, Tim. 2006. "Who Are the Recruits? The Demographic Characteristics of U.S. Military Enlistment, 2003–2005." Center for Data Analysis Report #06–09. The Heritage Foundation. Retrieved July 30, 2012, http://www.heritage.org/research/reports/2006/10/who-are-the-recruits-the-demographic-characteristics-of-us-military-enlistment-2003–2005.

Kang, Han K., and Tim A. Bullman. 1996. "Mortality among U.S. Veterans of the Persian Gulf War." *New England Journal of Medicine* 335 (20) (November 14): 1498–1504.

Kang, Han K., Nancy Dalager, Clare Mahan, and Erick Shii. 2005. "The Role of Sexual Assault on the Risk of PTSD among Gulf War Veterans." *Annals of Epidemiology* 15 (3): 191–195.

Kaplan, Mark S., Nathalie Huguet, Bentson H. McFarland, and Jason T. Newsom. 2007. "Suicide among Male Veterans: A Prospective Population Based Study." *Journal of Epidemiology and Community Health* 61 (7): 619–624.

Karney, Benjamin R., and John S. Crown. 2007. *Families under Stress: An Assessment of Data, Theory, and Research on Marriage and Divorce in the Military*. Santa Monica, CA: RAND.

Karney, Benjamin R., David S. Loughlin, and Michael S. Pollard. forthcoming. "Comparing Marital Status and Divorce Status in Civilian and Military Populations." *Journal of Family Issues*. Published online April 4, 2012.

Katz, Jonathan. 1976. *Gay American History: Lesbians and Gay Men in the U.S.A., A Documentary*. New York: Crowell.

Katznelson, Ira. 2005. *When Affirmative Action Was White: An Untold History of Racial Inequality in Twentieth-Century America*. New York: W.W. Norton & Company.

Keehn, Robert J. 1978. "Military Rank at Separation and Mortality." *Armed Forces & Society* 4 (2): 283–292.

Keene, Jennifer D. 2001. *Doughboys, the Great War, and the Remaking of America*. Baltimore, MD: Johns Hopkins University Press.

Kelley, Michelle L., Lisa B. Finkel, and Jayne Ashby. 2003. "Geographic Mobility, Family, and Maternal Variables as Related to the Psychosocial Adjustment of Military Children." *Military Medicine* 168 (12): 1019–1024.

Kelty, Ryan. 2008. "The US Navy's Maiden Voyage—Effects of Integrating Sailors and Civilian Mariners on Deployment." *Armed Forces & Society* 34 (4): 536–564.

Kelty, Ryan. 2009. "Citizen Soldiers and Civilian Contractors: Soldiers' Unit Cohesion and Retention Attitudes in the 'Total Force.'" *Journal of Political and Military Sociology* 37 (2) (January): 133–159.

Kelty, Ryan, Meredith A. Kleykamp, and David R. Segal. 2010. "The Military and the Transition to Adulthood." *Future of Children* 20 (1): 181–207. ISI:000277024900009.

Kelty, Ryan, and Darcy Schnack. 2012. "Attitudes on the Ground: What Soldiers Think about Civilian Contractors." In *Contractors and War: The Transformation of United States' Expeditionary Operations*, edited by Kinsey Christopher and Malcolm Patterson. Stanford, CA: Stanford University Press.

Kelty, Ryan, and David R. Segal. 2007. "The Civilianization of the U.S. Military: Army and Navy Case Studies of the Effects of Civilian Integration on Military Personnel." In *Private Military and Security Companies: Chances, Problems, Pitfalls and Prospects*, edited by Thomas Jäger and Gerhard Kümmel, pp. 213–240. Wiesbaden, Germany: VS Verlag für Sozialwissenschaften.

Kennedy, Peter E. 1998. *A Guide to Econometrics*. 4th ed. Cambridge, MA: MIT Press.

Kenney, Genevieve M., and Douglas A. Wissoker. 1994. "An Analysis of the Correlates of Discrimination Facing Young Hispanic Job-Seekers." *The American Economic Review* 84 (3) (June): 674–683. http://www.jstor.org/stable/2118075.

Kestnbaum, Meyer. 2000. "Citizenship and Compulsory Military Service: The Revolutionary Origins of Conscription in the United States." *Armed Forces & Society* 27 (1): 7–36.

Kier, Elizabeth. 1999. "Discrimination and Military Cohesion: An Organizational Perspective." In *Beyond Zero Tolerance: Discrimination in Military Culture*, edited by Mary Fainsod Katzenstein and Judith Reppy, pp. 25–52. New York: Rowman & Littlefield Publishers.

Kilburn, M. Rebecca, and Jacob Alex Klerman. 1999. *Enlistment Decisions in the 1990s: Evidence from Individual-Level Data*. Santa Monica, CA: RAND.

Kimerling, Rachel, Kristian Gima, Mark W. Smith, Amy Street, and Susan Frayne. 2007. "The Veterans Health Administration and Military Sexual Trauma." *American Journal of Public Health* 97 (12): 2160–2166.

King, Martin Luther Jr. 1998[1963]. "I Have a Dream." In *The Autobiography of Martin Luther King, Jr.*, edited by Clayborne Carson, pp. 223–227. New York: Warner Books.

Kirby, Sheila Natraj, Margaret Cecchine Harrell, and Jennifer Sloan. 2000. "Why Don't Minorities Join Special Operations Forces?" *Armed Forces & Society* 26: 523–545.

Kirschenman, Joleen, and Kathryn M. Neckerman. 1991. "'We'd Love to Hire Them, But . . . ': The Meaning of Race for Employers." In *The Urban Underclass*, edited by Christopher Jencks and Paul E. Peterson, pp. 203–234. Washington, DC: Brookings Institution.

Kleykamp, Meredith A. 2006. "College, Jobs, or the Military? Enlistment during a Time of War." *Social Science Quarterly* 87 (2): 272–290.

Kleykamp, Meredith A. 2007. "Military Service as a Labor Market Outcome." *Race, Gender & Class* 14 (3–4): 65–76.

Kleykamp, Meredith A. 2009a. "A Great Place to Start? The Effect of Prior Military Service on Hiring." *Armed Forces & Society* 35 (2): 266–285.

Kleykamp, Meredith A. 2009b. "Women's Work after War." Paper presented at the 2009 annual meeting of the Population Association of America, April 30–May 2, Detroit, Michigan.

Kleykamp, Meredith A. 2010. "Where Did the Soldiers Go? The Effects of Military Downsizing on College Enrollment and Employment." *Social Science Research* 39: 477–490.

Knapp, Gretchen. 2000. "Experimental Social Policymaking during World War II: The United Service Organizations (USO) and American War-Community Services (AWCS)." *Journal of Policy History* 12 (3) (November 3): 321–338.

Knights Out. 2010. "Knights Out—West Point Alumni Supporting LGBT Soldiers." Retrieved July 30, 2012, http://www.knightsout.org.

Kochavi, Arieh J. 2005. *Confronting Captivity: Britain and the United States and Their POWs in Nazi Germany*. Chapel Hill: The University of North Carolina Press.

Kohli, M. 1986. "The Worlds We Forgot: A Historical Review of the Life Course." In *Later Life*, edited by V. W. Marshall, pp. 271–303. Beverly Hills, CA: Sage Publications.

Kohli, M. 1988. "Social Organization and Subjective Construction of the Life Course." In *Human Development and the Life Cycle*, edited by A. B. Sorensen, F. E. Weiner, and L. R. Sherrod, pp. 271–292. Hillsdale, NJ: Lawrence Erlbaum Associates.

Kohli, M. 2007. "The Institutionalization of the Life Course: Looking Back to Look Ahead." *Research in Human Development* 4: 253–271.

Krebs, Ronald R. 2004. "A School for the Nation? How Military Service Does Not Build Nations, and How It Might." *International Security* 28 (4): 85–124.

Kuh, Diana, Chris Power, David Blane, and Mel Bartley. 1997. "Social Pathways between Childhood and Adult Health." In *A Life Course Approach to Chronic Disease Epidemiology*, edited by Diana Kuh and Yoav Ben Schlomo, pp. 169–198. Oxford, UK: Oxford University Press.

Kulka, Richard A., William E. Schlenger, John A. Fairbank, Richard L. Hough, B. Kathleen Jordan, Charles R. Marmar, Daniel S. Weiss, David A. Grady, and Senator Alan Cranston. 1990. *Trauma and the Vietnam War Generation: Report of Findings from the National Vietnam Veterans Readjustment Study*. New York: Brunner/Mazel.

LaRossa, Ralph. 2011. *Of War and Men: World War II in the Lives of Fathers and Their Families*. Chicago: University of Chicago Press.

Laub, John H., and Robert J. Sampson. 1993. "Turning Points in the Life Course—Why Change Matters to the Study of Crime." *Criminology* 31 (3): 301–325.

Laub, John H., and Robert J. Sampson. 2003. *Shared Beginnings, Divergent Lives: Delinquent Boys to Age 70*. Cambridge, MA: Harvard University Press.

Laufer, Robert S., and M. S. Gallops. 1985. "Life-Course Effects of Vietnam Combat and Abusive Violence—Marital Patterns." *Journal of Marriage and the Family* 47 (4): 839–853.

Laufer, Robert S., Thomas Yager, Ellen Frey-Wouters, and Joan Donnellan. 1981. "Postwar Trauma: Social and Psychological Problems of Vietnam Veterans in the Aftermath of the Vietnam War." In *Legacies of Vietnam: Comparative Adjustment of Veterans and Their Peers*, edited by Arthur Egendorf, Charles Kadushin, Robert S. Laufer, George Rothbart, and Lee Sloan, pp. 19–44. New York: Center for Policy Research.

Laumann, Edward O., John H. Gagnon, Robert T. Michael, and Stuart Michaels. 1994. *The Social Organization of Sexuality: Sexual Practices in the United States*. Chicago: University of Chicago Press.

LaVerda, Nancy, Andrea Vessey, and William F. Waters. 2006. "Use of the Veterans History Project to Assess World War II Veterans' Perceptions of Military Experiences and Health." *Military Medicine* 171 (11): 1076–1082.

Leal, David L. 1999. "It's Not Just a Job: Military Service and Latino Political Participation." *Political Behavior* 21 (2): 153–174.

Lee, Erika, and Judy Yung. 2010. *Angel Island: Gateway to America*. Oxford, UK: Oxford University Press.

Lee, Kimberly A., George E. Vaillant, William C. Torrey, and Glen H. Elder Jr. 1996. "A 50-Year Prospective Study of the Psychological Sequelae of World War II Combat." ARI Research Note 96–19. Alexandria, VA: U.S. Army Research Institute for the Behavioral and Social Sciences. Retrieved July 30, 2012, http://www.dtic.mil/cgi-bin/GetTRDoc?Location=U2&doc=GetTRDoc.pdf&AD=ADA319601.

Lee, Robert E., and Clifford Dowdey (eds.). 1961. *The Wartime Papers of R. E. Lee*. New York: Little, Brown.

Legree, Peter J., Paul A. Gade, Daniel E. Martin, M. A. Fischl, Michael J. Wilson, Veronica F. Nieva, Rod McCloy, and Janice Laurence. 2000. "Military Enlistment and Family Dynamics: Youth and Parental Perspectives." *Military Psychology* 12 (1): 31–49.

Lehring, Gary L. 2003. *Officially Gay: The Political Construction of Sexuality by the U.S. Military*. Philadelphia: Temple University Press.

Leland, Anne, and Mari-Jana Oboroceanu. 2010. "American War and Military Operations Casualties: Lists and Statistics." CRS Report RL32492. Washington DC: Congressional Research Service.

Levy, Yagil. 1998. "Militarizing Inequality: A Conceptual Framework." *Theory and Society* 27 (6): 873–904.

Lin, Nan. 1999. "Social Networks and Status Attainment." *Annual Review of Sociology* 25: 467–487.

Link, Bruce, and Jo Phelan. 2010. "Social Conditions as Fundamental Causes of Health Inequalities." In *Handbook of Medical Sociology*, edited by Chloe E. Bird, Peter Conrad, Allen M. Freemont, and Stefan Timmermans, pp. 3–17. Nashville, TN: Vanderbilt University Press.

Lipari, Rachel N., Paul J. Cook, Lindsay M. Rock, and Kenneth Matos. 2008. "2006 Gender Relations Survey of Active Duty Members (WGRA2006)." No. A166674. Arlington, VA: Defense Manpower Data Center.

Little, Roger D., and John Eric Fredland. 1979. "Veteran Status, Earnings, and Race—Some Long-Term Results." *Armed Forces & Society* 5 (2): 244–260.

Little, Roger D., and John J. Hisnanick. 2007. "The Earnings of Tied-Migrant Military Husbands." *Armed Forces & Society* 33 (4): 547–570.

Liu, Xian, Charles C. Engel, Han K. Kang, and David Cowan. 2005. "The Effect of Veteran Status on Mortality among Older Americans and Its Pathways." *Population Research and Policy Review* 24 (6): 573–592. ISI:000235138500002.

Logue, Larry, and Peter Blanck. 2008. "'Benefit of the Doubt': African-American Civil War Veterans and Pensions." *Journal of Interdisciplinary History* 28: 377–399.

London, Andrew S. and Nancy A. Myers. 2006. "Race, Incarceration, and Health: A Life Course Approach." *Research on Aging* 28(3): 409–422.

London, Andrew S., Elizabeth Allen, and Janet M. Wilmoth. forthcoming. "Veteran Status Extramarital Sex, and Divorce: Findings from the 1992 National Health and Social Life Survey." *Journal of Family Issues*.

London, Andrew S., Colleen Heflin, and Janet M. Wilmoth. 2011. "Work-Related Disability, Veteran Status, and Poverty: Implications for Family Well-Being." *Journal of Poverty* 15: 1–20.

London, Andrew S., and Janet M. Wilmoth. 2006. "Military Service and (Dis)Continuity in the Life Course—Evidence on Disadvantage and Mortality from the Health and Retirement Study and the Study of Assets and Health Dynamics among the Oldest-Old." *Research on Aging* 28 (1): 135–159.

Lopreato, Sally C., and Dudley L. Poston. 1977. "Differences in Earnings and Earnings Ability between Black Veterans and Non-Veterans in the United States." *Social Science Quarterly* 57 (4): 750–766.

Loughran, David S. 2002. *Wage Growth in the Civilian Careers of Military Retirees*. Santa Monica, CA: RAND.

Loughran, David S., Jacob Alex Klerman, and Craig W. Martin. 2006. *Activation and the Earnings of Reservists*. Santa Monica, CA: RAND.

Louis Harris and Associates. 1980. "Myths and Realities: A Study of Attitudes toward Vietnam Era Veterans, Submitted by the Veterans' Administration to the Committee on Veterans' Affairs, United States Senate." 96th Congress, 2d session. Senate Committee Print No. 29; GPO Item No: 1046-A. Washington, DC: Government Printing Office.

Louis Harris and Associates. 1985. "Survey of Female Veterans: A Study of the Needs, Attitudes, and Experiences of Women Veterans." Study No. 843002, Item 985. Washington, DC: Veterans Administration, Office of Information Management and Statistics, Statistical Policy and Research Service, Research Division.

Lumey, L. H., and Frans W. A. Vanpoppel. 1994. "The Dutch Famine of 1944–45—Mortality and Morbidity in Past and Present Generations." *Social History of Medicine* 7 (2): 229–246. ISI:A1994PE53600003.

Lundquist, Jennifer Hickes. 2004. "When Race Makes No Difference: Marriage and the Military." *Social Forces* 83 (2): 731–757.

Lundquist, Jennifer Hickes. 2006. "The Black-White Gap in Marital Dissolution among Young Adults: What Can a Counterfactual Scenario Tell Us?" *Social Problems* 53 (3): 421–441.

Lundquist, Jennifer Hickes. 2007. "A Comparison of Civilian and Enlisted Divorce Rates during the Early All Volunteer Force Era." *Journal of Political and Military Sociology* 35 (2) (December 1): 199–217.

Lundquist, Jennifer Hickes. 2008. "Reevaluating Ethnic and Gender Satisfaction Differences:The Effect of a Meritocratic Institution." *American Sociological Review* 73 (3): 447–496.

Lundquist, Jennifer Hickes, Irma T. Elo, Wanda Barfield, and Zhun Xu. 2010. "Race and Preterm Births: A Protective Effect of the Military?" Nationwide Scientific Broadcast for CDC's Division of Reproductive Health, Atlanta, GA.

Lundquist, Jennifer Hickes, and Herbert L. Smith. 2005. "Family Formation among Women in the US Military: Evidence from the NLSY." *Journal of Marriage and the Family* 67 (1): 1–13.

Lutz, Amy. 2008. "Who Joins the Military: A Look at Race, Class, and Immigration Status." *Journal of Political and Military Sociology* 36 (2): 167–188.

Lyson, Thomas A., and Charles M. Tolbert. 1996. "Small Manufacturing and Nonmetropolitan Socioeconomic Well-Being." *Environment and Planning* A28 (10) (October): 1779–1794.

MacGregor, Morris J. 1981. *Integration of the Armed Forces, 1940–1965*. Washington, DC: United States Army, Center of Military History.

MacLean, Alair. 2005. "Lessons from the Cold War: Military Service and College Education." *Sociology of Education* 78 (3): 250–266.

MacLean, Alair. 2010. "The Things They Carry: Combat, Disability, and Unemployment among U.S. Men." *American Sociological Review* 75 (4): 563–585.

MacLean, Alair, and Ryan D. Edwards. 2010. "The Pervasive Role of Rank in the Health of US Veterans." *Armed Forces & Society* 36 (5) (October): 765–785.

MacLean, Alair, and Glen H. Elder Jr. 2007. "Military Service in the Life Course." *Annual Review of Sociology* 33: 175–196.

Mahon, John K. 1960. *The American Militia Decade of Decision 1789–1800*. Gainesville: University Press of Florida.

Mahon, John K. 1983. *History of the Militia and the National Guard*. New York: Macmillan.

Mangione, Jerre, and Ben Morreale. 1992. *La Storia: Five Centuries of the Italian American Experience*. New York: HarperPerennial.

Mangum, Stephen L., and David E. Ball. 1987. "Military Skill Training—Some Evidence of Transferability." *Armed Forces & Society* 13 (3): 425–441.

Mangum, Stephen L., and David E. Ball. 1989. "The Transferability of Military-Provided Occupational Training in the Post-Draft Era." *Industrial & Labor Relations Review* 42 (2): 230–245.

Manning, Lory. 2005. *Women in the Military: Where They Stand*. Washington, DC: Women's Research and Education Institute.

Manski, Charles F., and David A. Wise. 1983. *College Choice in America*. Cambridge, MA: Harvard University Press.

Marchant, Karen H., and Frederic J. Medway. 1987. "Adjustment and Achievement Associated with Mobility in Military Families." *Psychology in the Schools* 24 (3): 289–294.

Marcus, Eric. 2002. *Making Gay History: The Half-Century Fight for Lesbian and Gay Equal Rights*. New York: HarperCollins.

Mare, Robert D., and Christopher Winship. 1984. "The Paradox of Lessening Racial Inequality and Joblessness among Black Youth—Enrollment, Enlistment, and Employment, 1964–1981." *American Sociological Review* 49 (1): 39–55.

Mare, Robert D., Christopher Winship, and Warren N. Kubitschek. 1984. "The Transition from Youth to Adult—Understanding the Age Pattern of Employment." *American Journal of Sociology* 90 (2): 326–358.

Mariscal, George. 1999. *Aztlán and Viet Nam: Chicano and Chicana Experiences of the War.* Berkeley: University of California Press.

Markusen, Ann R., Patrick Hall, Scott Campbell, and Sabrina Detrick. 1991. *The Rise of the Gunbelt: The Military Remapping of Industrial America.* New York: Oxford University Press.

Marmion, Harry A. 1971. *The Case against a Volunteer Army.* Chicago: Quadrangle Books.

Marmot, Michael G., George D. Smith, Stephen Stansfeld, Chandra Patel, Fiona North, Jenny Head, Ian White, Eric Brunner, and Amanda Feeney. 1991. "Health Inequalities among British Civil Servants—the Whitehall II Study." *Lancet* 337 (8754): 1387–1393.

Martindale, Melanie, and Dudley L. Poston. 1979. "Variations in Veteran-Nonveteran Earnings Patterns among World War II, Korea, and Vietnam War Cohorts." *Armed Forces & Society* 5 (2): 219–243.

Massey, Douglas S. 1990. "Social Structure, Household Strategies, and the Cumulative Causation of Migration." *Population Index* 56 (1): 3–26. ISI:A1990DF49300001.

Massey, Douglas S., and Nancy A. Denton. 1993. *American Apartheid: Segregation and the Making of the Underclass.* Cambridge, MA: Harvard University Press.

Massie, Dawn L., and Kenneth L. Campbell. 1993. *Analysis of Accident Rates by Age, Gender, and Time of Day Based on the 1990 Nationwide Personal Transportation Survey.* Ann Arbor: University of Michigan Transportation Research Institute.

Mattila, J. Peter. 1978. "GI Bill Benefits and Enrollments—How Did Vietnam Veterans Fare." *Social Science Quarterly* 59 (3): 535–545. ISI:A1978GG29700009.

Mayer, Albert J., and Thomas Ford Hoult. 1955. "Social Stratification and Combat Survival." *Social Forces* 34 (2): 155–159.

Mayer, Karl Ulrich. 2009. "New Directions in Life Course Research." *Annual Review of Sociology* 35: 413–433.

McCall, Leslie. 2005. "The Complexity of Intersectionality." *Signs* 30 (3): 1771–1800.

McCarthy, John F., Marcia Valenstein, and Frederic C. Blow. 2007. "Residential Mobility among Patients in the VA Health System: Associations with Psychiatric Morbidity, Geographic Accessibility, and Continuity of Care." *Administration and Policy in Mental Health and Mental Health Services Research* 34 (5): 448–455.

McClintock, Megan J. 1996. "Civil War Pensions and the Reconstruction of Union Families." *Journal of American History* 83 (2): 456–480.

McClintock, Megan J. 2002. "The Impact of the Civil War on Nineteenth-Century Marriages." In *Union Soldiers and the Northern Home Front: Wartime Experiences, Postwar Adjustments*, edited by Paul Alan Cimbala and Randall M. Miller, pp. 395–416. New York: Fordham University Press.

McDonagh, Edward C. 1946. "The Discharged Serviceman and His Family." *American Journal of Sociology* 51 (5): 451–454. ISI:000205009000015.

McGuire, S. H., and Dorothy W. Conrad. 1946. "Postwar Plans of Army and Navy Nurses." *American Journal of Nursing* 46 (5): 305–306.

McKain, Jerry Lavin. 1973. "Relocation in the Military—Alienation and Family Problems." *Journal of Marriage and the Family* 35 (2): 205–209.

McMinn, John H., and Max Levin. 1963. *Personnel in World War II.* Washington, DC: Department of the U.S. Army.

Meadows, William C. 1999. *Kiowa, Apache, and Comanche Military Societies.* Austin: University of Texas Press.

Meadows, William C. 2002. *The Comanche Code Talkers of World War II.* Austin: University of Texas Press.

Mehay, Stephen L., and Barry T. Hirsch. 1996. "The Postmilitary Earnings of Female Veterans." *Industrial Relations* 35 (2): 197–217.

Mehay, Stephen L., and Paul F. Hogan. 1998. "The Effect of Separation Bonuses on Voluntary Quits: Evidence from the Military's Downsizing." *Southern Economic Journal* 65 (1): 127–139.

Meid, Pat. 1964. *Marine Corps Women's Reserve in World War II.* Washington, DC: U.S. Marine Corps.

Mental Health Advisory Team. 2008. "Mental Health Advisory Team (MHAT) V: Operation Iraqi Freedom 06–08: Iraq; Operation Enduring Freedom 8: Afghanistan." Retrieved July 30, 2012, http://www.armymedicine.army.mil/reports/mhat/mhat_v/Redacted1-MHATV-4-FEB-2008-Overview.pdf.

Mershon, Sherie, and Steven Schlossman. 1998. *Foxholes and Color Lines: Desegregating the U.S. Armed Forces.* Baltimore, MD: The Johns Hopkins University Press.

Merton, Robert King. 1968. "Matthew Effect in Science." *Science* 159 (3810): 56+. ISI:A1968A419500007.

Mettler, Suzanne. 2002. "Bringing the State Back in to Civic Engagement: Policy Feedback Effects of the GI Bill for World War II Veterans." *American Political Science Review* 96 (2): 351–365.

Mettler, Suzanne. 2005. *Soldiers to Citizens: The G.I. Bill and the Making of the Greatest Generation.* New York: Oxford University Press.

Meyer, Denny. 2010. "Interview with Lt. Dan Choi." July 22. Gay Military Signal. http://www.gaymilitarysignal.com/1008Choi.html.

Meyer, J. 1986. "The Self and the Life Course: Institutionalization and Its Effects." In *Human Development and the Life Cycle*, edited by A. B. Sorensen, F. E. Weiner, and L. R. Sherrod, pp. 199–216. Hillsdale, NJ: Lawrence Erlbaum Associates.

Miles, Donna. 2004. "DoD Aims to Attract More Hispanics to Its Work Force." U.S. Department of Defense, American Forces Press Service News Articles. Retrieved June 4, 2008, http://www.defense.gov/news/newsarticle.aspx?id=25079.

Military Family Resource Center. 2000. *Military Families in the Millennium.* March 1. Arlington, VA: MFRC. Retrieved July 19, 2012, http://www.militaryhomefront.dod.mil/dav/lsn/LSN/BINARY_RESOURCE/BINARY_CONTENT/1725341.pdf.

Miller, Ann R. 1969. "Note on Some Problems in Interpreting Migration Data from 1960 Census of Population." *Demography* 6 (1): 13–16.

Miller, Laura L. 1997. "Not Just Weapons of the Weak: Gender Harassment as a Form of Protest for Army Men." *Social Psychology Quarterly* 60 (3): U3.

Miller, Randall M., Harry S. Stout, and Charles Reagan Wilson. 1998. *Religion and the American Civil War.* New York: Oxford University Press.

Mission: Readiness. 2010. "Too Fat to Fight: Retired Military Leaders Want Junk Food Out of America's Schools." Retrieved May 1, 2012, http://cdn.missionreadiness.org/MR_Too_Fat_to_Fight-1.pdf.

Mitchell, Reid. 1988. *Civil War Soldiers.* New York: Viking.

Mitchell, Reid. 1995. *The Vacant Chair: The Northern Soldier Leaves Home.* New York: Oxford University Press.

Modell, John. 1989. *Into One's Own: From Youth to Adulthood in the United States.* Berkeley: University of California Press.

Modell, John. 1995. "Did the Good War Make Good Workers?" In *The Home-Front War: World War II and American Society*, edited by Kenneth Paul O'Brien and Lynn H. Parsons, pp. 139–156. Westport, CT: Greenwood Press.

Modell, John, and Timothy Haggerty. 1991. "The Social Impact of War." *Annual Review of Sociology* 17: 205–224. http://www.jstor.org/stable/2083341.

Moody, James. 2005. "Fighting a Hydra: A Note on the Network Embeddedness of the War on Terror." *Structure and Dynamics* 1 (2). Retrieved May 1, 2012, http://escholarship.org/uc/item/7x3881bs.

Morin, Raul. 1963[2008]. "Among the Valiant: Mexican Americans in WWII and Korea." In *World War II and Mexican American Civil Rights*, edited by Richard Griswold del Castillo and Gris. Austin: University of Texas Press.

Mortimer, Jeylan T., and Michael J. Shanahan. 2003. *Handbook of the Life Course*. New York: Kluwer Academic/Plenum Publishers.

Morton, John. 2011. "Exercising Prosecutorial Discretion Consistent with the Civil Immigration Enforcement Priorities of the Agency for the Apprehension, Detention, and Removal of Aliens." June. Department of Homeland Security, U.S. Immigration and Customs Enforcement. Retrieved July 31, 2012, http://www.ice.gov/doclib/secure-communities/pdf/prosecutorial-discretion-memo.pdf.

Moskos, Charles C. Jr., and John Sibley Butler. 1996. *All That We Can Be: Black Leadership and Racial Integration the Army Way*. New York: Basic Books.

Moss, Philip, and Chris Tilly. 1996. "'Soft' Skills and Race: An Investigation of Black Men's Employment Problems." *Work and Occupations* 23 (3): 252–276.

Mouw, Ted. 2000. "Job Relocation and the Racial Gap in Unemployment in Detroit and Chicago, 1980 to 1990." *American Sociological Review* 65 (5): 730–753.

Muller, Eric L. 2001. *Free to Die for Their Country: The Story of the Japanese American Draft Registers in World War II*. Chicago: University of Chicago Press.

Murdoch, Maureen, M. van Ryn, J. Hodges, and Diane C. Cowper. 2005. "Mitigating Effect of Department of Veteran Affairs Disability Benefits for Post-Traumatic Stress Disorder on Low Income." *Military Medicine* 170 (2): 137–140.

Nakano, Satoshi. 2006. "The Filipino World War II Veterans Equity Movement and the Filipino American Community." *Pacific and American Studies* 6: 53–81.

Nakasone, Edwin M. 1999. *The Nisei Soldier: Historical Essays on World War II and the Korean War*. 2nd ed. White Bear Lake, MN: J-Press Publishing.

National Research Council. 2003. "Determinants of Intention or Propensity." In *Attitudes, Aptitudes, and Aspirations of American Youth: Implications for Military Recruitment*, edited by National Research Council, pp. 190–217. Washington, DC: National Academies Press.

National Research Council. 2006. *Assessing Fitness for Military Enlistment: Physical, Medical, and Mental Health Standards*. Washington, DC: National Academies Press.

Naval History and Heritage Command. 2010. "Navajo Code Talkers: World War II Fact Sheet." Naval History and Heritage Command. Retrieved August 22, 2010, http://www.history.navy.mil/faqs/faq61–2.htm.

Nayback, Ann Marie. 2008. "Health Disparities in Military Veterans with PTSD— Influential Sociocultural Factors." *Journal of Psychosocial Nursing and Mental Health Services* 46 (6): 43–51.

Neckerman, Kathryn M., and Joleen Kirschenman. 1991. "Hiring Strategies, Racial Bias, and Inner-City Workers." *Social Problems* 38 (4): 433–447.

Neimeyer, Charles Patrick. 1996. *America Goes to War: A Social History of the Continental Army*. New York: University Press.

Nelson, Joel I., and Jon Lorence. 1988. "Metropolitan Earnings Inequality and Service Sector Employment." *Social Forces* 67 (2): 492–511. ISI:A1988R840200010.

Nesbit, Rebecca, and David A. Reingold. 2008. "Soldiers to Citizens: The Link between Military Service and Volunteering." Working Paper 10, RGK Center for Philanthropy and Community Service, University of Texas at Austin, Austin,

Texas. Retrieved June 15, 2009, www.utexas.edu/lbj/rgk/fellowship/2008papers/Nesbitt.pdf.

Norman, Elizabeth M. 1999. *We Band of Angels: The Untold Story of American Nurses Trapped on Bataan by the Japanese.* New York: Random House.

O'Brien, Marco. 2008. "5 Military Myths—BUSTED!" Military.com. Retrieved December 3, 2009, http://www.military.com/Recruiting/Content/0,13898,02262008-military-myths.htm.

O'Hare, William, and Bill Bishop. 2007. "Rural Soldiers Continue to Account for a Disproportionately High Share of U.S. Casualties in Iraq and Afghanistan." Fact Sheet No. 9, Fall. Durham: University of New Hampshire Carsey Institute.

O'Rand, Angela M. 1996. "The Precious and the Precocious: Understanding Cumulative Disadvantage and Cumulative Advantage over the Life Course." *Gerontologist* 36 (2) (April): 230–238.

O'Rand, Angela M. 2002. "Cumulative Advantage Theory in Life Course Research." *Annual Review of Gerontology and Geriatrics* 22: 14–30.

O'Rand, Angela M., and M. L. Krecker. 1990. "Concepts of the Life Cycle: Their History, Meanings, and Uses in the Social Sciences." *Annual Review of Sociology* 16: 241–262.

Obama, Barack. 2009. "Remarks by the President to the Hispanic Chamber of Commerce on a Complete and Competitive American Education, March 10." Washington, DC: The White House, Office of the Press Secretary.

Office of the Deputy Under Secretary of Defense—Installations and Environment. 2008. "U.S. Military Installations, Ranges, and Training Areas." Retrieved December 10, 2009, https://www1.nga.mil/ProductsServices/TopographicalTerrestrial/PublishingImages/8205XMILINST_049.jpg.

Oi, Walter Y. 1996. "Historical Perspectives on the All-Volunteer Force: The Rochester Connection." In *Professionals on the Front Line: Two Decades of the All-Volunteer Force,* edited by John Eric Fredland, Roger D. Little, Curtis L. Gilroy, and W. S. Sellman, pp. 37–54. Washington, DC: Brassey's Inc.

Okazawa-Rey, Margo. 1997. "Amerasian Children of GI Town: A Legacy of US Militarism in South Korea." *Asian Journal of Women's Studies* 3 (1): 71–102.

Olson, Keith W. 1974. *G.I. Bill, the Veterans and the Colleges.* Lexington: University Press of Kentucky.

Onkst, David H. 1998. "'First a Negro . . . Incidentally a Veteran': Black World War Two Veterans and the GI Bill of Rights in the Deep South, 1944–1948." *Journal of Social History* 31 (3) (Spring): 517–519.

Orfield, Gary. 1992. "Money, Equity, and College Access." *Harvard Educational Review* 62 (3): 337–372.

Orvis, Bruce R., and Beth J. Asch. 2001. *Military Recruiting: Trends, Outlook, and Implications.* Santa Monica, CA: RAND.

Pager, Devah. 2007. *Marked: Race, Crime, and Finding Work in an Era of Mass Incarceration.* Chicago: The University of Chicago Press.

Pager, Devah, Bruce Western, and Bart Bonikowski. 2009. "Discrimination in a Low-Wage Labor Market: A Field Experiment." *American Sociological Review* 74 (5):777–799.

Palloni, Alberto, Mary McEniry, Ana Luisa Dávila, and Alberto García Gurucharri. 2005. "The Influence of Early Conditions on Health Status among Elderly Puerto Ricans." *Biodemography and Social Biology* 52: 132–163.

Parker, Michael W., Vaughn R. A. Call, and William F. Barko. 1999. "Soldier and Family Wellness across the Life Course: A Developing Role for Social Workers." In *Social Work Practice in the Military,* edited by James G. Daley, pp. 255–274. New York: Haworth Press.

Parker, Michael W., Vaughn R. A. Call, Ronald W. Toseland, Mark Vaitkus, Lucinda Lee Roff, and James A. Martin. 2002. "Employed Women and Their

Aging Family Convoys: A Life Course Model of Parent Care Assessment and Intervention." *Journal of Gerontological Social Work* 40 (1/2): 101–121.

Parker, Michael W., George F. Fuller, Harold G. Koenig, Jeffrey M. Bellis, Mark A. Vaitkus, William F. Barko, and Joan Eitzen. 2001. "Soldier and Family Wellness across the Life Course: A Developmental Model of Successful Aging, Spirituality, and Health Promotion, Part II." *Military Medicine* 166 (7) (July): 561–570.

Parker, Michael W., George F. Fuller, Harold G. Koenig, Mark A. Vaitkus, Jeffrey M. Bellis, William F. Barko, Joan Eitzen, and Vaughan R. Call. 2001. "Soldier and Family Wellness across the Life Course: A Developmental Model of Successful Aging, Spirituality, and Health Promotion. Part I." *Military Medicine* 166 (6) (June): 485–489.

Parker, Michael W., L. Roff, D. Klemmack, Harold G. Koenig, P. Baker, and R. Allman. 2003. "Religiosity and Mental Health in Southern, Community-Dwelling Older Adults." *Aging & Mental Health* 7 (5): 390–397.

Paskoff, Paul F. 2008. "Measures of War: A Quantitative Examination of the Civil War's Destructiveness in the Confederacy." *Civil War History* 54 (1): 35–62.

Pattillo, Mary, David Weiman, and Bruce Western (eds.). 2004. *Imprisoning America: The Social Effects of Mass Incarceration*. New York: Russell Sage Foundation.

Paulson, Don, and Roger Simpson. 1996. *An Evening at the Garden of Allah: A Gay Cabaret in Seattle*. New York: Columbia University Press.

Pavalko, E. K., and Glen H. Elder Jr. 1990. "World War II and Divorce—A Life-Course Perspective." *American Journal of Sociology* 95 (5): 1213–1234.

Payne, Deborah M., John T. Warner, and Roger D. Little. 1992. "Tied Migration and Returns to Human-Capital—the Case of Military Wives." *Social Science Quarterly* 73 (2): 324–339.

Pearlin, Leonard I., Elizabeth G. Menaghan, Morton A. Lieberman, and Joseph T. Mullan. 1981. "The Stress Process." *Journal of Health and Social Behavior* 22 (4): 337–356. ISI:A1981MU21000002.

Pema, Elda, and Stephen L. Mehay. 2009. "The Effect of High School JROTC on Student Achievement, Educational Attainment, and Enlistment." *Southern Economic Journal* 76 (2): 533–552.

Pencak, William. 2009. *Encyclopedia of the Veteran in America*. Vol. 1. Santa Barbara, CA: ABC-CLIO.

Pettit, Beck, and Bruce Western. 2004. "Mass Imprisonment and the Life Course: Race and Class Inequality in US Incarceration." *American Sociological Review* 69 (2): 151–169.

Pew Hispanic Center. 2003. "Hispanics in the Military." Retrieved August 21, 2008, http://pewhispanic.org/files/reports/17.pdf.

Pew Research Center. 2011. "Pew Social and Demographic Trends Project, War and Sacrifice in the Post-9/11 Era: The Military-Civilian Gap." October 5, 2011. Washington, DC: Pew Research Center. Retrieved July 31, 2012, http://www.pewsocialtrends.org/2011/10/05/war-and-sacrifice-in-the-post-911-era/.

Phelan, S. M., J. M. Griffin, W. L. Hellerstedt, N. A. Sayer, A. C. Jensen, D. J. Burgess, and M. van Ryn. 2011. "Perceived Stigma, Strain, and Mental Health among Caregivers of Veterans with Traumatic Brain Injury." *Disability and Health Journal* 4: 177–184.

Phillips, Robert L., Paul J. Andrisani, Thomas N. Daymont, and Curtis L. Gilroy. 1992. "The Economic Returns to Military Service—Race-Ethnic Differences." *Social Science Quarterly* 73 (2): 340–359.

Pizarro, Judith, Roxane Cohen Silver, and JoAnn Prause. 2006. "Physical and Mental Health Costs of Traumatic War Experiences among Civil War Veterans." *Archives of General Psychiatry* 63 (2): 193–200.

Plane, David Allen, Chris J. Henrie, and Marc J. Perry. 2005. "Migration up and down the Urban Hierarchy and across the Life Course." *Proceedings of the National Academy of Sciences of the United States of America* 102 (43) (August 29): 15313–15318.

Plank, Stephen B., and Will J. Jordan. 2001. "Effects of Information, Guidance, and Actions on Postsecondary Destinations: A Study of Talent Loss." *American Educational Research Journal* 38 (4): 947–979.

Polich, J. Michael, James N. Dertouzos, and S. James Press. 1986. "The Enlistment Bonus Experiment." R-3353-FMP, March. Santa Monica, CA: RAND. http://www.dtic.mil/cgi-bin/GetTRDoc?AD=ADA167428&Location=U2&doc=GetTRDoc.pdf.

Pollard, Michael S., Benjamin R. Karney, and David S. Loughran. 2008. "Comparing Rates of Marriage and Divorce in Civilian, Military, and Veteran Populations." Paper presented at the annual meeting of the Population Association of America, April 17–19, New Orleans, Louisiana.

Polusny, Melissa A., and Maureen Murdoch. 2005. "Sexual Assault among Male Veterans." *Psychiatric Times* 22 (4) (April 1): 34–38.

Portes, Alejandro. 1998. "Social Capital: Its Origins and Applications in Modern Sociology." *Annual Review of Sociology* 24: 1–24.

Portes, Alejandro, and Ruben Rumbaut. 2006. *Immigrant America*. Berkeley: University of California Press.

Portes, Alejandro, and Min Zhou. 1993. "The New Second Generation—Segmented Assimilation and Its Variants." *Annals of the American Academy of Political and Social Science* 530: 74–96.

Posadas, Barbara Mercedes. 1999. *The Filipino Americans*. Westport, CT: Greenwood Press.

Powers, William K. 1980. "Plains Indians Music and Dance." In *Anthropology of the Great Plains*, edited by W. Raymond Wood and Margot Liberty, pp. 212–229. Lincoln: University of Nebraska Press.

Pozetta, George. 1995. "My Children Are My Jewels: Italian American Generations during World War II." In *The Home-Front War: World War II and American Society*, edited by Kenneth Paul O'Brien and Lynn H. Parsons, pp. 63–82. Westport, CT: Greenwood Press.

Preston, Julia. 2010. "Immigration Status of Army Spouses Often Leads to Snags." *The New York Times*, May 7.

Preston, Samuel H., Mark E. Hill, and Greg L. Drevenstedt. 1998. "Childhood Conditions That Predict Survival to Advanced Ages among African-Americans." *Social Science & Medicine* 47 (9): 1231–1246.

Pribesh, Shana, and Douglas B. Downey. 1999. "Why Are Residential and School Moves Associated with Poor School Performance?" *Demography* 36 (4) (November): 521–534.

Prokos, Anastasia, and Irene Padavic. 2000. "Earn All That You Can Earn: Income Differences between Women Veterans and Non-Veterans." *Journal of Political & Military Sociology* 28 (1): 60–74.

Putnam, Robert D. 2000. *Bowling Alone: The Collapse and Revival of American Community*. New York: Simon & Schuster.

Quarles, Benjamin. 1959. "The Colonial Militia and Negro Manpower." *Mississippi Valley Historical Review* 45 (4): 643–652. ISI:A1959CBG7100005.

Rable, George C. 1989. *Civil Wars: Women and the Crisis of Southern Nationalism*. Urbana: University of Illinois Press.

Radford, Alexandria Walton. 2009. *Military Service Members and Veterans in Higher Education: What the New GI Bill May Mean for Postsecondary Institutions*. Washington, DC: American Council on Education.

Radford, Alexandria Walton, and Thomas Weko. 2011. *Military Service Members and Veterans: A Profile of Those Enrolled in Undergraduate and Graduate Education in 2007–08. Stats in Brief*, 2011–163. Washington, DC: U.S. Department of Education, National Center for Education Statistics.

Ramirez, Roberto R. 2004. "We the People: Hispanics in the United States." Census 2000 Special Reports, CENSR-18. Washington, DC: United States Census Bureau.

Ramos, Henry A. J. 1998. *The American GI Forum: In Pursuit of the Dream, 1948–1983.* Houston, TX: Arte Público Press.

RAND Corporation. 2008. "Post-Deployment Stress: What Families Should Know, What Families Can Do." CP-535, March. Santa Monica, CA: RAND. http://www.rand.org/pubs/corporate_pubs/CP535-2008–03.html.

Randolph, Mary Walker. 1946. "What Army Nurses Expect from the Profession." *American Journal of Nursing* 46 (2): 95–97. ISI:000203562500007.

Ransom, Roger L., and Richard Sutch. 2001. *One Kind of Freedom: The Economic Consequences of Emancipation.* 2nd ed. New York: Cambridge University Press.

Raphael, Steven, and Michael A. Stoll. 2006. "Modest Progress: The Narrowing Spatial Mismatch between Blacks and Jobs in the 1990s." In *Redefining Urban and Suburban America: Evidence from Census 2000*, edited by Bruce Katz and Robert E. Lang, pp. 119–142. Washington, DC: The Brookings Institute.

Ren, Xinhua S., Katherine Skinner, Austin Lee, and Lewis Kazis. 1999. "Social Support, Social Selection and Self-Assessed Health Status: Results from the Veterans Health Study in the United States." *Social Science & Medicine* 48 (12): 1721–1734.

Renshaw, K. D., E. S. Allen, G. K. Rhoades, and R. K. Blais. 2011. "Distress in Spouses of Service Members with Symptoms of Combat-Related PTSD: Secondary Trauma or General Psychological Distress?" *Journal of Family Psychology* 25 (461): 469.

Rentz, E. Danielle, Stephen W. Marshall, Dana Loomis, Carri Casteel, Sandra L. Martin, and Deborah A. Gibbs. 2007. "Effect of Deployment on the Occurrence of Child Maltreatment in Military and Nonmilitary Families." *American Journal of Epidemiology* 165 (10): 1199–1206.

Reskin, Barbara F. 2003. "Including Mechanisms in our Models of Ascriptive Inequality." *American Sociological Review* 68 (1): 1–21.

Richardson, Christy, and Judith Waldrop. 2003. "Veterans: 2000." Census 2000 Brief, C2KBR-22. Washington, DC: United States Census Bureau.

Ricks, Thomas. 1997. "The Widening Gap between the Military and Society." *The Atlantic* July: 66–78.

Riley, Matilda White, and John Riley. 1994. "Age Integration and the Lives of Older People." *The Gerontologist* 24: 110–115.

Rimmer, Peter J. 1997. "US Western Pacific Geostrategy: Subic Bay before and after Withdrawal." *Marine Policy* 21 (4): 325–344.

Rimmerman, Craig A. 1996. *Gay Rights, Military Wrongs: Political Perspectives on Lesbians and Gays in the Military.* New York: Garland Publishing.

Rindfuss, Ronald. 1991. "The Young Adult Years: Diversity, Structural Change, and Fertility." *Demography* 28 (4): 493–512.

Rindfuss, Ronald, Gray C. Swicegood, and Rachel Rosenfeld. 1987. "Disorder in the Life Course: How Common and Does it Matter?" *American Sociological Review* 52: 785–801.

Ritchey, Julia. 2009. "US Army, Mental Health Experts Team Up to Fight Rising Suicide Rate." Voice of America News. Retrieved February 5, 2009, http://www.voanews.com/english/news/a-13–2009–01–30-voa59–68626972.html?renderforprint=1.

Rochin, Refugio I., and Lionel Fernandez. 2002. "U.S. Latino Patriots: From the American Revolution to Afghanistan, An Overview." Retrieved August 21, 2008, https://pewhispanic.org/files/reports/17.3.pdf.

Roman, Peter J., and David W. Tarr. 2001. "Military Professionalism and Policymaking: Is There a Civil-Military Gap at the Top? If So, Does It Matter?" In *Soldiers and Civilians: The Civil-Military Gap and American National Security*, edited by Peter D. Feaver and Richard H. Kohn, pp. 403–428. Cambridge, MA: MIT Press.

Rosen, Sherwin, and Paul Taubman. 1982. "Changes in Life-Cycle Earnings— What Do Social Security Data Show." *Journal of Human Resources* 17 (3): 321–338.

Rosen, Steve (writer and director), and Pat Morita (narrator). 1997. *Beyond Barbed Wire*. VCI Video. Turner Classic Movies.

Rosenbaum, James E. 2001. *Beyond College for All: Career Paths for the Forgotten Half*. New York: Russell Sage Foundation.

Rosenheck, Robert, Linda Frisman, and An Me Chung. 1994. "The Proportion of Veterans among Homeless Men." *American Journal of Public Health* 84 (3): 466–469.

Rosnick, David, and Dean Baker. 2010. "The Impact of the Housing Crash on the Wealth of the Baby Boom Cohorts." *Journal of Aging & Social Policy* 22 (2): 117–128.

Rossi, Alice. 1985. *Gender and the Life Course*. New York: Aldine de Gruyter.

Rothberg, Joseph M. 1991. "Stress and Suicide in the United States Army—Effects of Relocation on Service Members Mental Health." *Armed Forces & Society* 17 (3): 449–458.

Rowe, Michael. 2009. "Remembering Pfc. Barry Winchell on the 10th Anniversary of His Murder." Servicemembers Legal Defense Network. Retrieved July 30, 2012, http://www.sldn.org/blog/archives/remembering-pfc-barry-winchell-on-the-10th-anniversary-of-his-murder.

Ruger, William, Sven E. Wilson, and Shawn L. Waddoups. 2002. "Warfare and Welfare: Military Service, Combat, and Marital Dissolution." *Armed Forces & Society* 29 (1): 85–107.

Ruggles, Steven, J. Trent Alexander, Katie Genadek, Ronald Goeken, Matthew B. Schroeder, and Matthew Sobek. 2010. "Integrated Public Use Microdata Series: Version 5.0 [Machine-readable database]." Minneapolis, MN: University of Minnesota. Retrieved August 16, 2010, http://usa.ipums.org/usa.

Ruggles, Steven, Matthew Sobek, J. Trent Alexander, Catherine A. Fitch, Ronald Goeken, Patricia Kelly Hall, Miriam King, and Chad Ronnander. 2008. "Integrated Public Use Microdata Series: Version 4.0 [Machine-readable database]." Minneapolis: University of Minnesota. Retrieved May 6, 2010, http://usa.ipums.org/usa/ipums_4_point_0.shtml.

Rupp, Leila J., and Verta A. Taylor. 1987. *Survival in the Doldrums: The American Women's Rights Movement, 1945 to the 1960s*. New York: Oxford University Press.

Ryan, Kathleen M. 2008. "'When Flags Flew High': Propaganda, Memory, and Oral History for World War II Female Veterans." Ph.D. Dissertation, School of Journalism and Communication, University of Oregon, Eugene, Oregon.

Ryder, Norman B. 1965. "The Cohort as a Concept in the Study of Social Change." *American Sociological Review* 30 (6) (December): 843–861.

Sabol, William J., Heather C. West, and Matthew Cooper. 2009. "Prisoners in 2008." Bureau of Justice Statistics Bulletin, NCJ 228417. Washington, DC: U.S. Department of Justice.

Sampson, Robert J., and John H. Laub. 1996. "Socioeconomic Achievement in the Life Course of Disadvantaged Men: Military Service as a Turning Point, circa 1940–1965." *American Sociological Review* 61 (3): 347–367.

Sampson, Robert J., Jeffrey D. Morenoff, and Thomas Gannon-Rowley. 2002. "Assessing 'Neighborhood Effects': Social Processes and New Directions in Research." *Annual Review of Sociology* 28: 443–478.

Sanders, John W., Shannon D. Putnam, Carla Frankart, Robert W. Frenck, Marshall R. Monteville, Mark S. Riddle, David M. Rockabrand, Trueman W. Sharp, and David R. Tribble. 2005. "Impact of Illness and Non-Combat Injury during Operations Iraqi Freedom and Enduring Freedom (Afghanistan)." *American Journal of Tropical Medicine and Hygiene* 73 (4): 713–719.

Sarnecky, Mary T. 1999. *A History of the U.S. Army Nurse Corps.* Philadelphia: University of Pennsylvania Press.

Sassen, Saskia. 1990. "Economic Restructuring and the American City." *Annual Review of Sociology* 16: 465–490.

Savoca, Elizabeth, and Robert Rosenheck. 2000. "The Civilian Labor Market Experiences of Vietnam-Era Veterans: The Influence of Psychiatric Disorders." *Journal of Mental Health Policy and Economics* 3 (4) (December): 199–207.

Savych, Bogdan. 2008. "Effects of Deployments on Spouses of Military Personnel." Ph.D. Dissertation, Policy Analysis, RAND Graduate School, Santa Monica, California.

Scholz, John Karl, and Ananth Seshadri. 2009. "Children and Household Wealth." Retrieved September 27, 2011, http://www.ssc.wisc.edu/~scholz/Research/Children.pdf.

Schwab, Stephen. 2002. "The Role of the Mexican Expeditionary Air Force in World War II." *The Journal of Military History* 66: 115–140.

Schwalm, Leslie A. 1997. "'Sweet Dreams of Freedom'': Freedwomen's Reconstruction of Life and Labor in Lowcountry South Carolina." *Journal of Women's History* 9 (1): 9–38.

Schwartz, J. Brad, Lisa L. Wood, and Janet D. Griffith. 1991. "The Impact of Military Life on Spouse Labor-Force Outcomes." *Armed Forces & Society* 17 (3): 385–407.

Scott, Sean A. 2008. "'Earth Has No Sorrow That Heaven Cannot Cure': Northern Civilian Perspectives on Death and Eternity during the Civil War." *Journal of Social History* 41 (4): 843–866.

Scott, Wilbur J. 1992. "PTSD and Agent Orange—Implications for a Sociology of Veterans Issues." *Armed Forces & Society* 18 (4): 592–612.

Seeborg, Michael C. 1994. "Race, Poverty, and Enlistment: Some Evidence from the National Longitudinal Survey of Youth." *Journal of Economics* 20 (1): 15–24.

Segal, David R. 1989. *Recruiting for Uncle Sam: Citizenship and Military Manpower Policy.* Lawrence: University Press of Kansas.

Segal, David R., Jerald G. Bachman, Peter Freedman-Doan, and Patrick M. O'Malley. 1999. "Propensity to Serve in the US Military: Temporal Trends and Subgroup Differences." *Armed Forces & Society* 25 (3): 407–427.

Segal, David R., Thomas J. Burns, William W. Falk, Michael P. Silver, and Bam Dev Sharda. 1998. "The All-Volunteer Force in the 1970s." *Social Science Quarterly* 79 (2): 390–411.

Segal, David R., Peter Freedman-Doan, Jerald G. Bachman, and Patrick M. O'Malley. 2001. "Attitudes of Entry-Level Enlisted Personnel: Pro-Military and Politically Mainstreamed." In *Soldiers and Civilians: The Civil-Military Gap and American National Security*, edited by Peter D. Feaver, Richard H. Kohn, and Triangle Institute for Security Studies, pp. 163–212. Cambridge, MA: Belfer Center for Science and International Affairs.

Segal, David R., and Mady Wechsler Segal. 2004. "America's Military Population." *Population Bulletin* 59 (4): 3–6.

Segal, David R., and Mady Weehler Segal. 2005. "U.S. Military's Reliance on the Reserves." Population Reference Bureau. Retrieved February 7, 2012, http://www.prb.org/Articles/2005/USMilitarysRelianceontheReserves.aspx.

Segal, Mady Wechsler. 1986. "The Military and the Family as Greedy Institutions." *Armed Forces & Society* 13 (1): 9–38.

Segal, Mady Wechsler, and Chris Bourg. 2002. "Professional Leadership and Diversity in the Army." Chapter 23 in *The Future of the Army Profession*, edited by Lloyd J. Matthews, pp. 505–520. Boston: McGraw-Hill.

Segal, Mady Wechsler, David R. Segal, Jerald G. Bachman, Peter Freedman-Doan, and Patrick M. O'Malley. 1998. "Gender and the Propensity to Enlist in the U.S. Military." *Gender Issues* 16 (3) (Summer): 65–87.

Segal, Mady Wechsler, Meridith Hill Thanner, and David R. Segal. 2007. "Hispanic and African American Men and Women in the U.S. Military: Trends in Representation." *Race, Gender & Class* 14 (3–4): 48–64.

Seidman, Steven. 2002. *Beyond the Closet: The Transformation of Gay and Lesbian Life*. New York: Routledge.

Selective Service System. 1971. "Semiannual Report of the Director of Selective Service for the Period July 1 to December 31, 1970." Washington, DC: U.S. Government Printing Office.

Selective Service System. 2008. "Effects of Marriage and Fatherhood on Draft Eligibility." Retrieved August 19, 2010, http://www.sss.gov/FSeffects.htm.

Selective Service System. 2009. "History and Records: The Vietnam Lotteries." Retrieved October 21, 2009, http://www.sss.gov/lotter1.htm.

Servicemembers Legal Defense Network. 2009a. "About 'Don't Ask, Don't Tell.'" SLDN Reports. Retrieved December 21, 2009, http://www.sldn.org/pages/about-dadt.

Servicemembers Legal Defense Network. 2009b. "Transgender Issues." Retrieved December 16, 2009, http://www.sldn.org/pages/transgender-issues.

Servicemembers United. 2011. "DOD and DHS Release Dates DADT Discharge Numbers." Retrieved July 30, 2012, http://www.servicemembers.org/2011/department-of-defense-and-department-of-homeland-security-release-latest-dadt-discharge-numbers.

Settersten, Richard A. 1999. *Lives in Time and Place: The Problems and Promises of Developmental Sciences*. Amityville, NY: Baywood Publishing.

Settersten, Richard A. 2003. "Propositions and Controversies in Life-Course Scholarship." Chapter 1 in *Invitation to the Life Course: Toward New Understandings of Later Life*, edited by Richard A. Settersten, pp. 15–48. Amityville, NY: Baywood Publishing.

Settersten, Richard A. 2006. "When Nations Call—How Wartime Military Service Matters for the Life Course and Aging." *Research on Aging* 28 (1): 12–36.

Settersten, Richard A., and Robin S. Patterson. 2006. "Military Service, the Life Course, and Aging: An Introduction." *Research on Aging* 28 (1): 5–11.

Settersten, Richard A., and Barbara Ray. 2010. "What's Going On with Young People Today? The Long and Twisting Path to Adulthood." *The Future of Children* 20 (1): 19–41.

Shadish, William R., Thomas D. Cook, and Donald Thomas Campbell. 2002. *Experimental and Quasi-Experimental Designs for Generalized Causal Inference*. Boston: Houghton Mifflin.

Shanahan, Michael J. 2000. "Pathways to Adulthood in Changing Societies: Variability and Mechanisms in Life Course Perspective." *Annual Review of Sociology* 26: 667–692.

Sharritt, Edna E. 1946. "Where Are the Ex-Service Nurses?" *American Journal of Nursing* 46 (12): 849–851.

Shawver, Lois. 1995. *And the Flag Was Still There: Straight People, Gay People, and Sexuality in the U.S. Military*. New York: Haworth Press.

Shay, Jonathan. 2002. *Odysseus in America: Combat Trauma and the Trials of Homecoming*. New York: Scribner.

Sheets, C. J., and H. Mahoney-Gleason. 2010. "Caregiver Support in the Veteran Health Administration: Caring for Those Who Care." *Journal of the American Society of Aging* 34: 92–98.

Shen, Yu-Chu, Jeremy Arkes, Boon Wah Kwan, Lai Yee Tan, and Thomas V. Williams. 2009. "The Effect of OEF/OIF Deployment Intensity on the Rate of Posttraumatic Stress Disorder among Active Duty Population." NBER Working Paper No. w15203. Cambridge, MA: National Bureau of Economic Research.

Shilts, Randy. 1993. *Conduct Unbecoming: Gays and Lesbians in the U.S. Military*. New York: St. Martin's Press.

Shipherd, Jillian C., Jane Stafford, and Lynlee R. Tanner. 2005. "Predicting Alcohol and Drug Abuse in Persian Gulf War Veterans: What Role Do PTSD Symptoms Play?" *Addictive Behaviors* 30 (3): 595–599.

Siebold, Guy L. 2001. "Core Issues and Theory in Military Sociology." *Journal of Political & Military Sociology* 29 (1): 140–159.

Sigelman, Lee, and Susan Welch. 1993. "The Contact Hypothesis Revisited: Black-White Interaction and Positive Racial Attitudes." *Social Forces* 71 (3): 781–795.

Sims, Carra S., Fritz Drasgow, and Louise F. Fitzgerald. 2005. "The Effects of Sexual Harassment on Turnover in the Military: Time-Dependent Modeling." *Journal of Applied Psychology* 90 (6): 1141–1152.

Sinclair, G. Dean. 2009. "Homosexuality and the Military: A Review of the Literature." *Journal of Homosexuality* 56 (6): 701–718. ISI:000268702300002.

Skocpol, Theda. 1992. *Protecting Soldiers and Mothers: The Political Origins of Social Policy in the United States*. Cambridge, MA: Belknap Press of Harvard University Press.

Skocpol, Theda. 1997. "The GI Bill and US Social Policy, Past and Future." *Social Philosophy & Policy* 14 (2): 95–115.

Skrentny, John D. 2002. *The Minority Rights Revolution*. Cambridge, MA: Belknap Press of Harvard University Press.

Smith, David G. 2010. "Developing Pathways to Serving Together: Dual Military Couples' Life Course and Decision-Making." Ph.D. Dissertation, Department of Sociology, University of Maryland, College Park, Maryland.

Smith III, Irving, Kris Marsh, and David R. Segal. 2011. "The World War II Veteran Advantage? A Lifetime Cross-Sectional Study of Social Status Attainment." *Armed Forces & Society* 38 (1): 5–26.

Smith, Kirsten P., and Nicholas A. Christakis. 2008. "Social Networks and Health." *Annual Review of Sociology* 34: 405–429.

Smith, Tom W. 1984. "Recalling Attitudes—An Analysis of Retrospective Questions on the 1982 GSS." *Public Opinion Quarterly* 48 (3): 639–649. ISI:A1984TL32600009.

Snyder, R. Claire. 2003. "The Citizen-Soldier Tradition and Gender Integration of the US Military." *Armed Forces & Society* 29 (2): 185–204.

Sobol, William J., Heather C. West, and Matthew Cooper. 2010[2009]. "Prisoners in 2008." Washington, DC: U.S. Department of Justice, Bureau of Justice Statistics. Retrieved July 31, 2012, http://bjs.ojp.usdoj.gov/content/pub/pdf/p08.pdf.

Social Security Administration. 2010. "Income of the Population 55 or Older, 2008." Social Security Online. Retrieved July 17, 2012, http://www.socialsecurity.gov/policy/docs/statcomps/income_pop55/2008.

Spiro, Avron, Paula P. Schnurr, and Carolyn M. Aldwin. 1997. "A Life-Span Perspective on the Effects of Military Service." *Journal of Geriatric Psychiatry* 30 (1): 91–128.

Sprey, Pierre M. 2011. "Evaluating Weapons: Sorting the Good from the Bad." Essay 9 in *The Pentagon Labyrinth: 10 Short Essays to Help You through It*, edited by Winslow T. Wheeler. Washington, DC: World Security Institute, Center for Defense Information.

St. John, Edward P. 2003. *Refinancing the College Dream: Access, Equal Opportunity, and Justice for Taxpayers*. Baltimore, MD: The Johns Hopkins University Press.

Stanley, Marcus. 2003. "College Education and the Midcentury GI Bills." *Quarterly Journal of Economics* 118 (2): 671–708.

Stanton-Salazar, Ricardo D. 1997. "A Social Capital Framework for Understanding the Socialization of Racial Minority Children and Youths." *Harvard Educational Review* 67 (1): 1–41.

Starr, Paul, Ralph Nader, James F. Henry, and Raymond P. Bonner. 1974. *The Discarded Army: Veterans after Vietnam; The Nader Report on Vietnam Veterans and the Veterans Administration*. New York: Charterhouse.

Steele, Richard. 2008. "The Federal Government Discovers Mexican Americans." In *World War II and Mexican American Civil Rights*, edited by Richard Griswold del Castillo. Austin: University of Texas Press.

Steele, Richard, and Richard Griswold del Castillo. 2008. "Civil Rights and the Legacy of War." In *World War II and Mexican American Civil Rights*, edited by Richard Griswold del Castillo. Austin: University of Texas Press.

Sterba, Christopher M. 2003. *Good Americans: Italian and Jewish Immigrants during the First World War*. New York: Oxford University Press.

Stern, Sol. 1971. "When the Black G.I. Comes Home from Vietnam." In *The Black Soldier: From the American Revolution to Vietnam*, edited by Jay David and Elaine Forman Crane, pp. 215–227. New York: Morrow.

Sterner, C. Douglas. 2008. *Go For Broke. The Nisei Warriors of World War II Who Conquered Germany, Japan, and American Bigotry*. Clearfield, Utah: American Legacy Historical Press.

Stewart, James B., and Juanita M. Firestone. 2001. "Looking for a Few Good Men: Predicting Patterns of Retention, Promotion, and Accession of Minority and Women Officers." In *Managing Diversity in the Military*, edited by Mickey R. Dansby, James B. Stewart, and Schulyer C. Webb, pp. 231–256. New Brunswick, NJ: Transaction Publishers.

Stock, Lt. Col. Margaret D. 2006. "Essential to the Fight: Immigrants in the Military, Five Years after 9/11." *Immigration Policy in Focus* 5 (9). Washington, DC: American Immigration Law Foundation, Immigration Policy Center.

Stock, Lt. Col. Margaret D. 2009. "Essential to the Fight: Immigrants in the Military Eight Years after 9/11." Special Report. Washington, DC: American Immigration Law Foundation, Immigration Policy Center.

Stoll, Michael A. 1998. "When Jobs Move, Do Black and Latino Men Lose? The Effect of Growth in Job Decentralisation on Young Men's Jobless Incidence and Duration." *Urban Studies* 35 (12): 2221–2239.

Stouffer, Samuel A., Arthur A. Lumsdaine, Marion Harper Lumsdaine, Robin M. Williams Jr., M. Brewster Smith, Irving L. Janis, Shirley A. Star, and Leonard S. Cottrell Jr. 1945. "The American Soldier in World War II": "Attitudes of WACs" (Survey 194, February), "Attitudes of Army Nurses" (Survey 192A, January), "Attitudes of Nurses" (Survey 192B, January).

Stouffer, Samuel A., Arthur A. Lumsdaine, Marion Harper Lumsdaine, Robin M. Williams Jr., M. Brewster Smith, Irving L. Janis, Shirley A. Star, and Leonard S.

Cottrell Jr. 1949a. *The American Soldier,* Vol. 1: *Adjustment during Army Life.* Princeton, NJ: Princeton University Press.

Stouffer, Samuel A., Arthur A. Lumsdaine, Marion Harper Lumsdaine, Robin M. Williams Jr., M. Brewster Smith, Irving L. Janis, Shirley A. Star, and Leonard S. Cottrell Jr. 1949b. *The American Soldier,* Vol. 2: *Combat and Its Aftermath.* Princeton, NJ: Princeton University Press.

Strasser, William A. 1999. "'A Terrible Calamity Has Befallen Us': Unionist Women in Civil War East Tennessee." *Journal of East Tennessee History* 71 (January): 66–88.

Street, Debra. 2007a. "Too Much, Too Little, Just Right? Policy Disconnects in an Aging Society." *Public Policy and Aging Report* 17(3): 7–10.

Street, Debra. 2007b. "Aging and Social Policy." In *The Blackwell Encyclopedia of Sociology,* edited by George Ritzer, pp 84–88. Oxford: Blackwell Publishing.

Street, Debra, and Sarah Desai. 2011. "Planning for Old Age." In *Handbook of the Sociology of Aging,* edited by Jacqueline L. Angel and Richard A. Settersten, pp. 379–398. New York: Springer.

Street, Debra, and Janet M. Wilmoth. 2001. "Social Insecurity: Women and Pensions in the US." *Women, Work and Pensions: International Issues and Prospects,* edited by Jay Ginn, Debra Street, and Sara Arber, pp. 120–141. Buckingham, UK: Open University Press.

Sturdevant, Saundra Pollock, and Brenda Stoltzfus (eds.). 1992. *Let the Good Times Roll: Prostitution and the U.S. Military in Asia.* New York: New Press.

Suris, Alina, and Lisa Lind. 2008. "Military Sexual Trauma—A Review of Prevalence and Associated Health Consequences in Veterans." *Trauma, Violence, and Abuse* 9 (4): 250–269.

Suris, Alina, Lisa Lind, T. Michael Ashner, Patricia D. Orman, and Frederick Etty. 2004. "Sexual Assault in Women Veterans: An Examination of PTSD Risk, Health Care Utilization, and Cost of Care." *Psychosomatic Medicine* 66 (5): 749–756.

Takaki, Ronald T. 2000. *Double Victory: A Multicultural History of America in World War II.* New York: Back Bay Books.

Tanielian, Terri L., and Lisa H. Jaycox. 2008. *Invisible Wounds of War: Psychological and Cognitive Injuries, Their Consequences, and Services to Assist Recovery.* Santa Monica, CA: RAND.

Teachman, Jay D. 2004. "Military Service during the Vietnam Era: Were There Consequences for Subsequent Civilian Earnings?" *Social Forces* 83 (2): 709–730.

Teachman, Jay D. 2005. "Military Service in the Vietnam Era and Educational Attainment." *Sociology of Education* 78 (1): 50–68.

Teachman, Jay D. 2007a. "Military Service and Educational Attainment in the All-Volunteer Era." *Sociology of Education* 80 (4): 359–374.

Teachman, Jay D. 2007b. "Race, Military Service, and Marital Timing: Evidence from the NLSY-79." *Demography* 44 (2): 389–404.

Teachman, Jay D. 2010. "Are Veterans Healthier?: Military Service and Health at Age 40 in the All-Volunteer Force Era." *Social Science Review* 40: 326–335.

Teachman, Jay D., and Vaughn R. A. Call. 1996. "The Effect of Military Service on Educational, Occupational, and Income Attainment." *Social Science Research* 25 (1): 1–31.

Teachman, Jay D., Vaughn R. A. Call, and Mady Wechsler Segal. 1993a. "Family, Work, and School Influences on the Decision to Enter the Military." *Journal of Family Issues* 14 (2): 291–313.

Teachman, Jay D., Vaughn R. A. Call, and Mady Wechsler Segal. 1993b. "The Selectivity of Military Enlistment." *Journal of Political & Military Sociology* 21 (2): 287–309.

Teachman, Jay D., and Lucky M. Tedrow. 2004. "Wages, Earnings, and Occupational Status: Did World War II Veterans Receive a Premium?" *Social Science Research* 33 (4): 581–605.

Teachman, Jay D., and Lucky M. Tedrow. 2007. "Joining Up: Did Military Service in the Early All Volunteer Era Affect Subsequent Civilian Income?" *Social Science Research* 36 (4): 1447–1474.

Teachman, Jay D., and Lucky M. Tedrow. 2008. "Divorce, Race, and Military Service: More Than Equal Pay and Equal Opportunity." *Journal of Marriage and the Family* 70 (4): 1030–1044.

Teigen, Jeremy M. 2006. "Enduring Effects of the Uniform: Previous Military Experience and Voting Turnout." *Political Research Quarterly* 59 (4): 601–607.

Terry, Wallace. 1971. "The Angry Blacks in the Army." In *Two, Three . . . Many Vietnams: A Radical Reader on the Wars in Southeast Asia and the Conflicts at Home*, edited by Editors of Ramparts with Banning Garrett and Katherine Barkley, pp. 222–231. San Francisco: Canfield Press.

Tessler, Richard, Robert Rosenheck, and Gail Amache. 2003. "Homeless Veterans of the All-Volunteer Force: A Social Selection Perspective." *Armed Forces & Society* 29 (4): 509+.

Theriot, Matthew T. 2009. "School Resource Officers and the Criminalization of Student Behavior." *Journal of Criminal Justice* 37 (3): 280–287.

Titunik, Regina F. 2000. "The First Wave: Gender Integration and Military Culture." *Armed Forces & Society* 26 (2): 229–257.

Toppin, Edgar A. 1975. "Blacks in the American Revolution." *Crisis* 82 (7) (August–September): 249–255.

Treadwell, Mattie E. 1954. *United States Army in World War II: Special Studies: The Women's Army Corps*. Washington, DC: Department of the Army.

TRICARE. 2010. "What is TRICARE?" Retrieved December 1, 2010, http://www.tricare.mil/mybenefit/home/overview/WhatIsTRICARE?

Truman, Harry S. 1948. "Executive Order 9981." July 26. Retrieved July 30, 2012, http://www.trumanlibrary.org/9981.htm.

Tully, Meg. 2009. "Frederick County Takes Stand against Illegal Immigrant Workers." Frederick (MD) *News Post*, December 16. http://www.fredericknewspost.com/sections/archives/display_detail.htm?StoryID=105306.

Turner, C., Susan Frayne, and Editors. 2004. "Veterans Health Initiative: Military Sexual Trauma." TRACE Code 03.VHI.SH&T.P.A. Washington, DC: Department of Veteran Affairs.

Turner, Sarah, and John Bound. 2003. "Closing the Gap or Widening the Divide: The Effects of the GI Bill and World War II on the Educational Outcomes of Black Americans." *Journal of Economic History* 63 (1): 145–177.

Tyson, Ann Scott. 2005. "Youths in Rural U.S. Are Drawn to Military: Recruits' Job Worries Outweigh War Fears." *Washington Post*, November 4, A1. http://www.washingtonpost.com/wp-dyn/content/article/2005/11/03/AR2005110302528.html.

U.S. Air Force Academy. 2010. "Academy Vision Statement." Retrieved April 23, 2010,http://www.mybaseguide.com/air-force/academy.

U.S. Army Medical Services. 2010. "Standards of Medical Fitness." Army Regulation 40–501, 23 August. Washington, DC: Department of the Army. http://armypubs.army.mil/epubs/pdf/r40_501.pdf.

U.S. Bureau of Labor Statistics. 2010. "National Compensation Survey: Employee Benefits in the United States, March 2010." Bulletin 2752. Washington, DC: U.S. Department of Labor. http://www.bls.gov/ncs/ebs/benefits/2010/ebbl0046.pdf.

U.S. Bureau of Labor Statistics. 2011a. "Unemployment Rates." Series ID LNU04000003, LNU04000006, LNU04000009. Washington, DC: U.S. Bureau of the Census, Division of Labor Force Statistics.

U.S. Bureau of Labor Statistics. 2011b. "Employment Population Ratios." Series ID LNU02300003, LNU02300006, LNU02300009. Washington, DC: U.S. Bureau of the Census, Division of Labor Force Statistics.

U.S. Bureau of Labor Statistics. 2011c. "Employee Benefits in the United States: March 2011." January 14, 2011. http://www.bls.gov/news.release/pdf/ebs2.pdf.

U.S. Census Bureau. 1940. "Census of Population and Housing, 1940 Census." Retrieved February 7, 2012, http://www.census.gov/prod/www/abs/decennial/1940.html.

U.S. Census Bureau. 2003. *Statistical Abstract of the United States*. Washington, DC: Department of Commerce.

U.S. Census Bureau. 2007. "The 2007 Statistical Abstract: National Security and Veterans Affairs." Table 507, Veterans by Sex, Period of Service, and State, 2005. Washington, DC: Government Printing Office. Retrieved July 31, 2012, http://www.census.gov/prod/2006pubs/07statab/defense.pdf.

US Census Bureau. 2008. *Statistical Abstracts 1951–1994*. Retrieved August 21, 2008, http://www.census.gov/prod/www/abs/statab1951–1994.htm

U.S. Census Bureau. 2009. "Montana: Selected Economic Characteristics: 2006–2008." Retrived December 10, 2009, http://factfinder.census.gov/servlet/ADPTable?_bm=y&-geo_id=04000US30&-qr_name=ACS_2008_3YR_G00_DP3YR3&-ds_name=ACS_2008_3YR_G00_&-lang=en&-redoLog=false&-_sse=

U.S. Census Bureau. 2010. "Veteran Status: 2010 American Community Survey 1-Year Estimates." Retrieved March 3, 2012, http://factfinder2.census.gov/faces/tableservices/jsf/pages/productview.xhtml?pid=ACS_10_1YR_S2101&prodType=table.

U.S. Census Bureau. 2011. "Housing Vacancies and Homeownership." Retrieved February 29, 2012, http://www.census.gov/hhes/www/housing/hvs/qtr410/q410ind.html.

U.S. Citizenship and Immigration Services. 2010. "USCIS Naturalizes Largest Number of Service Members since 1955: Agency Continues Outreach to Members of the Military and Their Families." Retrieved February 7, 2012, http://www.uscis.gov/portal/site/uscis/menuitem.5af9bb95919f35e66f614176543f6d1a/?vgnextoid=628d8ef34e03c210VgnVCM100000082ca60aRCRD&vgnextchannel=6a6e25b763b17210VgnVCM100000082ca60aRCRD.

U.S. Citizenship and Immigration Services. 2011a. "E-Verify User Manual for Employers." Retrieved July 31, 2012, http://www.uscis.gov/USCIS/E-Verify/Customer%20Support/E-Verify%20User%20Manual%20for%20Employers%20R3%200-%20Final.pdf.

U.S. Citizenship and Immigration Services. 2011b. "What is E-Verify?" Retrieved July 31, 2012, http://www.uscis.gov/portal/site/uscis/menuitem.eb1d4c2a3e5b9ac89243c6a7543f6d1a/?vgnextoid=e94888e60a405110VgnVCM1000004718190aRCRD&vgnextchannel=e94888e60a405110VgnVCM1000004718190aRCRD.

U.S. Department of Labor. 1948. "Economic Status of Registered Professional Nurses 1946–47." Bulletin No. 931. Washington, DC: Department of Labor.

U.S. Department of Veterans Affairs. 2010. "The Post-9/11 GI-Bill." Retrieved December 8, 2010, http://gibill.va.gov/post-911/post-911-gi-bill-summary.

U.S. Department of Veterans Affairs. 2011a. "VHA Directive 2011–024: Providing Health Care for Transgender and Intersex Veterans." Retrieved June 15, 2011, http://www.va.gov/vhapublications/ViewPublication.asp?pub_ID=2416.

U.S. Department of Veterans Affairs. 2011b. "Federal Benefits for Veterans, Dependents, and Survivors 2011 Edition." Retrieved December 14, 2011, http://www.va.gov/opa/publications/benefits_book.asp.

U.S. Office of Personnel Management. 2012. "Historical Federal Workforce Tables. Total Government Employment since 1962." Washington, DC: U.S. Office of Personnel Management.

U.S. War Department. 1888. *The War of the Rebellion: A Compilation of the Official Records of the Union and Confederate Armies*. Washington, DC: Government Printing Office.

Ulrich, Marybeth Peterson. 2002. "Infusing Civil-Military Relations Norms in the Officer Corps." In *The Future of the Army Profession*, edited by Lloyd J. Matthews, pp. 245–270. Boston: McGraw-Hill.

United Nations. 1983. "Estimation of Adult Mortality Using Successive Census Age Distributions." In *Manual X: Indirect Techniques for Demographic Estimation*, United Nations publication, Sales No. E.83.XIII.2, pp. 196–222. New York: United Nations, Department of Economic and Social Affairs, Population Division. http://www.un.org/esa/population/publications/Manual_X/Manual_X_Chapter_9.pdf.

Usdansky, Margaret L., Andrew S. London, and Janet M. Wilmoth. 2009. "Veteran Status, Race-Ethnicity, and Marriage among Fragile Families." *Journal of Marriage and the Family* 71 (3): 768–786.

Useem, Ruth Hill. 1993. "Third Culture Kids: Focus of Major Study—TCK 'Mother' Pens History of Field." *NewsLinks* 12 (3) (April 11) http://www.tckworld.com/useem/art1.html.

Vaidyanathan, K. E. 1969. "Comparison of CSR Estimates of Net Migration, 1950–1960 and Census Estimates, 1955–1960 for United States." *Social Forces* 48 (2): 233–243.

Veterans Administration. 1977. *VA History in Brief*. GovDoc: VA 1.19:06–77–1; GPO Item No: 988. Washington, DC: U.S. Government Printing Office.

Villahermosa, Gilberto. 2002. "America's Hispanics in America's Wars." *Army Magazine*. Retrieved July 30, 2012, http://www.valerosos.com/HispanicsMilitary.html.

Villemez, Wayne J., and John D. Kasarda. 1976. "Veteran Status and Socioeconomic Attainment." *Armed Forces & Society* 2 (Spring): 407–420.

Vine, David. 2004. "War and Forced Migration in the Indian Ocean: The US Military Base at Diego Garcia." *International Migration* 42 (3): 111–143.

Wake, Naoko. 2007. "The Military, Psychiatry, and 'Unfit' Soldiers, 1939–1942." *Journal of the History of Medicine and Allied Sciences* 62 (4): 461–494.

Wald, Johanna and Daniel J. Losen. 2003. "Defining and Re-Directing a School-to-Prison Pipeline." *New Directions for Youth Development* 2003 (99): 9–15.

Waller, Willard. 1944. *The Veteran Comes Back*. New York: Dryden Press.

Wardynski, Casey. 2000. *Military Compensation in the Age of Two-Income Households: Adding Spouses' Earnings to the Compensation Policy Mix*. Santa Monica, CA: RAND.

Warner, Rebecca Lynn. 1985. "The Impact of Military Service on the Early Career: An Extension of the Bridging Environment Hypothesis to Women (Stratification)." Ph.D. Dissertation, University of Washington, Pullman.

Warren, John Robert, and Elaine M. Hernandez. 2007. "Did Socioeconomic Inequalities in Morbidity and Mortality Change in the United States over the Course of the Twentieth Century?" *Journal of Health and Social Behavior* 48: 335–351.

Washington, Booker T. 1901. *Up from Slavery: An Autobiography*. New York: Doubleday, Page & Co.

Watanab, Henry, Peter S. Jensen, Leora N. Rosen, John Newby, John E. Richters, and Rosa M. Cortes. 1995. "Soldier Functioning under Chronic Stress—Effects of Family Member Illness." *Military Medicine* 160 (9): 457–461. ISI:A1995RU74400009.

Weber, Eve Graham, and David Kevin Weber. 2005. "Geographic Relocation Frequency, Resilience, and Military Adolescent Behavior." *Military Medicine* 170 (7): 638–642.

Weller, Christian, Jeffrey Brian Wenger, and Elise Gould. 2004. *Health Insurance Coverage in Retirement: The Erosion of Retiree Income Security.* Washington, DC: Economic Policy Institute.

Wertsch, Mary Edwards. 1991. *Military Brats: Legacies of Childhood inside the Fortress.* New York: Harmony Books.

WESTAT. 1986. "The 1985 Army Experience Survey. Data Sourcebook and User's Manual." ADA173826, January. Rockville, MD: WESTAT Inc. http://handle. dtic.mil/100.2/ADA173826.

White, C. Todd. 2009. *Pre-Gay L.A.: A Social History of the Movement for Homosexual Rights.* Champaign: University of Illinois Press.

White, Lynn K. 1990. "Determinants of Divorce: A Review of Research in the Eighties." *Journal of Marriage and Family* 52 (4) (November): 904–912.

White, Lynn K., and Naomi Lacy. 1997. "The Effects of Age at Home Leaving and Pathways from Home on Educational Attainment." *Journal of Marriage and the Family* 59 (4): 982–995.

White, Michael D. 2008. "Identifying Good Cops Early: Predicting Recruit Performance in the Academy." *Police Quarterly* 11: 27–49.

Whites, LeeAnn. 1995. *The Civil War as a Crisis in Gender: Augusta, Georgia, 1860–1890.* Athens: University of Georgia Press.

Wiley, Bell Irvin. 1943. *The Life of Johnny Reb: The Common Soldier of the Confederacy.* Baton Rouge: Louisiana State University Press.

Wiley, Bell Irvin. 1975. *Confederate Women.* Westport, CT: Greenwood Press.

Williams, Colin J., and Martin S. Weinberg. 1971. *Homosexuals and the Military: A Study of Less Than Honorable Discharge.* New York: Harper & Row.

Williams, David, and Teresa Crisp Williams. 2002. "'The Women Rising': Cotton, Class, and Confederate Georgia's Rioting Women." *Georgia Historical Quarterly* 86 (1) (Spring): 49–83.

Williams, Lindy, Linda Piccinino, Joyce Abma, and Florio Arguillas. 2001. "Pregnancy Wantedness: Attitude Stability over Time." *Social Biology* 48 (3–4): 212–233.

Williams, Robin M. 1989. "The American Soldier—An Assessment, Several Wars Later." *Public Opinion Quarterly* 53 (2): 155–174. ISI:A1989AE25900001.

Williams, Robin M. 2006. "The Long Twentieth Century in American Sociology: A Semiautobiographical Survey." *Annual Review of Sociology* 32: 1–23.

Willson, Andrea E., Kim M. Shuey, and Glen H. Elder Jr. 2007. "Cumulative Advantage Processes as Mechanisms of Inequality in Life Course Health." *American Journal of Sociology* 112 (6): 1886–1924. ISI:000247866000007.

Wilmoth, Janet M., and Andrew S. London. 2011. "Aging Veterans: Needs and Provisions." In *Handbook of the Sociology of Aging*, edited by Jacqueline L. Angel and Richard Settersten, pp. 445–461. New York: Springer.

Wilmoth, Janet M. and Charles F. Longino, Jr. 2006. "Demographic Trends That Will Shape U.S. Policy in the 21st Century." *Research on Aging.* 28(3): 269–288.

Wilmoth, Janet M., Andrew S. London, and Wendy Parker. 2010. "Military Service and Men's Health Trajectories in Later Life." *Journal of Gerontology: Social Sciences* 56 (6): 744–755.

Wilmoth, Janet M., Andrew S. London, and Wendy Parker. 2011. "Sex Differences in the Relationship between Veteran Status and Functional Limitations and Disabilities." *Population Research and Policy Review* 30: 333–354.

Wilson, Reginald. 1995. "The G.I. Bill and the Transformation of America." *National Forum* 75 (4) (Fall): 20–22.

Wilson, William Julius. 1987. *The Truly Disadvantaged: The Inner City, the Underclass, and Public Policy.* Chicago: The University of Chicago Press.

Wilson, William Julius. 1996. *When Work Disappears: The World of the New Urban Poor.* New York: Alfred A. Knopf.

Wing, Coady, Douglas A. Wolf, Andrew S. London, and Janet M. Wilmoth. 2009. "Military Service and Later Labor Force Outcomes: A Life Course Approach." Paper presented at the 2009 annual meeting of the Population Association of America, April 30–May 2, Detroit, Michigan.

Witten, Tarynn M. 2005. "Gender Identity and the Military—Transgender, Transsexual and Intersex-Identified Individuals in the Armed Forces—Part 1." Santa Barbara: University of California at Santa Barbara, Center for the Study of Sexual Minorities in the Military.

Wolfe, Jessica, Erica J. Sharkansky, Jennifer P. Read, Ree Dawson, James A. Martin, and Paige C. Ouimette. 1998. "Sexual Harassment and Assault as Predictors of PTSD Symptomatology among US Female Persian Gulf War Military Personnel." *Journal of Interpersonal Violence* 13 (1): 40–57.

Worden, William. 1996. *Children and Grief: When a Parent Dies.* New York: Guilford Press.

Wright, John Paul, David E. Carter, and Francis T. Cullen. 2005. "A Life-Course Analysis of Military Service in Vietnam." *Journal of Research in Crime and Delinquency* 42 (1): 55–83.

Wyler, William (director), Robert E. Sherwood (screenplay), and McKinlay Kantor (author of novel). 1946. *The Best Years of Our Lives.* Film with Fredric March, Dana Andrews, and Myrna Loy. Hollywood, CA: Samuel Goldwyn Company.

Wyman, Mira, Megan Lemmon, and Jay D. Teachman. 2010. "Non-Combat Military Service in the United States and Its Effects of Depressive Symptoms among Men." *Social Science Research* 40: 695–703.

Xie, Yu. 1992. "The Socioeconomic-Status of Young Male Veterans, 1964–1984." *Social Science Quarterly* 73 (2): 379–396.

Yang, Yang, and Kenneth Land. 2006. "A Mixed Models Approach to the Age-Period-Cohort Analysis of Repeated Cross-Section Surveys, with an Application to Data on Trends." *Sociological Methodology* 36: 75–97.

Yang, Yang, and L. C. Lee. 2009. "Sex and Race and Disparities in Health: Cohort Variations in Life Course Patterns." *Social Forces* 87: 2091–2124.

Yang, Yang, Sam Schulhofer-Wohl, J. Fu Wenjaing, and Kenneth Land. 2008. "The Intrinsic Estimator for Age-Period-Cohort Analysis: What It Is and How to Use It." *American Journal of Sociology* 113 (6): 1697–1736.

Ybarra, Lea. 2004. *Vietnam Veteranos: Chicanos Recall the War.* Austin: University of Texas Press.

Yingling, Paul. 2007. "A Failure in Generalship." Armed Forces Journal. Retreived November 2, 2009, http://www.armedforcesjournal.com/2007/05/2635198.

Young, Warren L. 1982. *Minorities and the Military: A Cross-National Study in World Perspective.* Westport, CT: Greenwood Press.

Zamora, Emilio. 2005. "Mexico's Wartime Intervention on Behalf of Mexicans in the United States: A Turning of Tables." In *Mexican Americans and World War II*, edited by Maggie Rivas-Rodriguez. Austin: University of Texas Press.

Zeeland, Steven. 1993. *Barrack Buddies and Soldier Lovers: Dialogues with Gay Young Men in the U.S. Military.* New York: Haworth Press.

Zeeland, Steven. 1996. *The Masculine Marine: Homoeroticism in the U. S. Marine Corps.* New York: Haworth Press.

Zeeland, Steven. 1999. *Military Trade.* New York: Haworth Press.

Zeiss, Antonette M. 2009. "Veterans Health Administration Care for Mental Health Problems Related to Military Sexual Trauma." Unpublished data from Office of Mental Health Services, Department of Veterans Affairs, Washington,

DC. Retrieved February 6, 2009, www.militarysexualtrauma.org/files/Veterans_Administration_Care_for_Mental_Health_Proble   ms_Related_to_Military_Sexual_Trauma_DTFSAM.ppt.

Zeitlin, Maurice, Kenneth G. Lutterman, and James W. Russell. 1973. "Death in Vietnam: Class, Poverty, and the Risks of War." *Politics & Society* 3 (3): 313–328.

Zweig, Michael, Michael Porter, and Yuxiang Huang. 2011. *American Military Deaths in Afghanistan, and the Communities from Which These Soldiers, Sailors, Airmen, and Marines Came.* State University of New York. Stonybrook, New York: Center for Study of Working Class Life.

Contributors

Amy Kate Bailey earned her Ph.D. in Sociology at the University of Washington, with concentrations in Demography and Racial Stratification. She is an Assistant Professor of Sociology at Utah State University, and was a NIH-funded Postdoctoral Research Fellow at Princeton University's Office of Population Research from 2008–2010. Her research examines migration among veterans, the effects of military-linked migration on both local communities and broader processes of population distribution, and the educational and occupational attainment of veterans. She also conducts research on lynching the in American South. Bailey's research is currently funded through the Utah Agricultural Experiment Station for projects exploring the reintegration of students who are veterans of the conflicts in Iraq and Afghanistan, the characteristics of communities most heavily affected by National Guard deployments, and the ways in which community-level social and economic changes affect the human capital characteristics of military enlistees. Her work has been published in *American Journal of Sociology, American Sociological Review, Historical Methods, Journal of Family History, Population Research and Policy Review*, and *Sociology of Education*.

Pamela R. Bennett has a Ph.D. in Sociology from the University of Michigan–Ann Arbor. She is Associate Professor of Sociology at Queens College, City University of New York. Her research interests include race, ethnic, and nativity differences in postsecondary outcomes and the consequences of racial residential segregation. Her current work investigates Black immigrants' relationships to Historically Black Colleges and Universities. She is also currently conducting research with Robert Nathenson on Hispanic-Serving Institutions in an effort to develop a more substantive definition of those institutions to replace the current demographic and statistical definition used by the federal government and, consequently, academics. Their research will examine how the college outcomes of Latino students vary across college types, including those in the typology she and Nathenson create. Bennett's work has been funded by the Spencer Foundation through Dissertation and Postdoctoral fellowships, the National Science Foundation, the American Sociological Association's Fund for the Advancement of the Discipline, and the Poverty & Race Research Action Council. Her work has been published in *American Sociological Review, Sociology of Education, Ethnic and Racial Studies, Social Science Research, Social Science Quarterly,* and *Du Bois Review: Social Science Research on Race.* During the 2012–13 academic year, she will be a Visiting Scholar at the Russell Sage Foundation where she will co-author with Amy C. Lutz a book on the sources of variation in educationally-relevant parenting strategies across race, nativity, and social class.

Maria T. Brown has a Ph.D. in Social Science and a Master's degree in Social Work from Syracuse University. She is a Social Gerontologist who uses the life course perspective to research the later-life experiences of socioeconomically disadvantaged individuals, women, and racial, ethnic, and sexual minorities. She has published in the areas life course impacts on cognitive function in later life, economics of aging, social security and early retirement, and lesbian, gay, bisexual, and transgender (LGBT) aging. Her current research (in collaboration with Janet M. Wilmoth and Andrew S. London) examines how military service shapes life course outcomes in terms of cognitive function and mental health. In a separate project (with Brian Grossman), she is exploring the relationship between same-sex sexual history, social support and isolation, and physical and mental health outcomes in older adults. Brown was a 2008–2010 John A. Hartford Foundation Doctoral Fellow in Geriatric Social Work, and was the recipient of the 2007 pre-dissertation- and 2010 dissertation-level student research awards from the Behavioral and Social Sciences Section of the Gerontological Society of America. Her work has been published in *The Gerontologist, Journal of Sexuality Research and Social Policy,* and the *Encyclopedia of Health and Aging.* She currently serves as Co-Convener of the Rainbow Research Interest Group of the Gerontological Society of America.

Daniel Burland has a Ph.D. in Sociology from the University of Massachusetts—Amherst and a Ph.D. in Comparative Literature from the University of Chicago. Between these two periods of graduate study, he served for four years as a medic in the U.S. Army, 307th Forward Support Battalion, 82nd Airborne Division, and was deployed to Afghanistan. He is currently Visiting Assistant Professor in the Legal Studies Program at the University of Massachusetts–Amherst, where he teaches courses on military law, civil rights law, and the correlation between changes in legislation and in social norms. In an article recently published in the journal *Armed Forces & Society*, he and Jennifer Lundquist analyzed data from a large-scale survey of military personnel in order to test the widespread notion in Military Sociology that soldiers serving in combat roles are motivated by different values from those held by soldiers serving in support roles. His current book project draws upon diverse sources— interviews, historical archives, museum displays and commemorative art, among others—in order to document cultural representations and perceptions of the 21st century military in the United States, with a particular focus on the resulting identity issues for different populations of soldiers and veterans.

D'Ann Campbell has a Ph.D. in American History, with a minor in Family Sociology, from The University of North Carolina at Chapel Hill. She is a Professor of History at Culver Stockton College, Canton, Missouri. She began her career at the Newberry Library in 1976 as Associate Director of the Family and Community History Center. Then, she taught and was an administrator at Indiana University, Austin Peay State University (TN), The Sage Colleges (NY), Southern New Hampshire University (NH), Chester College of New England (NH), the Coast Guard Academy, and Montana State University Billings before coming to Culver Stockton College. She served as the Distinguished Visiting Professor in History at the United States Military Academy 1989–1991. She was the first woman academic dean of any of the service academies and the first woman to teach Mil Art at West Point. Her areas of interest include American social history, women's history and military history. She is the author of *Women at War with America: Private Lives in a Patriotic Era* (Harvard University Press, 1984) and *Americans at War: Society, Culture, and the Homefront* (Macmillan, 2005; coeditor of volume 4). She has received a dozen grants and written over two dozen scholarly articles including: "Women in Combat: The World War Two Experience in the United States, Great Britain, Germany, and the Soviet Union" (*Journal of Military History*, 1993), which was awarded the Moncado Prize of the Society of Military History for "Best Article." She is currently writing a book on the roles that women played worldwide during the Second World War.

Glen H. Elder, Jr. is the Howard W. Odum Distinguished Research Professor of Sociology at The University of North Carolina at Chapel Hill where he manages a research program on life course studies at the Carolina Population Center. His books (authored, co-authored, edited) include: *Children of the Great Depression, Children in Time and Place, Children of the Land,* and *The Craft of Life Course Research.* He is currently engaged in studies of pathways to higher education, military service, effects of socioeconomic change on the life course and health, and linking early experience with late-life outcomes.

Paul Gade is a U.S. Air Force veteran and received his Ph.D. in Experimental Psychology from Ohio University. He recently retired from his position as Senior Research Psychologist and the Chief of Basic Research from the U.S. Army Research Institute for the Behavioral and Social Sciences after 36 years of service. He is currently a Research Professor of Organizational Sciences in the Department of Organizational Sciences and Communications at the George Washington University and Senior Research Fellow at the U.S. Army Research Institute for the Behavioral and Social Sciences. He is a fellow of the American Psychological Association and Past President of the Society for Military Psychology. He is also a member of the Association for Psychological Science, the International Society for Intelligence Research, and a fellow of the Inter-University Seminar on Armed Forces and Society. He has published more than sixty book chapters, journal articles, magazine articles, and technical reports. He is member of the Editorial Board and past Associate Editor of the journal *Military Psychology*. He was the Guest Editor for and a contributor to the first special issue of *Military Psychology*, which focused on military service and the life course. Gade's current professional interests are in: life course research and its history; military psychology history; theories and applications of intelligence and individual differences; and neuroscience in behavioral and social sciences and how the brain generates the mind.

Jessica Hoffman is a Doctoral Candidate in Sociology (The State University of New York at Buffalo), whose areas of specialization include law and society, gender, and the life course. Her dissertation research, *Narratives of Social Change and "Don't Ask Don't Tell": How Relationships to Law Shape Legal Consciousness*, explores how service members of different genders, ranks, tenures of service, and sexualities express legal consciousness in the aftermath of policy changes associated with "Don't Ask Don't Tell."

Ryan Kelty is an Associate Professor of Sociology at Washington College. His research interests include the effects of civilian contractor integration on military personnel, diversity in the military, and the role of military service in the life course. His research has appeared in *Armed Forces & Society*, *The Future of Children*, *Annual Review of Political and Military Sociology*, and several edited volumes.

Meredith Kleykamp is an Assistant Professor of Sociology at the University of Maryland-College Park. She holds a Ph.D. in Sociology from Princeton University. Her research centers on the social demography of the military and the social and economic consequences of military service. She has previously taught at the University of Kansas and the United States Military Academy at West Point. Her published research includes studies on what influences military enlistment and how those influences differ across various population segments. Recently, she has examined how military service influences veterans' employment using a field experiment of hiring and in-depth interviews with selected employers. She is currently investigating public attitudes toward veterans using experimental survey techniques. Her research has been funded by the National Science Foundation, the American Sociological Association's Fund for the Advancement of the Discipline, and the Time Sharing Experiments for the Social Sciences program. Her work has been published in the *American Journal of Sociology, American Sociological Review, Armed Forces & Society, Social Science Quarterly, Social Science Research,* and *Social Forces.*

Andrew S. London has a Ph.D. in Sociology and Demography from the University of Pennsylvania. He is Chair and Professor of Sociology, Senior Research Associate in the Center for Policy Research, Senior Fellow in the Institute for Veterans and Military Families, and Faculty Affiliate in the Aging Studies Institute at Syracuse University. For six years, he served as a founding Co-Director of Syracuse University's Lesbian, Gay, Bisexual, and Transgender (LGBT) Studies Program. His research focuses on the health, care, and well-being of stigmatized and vulnerable populations, including: persons living with HIV/AIDS and their caregivers; welfare-reliant and working poor women and their children; the formerly incarcerated; the elderly; and LGBT persons. He has received funding from the National Institute on Aging, the Social Security Administration's Boston College Retirement Research Consortium, the American Sociological Association's Fund for the Advancement of the Discipline, the National Poverty Center at the University of Michigan, the Northwestern University/University of Chicago Joint Center for Poverty Research, the Center for Demography and Ecology at University of Wisconsin-Madison, MDRC, AIDS Community Research Initiative of America (ACRIA), the Joyce Foundation, and the George Gund Foundation. His research related to military service and the life course has been published in *Journal of Family Issues, Journal of Marriage and Family, Journal of Poverty, Journals of Gerontology: Social Sciences, Population Research and Policy Review, Research on Aging,* and *Social Service Review,* as well as the *Handbook of Sociology of Aging* and the *Encyclopedia of the Life Course and Human Development.*

Leonard M. Lopoo is an Associate Professor of Public Administration and International Affairs and Senior Research Associate at the Center for Policy Research in the Maxwell School of Citizenship & Public Affairs at Syracuse University. He received his Ph.D. from the Harris School at the University of Chicago and completed a Postdoctoral Fellowship at the Woodrow Wilson School of Public and International Affairs at Princeton University. Lopoo's research interests primarily involve the family: fertility, marriage, maternal employment, and the public policies designed to assist the low-income population, and he has published in *Demography, Journal of Health Economics, Journal of Human Resources, Journal of Marriage and Family, Journal of Policy Analysis and Management,* and *Journal of Public Economics,* among many others. He has received funding from the Eunice Kennedy Shriver National Institute of Child Health and Human Development, the National Institute on Aging, the Pew Charitable Trusts, the Smith Richardson Foundation, and the University of Kentucky Center for Poverty Research. Lopoo is currently the Social Policy Co-Editor of the *Journal of Policy Analysis and Management,* a post he has held since 2008. He is the recipient of numerous awards for his research and teaching, including the Birkhead-Burkhead Teaching Excellence Award, a Meredith Professors Recognition Award, and the Daniel Patrick Moynihan Prize.

Jennifer Lundquist has a Ph.D. in Sociology and Demography from the University of Pennsylvania. She is an Associate Professor of Sociology, Director of Research Initiatives, and Acting Director of the Institute for Social Science Research at the University of Massachusetts, Amherst. Her research explores racial disparities in health and socioeconomic status, interracial dating and relationships, family formation patterns, and the military. She has received funding from the National Science Foundation and her work has been published in *American Sociological Review, Social Forces, Journal of Marriage and Family, Social Problems, Armed Forces & Society, the Journal of Political and Military Sociology, Sociological Forum, Academe,* and *Journal of Latin American Studies.* She also co-wrote *Demography: The Study of the Human Population, 3rd Edition.*

Amy C. Lutz has a Ph.D. in Sociology, a Master's degree in Latin American and Caribbean Studies, and a Graduate Certificate in Demography from The University at Albany, SUNY. She also held Postdoctoral Fellowships at the Center for Social Organization of Schools and Sociology Department at the Johns Hopkins University and Centre Maurice Halbwachs- CNRS—Ecole Normale Supérieure in Paris, France. She is an Associate Professor of Sociology and Cultural Foundations of Education and a Senior Research Associate at the Center for Policy Research at Syracuse University. Her research focuses on immigrants and children of immigrants, inequalities across race-ethnicity and social class, secondary and postsecondary education, and the transition from school to work. She has recently been working on collaborative projects comparing educational and early labor market outcomes among children of immigrant and native-born parents in Europe and North America. She is currently working on research with Yingyi Ma that investigates differences across immigrant generation in the propensity to enter the STEM pipeline through high school math course taking and completion of postsecondary degrees in math, science, and engineering. She is also working on a collaborative project about parenting variations across race, immigrant generation, and social class and their educational relevance for urban eighth graders and will spend the 2012–2013 academic year at the Russell Sage Foundation to complete a book based on the project. Lutz's research has been funded by the American Education Research Association, the Spencer Foundation, the Social Science Research Council, the American Sociological Association's Fund for the Advancement of the Discipline, and the Poverty & Race Research Action Council. Her research has appeared in *Ethnic and Racial Studies, Demography, Social Forces, Sociology of Education, Youth and Society, Ethnicities, Journal of Political and Military Sociology, Migraciones Internacionales*, and others.

Alair MacLean has a Ph.D. in Sociology from the University of Wisconsin-Madison. She is an Associate Professor of Sociology at Washington State University-Vancouver. Her research explores questions related to social inequality. She is currently evaluating how military service affects peoples' lives. Her work has been funded by the National Institute on Aging and the National Science Foundation. She has written articles that have been published in *Annual Review of Sociology* and the *American Sociological Review*, among many other journals. She is also co-editing a book (with David Grusky) that examines how increased inequality over the last thirty years has affected a variety of institutions, including the family and the labor market.

Katrina McDonald is an Associate Professor of Sociology, and she served as Associate Dean of Multicultural Affairs from 2008–2011, at Johns Hopkins University. Dr. McDonald earned a Bachelor of Arts degree with honors in Written Communication from Mills College in 1983 (Oakland, CA); a Master of Arts degree in Applied Communication Research from Stanford University in 1984 (Palo Alto, CA); a Master of Arts degree in Sociology from the University of California, Davis in 1990; and a Ph.D. in Sociology from UC Davis in 1995. She became tenured in the spring of 2006, the second black female ever to be awarded tenure in the School of Arts and Sciences or the School of Engineering. Her recent book, *Embracing Sisterhood: Class, Identity, and Contemporary Black Women* (Rowman & Littlefield, 2006), analyzes how contemporary black women's ideas of black womanhood and sisterhood merge with social class status to shape certain attachments and detachments among them. In collaboration Dr. Caitlin Cross-Barnett, McDonald is currently crafting research on contemporary marriage among African Americans, and with Daniel Pasciuti is constructing a social statistics textbook.

Brandis Ruise has a Master's degree in Personality and Social Psychology from American University. As a Consortium Research Fellow, she worked under Dr. Paul Gade, researching the impact of military enlistment on the lives of soldiers and their families from a life course perspective. She has contributed to publications and presentations in the areas of gender identity and cultural awareness. Currently, she is pursuing her doctoral degree in School Psychology at the University of Rhode Island, where her research will examine early intervention and psycho-educational assessment of at-risk populations.

David R. Segal has a Ph.D. in Sociology from the University of Chicago. He is Professor of Sociology, Director of the Center for Research on Military Organization, Faculty Associate in the Maryland Population Research Center, and Faculty Affiliate in the Department of Government and Politics and the School of Public Policy at the University of Maryland College Park. His research focuses on military personnel, organizational, and operational issues. Prior to joining the Maryland faculty he taught at the University of Michigan, and directed the sociological research program at the Army Research Institute for the Behavioral and Social Sciences during the first years of the current volunteer force. His research has been funded by the National Science Foundation, the Army Research Institute, and private foundations, and has been published in *The American Sociological Review, The American Journal of Sociology, Social Forces, Social Science Quarterly, Armed Forces & Society, Military Psychology,* and *Journal of Political and Military Sociology,* among others. His books include *Life in the Rank and File, Recruiting for Uncle Sam, Peacekeepers and their Wives,* and *The Postmodern Military.*

Debra Street has a Ph.D. in Sociology from Florida State University. She is Professor and Chair of the Department of Sociology at the University at Buffalo, SUNY, Fellow of the Gerontological Association of America, member of the National Academy of Social Insurance, and Visiting Senior Research Fellow (2011–2013) at the Institute of Gerontology, King's College, London. Her publications range from research on comparative public policy and the health professions, to health and income security in old age, planning for later life, and issues associated with assisted living and long term care. In separate projects, she is working with Stephanie Burge to better understand individual and institutional experiences in the evolving assisted living industry and with Debora Price on the *Behind Closed Doors* pilot project, which aims to develop a cross-national survey (U.S., Canada, U.K., and Singapore) to explore older couples' financial decision-making in different political economies. Street's research has been funded by the National Institute on Aging, the National Science Foundation, and the Robert Wood Johnson Foundation. Findings from her research have appeared in the *Journals of Gerontology: Social Sciences, The Gerontologist, Research* *on Aging, Social Problems, Journal of Sociology and Social Welfare, International Journal of Health Services, Journal of Health Care for the Poor and Underserved, Canadian Journal of Aging,* and *International Journal of Sociology and Social Policy.* With Jay Ginn and Sara Arber, she edited the book *Women, Work and Pensions: International Issues and Prospects.*

Jay Teachman is a Professor of Sociology at Western Washington University. He received his Ph.D. in sociology from the University of Chicago where he specialized in Statistical Methodology and Demography. His research interests focus around statistical methodologies, marital formation and dissolution, and the multifaceted consequences of military service for young men and women. Teachman is a Fellow of the National Council on Family Relations, and recently served as Chair of the Family Section of the American Sociological Association. He has received support for his research on veterans in the form of several grants from the National Science Foundation and the National Institutes of Health. His most recent grant provides funding for examining the ways in which military service may alter the trajectory of troubled behaviors (e.g., drug and alcohol abuse, violent behavior) that sometimes occur in young adulthood. Professor Teachman's work has been published in journals such as *American Sociological Review, Demography, Journal of Marriage and Family, Sociology of Education, Social Forces, Social Science Research, Journal of Family Issues, Sociological Methods and Research,* and *Population Research and Policy Review.*

Janet M. Wilmoth has a Ph.D. in Sociology and Demography, with a minor in Gerontology, from the Pennsylvania State University. She is a Professor of Sociology, Director of the Aging Studies Institute, Senior Research Associate in the Center for Policy Research, and Senior Fellow in the Institute for Veterans and Military Families at Syracuse University. Her research utilizes quantitative methods to understand later-life well-being from a life course perspective. She has published in the areas of older adult migration and living arrangements, health status, and financial security. Her current research (conducted in collaboration with Andrew S. London and others) examines how military service shapes various life course outcomes. In a separate project, she is developing daily assessments of physical functioning, self-care, and social engagement among older adults. She has received funding from the National Institute on Aging, the Social Security Administration's Boston College Retirement Research Consortium, the Gerontological Society of America's Hartford Foundation Doctoral Program, the American Sociological Association's Fund for the Advancement of the Discipline, the National Poverty Center at the University of Michigan, and the Center for Demography and Ecology at University of Wisconsin-Madison. Her work has been published in *Journals of Gerontology: Social Sciences, The Gerontologist, Research on Aging, the Journal of Aging and Health, Population Research and Policy Review, Journal of Marriage and Family, Journal of Family Issues, Journal of Poverty,* and *Social Service Review.* She also edited (with Ken Ferraro) *Gerontology: Perspectives and Issues, 3rd Edition.*

Coady Wing received his Ph.D from the Maxwell School of Citizenship and Public Affairs at Syracuse University, and was a post-doctoral fellow at the Institute for Policy Research at Northwestern University. He is an Assistant Professor of Health Policy and Administration at the University of Illinois at Chicago. His research interests include econometric evaluations of social programs and policies, applications and empirical tests of quasi-experimental research designs, the effects of occupational licensing restrictions in the health care sector, and the health and economic outcomes of military veterans.

Douglas A. Wolf has a Ph.D. in Public Policy Analysis from the University of Pennsylvania and is the Gerald B. Cramer Professor of Aging Studies and a Senior Research Fellow in the Center for Policy Research at Syracuse University. He is also Director of the Center for Aging and Policy Studies, which is supported by the National Institute on Aging. His research deals primarily with late-life health, disability, and family issues, and he approaches these issues from the perspectives of Demography and Gerontology. His current research includes a study of end-of-life patterns of change in disability, physical functioning, and Medicare costs, and projects addressing the factors that influence family members' patterns of provision of care to their elderly parents, as well as the consequences of being a "family caregiver." He is one of the investigators responsible for the National Health and Aging Trends Study (NHATS), a new national-level survey project aimed at developing data for studying trends in the prevalence and incidence of late-life disability. He is a member of the Russell Sage Foundation-supported Working Group on Care, the TRENDS network (housed at the University of Michigan), and the Scholars Strategy Network (housed at Harvard University). His work has appeared in several journals including *Demography, Population and Development Review, Evaluation Review, The Gerontologist, Journals of Gerontology: Social Sciences, Health Affairs, The Milbank Quarterly,* and *Public Administration Review.*

Index

Lincoln, Abraham, 55; administration
of, 50
linked lives: and geographic mobility, 191–194; as an approach
to research, 49, 157, 164,
255; as a principle of the life
course perspective, 4, 6, 13, 49,
157, 164, 243, 250, 256, 276;
between military personnel,
veterans, and family mem-
bers, xxii, 2, 4, 10, 12–13, 19,
23–24, 34, 40–41 50, 66, 130,
144–145,173, 179, 209, 212,
216, 219, 230, 239; inter- and
intra-generational ties, 6, 15,
120, 127, 140, 174, 177, 179,
195, 249, 281; need for research
on, xxii, 15, 67, 95, 98, 117,
157, 196–199, 241, 250–251,
275, 280–283, 287–288, 290;
social convoy, 6
location in time and place, as a principle of the life course perspective, 4–5, 243, 249, 276, 280,
London, Andrew S., xvii–xviii, 1–18,
66–67, 75, 78, 140, 142, 145,
174–176, 183, 195, 197, 200,
202–207, 216, 218–222, 224,
234, 238–240, 243, 249,
252, 254–255, 270, 276–277,
281–282
Lopoo, Leonard M., 10, 14, 144,
146, 200, 204, 206, 216–217,
220, 223, 240, 254–274, 279,
284–285
"Lost Cause" myth, the, 65
Luce-Cellar Act, the, 80
Lundquist, Jennifer Hickes, xxii, 13,
23, 34–36, 95, 98, 159, 163,
165–184, 191, 205, 249, 252,
254, 276–277, 279, 281
Lutz, Amy C., 12, 21, 68–96, 119–
120, 129, 137–138, 148, 156,
170, 178, 234, 256, 279

M

MacLean, Alair, 2, 13, 25, 39, 136,
152, 166, 174, 176, 200–242,
250, 254, 276–277, 281
Manhattan Project, the, 84
Marine Corps, the: bases, 190–191;
career service in, 32; race and
ethnic composition of, 71, 92;
race and ethnic personnel in,

78, 88, 90; returns in earnings
among veterans of the, 151;
segregation within and integration of, 72; women in, 12, 30,
60, 61, 64–65, 66, 107
marriage, 43, 52, 108, 173, 179–180,
205, 250–251, 258, 265,
276–277, 281–283, 286–287;
age-patterning of, 148; among
women veterans of World War
II, 64; and the linked lives
perspective, 66–67, 98, 157,
164; and stress, 35, 173–177;
behavior, 254; disruption/
divorce/dissolution, 7, 281;
dual-service/joint-service, 34,
175, 181; effects of military service on, 11–12, 15, 25, 33–36,
43, 98; extramarital affairs/sex,
176, 197; historical research on,
65; interracial, 178, 198; rates
of, 34, 198; same-sex, 114, 227;
selection into military, 163; stability, 281; status 36, 42, 170,
260, 282; timing of, 144
marriage markets, local, 198
Marsh, Jr., John O., 244–245
Marshall, George C., 38
material hardship, 140, 175, 183, 216,
239, 241, 252, 277
Matthew Effect, the, 201
Maxwell School of Citizenship and
Public Affairs, xvii–xviii
McCarthy era, 106
McDonald, Katrina Bell, 3, 7, 12, 24,
109, 119–143, 144, 147–149,
155, 170, 174, 186, 203, 205,
230, 233, 240, 246, 250, 252,
258, 275–278, 283, 286
McGovern, George, 77
medals, awarded for service, xix, 84
Medicaid, 229, 235–236, 238
Medicare, 221, 227–229, 232–233,
235, 237–241
Medigap insurance, 229, 232, 235–
236, 238
mental health: among LGBT veterans,
114, 116–117; among veterans
215–217; and the transition
to adulthood, 25, 44; and
migration, 189, 193, 196; and
wartime service, 200, 209–211,
214, 219; anxiety, 42; depression 40–41, 50, 171, 176–177,

deployment during, 177; exposure to environmental toxins
during, 208; number of deaths
during, 212–213, 284; number
serving during, 213; number
wounded during, 213; percentage of current veterans who
served during, 3; risk of combat
during, 140–141; veterans'
children's stress and depression
during, 177; veterans' later-life
service-related needs from, 224;
young adult involvement in, 203
Peterson Air Force Base, 191
Philippine(s), 78–81, 85; -American
War, 79; Scouts, 79
Philippine Military Bases Agreement,
the, 80, 85
physical exam: pre-induction failure
rate, 261
postdoctoral fellows and fellowships: involvement in military
research, 11, 245; Hartford
Foundation Geriatric Scholar,
247; National Institute of Aging
Postdoctoral Fellowship, 247;
National Research Council
Postdoctoral Fellowship, 247;
Secretary of the Army Research
and Study Fellowship, 245
post-traumatic stress disorder (PTSD):
among LGBT veterans, 114;
among Native Americans and
Native Hawaiians, 89–90; and
child, spouse, and family well-
being, 171, 176–177, 182, 219,
251; and increased risk of death
and suicide, xxii, 40–41, 217;
and positive combat experiences, 152; and use of treatment
services, 41, 114, 210–211; as a
negative turning point, 203–
204; delayed-onset, 211, 216;
in relation to military sexual
trauma, 42; in relation to social
network ties, 217; in relation
to war and combat, xxii, 42,
89–90, 114, 152, 176, 203–204,
217, 220, 251; linked to risk of
cardiovascular disease, xxii;
prevalence of, 40, 42, 89–90,
176, 211, 216–217; symptoms
of, 211, 216

poverty: among Filipino veterans, 81;
and cumulative inequality, 239,
241; and military service by
Latinos, 77; combat veterans'
spouses' risk of, 197; in households with disabled veterans,
140, 175, 183, 216, 239, 252,
277; military service as a route
out of, xxi, 77; post-Civil War,
52. *See also* material hardship;
War on Poverty
Powell, General Colin, 38
Presidio, the, 84
prisoners of war (POWs), 65, 84
private health insurance, 221, 226–
229, 233–238
private sector: colleges and universities, 133, 136; employees and
employers, 228, 231, 240;
employment and jobs, 233, 238;
military contractors and security firms, 29, 152; retirement
income and health programs,
228–229, 232–233, 238, 240
Project 100,000, 77
propaganda, 81
psychiatry: adoption of the term post-
traumatic stress disorder (PTSD),
211; assessments of WWII
veteran adjustment, 63; role in
defining military policy regarding homosexuality, 100–101
psychiatric disorders. *See* mental health
Puerto Ricans, 75–77, 92, 170, 273
Pulaski, as a well-known Revolutionary War leader, 69
Purple Heart, 84

Q

quotas associated with immigration,
69–70, 79

R

race and ethnic groups, military service
among 68–96. *See also* American, race and ethnic groups
racism, 83–85, 103, 118, 171. *See also*
discrimination
RAND Corporation, the, 40, 266
rape. *See* sexual trauma
rank: and authority, 95; and divorce,
34; and duty-station assignments, 163; and health

Ruise, Brandis, 2, 14, 18, 242–253, 286

S

Sanitary Commission, 49, 66
sample: attrition from, 255; convenience, 246; experiment, 161; later-life, 223; longitudinal, xix; of gay men and lesbians, 110; representativeness, 277, 284; simple random, 286–287; size of, 161, 196, 286; snowball, 60; subsamples of military respondents, 287; statistical independence of members within, 255
satisfaction: spousal, 189, 196; with career, 27, 246; with finances, 27, 246; with life, 219, 223, 246; with male friendships, 247; with the military, 196, 245; with military housing, 95; with military lifestyle, 72, 158, 189, 192–193, 196
Second Great Awakening, the, 55
school system: military, 179, 193
Schriever Air Force Base, 191
screening: among employers, 132; health-care related, 117; pre-combat, 206; pre-enlistment, 4, 99–101, 105, 204, 261–262, 277–279. *See also*, recruitment
Secretary of the Army, the, 244–245
Secretary of Defense, the, 47, 111
Secretary of War, the, 86
security: financial and health, 14, 28, 45, 50, 102, 132, 142, 221–242, 250, 256; national, 33, 73, 151; private firms, 29; job-related, 79
Segal, David R., xvii, 7, 11, 19–47, 67, 79, 95, 120, 128, 144, 149, 152, 157–158, 168–170, 174, 186–187, 189, 205, 207, 229–231, 233–234, 240, 246, 251–252, 275–276, 278–279
segregation, in the armed forces, 17, 21, 46, 71–73, 75–76, 79–80, 82–83, 94, 119, 170; in society, 17, 46, 70–71, 73, 119, 123, 137, 177, 198. *See also* desegregation
Selective Service, 22, 93, 186. *See also* conscription; draft
selection: and research methods, 4, 14, 146, 196, 223, 255–261,

272–274, 279–280, 282, 285; and the start of data collection, 285; as a problem for causal attribution, 255, 260–261; as threat to internal validity, 255; as threat to sample representativeness, 220, 255, 268; at different points in the life course, 286; bias, 144; controls for, 277, 285; into the civilian population, 223, 257, 272; into the military, 7, 10–11, 13, 30, 32, 147–148, 153, 163, 195, 200, 204–207, 216, 223, 257, 272; models of, 286; on prior mortality, 220, 257, 269–272
service academies: admission of women into, 23, 66, 170; and moral-ethical development, 39; and service as a military officer, 25; Air Force, 39, 191; Naval, 88, 97; West Point, 39, 112;
servicewomen: and civilian careers, 63; and education, 61; and social integration after service, 64; in the Coast Guard *Semper Paratus*/Always Ready (SPARs), 12, 60–61, 66; in the Navy Women Accepted for Voluntary Emergency Service (WAVES), 12, 60–61, 66; in the Women's Army Corps (WACS) 12, 60–62, 66, 107; in the Women Marines, 12, 61, 107
Service Members Legal Defense Network (SLDN), the, 111, 115–116
service-connected disability. *See* disability
Servicemen's Readjustment Act of 1944, the, 22, 132. *See also* GI Bill
sexual assault. *See* sexual trauma
sexual harassment. *See* sexual trauma
sexual orientation: and dishonorable discharge, 12, 99, 111; and exclusion from military service, 101; and military policy, 32–33, 113, 117; and selection into military service, 11, 30; and the composition of the armed services, 11; and use of Veterans Administration services, 113–114; and veterans' mental health, 114; as distinct from